ANALECTA BIBLICA
INVESTIGATIONES SCIENTIFICAE IN RES BIBLICAS

126

FEARGHUS Ó FEARGHAIL

THE INTRODUCTION TO LUKE-ACTS

A Study of the Role of Lk 1,1-4,44 in the Composition of Luke's Two-Volume Work

EDITRICE PONTIFICIO ISTITUTO BIBLICO – ROMA 1991

IMPRIMI POTEST
Romae, die 12 Iunii 1991

R. P. KLEMENS STOCK, S.J.
Rector Pontificii Instituti Biblici

ISBN 88-7653-126-2

EDITRICE PONTIFICIO ISTITUTO BIBLICO
Piazza della Pilotta, 35 - 00187 Roma

To the memory of Peter Birch, Bishop of Ossory († 1981)
and of
John Farrell, my father († 1988)

PREFACE

The present work is a slightly revised version of a dissertation defended in the Pontifical Biblical Institute, Rome, in February 1987, with account taken of issues raised at the defence and of more recent literature where possible. Its publication affords me the opportunity of thanking Fritzleo Lentzen-Deis S.J. and Albert Vanhoye S.J. for their stimulating direction of my thesis which benefitted greatly from their many penetrating comments and helpful criticisms. My thanks too to my scripture colleague in Kilkenny, Dr James Brennan, for his invaluable assistance, and also to my scripture colleagues in St. Patrick's College, Carlow, for their help.

The authorities of the Irish College and S. Maria dell'Anima, Rome, and the Hochschule Sankt Georgen, Frankfurt, were generous in their hospitality during my years of study; the staff and students of St. Kieran's College, Kilkenny, generous in their patience.

A debt of gratitude is owed to the late Bishop Peter Birch with whose encouragement my doctoral studies began, to the late Cardinal Tomás Ó Fiaich for his help and encouragement, and to Bishop Laurence Forristal for the time and support given to complete the work.

There are many others who should be thanked, particularly those whose generous contributions have made this publication possible, and the first year students of St. Kieran's College who helped with the indices. May I express to all of them my deep gratitude.

FÓF

TABLE OF CONTENTS

PROLOGUE

The past thirty five years or so have seen a great proliferation of writings on Luke–Acts, as the works of Rasco and Bovon abundantly demonstrate.[1] Redactional for the most part, these studies have produced many new insights into the author's thought and method of composition, and, refined in the cauldron of controversy, they have added greatly to Cadbury's perennially valuable contributions of over half a century ago.[2] And the debate surrounding Luke–Acts shows little sign of flagging.[3]

The redactional method has surely proved its worth, and it continues to do so despite the inherent limitation involved in the inability to identify Lucan sources with any appreciable certainty. But it could with considerable profit be complemented by a compositional approach which concentrates more on the evangelist's arrangement and general organization of the material at his disposal. The literary structure imposed on the work as a whole and on its individual parts offers an invaluable indication of the writer's thought and purpose and can be a decisive factor in interpreting Lucan composition, as for instance, at 3,20-21[4] or 4,14-44.[5] Such an approach affords an opportunity of throwing fresh light from a different perspective on some of the problems that continue to beset students of the Lucan corpus, especially a number

---

[1] E. Rasco, *La Teologia de Lucas: Origen, Desarollo, Orientaciones*, AnGreg 201: Rome 1976; F. Bovon, *Luc le théologien, Vingt-cinq ans de recherches (1950-1975)*, Neuchatel-Paris 1978. See also E. Grässer, "Die Apostelgeschichte in der Forschung der Gegenwart", *TRu* 26 (1960) 93-167; idem, "Acta-Forschung seit 1960", *TRu* 41 (1976) 141-194.259-290; 42 (1977) 1-68.

[2] *The Making of Luke-Acts*, London 1968[2] (1927); *The Style and Literary Method of Luke*, HTS VI: New York 1969 (repr. Cambridge, Mass. 1920).

[3] See, for example, J. A. Fitzmyer, *The Gospel According to Luke (I-IX)*, AB 28: Garden City 1981, 3-283, esp. 3-34; F. Plümacher, "Acta-Forschung 1974-1982", *TRu* 48 (1983) 1-56; 49 (1984) 105-169.

[4] See ch. I, pp. 21-22; also H. von Baer, *Der Heilige Geist in den Lukasschriften*, BWANT III.3: Stuttgart 1926, 55-56; 56 n. 11; H. Conzelmann, *Die Mitte der Zeit*, Tübingen (1954) 1965[5], 14-15.

[5] See ch. I, pp. 9-10; also H. Schürmann, *Das Lukasevangelium* I, HTKNT 3.1: Freiburg 1969, 221. F. Giancotti, *Strutture delle Monografie di Sallustio e di Tacito*, BCC 108: Messina-Florence 1971, 7, uses the expression *struttura compositiva* in the context of the literary arrangement or design of a work.

of those raised by Hans Conzelmann's influential work *Die Mitte der Zeit*.[6]

The present study offers a contribution towards the compositional study of Luke–Acts with an examination of the role of Lk 1,1–4,44 in the work as a whole. This choice of vantage point from which to conduct such a study is due in no small measure to the intrinsic importance for the interpretation of any literary work of its opening section, and its proemium in particular. Two other factors govern this choice, both demonstrated in the literary analysis, namely, that 1,5–4,44 constitutes the gospel's first major section and that a major break in the gospel narrative may be placed at 4,44. It is the relationship between the initial four chapters and the remainder of Luke–Acts that is the focus of the present study.

This relationship has been perceived in different ways. The implications of the secular style and motifs of Lk 1,1-4 for the work these verses introduce,[7] the significance of the programme outlined here for Luke's method of composition,[8] and the application of these verses to Luke–Acts as a whole[9] or to the gospel alone[10] — these are all issues that continue to raise their heads with a certain frequency.

The infancy narrative has its own set of problems. Conzelmann's treatment or rather lack of treatment of these chapters implies the absence of an organic relationship between them and the rest of the work, if not the existence of outright conflict.[11] Conybeare had earlier regarded the *Diatessaron* as witnessing to a text of Luke that did not contain these chapters,[12] while Streeter took Lk 1-2 to be a later addition to a gospel that originally began with 3,1, added, it would seem, as an afterthought, when the two-volume work was complete.[13]

---

[6] Cited n. 4.

[7] See ch. V, p. 155.

[8] See ch. III, pp. 107-114.

[9] See ch. III, n. 52.

[10] See ch. III, n. 51.

[11] Cf. *Mitte*, 16 n. 2; 19. It was not unknown for introductions to be composed independently of the works for which they were used. Demosthenes, for example, had a collection of ready made proemia to hand for use when the occasion demanded (*Proemia*), and Cicero remarked in a letter to Atticus (XVI,6.4) that he had a roll full of proemia; he even prefixed one by mistake to his work *De Gloria* which he sent to Atticus forgetting that he had already used it for the third volume of his *Academica*. Such pre-cast introductions would be unlikely to have a real organic relationship with the works to which they were prefixed.

[12] F. C. Conybeare, "Ein Zeugnis Ephräms über das Fehlen von c. 1 und 2 im Texte des Lucas", *ZNW* 3 (1902) 192-197, esp. 196; but see the criticism of D. Völter, "Das angebliche Zeugnis Ephräms über das Fehlen von c. 1 und 2 im Texte des Lucas", *ZNW* 10 (1909) 177-180.

[13] B. H. Streeter, *The Four Gospels. A Study of Origins*, London 1924, 209; cf. A.

For Schubert, though, Luke's infancy narrative was no afterthought. Indeed he was very emphatic about finding here the beginning of Luke's proof-from-prophecy theology which he saw as dominating the whole of Luke–Acts.[14] Nor was it for Audet and Minear who attributed to Lk 1-2 the function of an Hellenistic proemium and a prologue respectively.[15] While taking the narrative to be a later addition,[16] Brown regards it as having an introductory role in the gospel,[17] as does Schürmann, who describes it as a prelude.[18] Oliver, Tatum, Minear and Brown all stress the importance of the infancy narrative for any proper analysis of the thought of Luke.[19]

The following two chapters are usually taken to be more directly related to the ministry of Jesus and in some way preparatory to it, although the situation is complicated by the fact that the beginning of the account of Jesus' ministry is generally placed at some point within their confines. Many authors entitle the unit 3,1–4,13 "The Preparation of

---

Hilgenfeld, "Zu Lucas III,2", *ZWT* 44 (1901) 466-468; G. Erdmann, *Die Vorgeschichten des Lukas- und Matthäus-Evangeliums und Vergils vierte Ekloge*, FRLANT 48: Göttingen 1932, 7; see also P. Benoit, "L'Enfance de Jean-Baptiste selon Luc I", *NTS* 3 (1956-57) 173; W. G. Kümmel, *Introduction to the New Testament*, tr. by H. C. Kee, London 1975², 136-137; W. Wink, *John the Baptist in the Gospel Tradition*, SNTSMS 7: Cambridge 1968, 58 n. 1; Schürmann, *Lk* I, 141; R. E. Brown, *The Birth of the Messiah. A commentary on the infancy narratives in Matthew and Luke*, London 1977, 240-241; I. H. Marshall, *The Gospel of Luke. A Commentary on the Greek Text*, Exeter 1978, 157; L. Legrand, *L'Annonce a Marie (Lc 1,26-38). Une apocalypse aux origines de l'Évangile*, LD 106: Paris 1981, 312-313.

[14] P. Schubert, "The Structure and Significance of Luke 24", *Neutestamentliche Studien für R. Bultmann*, ed. W. Eltester, BZNW 21: Berlin 1954, 165-186.

[15] J.-P. Audet, "Autour de la théologie de Luc I-II", *ScEc* 11 (1959) 412; P. S. Minear, "Luke's Use of the Birth Stories", *Studies in Luke-Acts*, eds. L. E. Keck, J. L. Martyn, London 1968, 119; cf. X. Léon-Dufour, "Les Évangiles synoptiques", *Introduction à la Bible* II, *Nouveau Testament*, eds. A. Robert, A. Feuillet, Tournai 1959², 233; Fitzmyer, *Lk I-IX*, 184, describes it as "a sort of overture to the whole opus".

[16] Glued on, presumably, like the proemium sent by Cicero to Atticus (see n. 11 above).

[17] *Birth*, 242; cf. A. Loisy, *L'Évangile selon Luc*, Paris 1924, 24.

[18] *Lk* I, 18.204.

[19] H. H. Oliver, "The Lucan Birth Stories and the Purpose of Luke-Acts", *NTS* 10 (1963-64) 202-226; W. B. Tatum, "The Epoch of Israel: Luke I-II and the Theological Plan of Luke-Acts", *NTS* 13 (1966-67) 184-195; Minear, "Birth Stories", 112-118; Brown, *Birth*, 242. On the basis of vocabulary and style it was considered to form an integral part of the gospel by A. Harnack ("Das Magnificat der Elizabet (Luc 1,46-55) nebst einigen Bemerkungen zu Luc 1 und 2", *SPAW* 27 (1900) 538-556; *Lukas der Arzt. Beiträge zur Einleitung in das Neue Testament* I, Leipzig 1906, 69-75.138-152), H. Zimmermann ("Evangelium des Lukas Kap. 1 und 2", *TSK* 76 (1903) 249-290) and J. G. Machen (*The Virgin Birth of Christ*, New York-London 1930, 102-118); see also A. Plummer, *A Critical and Exegetical Commentary on the Gospel According to S. Luke*, ICC, Edinburgh 1922⁵, lxix; N. Turner, "The Relation of Luke I and II to Hebraic Sources and to the Rest of Luke-Acts", *NTS* 2 (1955-56) 100-109; Minear, "Birth Stories", 112-118.

Jesus' Ministry".[20] Loisy viewed 3,1–4,44 as a unit and took it to introduce Jesus' Galilean ministry of 5,1–9,50.[21] Schürmann, likewise, takes these chapters to form a unit, but sees them as describing "The Beginning from Galilee".[22] As for the Nazareth scene, it has long been regarded as programmatic for Jesus' ministry.[23] In the wake of Schürmann's treatment of Lk 4,14-44 a number of authors have come to regard this whole unit in a similar vein.[24]

Although the infancy narrative and the following two chapters are generally regarded by many as very much separate entities for reasons of style and content, quite a number of authors see the gospel's initial section as extending beyond the infancy narrative into the following chapters. Schanz, Wikenhauser and Schmid took 1,5–4,13 to form a unit, applying to it the term *Vorgeschichte* (Preliminary History).[25] The more

---

[20] Cf. J. Knabenbauer, *Evangelium Secundum Lucam, Commentarius in Quatuor S. Evangelia Domini N. Jesu Christi* III, Paris 1905², 155; F. Hauck, *Das Evangelium des Lukas*, Leipzig 1934, 47; A. Valensin, J. Huby, *Évangile selon Saint Luc*, VS 3: Paris 1927², 1; A. Wikenhauser, *Einleitung in das Neue Testament*, Freiburg 1953, 146; K. Staab, *Das Evangelium nach Markus und Lukas*, Würzburg 1956, 31; W. J. Harrington, *The Gospel according to St Luke*, London 1968, 76; C. Stuhlmueller, "The Gospel According to Luke", *The Jerome Biblical Commentary* II, eds. J. A. Fitzmyer, R. E. Brown, London 1970, 119; J. Ernst, *Das Evangelium nach Lukas*, Regensburg 1977, 135; J. P. Kealy, *Luke's Gospel Today*, Denville 1979, 156; J. Kremer, *Lukasevangelium*, Würzburg 1988, 45; R. J. Karris, "The Gospel According to Luke", *The New Jerome Biblical Commentary* II, eds. J. A. Fitzmyer, R. E. Brown, London 1990, 677; J. Weiss, *Die drei älteren Evangelien. Die Schriften des Neuen Testaments* I, ed. W. Bousset, Göttingen 1917³, 412, entitles it "The introduction to Jesus' public ministry".

[21] Loisy, *Lc*, 169.

[22] *Lk* I, 147.

[23] See, for example, H. J. Holtzmann, *Die Synoptischen Evangelien. Ihr Ursprung und Geschichtlicher Charakter*, Leipzig 1863, 214-215; F. Nicolardot, *Les Procédés de Rédaction des Trois Premiers Évangélistes*, Paris 1908, 174; E. Klostermann, *Das Lukasevangelium*, HNT 5: Tübingen 1975³, 61 ("...ein Vorspiel für sein Geschick überhaupt"); D. Hill, "The Rejection of Jesus at Nazareth (Luke iv 16-30)", *NT* 13 (1971) 170 ("...programmatic prologue to the ministry of Jesus"); also T. Zahn, *Das Evangelium des Lucas*, Leipzig 1913¹⁻², 239; H. Anderson, "Broadening Horizons. The Rejection of Nazareth Pericope of Luke 4:16-30 in Light of Recent Critical Trends", *Int* 18 (1964) 260.

[24] Cf. M. Völkel, "Zur Deutung des "Reiches Gottes" bei Lukas", *ZNW* 65 (1974) 63-65; U. Busse, *Die Wunder des Propheten Jesus. Die Rezeption, Komposition und Interpretation der Wundertradition im Evangelium des Lukas*, FzB 24: Stuttgart 1977, 58; idem, *Das Nazareth-Manifest Jesu. Eine Einführung in das lukanische Jesusbild nach Lk 4,16-30*, SBS 91: Stuttgart 1978, 77-81; A. del Agua Pérez, "El cumplimiento del Reino de Dios en la misión de Jesús: Programa del Evangelio de Lucas (Lc. 4,14-44)", *EstBib* 38 (1979) 271-273.

[25] P. Schanz, *Commentar über das Evangelium des heiligen Lucas*, Tübingen 1883, 39; Wikenhauser, *Einleitung*, 146; J. Schmid, *Das Evangelium nach Lukas*, RNT 3: Regensburg 1960⁴, 33; also Kümmel, *Introduction*, 125, who describes this unit as "prehistory and preparation for Jesus' ministry"; Knabenbauer, *Lk*, 42; J. Moffat, *An*

evocative term prologue, although without much specification, was applied by Davies to 1,1–3,38[26] and by Gibbs to 1,1–4,30.[27] In the more recent analyses of Wilkens,[28] and Bossuyt and Radermakers,[29] 1,5–4,44 is taken to form the gospel's opening section.

The variety of proposals for the extent of the gospel's first major section raises another question, namely, the extent of the introductory material in 1,1–4,44 and the point at which the gospel's narrative proper begins — at 1,5, 3,1, 3,21, 4,1, 4,14, 4,31, or at 5,1 as will be argued in the present study. There is certainly a great lack of unanimity on this point. Nevertheless, the views listed above clearly indicate the widespread feeling that a relationship exists between various parts of these initial four chapters and the remainder of Luke's work. The present study examines the nature and extent of this relationship, and it concludes that these chapters as a whole prepare the reader or hearer in a variety of ways for the rest of Luke–Acts.

A necessary preliminary to the study of 1,1–4,44 in its relationship to what follows is the determination of the literary structure of the two-volume work as a whole and of the gospel in particular. This has its own intrinsic value, as has been noted above. But a cursory survey of the literature shows how indispensable such a study is in any case, and particularly so given the need to justify the extension of the gospel's first major section to 4,44. Proposed literary structures range from the different four-part arrangements put forward by Schleiermacher, Ewald and others,[30] to the sixteen-part structure of Grimm,[31] and include

---

Introduction to the Literature of the New Testament, Edinburgh 1920[3], 264; A. Stöger, *Das Evangelium nach Lukas* I, Düsseldorf 1964, 15; R. Meynet, *Quelle est donc cette parole? Lecture "rhétorique" de L'évangile de Luc (1–9,22-24)* I, LD 99A: Paris 1979, 149; C. F.Evans, *Saint Luke*, London 1990, v. For C. H. Talbert, *Reading Luke. A Literary and Theological Commentary on the Third Gospel*, New York 1984, 15-17, 1,5–4,15 forms a unit; for A. Bisping, *Erklärung der Evangelien nach Markus und Lukas*, EHNT II: Münster 1868[2], 145, 1,1–4,13.

[26] J. H. Davies, "The Lucan Prologue (1-3): An attempt at objective redaction criticism", *SE* VI, ed. E. A. Livingstone, TU 112: Berlin 1973, 79-83.

[27] J. M. Gibbs, "Mark 1,1-15, Matthew 1,1–4,16, Luke 1,1–4,30, John 1,1-51. The Gospel Prologues and their Function", Livingstone (ed.), *SE* VI, 182.

[28] W. Wilkens, "Die theologische Struktur der Komposition des Lukasevangeliums", *TZ* 34 (1978) 1.6.

[29] P. Bossuyt, J. Radermakers, *Jésus Parole de la Grâce selon saint Luc* I (9-22), II (29-30), Brussels 1981.

[30] F. Schleiermacher, *Ueber die Schriften des Lukas, ein kritischer Versuch*, Berlin 1817, 18; H. Ewald, *Die drei ersten Evangelien und die Apostelgeschichte* I, Göttingen 1871[2], 95; cf. Bisping, *Mk und Lk*, 145; Léon-Dufour, "Évangiles", 233; E. E. Ellis, *The Gospel of Luke*, London 1966, 33-37; Harrington, *Lk*, 76; Evans, *Lk*, v-vi; Wilkens, "Struktur", 1.

[31] J. Grimm, *Die Einheit des Lukasevangeliums*, Regensburg 1863.

various five,[32] six[33] and seven-part[34] structures of the majority of exegetes. The picture for Acts is not much different,[35] and the same applies to individual sections of both volumes, 1,5–4,44 being no exception.[36]

The present study opens then with an analysis in chs. I and II which endeavours to establish the literary structure of Luke–Acts. Ch. I concentrates on 1,1–4,44, while ch. II looks at the remainder of Luke's work, and the gospel in particular. The study goes on in chs. III and IV to examine the roles of Lk 1,1-4 and 1,5–4,44 in Luke–Acts from various points of view. In the final chapter the literary form of the two-volume work, in which both these units play a decisive role, is discussed.

Before attempting to establish the literary structure of Luke–Acts a brief word on the subject of methodology is necessary. In the past, source criticism led many to propose arrangements of the gospel overly dependent on Luke's use or non-use of sources, especially those taken to be of Marcan provenance. The underlying assumption in such cases really was that the evangelist's sources controlled the order and arrangement of his own presentation. True, it was recognized that Luke's placing of the Nazareth pericope offered evidence of a Lucan overall design. But placing the conclusion of a major section at 8,3[37] or 18,14,[38] or taking the travel narrative to end at 19,27[39] or 19,28,[40] was often due more to

---

[32] Cf. Schanz, *Lc*; Knabenbauer, *Lc*, 21; Moffat, *Introduction*, 264; Loisy, *Lc*; Klostermann, *Lk*; J.M. Creed, *The Gospel According to Saint Luke*, London 1930, lvii; Ernst, *Lk*; Wikenhauser, *Einleitung*, 146-149; E. Schweizer, *Das Evangelium nach Lukas*, NTD 3: Göttingen 1982.

[33] Cf. Plummer, *Lk*, xxxviii-xl; Schmid, *Lk*; Stöger, *Lk* I, 15-19; II (Düsseldorf 1966), 7-10; G. Schneider, *Das Evangelium nach Lukas Kapitel 1-10*, ÖTK 3.1: Regensburg 1977, 25; Kremer, *Lk*, 16-20.

[34] Cf. Holtzmann, *Evangelien*, 206-242; J. Weiss, *Evangelien*, 392-511; M.-J. Lagrange, *Évangile selon Saint Luc*, Paris 1921², xxxiv-xxxv; Hauck, *Lk*, v-viii; Marshall, *Lk*, 7-11.

[35] See ch. II, pp. 67-69.

[36] See ch. I, pp. 9-10, and there nn. 2-18.

[37] Cf. Holtzmann, *Evangelien*, 220; Wikenhauser, *Einleitung*, 147; Stöger, *Lk* I, 172.

[38] Cf. Holtzmann, *Evangelien*, 225; J. Wellhausen, *Das Evangelium Lucae übersetzt und erklärt*, Berlin 1904, 45; Klostermann, *Lk*, 101; Léon-Dufour, "Évangiles", 233; Fitzmyer, *Lk I-IX*, 138.

[39] For this popular point of division see J. Weiss, *Evangelien*, 443; Knabenbauer, *Lc*, 330; K.L. Schmidt, *Der Rahmen der Geschichte Jesu. Literarkritische Untersuchungen zur ältesten Jesusüberlieferung*, Berlin 1919, 246-247; Moffat, *Introduction*, 264; Valensin, Huby, *Lc*, 1; Hauck, *Lk*, 134; C.C. McCown, "Gospel Geography: Fiction, Fact, and Truth", *JBL* 60 (1941) 14; Staab, *Mk und Lk*, 65; Schmid, *Lk*, 176; Harrington, *Lk*, 8; Schürmann, *Lk* I, 260-261; Stöger, *Lk* I, 272; Ernst, *Lk*, 314; Schneider, *Lk 1-10*, 225-226; Kremer, *Lk*, 18-19; Evans, *Lk*, vi; Karris, "Luke", 677; F. Bovon, *Das Evangelium nach Lukas* 1, EKKNT III.1: Zürich 1989, 15; A. Huck, H. Lietzmann, *Synopsis of the First Three Gospels*, ed. F.L. Cross, Oxford 1972, 153; A. Huck, H. Greeven, *Synopse der drei ersten Evangelien mit Beigabe der johanneischen Parallelstellen*, Tübingen 1981, 191; K.

considerations based on Luke's presumed use of sources than to indications from the evangelist's text.[41]

In a study such as the present one a knowledge of the exact relationship between the synoptics could be of great value, but it is not of vital importance. Given the continuing debate surrounding the various solutions to the synoptic problem,[42] it seems best to treat each of the synoptics as independent, while recognizing that they have a great deal of material in common. Even if it were true that Luke uses Mark's gospel and generally follows its order of pericopes, it still does not follow that this is determinative for the literary structure of Luke's work, no more than Livy's use of Polybius was for the arrangement of his work.[43] A comparison of the gospel of Luke with the other synoptics highlights its specifically Lucan elements, and this in turn helps one to see more clearly the particular arrangement that he gives his account. But it must be kept in mind that it is the text of Luke that is of primary importance for the determination of its literary structure.

Aland, *Synopsis Quattuor Evangeliorum*, Stuttgart 1973[8], 360; also the comment of I. de la Potterie, "Les deux noms de Jérusalem dans l'évangile de Luc", *RSR* 69 (1981) 66 n. 26.

[40] Cf. J. A. Bengel, *Gnomon Novi Testamenti*, Tübingen 1742, 202; Plummer, *Lk*, 260; Stuhlmueller, "Luke", 119; A. George, "Tradition et rédaction chez Luc. La construction du troisième Évangile", *ETL* 43 (1967) 109 (= *Études sur l'œuvre de Luc*, Paris 1978, 23).

[41] See, for example, the unit 5,17–6,11 proposed by Schmid, *Lk*, 123, and Wikenhauser, *Einleitung*, 250, due mainly to the fact that it is parallel to Mk 2,1–3,6 (cf. R. Pesch, *Das Markusevangelium* I, HTKNT II.I: Freiburg 1976, 33; J. Gnilka, *Das Evangelium nach Markus (Mk 1-8,26)*, EKKNT II.1: Zürich-Neukirchen 1978, 71. Marshall, *Lk*, 206, takes the unit 5,12–6,11 to reproduce the section Mk 1,40–3,6. One of the reasons Fitzmyer advances for treating 3,1 as the beginning of the Lucan gospel proper (*Lk I-IX*, 450) is its correspondence to Mk 1 at this point.

[42] The spate of articles and the number of books that have appeared on various aspects of the synoptic problem in recent years, occasioned especially by the important contributions of R. C. Butler, *The Originality of St. Matthew. A Critique of the Two-Document Hypothesis*, Cambridge 1951, and W. R. Farmer, *The Synoptic Problem. A Critical Analysis*, Dillsboro 1976[2] (1964), make it impossible, in the compass of a brief note, to give an overview of the present situation. One can only refer the reader to the following selection that should give an idea of the difficulties facing all current hypotheses: R. H. Fuller, "Die neuere Diskussion über das synoptische Problem", *TZ* 34 (1978) 129-148; J. A. Fitzmyer, "The Priority of Mark and the "Q" Source in Luke", *Jesus and man's hope* I, eds. D. G. Miller, D. Y. Hadidian, Pittsburg 1970, 131-170; M.-E. Boismard, "The Two-Source Theory at an Impasse", *NTS* 26 (1979-80) 1-17; B. Orchard, T. R. W. Longstaff (eds.), *J. J. Griesbach: Synoptic and Text-Critical Studies. 1776-1976*, SNTSMS 34: Cambridge 1979; W. O. Walker, Jr. (ed.), *The Relationships Among the Gospels. An Interdisciplinary Dialogue*, San Antonio 1978; W. R. Farmer (ed.), *New Synoptic Studies. The Cambridge Gospel Conference and Beyond*, Macon 1983; C. M. Tuckett (ed.), *Synoptic Studies. The Ampleforth Conferences of 1982 and 1983*, JSNTSS 7: Sheffield 1984, esp. vii-xii; F. G. Downing, "Compositional Conventions and the Synoptic Problem", *JBL* 107 (1988) 69-85.

[43] Cf. T. J. Luce, *Livy: The Composition of his History*, Princeton 1977, xxvi.3-7.25-32; P. G. Walsh, *Livy: His Historical Aims and Methods*, Cambridge 1961, 173-190; E. Burck, *Die Erzählungskunst des T. Livius*, Berlin-Zürich 1964[2].

CHAPTER I

THE LITERARY STRUCTURE OF LK 1,1–4,44

Introduction

Literary analyses of the first four chapters of Luke's gospel have produced quite a variety of results. Various two and three-part arrangements have been put forward for the infancy narrative to accommodate the parallel between the figures of John and Jesus that is clearly present.[1] Points of division are placed at 3,20/21,[2] 3,38/4,1,[3] 4,13/14[4] and 4,30/31[5] in the following two chapters, while units such as 1,1–2,52,[6] 1,1–3,38,[7] 1,1–4,30,[8] 1,5–4,13,[9] 1,5–4,15[10] and 1,5–4,44[11] are also proposed. Not surprisingly, the beginning of the gospel's narrative

---

[1] See the convenient summary of such arrangements in Brown, *Birth*, 248-249.

[2] Cf. George, "Construction" 106 (= *Études*, 20); N. Geldenhuys, *Commentary on the Gospel of Luke*, London 1965, 46; L. Morris, *Luke*, London 1974, 61; Meynet, *Parole* I, 169.

[3] Cf. Davies, "Prologue", 84.

[4] An important point of division in many commentaries; see those of Bisping, Schanz, Knabenbauer, J. Weiss, Lagrange, Valensin-Huby, Creed, Hauck, Schmid, Staab, Stöger, Harrington, Stuhlmueller, Ernst, Schneider, Marshall, Fitzmyer, Kremer and Evans; also F. Godet, *Commentaire sur l'Évangile de Saint Luc* I, Paris 1872², 205.287; Kümmel, *Introduction*, 125.

[5] Cf. W. Grundmann, *Das Evangelium nach Lukas*, THNT 3: Berlin 1974⁷, 98; Gibbs, "Prologues", 182; Schweizer, *Lk*, 10.44-45. Both Holtzmann, *Evangelien*, 211-214, and Wellhausen, *Lc*, 3, placed the division at 4,15/16.

[6] Cf. Audet, "Luc I-II", 412; Léon-Dufour, "Évangiles", 233; Minear, "Birth Stories", 119.

[7] Cf. Davies, "Prologue", 78-84.

[8] Cf. Gibbs, "Prologues", 182-186.

[9] See Prologue, n. 25; also R. Cornely, *Introductio Specialis in Singulos Novi Testamenti Libros*, Paris 1897², 161. Bisping, *Mk und Lk*, 145, took 1,1–4,13 to form a unit; likewise Evans, *Lk*, v.

[10] Cf. C. H. Talbert, *Luke*, 15-17; idem, "Prophecies of Future Greatness: The Contribution of Greco-Roman Biographies to an Understanding of Luke 1:5–4:15", *The Divine Helmsman: Studies on God's Control of Human Events*, Presented to L. H. Silberman, eds. J. L. Crenshaw, S. Sandmel, New York 1980, 129.

[11] Cf. Wilkens, "Struktur", 1.6; Bossuyt, Radermakers, *Luc* I, 9-22; II, 29-30.

proper is variously placed at 1,5,[12] 3,1,[13] 4,1,[14] 4,14[15] and 4,31.[16] Of particular note is the fact that Nestle, in his edition of the Greek New Testament, placed major breaks at 1,4/5 and 4,44/5,1.[17] Westcott and Hort did so at 1,4/5 and 2,52/3,1, and to a lesser, if still noticeable, degree at 4,44/5,1.[18] In the light of these various arrangements it is evident that the crucial points for any literary analysis of these chapters are 1,4/5, 2,52/3,1, 3,20/21, 3,38/4,1, 4,13/14, 4,30/31 and 4,44/5,1.

Style, content, form or genre and geography are the usual factors taken into account when the literary structure of these chapters is examined. The first three are decisive factors in delineating the units 1,1-4 and 1,5-2,52, while geographical considerations appear to carry the greatest weight in placing a beginning at 4,14 or a conclusion at 4,44. In the complex matter of determining literary structure these are certainly important considerations. But so too are other 'clues' left consciously or unconsciously by the author, repetitions of various kinds, time indications, summaries, pauses, narrative settings and developments, literary associations, and so on. Where possible, various indicators are taken into account when endeavouring to establish the extent of a particular unit and the principle of arrangement adopted in that unit. Bearing this in mind let us examine the literary structure of 1,1–4,44.

1. 1,1-4: Proemium

The gospel opens in impressive fashion with what Norden once described as the New Testament's best written period, 1,1-4.[19] Composed of one carefully written and unusually compressed sentence which is

---

[12] Cf. Ewald, *Evangelien*, 95; Godet, *Lc*, 81; Knabenbauer, *Lc*, 42; Hauck, *Lk*, 17; Ellis, *Lk*, 33; Harrington, *Lk*, 8; Wilkens, "Struktur", 1; Meynet, *Parole* I, 149.

[13] Cf. Schleiermacher, *Lukas*, 50; Wellhausen, *Lc*, 3; Klostermann, *Lk*, 48; Schürmann, *Lk* I, 146-147; Léon-Dufour, "Évangiles", 233; Huck, Lietzmann, *Synopsis*, 3; see also P. Rolland, "L'organisation du Livre des Actes et de l'ensemble de l'oeuvre de Luc", *Bib* 65 (1984) 83; Plummer, *Lk*, xxxviii; Schweizer, *Lk*, 44-45. George, "Construction", 105 (= *Études*, 20), takes 3,21–9,50 to form a unit.

[14] See n. 7 above.

[15] Cf. J. Weiss, *Evangelien*, 421; Wikenhauser, *Einleitung*, 146; Schneider, *Lk* I, 103; Ernst, *Lk*, 165.

[16] Cf. Gibbs, "Prologues", 183-184. Grundmann, *Lk*, 123, places the beginning of Jesus' Galilean ministry at 4,31.

[17] Cf. E. Nestle, *Novum Testamentum Graece*, Stuttgart 1908[7] (1898), and subsequent editions up to but excluding the latest (26) of K. Aland (Stuttgart 1979) in which the major break after 4,44 no longer appears.

[18] B.F. Wescott, F.J.A. Hort, *The New Testament in the Original Greek, Text*, Cambridge-London 1890[2] (1881).

[19] E. Norden, *Agnostos Theos. Untersuchungen zur Formengeschichte Religiöser Rede*, Leipzig-Berlin 1913, 316 n. 1.

clearly distinguishable in language, style and content from the following narrative, it contains not a few of the elements common to proemia of ancient prose writings.[20] The author refers to the subject matter of the work,[21] to earlier writings on the same subject,[22] and to the sources used.[23] He mentions his decision to write,[24] indicates the method, scope and accuracy of his investigations,[25] gives the reader information on his method of composition,[26] communicates the purpose of the work,[27] and dedicates it to Theophilus.[28] It has all the character of a self-contained proemium, a circumstance that distinguishes it further from what follows.

2. 1,5–2,52: Infancy Narrative

With an abrupt change in tone and style — likened by Plummer to the change from a chapter of Xenophon to one of the Septuagint[29] —

---

[20] On the proemium see the convenient collection of proemia of A. Toynbee, *Greek Historical Thought. From Homer to the Age of Heraclius*, New York 1952², 29ff.; see also H. Lieberich, *Studien zu den Proömien in der griechischen und byzantinischen Geschichtschreibung I. Teil. Die griechischen Geschichtschreiber*, Munich 1898; T. Janson, *Latin Prose Prefaces. Studies in Literary Conventions*, AUSSLS 13: Stockholm 1964; G. Engel, *De antiquorum epicorum didacticorum historicorum prooemiis*, Diss. Marburg 1910; A. D. Leeman, "Structure and meaning in the prologues of Tacitus", *YCS* 23 (1973) 169-208.

[21] Cf. Her., *Hist.* I,1; Thuc., *War* I,1.1; Pol., *Hist.* I,1.1; Diod., *Hist.* I,1.1; 3.2; Dion. Hal., *Ant. Rom.* I,3.6; 5.1-3; Appian, *Hist. Rom.* Pr. 1.13-14; Jos., *BJ* I,1; Livy, *Ab Urbe* Pr. 1; etc.

[22] See, for example, Her., *Hist.* I,1-5; Pol., *Hist.* I,1.1-2; 4.2-3; Diod., *Hist.* I,1.1-3; Dion. Hal., *Ant. Rom.* I,6.1-2; 7.1; Jos., *BJ* I,1-2; *C. Ap.* I,4-27; Tac., *Hist.* I,1; *Agric.* 1,1; Diosc., *De Mat. Med.* I Pr.; *Rhet. ad Her.* IV,1.1-7.10.

[23] Cf. Thuc., *War* I,22.1-3; Diod., *Hist.* I,4.1-5; Dion. Hal., *Ant. Rom.* I,7.1-3; Jos., *C. Ap.* I,4-5.59; Arrian, *An.* I Pr. 1.3; Phil., *Apoll.* I,2; etc.

[24] Cf. Diod., *Hist.* I,3.5; Dion. Hal., *Ant. Rom.* I,6.3; Jos., *BJ* I,3; *C. Ap.* I,3; Phil., *Apoll.* I,2.

[25] Cf. Thuc., *War* I,22.1-3; Diod., *Hist.* I,4.1-5; Dion. Hal., *Ant. Rom.* I,7.1-3; Arrian, *An.* I Pr. 1-3; Phil., *Apoll.* I,2-3; etc.

[26] Cf. Diod., *Hist.* I,3.5–6.8; Arrian, *An.* I Pr. 1; Appian, *Hist. Rom.* Pr. 13-15; Dio Cass., *Hist.* I,2; Livy, *Ab Urbe* Pr. 6; Jos., *Ant.* I,17; Phil., *Apoll.* I,2.

[27] Cf. Her., *Hist.* I,1; Thuc., *War* I,1.1; Pol., *Hist.* I,1.1–2.5; Dion Hal., *Ant. Rom.* I,5.1-3; 6.3-5; Jos., *C. Ap.* I,3; Phil., *Apoll.* I,2.

[28] Cf. J. Ruppert, *Quaestiones ad historiam dedicationis librorum pertinentes*, Diss. Leipzig 1911; Janson, *Prefaces*, passim; art. "Dedications", *OCD*, 259-260. The dedication is most common in didactic works; see, for example, the proemia of Dioscorides (*De Mat. Med.* I-V), the dedicatory letters to the scientific works of Archimedes (cf. *De Sph. et Cyl.*; *De Con. et Sph.*) and Apollonius of Perga (*Con.* I), the proemia of the rhetorical treatises of Quintilian (*Inst. Or.*) and Cicero (cf. *De Or.*; *Or.*), of *Rhet. ad Alex.* and *Rhet. ad Her.*, and of Varro's works on Agriculture and the Latin language; it is also to be found elsewhere, as in the writings of Isocrates (*Evag.*), Plutarch (*Dem.*; *Dion*; *Aratus*), Josephus (*C. Ap.* I-II) and Tacitus (*Agric.*; *Dial.*).

[29] *Lk*, 1.

Luke begins his account of the events surrounding the conception, birth and growth of both John and Jesus. The unity of these two chapters has long been recognized for reasons of content and style. So also has the careful arrangement of the material. It is commonly agreed, and brought out best perhaps in the literary structure proposed by Dibelius, that the author intended to draw a parallel between John and Jesus here.[30] But the same consensus does not apply to the extent of this parallel nor to the literary arrangement of these chapters.[31]

2.1 1,5-56: 'Annunciation' and Visitation

The first three literary units of the gospel are so closely linked as to give the impression of the unity of 1,5-56. The account of John's miraculous conception in 1,5-25 is framed by references to Elizabeth's sterility in vv. 7 and 25 (στεῖρα...ὄνειδος), by the time indications of vv. 5 and 25 (ἐν [ταῖς] ἡμέραις), and by the mention in vv. 5 and 24 of Elizabeth herself.[32]

The arrival and departure of the heavenly messenger frame the 'annunciation' scene of 1,26-38 (cf. vv. 27-28.38). It is closely linked to the previous scene by references to Elizabeth's pregnancy in vv. 26a (cf. v. 24b) and 36 and by the angel Gabriel who acts as the divine messenger in both cases (cf. vv. 19.26). Striking structural and thematic parallels between the two scenes have long been noted (see below).

The visitation scene of 1,39-56 is enclosed by Mary's movements — her departure from a city of Judah in v. 39 and her return to her home in v. 56b. From dramatic and thematic points of view it is closely linked to the previous two. References in vv. 24-25 to Elizabeth's pregnancy and to her five-month seclusion, together with the sign given to Mary in v. 36, clearly prepare for the visitation scene in which the dramatic movement begun in the first scene comes to an initial climax with the meeting of the two mothers and their unborn children. The immediacy of Mary's

---

[30] M. Dibelius, Die urchristliche Überlieferung von Johannes dem Täufer, FRLANT 15: Göttingen 1911, 67-68; cf. Plummer, Lk, 6; Klostermann, Lk, 4; Erdmann, Vorgeschichten, 10-11; F. Dornseiff, "Lukas der Schriftsteller. Mit einem Anhang: Josephus and Tacitus", ZNW 35 (1936) 129-130; E. Burrows, The Gospel of the Infancy and Other Biblical Essays, London 1940, 1-6; R. Laurentin, Structure et Théologie de Luc I-II, Paris 1957, 32-42; O. da Spinetoli, Introduzione ai Vangeli dell'Infanzia, Brescia 1967, 68, and there n. 4; Wink, Baptist, 58-60; 60 n. 1; A. George, "Le parallèle entre Jean-Baptiste et Jésus en Lc 1-2", Mélanges Béda Rigaux, eds. A. Descamps, A. de Halleux, Gembloux 1970, 147-171 (= Études, 43-65); Brown, Birth, 248-252; Legrand, L'Annonce, 50-53.

[31] Cf. Brown, Birth, 248-249; Wink, Baptist, 59.

[32] Note also the contrasting references to Elizabeth in vv. 7 and 24 (στεῖρα... συνέλαβεν) observed by Meynet, Parole II, A1.

reaction to the sign of v. 36 is highlighted by the phrase μετὰ σπουδῆς of v. 39. The angel's promise of v. 15 is fulfilled in v. 41, while Mary's faith and humility of the previous scene are recalled by Elizabeth's praise of v. 45 and her own description of herself as God's δούλη in the Magnificat (v. 48). These various considerations suggest that the events preceding the births of John and Jesus form something of a unity within the infancy narrative.[33] The arrangement of the rest of this narrative as set out below adds a confirmative note.

2.2 1,57-80: Birth and Growth of John

John is the focus of attention in this section which is framed by references to him in vv. 57 (ἐπλήσθη ὁ χρόνος τοῦ τεκεῖν αὐτήν... υἱόν) and 80 (τὸ δὲ παιδίον ηὔξανεν... ἕως ἡμέρας ἀναδείξεως αὐτοῦ). Canticle (1,68-79) and narrative (1,57-66) are linked by virtue of the address of v. 76, καὶ σὺ δέ, παιδίον, and by the final four verses of the canticle which may be seen as Zachary's response to the wonder expressed by the neighbours and others at the circumstances surrounding the naming of the child. With the notice in v. 80b that John spent his life up to the beginning of his mission to Israel in the desert, the reader is brought up to the point at which the story of John is resumed in 3,1-2. The author must now retrace his steps to give a parallel account of Jesus' birth and infancy.

The section has many links with the previous one. John's birth, his naming and the accompanying circumstances (cf. vv. 57.59b-64) represent obvious links with the first scene (cf. vv. 13.20.22). Zachary's inspired words of v. 76 (προπορεύσῃ γὰρ ἐνώπιον κυρίου ἑτοιμάσαι ὁδοὺς αὐτοῦ) echo those of the angel in v. 17 (προελεύσεται ἐνώπιον αὐτοῦ... ἑτοιμάσαι κυρίῳ λαόν), while the public recognition of the Lord's mercy to Elizabeth in v. 58 recalls Elizabeth's own words in v. 25 and those of Mary in the Magnificat (cf. vv. 47.50.54).

2.3 2,1-52: Birth and Growth of Jesus

Chronological and historical references in 2,1-3 signal a change of tone and the beginning of a new phase in the narrative devoted to Jesus' birth and early life. The two problematic verses for a literary analysis of this chapter are vv. 21 and 40.

---

[33] Cf. Burrows, *Infancy*, 4-5; Dibelius, *Überlieferung*, 68; P. Gaechter, *Maria im Erdenleben. Neutestamentliche Marienstudien*, Innsbruck 1953, 12; S. Lyonnet, "Le récit de l'Annonciation et la Maternité Divine de la Sainte Vierge", *AmiCl* 66 (1956) 36; Laurentin, *Luc I-II*, 32-33.

Tischendorf, Wescott and Hort, and Nestle leave v. 21 isolated in their editions of the text.[34] *The Greek New Testament* separates it from what follows.[35] It is more commonly taken to form part of the unit 2,21-40.[36] Since the birth, circumcision and naming are linked in the case of John, and the phrase ἐν τῇ κοιλίᾳ of v. 21 recalls οὔσῃ ἐγκύῳ of v. 5, it seems best to take 2,1-21[37] as a unit.

While Wescott and Hort, Nestle and *The Greek New Testament* print v. 40 along with v. 39 separately from the rest of the text, the two verses are usually taken to conclude a section.[38] The two have different roles, however. V. 39 functions as a conclusion, bringing the development begun in 2,4 to a close[39] and more importantly emphatically noting the return of Joseph and Mary to Nazareth. Notwithstanding its nature as a summary[40] v. 40 functions as an introduction, the reference to Jesus being filled with wisdom preparing the scene in the temple which illustrates this wisdom.[41] The repetition with progression in 2,52 of the terms σοφία, χάρις and θεός of 2,40 forms an inclusion for 2,40-52.[42]

The unit 2,1-39 is framed by the movements of Joseph and Mary with the child (cf. vv. 4.39b), and may be further divided into two closely linked units, 2,1-21 and 2,22-39.[43] The repetition of v. 21a in v. 22a marks the point of division between these two,[44] while references to the law in vv. 22 and 39 (κατὰ τὸν νόμον) form an inclusion for the latter.

---

[34] In addition to the editions of C. Tischendorf (*Novum Testamentum Graece* I, Leipzig 1869), Westcott and Hort, and Nestle (cited above), see also that of H. J. Vogels (*Novum Testamentum Graece*, Düsseldorf 1920).

[35] Eds. K. Aland, M. Black, C. M. Martini, et al., Stuttgart 1975³.

[36] See, for example, Plummer, *Lk*, 61; Klostermann, *Lk*, 39; Grundmann, *Lk*, 87; Ernst, *Lk*, 112; Schneider, *Lk* I, 69; Marshall, *Lk*, 114; Fitzmyer, *Lk I-IX*, 418; Schweizer, *Lk*, 36.

[37] Thus Erdmann, *Vorgeschichten*, 11; Gaechter, *Maria*, 12; Schürmann, *Lk* I, 97; George, "Parallèle", 151; Brown, *Birth*, 393; Meynet, *Parole* I, 158.

[38] See n. 36 above; 2,1-40 is taken to form a unit by Schmid, *Lk*, 63, Schürmann, *Lk* I, 97, and Brown, *Birth*, 408.

[39] Note the repetition in 2,4.39: ... ἀπὸ τῆς Γαλιλαίας ἐκ πόλεως Ναζαρὲθ εἰς τὴν Ἰουδαίαν εἰς πόλιν... εἰς τὴν Γαλιλαίαν εἰς πόλιν ἑαυτῶν Ναζαρέθ.

[40] A summary may act as an introduction (cf. 4,14-15; 8,1; 13,22; Acts 8,4; 11,19; etc.), as well as a conclusion (cf. 1,80; 2,52; 21,37-38; 24,53, etc.); see below.

[41] Cf. H. J. Holtzmann, *Die Synoptiker*, HCNT I.1: Tübingen-Leipzig 1901³, 322; Schmid, *Lk*, 79; Laurentin, *Luc I-II*, 135-141; Schürmann, *Lk* I, 132-133.

[42] For the unit 2,40-52 see Holtzmann, *Synoptiker*, 322; F. Christ, *Jesus Sophia. Die Sophia-Christologie bei den Synoptikern*, ATANT 57: Zürich 1970, 61; also Gaechter, *Maria*, 10.50.

[43] Note the repetition of Χριστὸς κύριος of 2,11 in 2,26, the proclamation of the presence of salvation in 2,11 (ἐτέχθη ὑμῖν σήμερον σωτήρ) and 2,29-30 (Νῦν...τὸ σωτήριόν σου), and references to the first-born in 2,7 and 2,23.

[44] Καὶ ὅτε ἐπλήσθησαν (αἱ) ἡμέραι (ὀκτὼ) τοῦ...: vv. 21a.22a; on this type of repetition see H. Lausberg, *Handbuch der Literarischen Rhetorik. Eine Grundlegung der Literaturwissenschaft*, Munich 1973², 311-315.

It should be noted that 2,40-52, and not simply 2,40,[45] is parallel to 1,80a-80b, and, as in the case of this verse and John, brings the narrative about Jesus up to the point at which it is resumed in 3,21 (cf. 2,51-52). This suggests that the parallel between John and Jesus runs right through the chapter. There is, to be sure, a patent imbalance between 2,40-52 and 1,80, but such an imbalance is equally present in the accounts of their births and naming.

Indications of the closely-knit nature of the infancy narrative as a whole continue to be found here. Associations between 2,1-21 and the preceding chapter include references to Mary's betrothal (2,7; cf. 1,27), to David (2,4; cf. 1,32), and to the praise of God (2,28.30; cf. 1,67-79).[46] The fulfilment of the words of Gabriel to Mary (1,31) is underlined by the use of the verb τίκτω in 2,7. The three angelophanies of 1,11-20, 1,26-38 and 2,8-13 represent striking parallels.[47]

The final scene is linked to other parts of the narrative particularly by its temple setting, a setting that looms large throughout the infancy narrative and provides it with a framework (cf. 1,5-25; 2,40-52). Its conclusion in Nazareth (cf. vv. 51-52) recalls 2,39 and the 'annunciation' to Mary (cf. 1,27). The astonishment of those who heard Jesus in the temple (cf. 2,47) recalls similar reactions in the accounts of John's naming (cf. 1,63) and Jesus' birth (cf. 2,18). Mary's meditative reaction of 2,51b recalls 2,19 and 1,66.

2.4 *The parallel in 1,5–2,52*

The parallel in 1,5–2,52 between John and Jesus, in which the superiority of Jesus is clearly implied, is a commonplace of Lucan exegesis.[48] There is little agreement though on the actual extent of this parallel and on the motif-arrangement of these chapters.[49] The following arrangement, based in part on the literary analysis conducted above, suggests that the parallel runs right through the infancy narrative:

---

[45] On the parallel between 2,22-39 and 1,67-79 see Gaechter, *Maria*, 10; George, "Parallèle", 153; for Wink, *Baptist*, 59, Dibelius, *Überlieferung*, 67, and Erdmann, *Vorgeschichten*, 11, the parallel is between 2,22-40 and 1,67-80.

[46] Cf. Brown, *Birth*, 156.409.424.

[47] It is true that 2,40a and 1,80a are parallel, but not 2,40b and 1,80b; whereas the latter contains a time indication that covers the span of life from John's childhood to the beginning of his public ministry, not so the former which merely refers to the growth of Jesus and to the favour of God on him. The septuagintal parallels for 1,80b and 2,40b are represented by Gen 21,20b and 1 Kgs 3,19 respectively; for 2,52b, by 1 Kgs 2,26.

[48] See n. 30 above.

[49] Cf. Brown, *Birth*, 248-249; Burrows, *Infancy*, 4-6; Dibelius, *Überlieferung*, 67; George, "Parallèle", 147-148; Erdmann, *Vorgeschichten*, 11.

Announcement of Conception, etc.[50]	1,5-25	1,26-38
Visitation	1,39-56	
Birth	1,57-58	2,1-20
Circumcision and Naming	1,59-66	2,21
Praise & Prophecy	1,67-79	2,22-39
Growth; Life prior to public ministry	1,80	2,40-52

One can readily see from this table that the parallel is rarely balanced. Two verses, for example, are devoted to John's birth, twenty to that of Jesus. The proportion in the case of the circumcision and naming is eight to one in favour of John. It is very much the other way in the case of their growth and life prior to the beginning of their ministries — one to thirteen. Despite this imbalance, Luke's desire to parallel the two figures is evident right through.

The parallel is perhaps most evident in the first two scenes which despite their different literary forms[51] contain many points of similarity. These include: the angelophanies; the birth oracles with their references to extraordinary conceptions and to the identity and future of both figures;[52] significant linguistic links, such as the subtle use of ταράσσω and its compound διαταράσσω to characterize the different reactions of Zachary and Mary to the angelic visitor; septuagintal reminiscences, such as those recalling the conception of Isaac (cf. 1,7b.18b: Gen 18,11; 1,37: Gen 18,14).

The parallel is continued in the visitation scene where John's leap in his mother's womb indicates the presence and identity of Jesus. Elizabeth's hymn of praise (1,42-45) and Mary's own hymn of praise to God (1,47-55) highlight the great privilege that has been bestowed on Mary, a privilege that reflects the greatness of her son.

In 1,57-80 and 2,1-52 the sequence of motifs is similar, even if extra elements are found in the latter. Verbal similarities again underline the parallel. The actual birth reports are patterned in part on Gen 25,24 (cf. 1,57; 2,6),[53] while the accompanying reactions of joy, astonishment, praise of God and much thought are couched in similar terms.[54] Verbal

---

[50] The titles of the various sections are only roughly indicative of content here.

[51] The former is a miraculous birth story, the latter, a call narrative; cf. K. Stock, "Die Berufung Marias (Lk 1,26-38)", Bib 61 (1980) 461-465; G. M. Soares Prabhu, " 'Rejoice, Favored One!' Mary in the Annunciation Story of Luke", Biblebhashyam 3 (1977) 259-265; 271 n. 2; F. Ó Fearghail, "The Literary Forms of Lk 1,5-25 and 1,26-38", Marianum 43 (1981) 321-344.

[52] And patterned on Gen 16,11-12, 17,19 and Judg 13,3-5.7.

[53] Gen 25,24: καὶ ἐπληρώθησαν αἱ ἡμέραι τοῦ τεκεῖν αὐτήν.

[54] Cf. συνέχαιρον ... χάρα (1,58; 2,10); ἐθαύμασαν (1,63; 2,18); πάντα τὰ ῥήματα ταῦτα, καὶ ἔθεντο πάντες ... ἐν τῇ καρδίᾳ αὐτῶν ... ἡ δὲ Μαριὰμ πάντα συνετήρει τὰ ῥήματα ταῦτα συμβάλλουσα ἐν τῇ καρδίᾳ αὐτῆς (1,65-66; 2,19).

links are also to be found between the prophetic hymns of praise of Zachary and Simeon,[55] and between 1,80a and 2,40a.[56] Circumcision and naming are associated in the case of both (cf. 1,59-63; 2,21), and the author is concerned to bring his account of each up to the point at which their public ministries begin (cf. 1,80b; 2,51-52).[57]

The clearest indication of the author's desire to parallel John and Jesus in these two chapters is the awkwardly lying 2,21c which appears to have been inserted here, not without difficulty, to remind the reader that Jesus, like John, was given the name communicated by the angel before his conception.

While bringing out the similarities between the two figures, the parallel also highlights their differences, thus bringing out the uniqueness and superiority of Jesus. The conception of John, for example, is miraculous, but it has Old Testament parallels, particularly that of Isaac in which problems of barrenness and old age had also to be overcome (cf. 1,7b.18b; Gen 18,11-12). In the case of Jesus no such parallel exists, for it is unique.[58] Of note also is the fact that the conception of John was the result of prayer (cf. 1,13), while that of Jesus was completely unsought, being the result of the will of God and the positive response of Mary to his call.

The identity of the two figures is brought out especially in the birth oracles. In 1,14-17 John is presented as one who will be great before the Lord,[59] and something of a Nazarite who will be filled with the Spirit from his mother's womb (cf. 1,41). Of Jesus it is said that he will be great, Son of God and a royal figure whose reign will endure for ever. John appears as the precursor in 1,41-44, Jesus as the κύριος (cf. 1,43). While the story of John's naming brings out his unusual nature (cf. 1,65-66), the lengthy account of Jesus' birth proclaims him Χριστὸς κύριος and σωτήρ. And while John is described as a prophet of the most high (1,76), Jesus is described as God's salvation which is prepared before all peoples, a light of revelation to the Gentiles and the glory of Israel.

---

[55] Cf. πνεύματος (τοῦ) ἁγίου (1,67; 2,26); εὐλογητὸς κύριος ὁ θεὸς τοῦ 'Ισραήλ, ... εὐλόγησεν τὸν θεόν (1,68a; 2,28b); λύτρωσιν (1,68b; 2,38); note σωτηρία in 1,69.71.77, and σωτήριον in 2,30; εἰρήνη in 1,79 and 2,29.

[56] Τὸ δὲ παιδίον ηὔξανεν καὶ ἐκραταιοῦτο is found in both.

[57] Cf. 3,1-2.21-23.

[58] The difficulty is overcome here only by the unique action of the Spirit (cf. 1,35); on this point see the discussion between Brown (*Birth*, 299-301; "Luke's Description of the Virginal Conception", *TS* 35 (1974) 360-362) and J. A. Fitzmyer ("The Virginal Conception of Jesus in the New Testament", *TS* 34 (1973) 566-570; *Lk I-IX*, 337-341).

[59] That is, "in the eyes of the Lord"; cf. 4 Kgs 5,1; Dan Th Su 64; also Grundmann, *Lk*, 50; Marshall, *Lk*, 57.

Distinctive features of the missions of the two figures also emerge from the parallel. In making ready for the Lord a people prepared (cf. 1,17d) John's mission is directed solely to Israel, for he is to turn many of the sons of Israel to the Lord their God (1,16).[60] The reference in 1,80b to the ἡμέρας ἀναδείξεως αὐτοῦ πρὸς τὸν Ἰσραήλ corresponds to this limitation.[61]

The universal setting of the birth-narrative (cf. 2,1-2) and the cosmic significance of the child's birth expressed in the words of the heavenly messengers (cf. 2,10.14) suggest the universal significance of Jesus' mission.[62] Even the language and style of 2,1-20 correspond to this emphasis; for these verses contain less semitisms than the surrounding narrative,[63] and the public proclamation of Jesus' birth in 2,10-11 is couched in imperial tones[64] in marked contrast to the septuagintal language and style of 1,58. The universal implications present in these scenes are made quite explicit by the words of Simeon in 2,30-32.[65]

---

[60] On the eschatological nature of both their missions see p. 125 below; also G. Lohfink, *Die Sammlung Israels. Eine Untersuchung zur lukanischen Ekklesiologie*, SANT 39: Munich 1975, 22-23.

[61] Schürmann, *Lk* I, 94, translates it "Bestallung für Israel"; also W. Bauer, *Griechisch-Deutsches Wörterbuch zu den Schriften des Neuen Testaments und der übrigen urchristlichen Literatur*, Berlin 1952[4], 97, though not the English edition (W. F. Arndt, F. W. Gingrich, *A Greek-English Lexicon of the New Testament and Other Early Christian Literature*, Chicago 1974, 53) which renders it with 'manifested'. It could be translated with "commission", if this term were understood as a signal to begin his ministry and not as a conferral of office (see n. 74 below).

[62] It is possible that the birth oracle in 1,32-33 with its reference to the restoration of the Davidic throne may already imply the extension of salvation beyond Israel, for according to Acts 15,14-17, in which Amos 9,11-12 LXX is cited, the Gentile mission is associated with the restoration of the Davidic kingdom alluded to in the text of Amos. The re-erection of the fallen tent of David does not refer to the gathering and restoration of Israel, as Lohfink, *Sammlung Israels*, 59, suggests, not even in the Hebrew text where it refers to the restoration of Davidic rule over all the nations over which David ruled, including Edom (cf. J. L. Mays, *Amos. A Commentary*, London 1969, 163-164). As in Qumran (4QFlor 1.12-13), the citation from Amos in Acts 15 refers to an individual, to Jesus, in fact (cf. E. Haenchen, *The Acts of the Apostles. A Commentary*, Oxford 1971, 448).

[63] See the study of R. Morgenthaler, *Statistik des Neutestamentlichen Wortschatzes*, Zürich-Stuttgart 1973[2], 62-63, on 2,1-20.

[64] Cf. E. Norden, *Die Geburt des Kindes. Geschichte einer religiösen Idee*, Leipzig-Berlin 1924, 157, and there n. 2 where he cites the Priene inscription; for 2,10-11 see, apart from this inscription cited in ch. IV, n. 110 below, Plut., *Lyc.* 3,4, and Ditt., *Syll³*. 760,5, both cited in Klostermann, *Lk*, 37; *IGRR* III,715.718.

[65] Cf. S. G. Wilson, *The Gentiles and the Gentile Mission in Luke-Acts*, SNTSMS 23: Cambridge 1973, 36-38; Creed, *Lk*, 41; Marshall, *Lk*, 120-121; Fitzmyer, *Lk I-IX*, 428.

3. 3,1-4,44: Ministries of John and Jesus

The unity of chapters three and four is an important feature of Schürmann's analysis.[66] Wescott and Hort, and Nestle, in their editions of the text, had already suggested their unity, as had Loisy, if briefly and only in passing.[67] But Schürmann's work, which received strong support from Völkel and others,[68] has put it on a firmer footing, and this is the position of the present study.

Schürmann's view of the role of 3,1 in the gospel as the starting point of the narrative proper is by no means as secure.[69] The elaborate six-part synchronism of 3,1-2a, so elaborate, in fact, that Streeter regarded it as the "opening section of a book",[70] is indeed suitable for the beginning of a major section or of the narrative proper,[71] and certainly more suitable for the latter than 1,5, 4,14 and 4,31 that are assigned the role from time to time.[72] But a number of factors militate against taking this impressive opening, however unique in the New Testament, to introduce more than the following two chapters.

Synchronisms are used both in Hellenistic and Jewish literature, but the texts occasionally cited as parallels for Lk 3,1-2a do not mark the beginning of the narrative proper of their respective works. Pol., *Hist.* I,3.1-2 is part of the proemium in which it introduces 3.1–5.5 and justifies the point at which Polybius begins his history. Thuc., *War* II,2.1 marks the beginning not of the narrative proper but of the Peloponnesian war. And Pol., *Hist.* I,6.1-2 marks the beginning of the preparatory narrative that extends over the first two volumes of Polybius' history.[73] In the case of Jewish parallels the synchronism generally forms part of the title or prologue of the work (cf. Is 1,1; Jer 1,1-3; Hos 1,1; Amos 1,1).

---

[66] Cf. Schürmann, *Lk* I, 147.

[67] Loisy, *Lc*, 169; also Wilkens, "Struktur", 2.

[68] Cf. M. Völkel, "Der Anfang Jesu in Galiläa. Bemerkungen zum Gebrauch und zur Funktion Galiläas in den lukanischen Schriften", *ZNW* 64 (1973) 225-226; Lohfink, *Sammlung*, 39 n. 76; Agua Pérez, "Cumplimiento", 271 n. 10; Wilkens, "Struktur", 2.

[69] Cf. Schürmann, *Lk* I, 146-147, and the authors cited in n. 12 above.

[70] *Gospels*, 209; an observation owed, he states, to a conversation with J.C. Hawkins. See Fitzmyer, *Lk I-IX*, 310.

[71] In Diodorus' historical work synchronisms are frequently used to mark the beginning of the account of the year's events from the point where accurate dating is possible and where in consequence an annalistic arrangement is adopted (cf. XI,1.2; 27.1; 38.1; 41.1). The beginning of the narrative proper (I,6.1) is not marked with a synchronism.

[72] See nn. 12-16 above.

[73] Neither Polybius (*Hist.* III,6.1) nor Thucydides (*War* I,118.3; cf. I,24.1) begins the narrative proper with a synchronism. Synchronisms are used by Josephus in the course of the narrative (cf. *BJ* II,284; *Ant.* XVIII,106).

Partly responsible for the elaborate nature of the synchronism in 3,1-2a is the political situation in Palestine that had evolved quite a bit from the time of John's conception (cf. 1,5). The time indication of 1,5 and the synchronism of 3,1-2a are in fact closely related, the former indicating the political situation in Palestine at the time of John's conception, the latter, that at the beginning of his ministry.

With its additional references to the Roman emperor and the Jewish religious leadership, 3,1-2a is certainly more striking and elaborate than 1,5. But the force of the reference to the emperor in 3,1-2a is relativized somewhat by the fact that such a reference is already to be found in 2,1-2 which introduces a new section within the infancy narrative. The elaborate nature of 3,1-2a is justified to a certain extent by its immediate context. John's ministry has its own importance, as is underlined by the lengthy scriptural citation of 3,4-6. With the public appearance in Israel of this prophetic figure (cf. 3,2-3), the long-still voice of prophecy once again resounds in the land. The promise is being fulfilled (cf. 3,4-6). John's appearance also signals Jesus' proximate arrival on the public scene. The ministries of these two are inextricably linked, the former pointing towards the latter (cf. 3,15-17) and already awakening the firm hope of universal salvation (cf. 3,6).

The close links between this section and the preceding one should also be noted. The notice of the 'call' of John, son of Zachary, couched in terms reminiscent of Old Testament call narratives,[74] recalls the 'biblical' words of the angel in 1,17 and of the old priest in 1,76, and these prophetic words are presented by 3,4 as being fulfilled in John's ministry. The desert scene of the 'call' (cf. 3,2b) reminds the reader that the story of John resumes from where it left off in 1,80b.

Neither Acts 1,21-22 nor the summary of the gospel given in Acts 1,1-2 provides support for placing the beginning of the gospel's narrative proper at 3,1-2a. Both these texts indicate the beginning of Jesus's ministry as the earliest possibility for this point.[75]

---

[74] Cf. Jer 1,4; Hos 1,1; Mic 1,1; Joel 1,1; Zech 1,1; Hag 1,1; etc. Unlike the OT parallels John does not receive a revelation; the coming of the word of God refers to a single event at a definite place and time that initiated his ministry. John is equipped for his mission from his mother's womb and already begins his activity there (cf. 1,41.44); cf. A. Serra, "Le Madri d'Israele nell'antica letteratura giudaica e la Madre di Gesù. Prospettive di Ricerca", *Il Salvatore e la Vergine-Madre. La maternità salvifica di Maria e le cristologie contemporanee*, Atti del 3º Simposio Mariologico Internazionale, Rome-Bologna 1981, 343; Brown, *Birth*, 341.

[75] The beginning of Jesus' ministry is explicitly associated with discipleship in Acts 1,21-22; on Acts 1,1-2 see p. 96 below.

3.1 *3,1-20: Ministry of John*

The account of John's ministry in 3,1-20 exhibits a clear thematic unity. An inclusion which is formed between vv. 1-2 and 19-20 by references to Herod, during whose reign this ministry takes place (τετρααρχοῦντος ... Ἡρῴδης ὁ τετραάρχης), his brother Philip (Φιλίππου δὲ τοῦ ἀδελφοῦ αὐτοῦ ... τοῦ ἀδελφοῦ αὐτοῦ) and John himself (Ἰωάννην ... τὸν Ἰωάννην) underlines this unity.

The role of v. 18 in this section has been the subject of some debate. Is it to be taken with vv. 15-17 as part of the description of John's ministry, or with vv. 19-20 as part of the conclusion (cf. μέν ... δέ: vv. 18.19)?[76] The former appears more likely. As a summary, v. 18 rounds off the treatment of John's preaching, describing it as 'good news' (εὐαγγελίζετο) and indicating that much more was preached besides (πολλά ... καὶ ἕτερα). Of note is the fact that Luke uses not the simple μέν here but μὲν οὖν which has a resumptive force (cf. Acts 8,25; 9,31). V. 18 also acts as a transition to what follows, a role likewise accommodated by μὲν οὖν.[77] But neither its transitional role nor the presence of δέ in v. 19[78] necessitates that v. 18 be taken with vv. 19-20. The concluding two verses provide a contrast not only with v. 18 but with the whole preceding section on John's ministry.

3.2 *3,21–4,44: Ministry of Jesus*

With the removal of John from the scene in 3,20 and the arrival of Jesus in 3,21, a new section begins. As he did in the case of John, Luke now picks up the story of Jesus from where he left off in the infancy narrative and resumes the parallel between the two figures.

3.2.1 *3,21-38: The Initiation of Jesus' Ministry*

a) *3,21-22*

Although 3,21-22 introduces a new section, there is nonetheless an overlap with the previous one. For only in 3,21 is the climax of John's ministry reported with the completion of the baptism of 'all the people'

---

[76] For the former see Meynet, *Parole* II, A7, for the latter, Godet, *Lc* I, 225; Schanz, *Lk*, 167; Plummer, *Lk*, 96; eds. of Tischendorf, Wescott and Hort, Nestle and Vogels.

[77] On the transitional use of μὲν οὖν see J. D. Denniston, *The Greek Particles*, Oxford 1954², 471-472; also F. Blass, A. Debrunner, *A Greek Grammar of the New Testament and Other Early Christian Literature*, tr. R. W. Funk, Chicago-London 1975, 235 (451.1).

[78] The use of μὲν οὖν ... δέ should be distinguished from that of μέν ... δέ since the grammatical connection in the former case is much less strong due to the resumptive force of μὲν οὖν. This is borne out by Luke's own usage in Acts 8,25/26, 9,31/32 and 16,5/6.

and of Jesus in particular. That John is the agent in all cases is implied by the verbal relationships between 3,21 and 3,3-18 provided by βαπτισθῆναι (cf. vv. 4.12.16.21) and λαός (cf. vv. 15.18.21), and by the fact that John is the only one who baptizes here. The events of 3,19-20 represent an anticipation,[79] and a deliberate one at that, since Luke sees the two ministries as succeeding one another (cf. Acts 10,37; 13,24-25).

A great deal of theological weight has been attributed to the *caesura* between 3,1-20 and 3,21 ff. Von Baer interpreted this separation as a deliberate move on Luke's part to have Jesus alone on the centre of the stage as the one and only bearer of the Spirit, and the leading figure in salvation history.[80] Conzelmann found in it the key to Luke's composition, its intent apparently being, in view of the temporal overlap, to make clear the fundamental separation between John and Jesus.[81]

Signs of Lucan redaction in 3,18-22 are not lacking,[82] and the separation and overlap are undoubtedly due to the evangelist. Luke is known to round off one subject before beginning another (cf. 1,56.57.80b).[83] The overlap is significant since it underlines the preparatory role of John which reaches its climax in 3,21, emphasizes Jesus' solidarity with the people,[84] and has the people present at the epiphany of 3,22. But Luke's composition at this point does not imply a division of salvation history into different epochs, whether in von Baer's or Conzelmann's sense of that term.[85]

b) *3,23-38*

Without a change of scene, the evangelist makes an explicit reference to the beginning of Jesus's ministry in 3,23a[86] and links the genealogy

---

[79] Cf. Schürmann, *Lk* I, 189; L. Feldkämper, *Der betende Jesus als Heilsmittler nach Lukas*, St. Augustin 1978, 33; the lectionary has the reading 3,15f.21f. for the feast of Our Lord's baptism.

[80] *Heilige Geist*, 55-56 and 56 n. 11.

[81] *Mitte*, 14-15.

[82] Cf. J. Jeremias, *Die Sprache des Lukasevangeliums. Redaktion und Tradition im Nicht-Markusstoff des dritten Evangeliums*, Göttingen 1980, 112-114; for a penetrating criticism of Conzelmann's theory of the geographical separation between the ministries of John and Jesus see Wink, *Baptist*, 49-51; also the review of W. C. Robinson, Jr., in *Int* 16 (1962) 196.

[83] See also, for example, Acts 9,1-31; 9,32–11,18; 13,1–14,28; cf. C. M. Martini, *Atti degli Apostoli*, Rome 1974³, 20-21.

[84] Cf. Feldkämper, *Betende Jesu*, 47; Godet, *Lc* I, 230.

[85] See ch. IV, pp. 118-122.

[86] On ἦν... ἀρχόμενος see M. Zerwick, M. Grosvenor, *A Grammatical Analysis of the Greek New Testament* I, Rome 1974, 184; É. Samain, "La notion de APXH dans l'oeuvre lucanienne", *L'Évangile de Luc. Problèmes littéraires et théologiques*, Mémorial Lucien Cerfaux, ed. F. Neirynck, BETL 32: Gembloux 1973, 313 n. 43; I. de la Potterie, "La notion de "commencement" dans les écrits johanniques", *Die Kirche des Anfangs*, Fs

(3,23b-38) grammatically to it.[87] The phrase ὢν υἱός, ὡς ἐνομίζετο of v. 23b which recalls 3,22 (cf. υἱός) complements, and at the same time contrasts with, the words of the heavenly voice of 3,22a, adding the point of view of Jesus' contemporaries to that of the divine declaration. The genealogy complements the epiphany of 3,22 with respect to the mission of Jesus, for while the symbolism of the epiphany points towards a mission in Israel's favour,[88] the genealogy points towards a mission of universal significance.[89]

3.2.2 4,1-13: Temptation

A change of scene in 4,1a introduces the temptation story which concludes with the devil's departure in 4,13. It is framed by references to the devil's activity in vv. 2 and 13 (πειραζόμενος ὑπὸ τοῦ διαβόλου... συντελέσας πάντα πειρασμὸν ὁ διάβολος ἀπέστη) and by the verb συντελεῖν (vv. 2.13). As in the other synoptics it is closely related to the baptismal scene through the themes of divine sonship and the Spirit,[90] while the thoroughly Lucan phrase πλήρης πνεύματος ἁγίου[91] provides an extra link in the Lucan chain of relationships.

As has often been noted, the phrase ἄχρι καιροῦ points forward towards the passion narrative, and in particular towards 22,3 and 22,53.[92] This is a method of composition that is typical of Luke, as Dupont has

---

für H. Schürmann, eds. R. Schnackenburg, J. Ernst, J. Wanke, EThSt 38: Leipzig 1977, 380. The indication of age at the beginning of a reign or the assumption of a public office, etc., is not infrequent in the OT and elsewhere; cf. 2 Sam 5,4 (David), Gen 41,46 (Joseph), Num 4,3 (the Levites), Arrian, *An.* I,1.1 (Alexander); Diog. Laert., *Lives* II,5 (Anaxagoras). The close connection between 3,23a and the epiphany is further evidence that the epiphany represents a signal to Jesus to begin his ministry.

[87] Thus emphasizing the relationship between the genealogy and mission of Jesus; see nn. 89 and 126 below.

[88] In 3,22 the coming of the Spirit in bodily form like a dove suggests to the people present that Jesus is the anointed one whom they await, and thus one whose mission is in their favour.

[89] The genealogy implies that Jesus' mission is directed not only to the sons of Abraham, as in the case of John (cf. 3,8), but to all men (cf. Grundmann, *Lk*, 112; K. H. Rengstorf, *Das Evangelium nach Lukas*, NTD 3: Göttingen 1974[15], 61; Stöger, *Lk* I, 124-125; Ernst, *Lk*, 155). The genealogy of Moses is associated with his mission in favour of Israel in Ex 6,10-28.

[90] Cf. Feldkämper, *Betende Jesu*, 36.

[91] Cf. Jeremias, *Sprache*, 114-115.

[92] Note the explicit reference to Satan entering Judas in 22,3 and ὑμῶν ἡ ὥρα καὶ ἡ ἐξουσία τοῦ σκότους of 22,53 (cf. ἐξουσία: 4,6); cf. Staab, *Lk*, 37; Schürmann, *Lk* I, 214; 4,13 is taken to refer to 22,3 (J. Weiss, *Evangelien*, 421; Plummer, *Lk*, 114; Klostermann, *Lk*, 61), 22,53 (Zahn, *Lk*, 226 n. 9), Gethsemane (Godet, *Lc* I, 275; Loisy, *Lc*, 152), the passion (T. W. Manson, *The Sayings of Jesus*, London 1949, 45).

pointed out.[93] Conzelmann takes this phrase to indicate the beginning of a new epoch — that of Jesus — in the particular version of the three-part division of salvation history that he proposes. This point will be taken up in ch. IV. For the present it is sufficient to note how events of the passion narrative are foreshadowed in 4,13.

3.2.3 *4,14-44: Anticipation of Jesus' Ministry*

With the repetition in 4,14a of the verb ὑποστρέφειν of 4,1a, the scene changes rapidly from the desert to Galilee. Many authors take the notice of Jesus' return to Galilee and the first reference to his activity there in 4,14-15 to mark the beginning of a major section that extends to 9,50 and contains an account of Jesus' Galilean ministry.[94] Conzelmann regards the summary of 4,14-15 as a title for this section.[95] Ernst and Schneider go further and take it to mark the beginning of the gospel's narrative proper.[96] Schürmann restricts Jesus' specifically Galilean ministry to 4,14-44 and sees it as constituting the ἀρχή of Jesus' whole ministry.[97] The suggestion that 4,14-44 forms a unit is by no means a novel one. Godet, Schanz, Plummer and Lagrange had already treated it as such.[98] But Schürmann's analysis, and especially his treatment of the problematic Ἰουδαίας in 4,44, has persuaded a number of exegetes in recent years to adopt this position.[99]

Not the least of the reasons for treating 4,14-44 as a unit is the fact that Jesus' activity throughout is very much a synagogal activity. Almost half of all references in Luke's gospel to the synagogue are to be found here (cf. vv. 15.16.20.28.33.38.44), and two such references, ἐδίδασκεν ἐν ταῖς συναγωγαῖς αὐτῶν of v. 15 and ἦν κηρύσσων εἰς τὰς συναγωγὰς αὐτῶν of v. 44 form an inclusion for the unit. The anticipated reference to a Capernaum ministry of Jesus in 4,23 represents a significant link

---

[93] J. Dupont, "Les tentations de Jésus dans le récit de Luc (Luc, 4,1-13)", *ScEc* 14 (1962) 23, and there n. 71.

[94] See the commentaries of Bisping, Godet, Schanz, J. Weiss, Knabenbauer, Plummer, Lagrange, Staab, Creed, Leaney, Stuhlmueller, Stöger, Schmid, Marshall, Ernst, Fitzmyer, Kremer and Evans cited above; also Meynet, *Parole* I, 69.

[95] *Mitte*, 24; cf. Schmidt, *Rahmen*, 37-38.

[96] Ernst, *Lk*, 165; Schneider, *Lk* I, 103.

[97] *Lk* I, 221. Schürmann distinguishes it from the following phase 5,1–19,27 which he sees as extending over the whole land of the Jews.

[98] Godet, *Lc* I, 42; Schanz, *Lk*, 182; Plummer, *Lk*, xxxviii; Lagrange, *Lc*, xxxvi; also Grimm, *Einheit*, 42; Zahn, *Lk*, 248; Leaney, *Lk*, 115; Stuhlmueller, "Luke", 119.

[99] *Lk* I, 221.256-257; 4,14-44 constitutes a unit also for Schneider, *Lk* I, 103; Busse, *Nazareth-Manifest*, 20-21; Agua Pérez, "Cumplimiento", 270-271, and there n. 10; Ernst, *Lk*, 165-166; Wilkens, "Struktur", 2; Evans, *Lk*, 263.

between the Nazareth scene and the following account of a Capernaum based ministry of Jesus.[100] The scriptural reading of 4,18-19 serves to bind the whole together. The expression πνεῦμα κυρίου of v. 18a recalls πνεύματος of v. 14a; εὐαγγελίσασθαι ... ἀπέσταλκέν με κηρύξαι ... κηρύξαι of vv. 18cd and 19 is reproduced on the lips of Jesus in v. 43 and in the summary of 4,44 (εὐαγγελίσασθαί με ... ἀπεστάλην ... ἦν κηρύσσων); the verb ἔχρισεν of v. 18b is echoed in the reference to the demons' knowledge of v. 41 (τὸν Χριστόν). Although Jesus' message of the kingdom is mentioned explicitly for the first time in the gospel in v. 43, its content is already to be found in 4,18-21.

Two summaries, 4,14-15 and 4,44, provide an introduction and a conclusion for this unit which may be divided into two main parts, 4,16-30 and 4,31-43. The first of these is delineated by references to the arrival of Jesus in Nazareth and his departure therefrom (cf. vv. 16a.30) and is itself composed of two parts, 4,16-22 and 4,23-30.[101]

References in vv. 31 and 43 to Jesus' city-orientated ministry form an inclusion for the second part (πόλιν τῆς Γαλιλαίας ... καὶ ταῖς ἑτέραις πόλεσιν) which is set in Capernaum and its environs. Changes in setting from the synagogue of Capernaum (4,31-37) to Simon's house (4,38-41) to a desert place (4,42-43) suggest a three-part composition. The 'other cities' referred to in v. 43 may be Galilean (cf. vv. 14-15.31), though not necessarily so. Indeed given the general nature of the statement in v. 43, they are most likely not. Taking them to refer to the cities of Palestine provides a better transition to 4,44.

3.2.4 4,44: Problem of Judea

Lk 4,44 is of vital importance for Schürmann's analysis of the gospel and also for the present study. It is a verse that is not without its difficulties, as is demonstrated by its textual history. In the light of its importance for the literary analysis of Luke's work, a closer look at it is advisable.

The reading Γαλιλαίας is found in a whole host of manuscripts covering a wide geographical area, an area more impressive by far than those attesting the reading Ἰουδαίας. It can count on the support of the

---

[100] Cf. L. Brun, "Zur Kompositionstechnik des Lukasevangeliums", *SO* 9 (1930) 41: "Dass sie für ihn zusammengehörig sind, wird schon durch die Zusammenordnung der Städte 4,23 gewährleistet"; Busse, *Wunder*, 70.

[101] Thus L. Brun, "Der Besuch Jesu in Nazareth nach Lukas", *Serta Rudbergiana*, eds. H. Holst, H. Moland, Oslo 1931, 7; Schürmann, *Lk* I, 236; diff. R.C. Tannehill, "The Mission of Jesus according to Luke IV 16-30". *Jesus in Nazareth*, ed. W. Eltester, BZNW 40: Berlin-New York 1972, 53.63.

fifth century Codex Alexandrinus and the late fifth or early sixth century Codex Bezae, as well as an impressive number of Greek minuscules, Byzantine, Old Latin and Vulgate witnesses, and part of the Syriac tradition.[102] It is not surprising, then, that all the modern editions of the Greek New Testament and the commentaries prior to the publication of the mid-fourth century Codex Vaticanus considered Γαλιλαίας to be the authentic reading.

With the publication of Codex Vaticanus in 1857 and of Codex Sinaiticus six years later, the weight of the evidence changed dramatically in favour of the reading Ἰουδαίας.[103] Wescott and Hort, who laid great store on the combination B, included it in their edition of the text.[104] So too did Nestle, von Soden and Vogels.[105] Tischendorf remained unimpressed by the new evidence;[106] Godet considered it "absurde";[107] Hahn, an "arbitrary alteration";[108] and K. L. Schmidt, excluded by the context.[109]

The reading Ἰουδαίας nevertheless gradually gained acceptance, and it is not difficult to see why. It clearly represents the *lectio difficilior*, since it is difficult to fit into a Galilean ministry that is usually thought to begin in 4,14 and to extend to 9,50.[110] Moreover, the reading Γαλιλαίας can be explained as due to the influence of 4,14, or as a harmonization with Mt 4,23 or Mk 1,39.[111] Any doubts remaining as to which reading the external evidence supported should have been dispelled with the publication of the second or early third century Bodmer papyrus P[75], the earliest known witness to the text of Luke.[112] The variants τῶν Ἰουδαίων and αὐτῶν represent other attempts to resolve the difficulty caused by Ἰουδαίας for a Galilean ministry extending from 4,14 to 9,50.[113]

The problems of 4,44 do not end here. The meaning of Ἰουδαίας must be determined, since it may refer to the province of that name or the

---

[102] See the mss listed in Nestle or the *Greek New Testament* which include lectionary support.

[103] Cf. Schanz, *Lk*, 194.

[104] Cf. *New Testament* II, Introduction 210ff.; Appendix 57-58.

[105] Published in 1898, 1913 and 1920 respectively; see also Merk 1935[2].

[106] Preferring to adhere to his pre-1857 editions of the text in the case of this reading.

[107] *Lc* I, 315.

[108] G. L. Hahn, *Das Evangelium des Lucas* I, Breslau 1892, 335 n. 2.

[109] *Rahmen*, 61.

[110] See the authors listed in n. 94 above.

[111] Cf. B. M. Metzger, *A Textual Commentary on the Greek New Testament*, London-New York 1971, 137-138.

[112] In the light of the external and internal evidence it is surprising that E. Delebecque, *Évangile de Luc*, Paris 1976, 26, should prefer the reading Γαλιλαίας; see also A. Souter, *Novum Testamentum Graece*, Oxford 1950[2].

[113] The variants involving εἰς and ἐν (see W,1[18] and 1[34,48,1231]m) are not significant from the point of view of the gospel's composition.

whole of Palestine. If it is taken to refer to the province (cf. Lk 3,1), 4,44 would seem to suggest a ministry of Jesus in the south of Palestine 'sandwiched' between two stages of a Galilean ministry described in 4,14-43 and 5,1-9,50.[114] This is hardly likely, since Luke would surely have gone to greater lengths to describe it. In any case, such a ministry goes against the outline set forth in Lk 23,5, Acts 10,37 and 13,31 which has him beginning his activity in Galilee and later wending his way gradually to Jerusalem. Also of note is the general context of 4,44 (cf. v. 43) which points towards the broader sense for Ἰουδαίας in this verse.[115] The evidence is strongly in favour of taking Ἰουδαίας, with most commentaries, to refer to the whole land of Palestine (cf. Lk 1,5; 6,17; 7,17; 23,5; Acts 10,37).

The problem remains of fitting 4,44 with its reference to Palestine into a ministry confined to Galilee in 4,14-43 and again, apparently (see below), in 5,1–9,50. One could with Schürmann take the verse to be transitional and see it as concluding the initial stage of Jesus' ministry which is confined to Galilee ('time of beginning'), while at the same time introducing the next stage which extends to all Palestine (5,1–19,27).[116] In this case the only Galilean ministry strictly speaking is that of 4,14-44, and even this, according to Schürmann's analysis, is not confined to Galilee, since towards its conclusion (4,44) Jesus travels beyond its boundaries, teaching in the synagogues of Palestine.

Schürmann's analysis, however, overlooks the fact that associated with the ἀρχή of Jesus' ministry in Galilee are the motifs of αὐτοψία and the twelve (cf. Acts 1,21-22; 10,37-39), neither of which is present in 4,14-44 where Jesus is unaccompanied.[117] There is the further point that Luke manifestly intends to describe a Galilean ministry of Jesus in 5,1–9,50. In this section Jesus is presented as journeying almost all the

---

[114] In the manner of Jn 2,12–4,3.43-45; see Grundmann, *Lk*, 126; also Conzelmann, *Mitte*, 35 n. 1 and 61-62, with his interpretation of Ἰουδαίας as a province, an interpretation Zahn, *Lk*, 248, had regarded as "unerträglich".

[115] The sense accepted by most; cf. Schürmann, *Lk* I, 29 n. 12; George, "Construction", 106 (= *Études*, 20); Schanz, *Lk*, 194; Völkel, "Anfang", 226; Bauer, *Wörterbuch*, 687,2; Plummer, *Lk*, 141, who points out that classical authors used Judea in much the same manner, Strabo, for example, using it for all the regions from Lebanon southwards; diff. M. Bachmann, *Jerusalem und der Tempel. Die geographisch-theologischen Elemente in der lukanischen Sicht des jüdischen Kultzentrums*, BWANT 109: Stuttgart 1980, 121-126.

[116] Cf. Schürmann, *Lk* I, 146.256-257.

[117] Lagrange, *Lc*, xxxvi, entitles 4,14-44: "Jésus prêche seul"; cf. Godet, *Lc* I, 287.317; H. Schürmann, "L'Évangile (Lc 5,1-11): La promesse à Simon-Pierre", *ASeign* 58 (1964) 27; W. Dietrich, *Das Petrusbild der lukanischen Schriften*, BWANT 94: Stuttgart 1972, 87-88; Fitzmyer, *Lk I-IX*, 559.

time within the borders of the province.[118] It is here that he gathers
together the women who will be present at his death and burial, and who
will come first to the empty tomb (cf. 8,1-3: 23,49.54; 24,6). And it is here
in Galilee that the continual contact of the disciples with Jesus begins (cf.
Acts 1,21-22; 10,37-39; 13,31).[119] Given that Luke describes a Galilean
ministry of Jesus in 4,14-43 and 5,1–9,50, how does one resolve the
problem of 4,44?

The difficulty can be overcome if one accepts that 4,14-44 represents
an anticipation of Jesus' ministry which does not stand in a chronological
relationship to the immediately following narrative. In this case, 4,44
would have a chronological sense solely within the context of 4,14-44,
and then only insofar as it explicitly indicates a ministry of Jesus which,
having begun in Galilee (4,14-43), extends to all Palestine (cf. Lk 23,5;
Acts 10,37). This view of 4,14-44 implies that neither the ἀρχή of Jesus'
ministry as a whole, nor of its Galilean period, is recounted here. What
has happened is that traditions associated with a later stage of Jesus'
ministry have been used by Luke to compose an anticipation of that
ministry.[120] This ensures that the parallel with John's ministry is
completed, that John's relationship with Jesus is clarified, and that a
programmatic introduction to the ministry of Jesus is provided. This
latter aspect of 4,14-44 will be examined further in ch. IV.

The two 'pictures' of Jesus' activity presented in 4,16-30 and 4,31-43
suggest a further reason for taking 4,14-44 to form a unit. Jesus' words in
the former are complemented by his deeds in the latter, so that together
the two serve to characterize the ministry of Jesus as a whole, and in a
way that corresponds to the summary of Acts 1,1 (ποιεῖν τε καὶ
διδάσκειν: cf. Lk 24,19: δυνατὸς ἐν ἔργῳ καὶ λόγῳ). In addition, the
power and authority of Jesus' word are illustrated in the latter.[121] In their
descriptions of reaction to Jesus the two accounts stand in sharp contrast:

---

[118] The one time that Jesus journeys outside the borders of Palestine is presented by
Luke, and Luke alone, as an exception; see 8,26: χώραν τῶν Γερασηνῶν, ἥτις ἐστὶν
ἀντιπέρα τῆς Γαλιλαίας (diff. Mt 8,28; Mk 5,1).

[119] Although the "shared *anabasis*" from Galilee to Jerusalem represents an essential
qualification for a witness (cf. W. C. Robinson, Jr., *The Way of the Lord. A Study of
History and Eschatology in the Gospel of Luke*, Basle 1962, 60-61), it is the whole of Jesus'
ministry, and not simply the journey (cf. R. J. Dillon, *From Eye-Witnesses to Ministers of
the Word. Tradition and Composition in Luke 24*, AnBib 82: Rome 1978, 294), that
provides the witnesses' credentials.

[120] Jesus' visit to Nazareth is associated by the synoptics with a later stage of his
ministry (cf. Mt 13,53-58; Mk 6,1-6; Lk 4,23). Of note also is the fact that Mark's account
of Jesus' miracle working in Capernaum comes after the call of the first disciples (1,21-28)
and not before as in Luke.

[121] Cf. Busse, *Wunder*, 57-62.80; F. Prast, *Presbyter und Evangelium in nachapostolischer Zeit. Die Abschiedsrede des Paulus in Milet (Apg 20,17-38) im Rahmen der
lukanischen Konzeption der Evangeliumsverkündigung*, FzB 29: Stuttgart 1979, 276.

rejection in Nazareth by his own to the point of an attempt on his life, acceptance by the people of Capernaum culminating in an attempt to prevent his departure from their midst. The contrast is underlined by the use of the Lucan verb πορεύεσθαι.[122] From the opposition of Nazareth Jesus escapes in order to go on his way (ἐπορεύετο). The enthusiastic people of Capernaum (καὶ κατεῖχον αὐτὸν τοῦ μὴ πορεύεσθαι ἀπ' αὐτῶν) must be reminded of his divine mandate (δεῖ) to preach the kingdom in "the other cities". The decidedly negative reaction of the Nazareans and the positive reaction of the people of Capernaum offer an anticipation of a ministry that is characterized by rejection and acceptance (see ch. IV below).

3.3 Unity of 3,1–4,44

The foregoing analysis, in which the close links between the various scenes and literary units of 3,21–4,44 have been noted, as well as the significant presence throughout of the motifs of the Spirit (cf. 3,22; 4,1a.14.18ab) and of the divine sonship of Jesus (cf. 3,22.23-38; 4,3.9.41), suggests that 3,21–4,44 constitutes a literary unit. One can go further and affirm with Schürmann that 3,1-20 and 3,21–4,44 together form a literary unit.

The chronological and thematic overlap between 3,1-20 and 3,21–4,44, which sees the climax of John's ministry reported in 3,21 (cf. 3,3.7), points towards their unity. So too does the epiphany of 3,22 which in this context functions as a demonstration to the people present (cf. 3,15.18.21) that Jesus is the one about whom John has been preaching (cf. 3,15-16).[123] But the strongest evidence in favour of their unity comes from the presence in these chapters of a parallel between John and Jesus similar to that found in the infancy narrative. Morgenthaler and Grundmann observed the existence of such a parallel in part of these chapters.[124] It is present, in fact, right throughout 3,1-4,44. Both individuals receive divine signals to begin their ministries (cf. 3,2b.21-22), and their paternity is given at this point (cf. 3,2b.23b). Both are presented as prophetic figures (cf. 3,2b.7-20; 4,16-30) who spend time in the desert prior to the beginning of their ministries (cf. 3,2b; 4,1-13). Both preach "good news" (cf. 3,18; 4,43) and their ministries are shown to fulfil Isaian prophecies (cf. 3,4-6; 4,18–19.21). The parallel may be more clearly seen in the following disposition of the text:

---

[122] Mt-29, Mk-4, Lk-51, Jn-13, Acts-37, Paul-8; Rest-9; cf. Rasco, *Lucas*, 121.

[123] See n. 79 above.

[124] R. Morgenthaler, *Die lukanische Geschichtsschreibung als Zeugnis. Gestalt und Gehalt der Kunst des Lukas* I, Zürich 1949, 154-155; Grundmann, *Lk*, 119.

3,2b	'Commission'	3,21-22	'Commission'
3,2c	Son of Zachary	3,23-38	Son of Joseph; genealogy
3,2d	In the desert	4,1-13	In the desert; temptation
3,3-20	Ministry	4,14-44	Ministry
3a	Scene of ministry	14f.44	Scene of ministry
4-6	Fulfils Isaian prophecy	18f.21	Fulfils Isaian prophecy
7-19	Words (Deeds implied)	14-44	Words & Deeds
18	Εὐηγγελίζετο τὸν λαόν	43	Εὐαγγελίσασθαι ... τὴν βασιλείαν τοῦ θεοῦ
20	Ἐν φυλακῇ	44	Ἦν κηρύσσων ... Ἰουδαίας

As in the case of 1,5–2,52, the parallel is not balanced. The brief reference to John's paternity in 3,2c is paralleled by a sixteen verse genealogy (3,23b-38), the reference to John's period in the desert (3,2d), by the account of Jesus' temptation (4,1-13). 'Deeds' are not actually reported in John's case, though his work of baptizing is implied (cf. 3,7.16). Nevertheless, as the above disposition suggests, the parallel is present throughout. The most eloquent testimony to its deliberate nature is perhaps the use of the verb εὐαγγελίζεσθαι in relation to the preaching of John (3,18; cf. 4,43).

Just as in the infancy narrative, the similarities between the two figures bring their differences into sharper relief, and the uniqueness and superiority of Jesus are highlighted. While both are presented as prophets, John is merely the forerunner, Jesus, the 'stronger one', the anointed one, the beloved divine son, a royal prophetic figure.[125] The signal to John to begin his ministry is expressed in terms reminiscent of Old Testament call narratives, that for Jesus is contained in an epiphany in which a heavenly voice announces his identity and alludes to his mission.[126] John's ministry fulfils the prophecy of Isaiah (40,3-5) insofar as it is one of preparation for the Lord. That of Jesus fulfils Isaian prophecy (60,1-2; 58,6) insofar as he is the one through whom salvation is present. John's ministry as presented in 3,3-20 is directed to Israel (cf.

---

[125] Note the possible allusion to the royal prophetic-type figure of Is 42,1; cf. F. Lentzen-Deis, *Die Taufe Jesu nach den Synoptikern. Literarkritische und gattungsgeschichtliche Untersuchungen*, FTS 4: Frankfurt am Main 1970, 156-158.

[126] On 3,2b see n. 74 above. Jesus is not called to be something new either. His identity and mission are made known in various ways in the infancy narrative, and he is equipped at the moment of his conception for a mission of which he already shows an awareness (cf. 2,40-52). The epiphany of 3,22 has a demonstrative function (cf. Schürmann, *Lk* I, 192; M. Rese, *Alttestamentliche Motive in der Christologie des Lukas*, SNT 1: Gütersloh 1969, 148; Lentzen-Deis, *Taufe Jesu*, 265.270.272; Feldkämper, *Betende Jesu*, 44, and there n. 47); and given the fact that the notice of the beginning of Jesus' ministry follows on immediately without a change of scene, it also has an initiating function with respect to Jesus' ministry.

3,8) and is subordinate to that of Jesus (cf. 3,4.16). His preaching, which does not have the kingdom as its object, is meant to prepare the people for Jesus, the one who is to come. Jesus' ministry is also directed towards Israel (cf. 3,21-22), but it transcends it, since it is of universal significance (cf. 3,23-38; 4,25-27).[127] And unlike John, Jesus preaches the kingdom.

4. Unity of 1,5–4,44

From the above analysis it emerges that 1,5–2,52 and 3,1–4,44 form literary units. One can go further and affirm that these two sections together form the literary unit 1,5–4,44. A number of reasons may be adduced in favour of this position.

One fairly obvious link between the two sections is provided by the fact that the life-stories of both figures are taken up in the second from where they left off in the first. This is quite evident in John's case, as has been noted above (cf. 3,1-2a and 1,5; 3,2b and 1,80b; 3,4-6 and 1,17.76). In the case of Jesus a reference to his supposed paternity in 3,23 recalls the infancy narrative. The phrase οὗ ἦν τεθραμμένος of 4,16 recalls 2,40-52 and Jesus' early life in Nazareth. So too does the complex reaction of the Nazareth congregation in 4,22.[128]

The striking presence of the theme of the Spirit throughout these four chapters and its relative infrequency elsewhere in the gospel offer further support for their unity. Πνεῦμα ἅγιον is found on nine occasions in 1,5–4,44 (1,15.35.41.67; 2,25.26; 3,16.22; 4,1), but elsewhere in the gospel only in 10,21, 11,13, 12,10 and 12,12. Πνεῦμα without the adjective ἅγιος but with the same meaning is found in 2,27, 4,1b, 4,14

---

[127] Jesus' solidarity with "all the people" in his baptism (3,21), the symbolism of the epiphany, particularly that of the dove (cf. Lentzen-Deis, *Taufe Jesu*, 181.265-271.278), and the close relationship of the scene to what precedes, especially 3,15-18, suggest a mission for Jesus in favour of Israel at any rate. On the significance of the genealogy see n. 89 above; on Lk 4,25-27 see Wilson, *Gentiles*, 40-41; Schneider, *Lk* I, 110; Tannehill, "Mission", 60.

[128] The problems long associated with the meaning of 4,22 in the context of Luke's Nazareth scene (cf. Anderson, "Broadening Horizons", 259-275; Hill, "Rejection", 162-169; J. Nolland, "Impressed Unbelievers as Witnesses to Christ (Luke 4:22a)", *JBL* 98 (1979) 219-223) can be resolved by interpreting it against the background of the infancy narrative and 2,40-52 in particular. According to 4,22a the congregation reacts favourably to Jesus (μαρτυρεῖν with the dative carries a positive sense; cf. I. de la Potterie, *Excerpta Exegetica ex Evangelio Sancti Lucae*, Rome 1963-1964, 129; F. Ó Fearghail, "Rejection in Nazareth: Lk 4, 22", *ZNW* 75 (1984) 61-63). This favourable witness refers not to what Jesus has just said but to their personal experience of his extraordinary nature, his grace and favour before God and men (cf. 2,40-52). They are astonished, however, at the message he now preaches (4,22b: καί adversative; θαυμάζειν used with a negative sense; cf. Lk 11,38; Ó Fearghail, "Rejection", 67-71) since he is one of their own (4,22c; cf. 4,16a.24).

and 4,18 (πνεῦμα κυρίου). Of note also are the unique references to the guidance of the Spirit in 2,27 and 4,1b (cf. 4,14), and the association of Spirit and power (δύναμις) in 1,35 and 4,14, an association that recurs only in Acts 1,8 (cf. Lk 24,49) and 10,38.

The relationship between the references to the Spirit in 3,22, 4,1a.18 and 1,35 is of particular note. Since Jesus, unlike John, is already full of the Spirit from the moment of his conception, what is represented in 3,22 is not a new gift of the Spirit but a demonstration that Jesus is the one about whom John has been preaching (cf. 3,16), the anointed one whom the people expect (cf. 3,15). It is to 1,35 that 3,22 and 4,1a.18 primarily refer.[129]

The theme of divine sonship is also characteristic of these four chapters. It is present in the call of Mary (1,32.35), the finding in the temple (2,49), the words of the heavenly voice (3,22), the genealogy (3,23.38), the temptation account (4,3.9), and the story of the healing of many people in Simon's house (4,41; diff. Mk 1,34). The occurrences of the theme elsewhere in the gospel are easily listed: 8,28 on the lips of a demon, 9,35 in the words of the heavenly voice, and 22,70 in a sinister question on the lips of the members of the council. The theme links 3,22 closely to 1,35, for Jesus' divine sonship, which the heavenly voice makes known to the people in 3,22, has already been made known to the reader in 1,35.

Two verbs which play an important role in Luke's theology, δεῖ and εὐαγγελίζεσθαι, and the terms Χριστός and ἅγιος forge significant links between the infancy narrative and 3,1–4,44. Δεῖ is found on the lips of Jesus in 2,49 and 4,43 in reference to his mission. It does not occur again until 9,22 when Jesus uses it to indicate that his mission includes his passion and death. Thereafter it is used in reference to Jesus' mission in 13,33, 17,25, 22,37, 24,7.26 and 24,44 (cf. 24,46), in all of which it refers to the passion.

---

[129] While stressing the demonstrative nature of the epiphany of 3,22, Schürmann, Lk I, 192.194-195, holds, with most commentators, that an actual gift of the Spirit is involved here. This position appears to be based on the interpretation of πλήρης πνεύματος ἁγίου of 4,1 as indicating, in the light of 3,22, that Jesus has just been filled with the Spirit. But the parallel between John and Jesus which implies the superiority of the latter suggests that Jesus is equipped from the moment of his conception for his mission. Furthermore, it is arguable that 4,1a does not refer primarily to 3,22 but backwards to 1,35 and forwards to the temptation scene. In Luke-Acts πλήρης is used to indicate a state which has not arisen in the immediate past and does not arise there and then (cf. Acts 6,3.5.8; 7,55; 11,24; also Lk 5,12; Acts 9,36; 13,10). To express something that happens there and then in Acts 19,28 the verb γίνεσθαι is used with πλήρης. In this πλήρης differs from πίμπλημι which describes a gift, whether in the future (Lk 1,15), or in the immediate past, or there and then (cf. Lk 1,41.67; Acts 2,4; 4.8.31; 9,17; 13,9; also Lk 4,28; 5,26; 6,11; Acts 3,10; 5,17; 13,45). While recalling 1,35 and 3,22, the phrase πλήρης πνεύματος ἁγίου of 4,1a prepares principally for the following encounter with Satan in which Jesus, full of the Spirit, is assured of success. See also ch. IV, p. 133, and there n. 124.

Half of the gospel occurrences of the verb εὐαγγελίζεσθαι are found in 1,5–4,44 (elsewhere 7,22; 8,1; 9,6; 16,16; 20,1). On two occasions it is associated with John (1,19; 3,18), on three, with Jesus (2,10; 4,18.43). In all five cases the verb conveys the sense of 'good news'. The announcement of John's conception, identity and mission (1,13-17) constitutes the beginning of the 'good news' for Luke (cf. 1,19). And only in 4,43 is the content of Jesus' 'good news', the kingdom, first explicitly stated.

The title Χριστός is applied to Jesus four times in 1,5–4,44, directly in 2,11, 2,26 and 4,41, and indirectly in 3,15 (cf. ἔχρισεν: 4,18). It is not found again until Peter's 'confession' in 9,20, and thereafter only in the gospel's Jerusalem section (20,41; 22,67; 23,2.35.39; 24,26.46). The sole occurrences of the adjective ἅγιος in direct reference to Jesus in Luke–Acts are found in 1,35 and 4,34. An indirect, though no less important, reference occurs in 2,23.[130]

The most significant indication of the unity of these chapters is provided by the parallel between John and Jesus that runs not only through the infancy narrative but also through chapters three and four. This becomes even more evident when the exact nature of the parallel is considered.

Luke's infancy narrative is unique among infancy narratives of Jesus in devoting so much attention to the figure of John the Baptist who appears only briefly in the *Protevangelium of James* and not at all in Mt 1-2 or in the *Infancy Gospel of Thomas*. Greater space is also given to his ministry in Luke's account. Being Jesus' precursor, and as such intimately linked to him, John is a figure of importance in his own right, as the events surrounding his birth and the synchronism marking the beginning of his ministry testify. But is this enough to justify the attention devoted to him in 1,5–4,44? Is the parallel simply a parallel?

To the last question Erdmann would certainly have replied in the negative. He took the gospel's first three scenes to contain an implicit comparison between John and Jesus, a syncrisis,[131] in which the superiority of the latter was clearly implied.[132] Later writers brought Erdmann's suggestion a step further, arguing in favour of the presence of a comparison also in the accounts of the actual births and circumcisions, and in the notices of the children's growth in 1,80 and 2,40.[133]

---

[130] See ch. IV, p. 138.

[131] On the syncrisis see F. Focke, "Synkrisis", *Hermes* 58 (1923) 327-368; F. Leo, *Die Griechisch-Römische Biographie nach ihrer Literarischen Form*, Hildesheim 1965 (repr. Leipzig 1901), 149-152.

[132] *Vorgeschichten*, 9: "im stillen wertet".

[133] Cf. Grundmann, *Lk*, 46; George, "Parallèle", 149-154; W. Radl, *Paulus und Jesus im lukanischen Doppelwerk. Untersuchungen zu Parallelmotiven im Lukasevangelium und in der Apostelgeschichte*, EHS XXIII.49: Frankfurt am Main 1975, 352-353.

Grundmann noted its presence in chapters three and four.[134] The foregoing analysis suggests that the whole of 1,5–4,44 was composed in the form of a syncrisis.

The syncrisis is perhaps best known to us from Plutarch's famous syncrises. But long before he wrote, Isocrates published his eulogy of Evagoras in which the murdered king's praise was heightened and his superiority demonstrated by means of a comparison with King Cyrus.[135] The syncrisis was an invaluable tool for literary critics,[136] biographers[137] and historiographers.[138] Its use has been pointed out in the book of Wisdom[139] and in Jewish midrash.[140] Philo used it and wrote about it.[141] And it may underlie a number of texts from Paul's hand (cf. 1 Cor 15,45-49, Rom 5,12-21, Gal 4,21-31, 2 Cor 7,5-8)[142] and from Hebrews (cf. 3,1-6; 9,1-10.11-14; 12,18-24).[143]

That such a technique formed part of Luke's literary store should cause no undue surprise given its widespread use[144] and the fact that it

---

[134] *Lk*, 98-99: "Die Art, wie Lukas die Wirksamkeit des Täufers und die Anfänge des Wirkens Jesu darstellt, entspricht in Parallelität, Überbietung und Verknüpfung der Weise der Kindheitsgeschichten."

[135] *Evag.* §§ 34-38; cf. Focke, "Synkrisis", 335-336; J. Martin, *Antike Rhetorik. Technik und Methode*, HAW II.3: Munich 1974, 188-189; Leo, *Biographie*, 149. Xenophon employed this technique in his eulogy of Agesilaus for the same purpose; cf. *Ages.* 9,1-5; Focke, "Synkrisis", 337. Aristotle's teaching on the subject in *Rhet.* I,9.38-39.1368a corresponds to this use: "And you must compare (συγκρίνειν) him with illustrious personages for it affords ground for amplification and is noble, if he can be proved better than men of worth ... if you cannot compare him with illustrious personages, you must compare him with ordinary persons, since superiority (ὑπεροχή) is thought to indicate virtue"; (tr. J. H. Freese, LCL); see also Anax., *Rhet.* 35.13-14.

[136] Cf. Focke, "Synkrisis", 339-348.

[137] Syncrises were appended to most of Plutarch's parallel *Lives*; they are occasionally found in their introductions (e.g. *Dem.*; *Phoc.*); see Focke, "Synkrisis", 348-351.358-363.

[138] Cf. Her., *Hist.* II,35-37; Pol., *Hist.* I,2.1-7; VI,43.1-56; XXIV,11.1-13.10; Sall., *Cat.* 54; Appian, *Civil War* I Pr.; II,149-154; also I. Bruns, *Die Persönlichkeit in der Geschichtsschreibung der Alten. Untersuchungen zur Technik der antiken Historiographie*, Berlin 1898, 91; George, "Parallèle", 156-157.

[139] Wis 11-19; cf. F. Focke, *Die Entstehung der Weisheit Salomos. Ein Beitrag zur Geschichte des jüdischen Hellenismus*, FRLANT NF 5: Göttingen 1913, 12-20; J. M. Reese, *Hellenistic Influence on the Book of Wisdom and its Consequences*, AnBib 41: Rome 1970, 98.

[140] E. Stein, "Ein jüdisch-hellenistischer Midrasch über den Auszug aus Ägypten", *MGWJ* 78 (1934) 558-575.

[141] Cf. *De Ebr.* §§186-187; for theory see *De Abr.* §36; *De Vita Mos.* I,83; II,194; *De Sacr.* §14; *De Gig.* §§40-41.

[142] Cf. George, "Parallèle", 158.

[143] Cf. A. Vanhoye, *La structure littéraire de l'épître aux Hébreux*, Paris-Bruges 1976², 144-151.206-207.

[144] Examples are also to be found in early Syriac literature (cf. R. Murray, *Symbols of Church and Kingdom. A Study in Early Syriac Tradition*, Cambridge 1975, 42.336; idem,

was one of the *progymnasmata* or preliminary exercises that were studied in the elementary stages of instruction in the Hellenistic school.[145] In these exercises it formed part of the encomium and commonplace,[146] and at least by the time of Quintillian was an exercise in its own right.[147]

The type of syncrisis present in 1,5-4,44 must be distinguished, however, from those appended to Plutarch's parallel lives. Plutarch's are essentially comparisons between men of similar achievement and virtue.[148] Their purpose is not to show the overall superiority of one person over the other, but to complete the picture presented in the parallel lives by highlighting their differences and thus indicating their individual characteristics and achievement. They compare without showing ὑπεροχή.

Luke's use of the syncrisis in 1,5-4,44 to show the superiority of Jesus corresponds more to that found in the encomium or eulogy and in historiography where a person or subject is introduced in order to show the greatness and superiority of the person or subject under discussion.[149]

"Some Rhetorical Patterns in Early Syriac Literature", *A Tribute to A. Vööbus. Studies in Early Christian Literature and Its Environment, Primarily in the Syrian East*, ed. R. H. Fischer, Chicago 1977, 109-131), in Eusebius (cf. *Hist. Eccl.* IX,10.1), the Cappadocian Fathers (see, for example, John Crysostom's comparison of Jesus and Moses showing Jesus' superiority in *Catéchèse* III, 24-26 (*Sc* 50,165-167); also H. Hunger, *Aspekte der griechischen Rhetorik von Gorgias bis zum Untergang von Byzanz*, Vienna 1972, 50), and in Byzantine literature (cf. H. Hunger, *Die Hochsprachliche Profane Literatur der Byzantiner* I, HAW XII.5.1: Munich 1978, 106-108).

[145] Cf. G. A. Kennedy, *The Art of Persuasion in Greece*, Princeton 1963, 270; H. I. Marrou, *Histoire de l'Éducation dans l'Antiquité*, Paris 1948, 272-278; S. F. Bonner, *Education in Ancient Rome. From the elder Cato to the younger Pliny*, London 1977, 259-267; Hunger, *Literatur*, 92-108; D. L. Clark, *Rhetoric in Greco-Roman Education*, New York 1957, 177-212; W. Kroll, "Rhetorik", *PRE Suppl.* VII, 1117-1119; G. L. Kustas, *Studies in Byzantine Rhetoric*, AB 17: Thessalonika 1973, 22, and there n. 1; Focke, "Synkrisis", 331.

[146] See collections of Theon (i/ii), Aphthonius (iii) and Hermogenes (ii) in L. Spengel (ed.), *Rhetores Graeci* II, Leipzig 1854, 1-730.

[147] Cf. Quint., *Inst. Or.* II,4.20-21: "From this our pupil will begin to proceed to more important themes, such as the praise of famous men and the denunciation of the wicked... It is but a step from this to practice in the comparison of the respective merits of two characters"; (tr. H. E. Butler, LCL); also Clark, *Rhetoric*, 194-199; Focke, "Synkrisis", 330ff.

[148] Cf. H. Erbse, "Die Bedeutung der Synkrisis in den Parallelbiographien Plutarchs", *Hermes* 84 (1956) 398-424. This distinction is not observed by George, "Parallèle", 156ff., nor by Radl, *Paulus und Jesus*, 352-355, both of whom refer to examples from classical literature.

[149] That Luke's comparison is carried through not in the more 'rhetorical' manner of immediate comparisons within the sentence itself or in successive sentences, as in the case of Plutarch's syncrises or the examples from Syriac literature, but in blocks of material, section by section, is no militating factor. This method corresponds to the advice of Aphthonius (31,19) and to the use of the syncrisis in Appian, *Civil War* II,21.149-154, and to a lesser extent in Pol., *Hist.* I,2; see also the syncrises of poverty and wealth in *Teles* 33H-48H (cf. *Teles (The Cynic Teacher)*, ed. E. N. O'Neill, Missoula 1977).

By comparing the two figures with respect to their identity and mission Luke brings the uniqueness of Jesus into sharper focus. Indeed the greater the role attributed to John, the more the uniqueness of Jesus emerges. This is especially evident, for example, in the accounts of their conceptions[150] and of the beginning of their ministries.[151]

Support for the placing of a major division at 4,44 is forthcoming also from the remainder of the gospel narrative. It comes, in particular, from Luke's presentation of the associated themes of the apostles and their eyewitness-ship. The importance of the theme of the twelve in Luke's work, whatever the group's exact significance may be,[152] is clearly conveyed by the account of the restoration of the original number in Acts 1,15-26. The necessary qualification for membership of this group is that of continuous contact with Jesus throughout his public life, continuous eyewitness-ship from the beginning of his ministry up to his ascension (cf. Lk 1,2; Acts 1,21-22).[153] This continuity is preserved even in the face of Jesus' passion (diff. Mt 26,56; Mk 14,50).[154] Given Luke's interest in the continuous eyewitness-ship of the apostles "from the beginning" (cf. Lk 1,2; Acts 1,22), one would expect him to to pay particular attention to this in the narrative.

A comparison between the synoptics is instructive at this point. Both Matthew and Mark place the call of the first disciples (later appointed apostles) at the beginning of Jesus' ministry, after his baptism and temptation, the imprisonment of John and a brief summary of Jesus' preaching.[155] Before narrating the call of the first disciples, however, Luke tells of a visit by Jesus to his native town of Nazareth, surely an

---

[150] The comparison highlights the extraordinary nature of Jesus' conception; see especially 1,18.34.37 and Gen 18,14; also the discussion between Fitzmyer and Brown mentioned in n. 58 above.

[151] Note the difference in their 'commissions'; see nn. 74 and 126 above.

[152] On the significance of the twelve see K.H. Rengstorf, "δώδεκα", *TDNT* II, 326-328; S. Freyne, *The Twelve: Disciples and Apostles. A study in the theology of the first three gospels*, London-Sydney 1968, 45-48; P.-H. Menoud, "Les additions au groupe des douze apôtres, d'après le livre des Actes", *RHPR* 37 (1957) 78-79; Lohfink, *Sammlung*, 72; T. Holtz, "δώδεκα", *EWNT* I, 879.

[153] Cf. Freyne, *Twelve*, 220; G. Klein, *Die zwölf Apostel. Ursprung und Gehalt einer Idee*, FRLANT 77: Göttingen 1961, 204-208.

[154] Cf. G. Schneider, *Die Apostelgeschichte* I, HTKNT 5.1: Freiburg 1980, 219, and there n. 63. At the denial Jesus and Peter are in close proximity (cf. Lk 22,61; diff. Mt 26,75; Mk 14,72). Luke's interest in the motif of eyewitness-ship is evident also in his treatment of the Galilean women who are eyewitnesses of Jesus' death and burial and of the empty tomb (cf. Mt 27,55-56; Mk 15,40; Lk 24,49). Unlike Matthew and Mark, he portrays them as actual eyewitnesses of Jesus' Galilean ministry (8,1-3); cf. Schürmann, *Lk* I, 446.

[155] See, apropos of Mark, R. Pesch, *Das Markusevangelium* I, HTKNT II.1: Freiburg 1976, 114: "Der Evangelist macht wenigstens vier Jünger, und zwar die wichtigsten, von Anfang an zu Zeugen des Wirkens Jesu."

important event, especially since it contains a programmatic statement relating to his ministry. Then he gives an account of Jesus' activity in Capernaum where he teaches, expels demons, heals, has his identity proclaimed by demons, and makes a further programmatic statement in relation to his ministry (4,43). On these occasions Jesus is without disciples. The continuous presence associated with apostleship only begins in 5,1-11 with the call of the first three disciples (later apostles). It is true that Jesus is reported in 4,38-41 as visiting Simon's house. Significantly, though, there is no James or John or Andrew present, as in Mk 1,29, and in 4,42 it is not "Simon and those with him" who seek Jesus, as in Mk 1,36, but the ὄχλοι. In 4,44 even they are absent. The introduction of such an important Lucan theme as the eyewitness-ship of the apostles in 5,1-11 and its absence prior to that[156] represent further reasons for placing a major division at 4,44.

In the light of the above remarks on discipleship it is not surprising to find that the initial occurrence of the verb ἀκολουθεῖν in the gospel is to be found in 5,11 (cf. Mt 4,20; Mk 1,18). Nor is it surprising that the term ἐπιστάτα occurs in 5,5 for the first time. This form of address is confined almost exclusively to the disciples and apostles in Luke (Peter: 5,5; 8,45; 9,33; John: 9,49; the disciples in the boat: 8,24).[157] The theme of discipleship, which is intertwined with that of apostleship, is first introduced in 5,1-11. In this pericope, and in 5,27-28, Jesus is shown to be gathering round himself a nucleus of followers. It is no coincidence that the term μαθητής makes its first appearance in the gospel in 5,30.

It may also be pointed out that the expression ὁ λόγος τοῦ θεοῦ, which is found frequently in Acts, occurs for the first time in Luke's work in 5,1 (cf. 8,11.21; 11,28). The theme of hearing the word of God or hearing Jesus is, in fact, a theme upon which Luke lays particular stress in 5,1-9,50, as will be seen presently.[158]

Finally, as will be shown in the following chapter, the placing of a major division at 4,44 is also justified by the fact that 5,1–24,53, and more particularly 5,1-9,50, form literary units in their own right.

---

[156] See n. 117 above.

[157] Even in the case of the lepers in 17,13 it appears to imply some kind of relationship to Jesus; cf. Grundmann, *Lk*, 336-337; W. Bruners, *Die Reinigung der zehn Aussätzigen und die Heilung des Samaritars. Lk 17,11-19. Ein Beitrag zur lukanischen Interpretation der Reinigung von Aussätzigen*, FzB 23: Stuttgart 1977, 186-187; W. Grimm, "ἐπιστάτης", *EWNT* II, 94; see ch. IV, n. 168. Luke uses διδάσκαλος mostly as an address for non-disciples.

[158] The theme of the word of God is already found in Lk 1,2 where λόγος refers to the Christian message (cf. 1,4). It appears again in 4,22 where λόγοις τῆς χάριτος refers to Jesus' message of 4,18-21; in 4,32 λόγος refers to Jesus' teaching in Caphernaum, while in 4,36 it conveys the sense of a command.

Conclusion

From the literary analysis conducted above, it may be seen that the first four chapters of Luke's gospel are composed of a proemial period 1,1-4 and a narrative section 1,5–4,44. The unity of 1,5–4,44 and the existence of a major break in the gospel at 4,44 are suggested by a number of literary and thematic considerations that concern not only 1,5–4,44 but also the remainder of the gospel.

The unit 1,5–4,44 is shown to consist of two main parts, 1,5–2,52 and 3,1–4,44, the first of which may be divided into three parts, 1,5-56, 1,57-80 and 2,1-52, the second into two, 3,1-20 and 3,21–4,44, with 3,21–4,44 composed of three parts, 3,21-38, 4,1-13 and 4,14-44. The unit 4,14-44 does not narrate the 'beginning' of Jesus' ministry but represents an anticipation of that ministry which does not stand in a chronological relationship with what follows.

Implied in the foregoing remarks concerning the relationship between 4,14-44 and what follows is that 1,5–4,44 functions as a preliminary narrative section in the gospel. The literary analysis of 5,1–24,53 in the following chapter should throw further light on this. The function of 1,1-4 and 1,5–4,44 in Luke–Acts as a whole will be discussed in chs. III and IV respectively.

CHAPTER II

LITERARY STRUCTURE OF LK 5,1–ACTS 28,31

A. Lk 5,1–24,53

Preliminary Remarks

One of the reasons advanced in the previous chapter for placing a major division in Luke's gospel at 4,44 was that 5,1–24,53 forms a literary unit in its own right. Two significant indications of this are provided by literary relationships that exist between 5,1-11 and ch. 24. While carrying an evident reference to 22,31 and Peter's denial, the use of the name Simon in 24,34 clearly recalls 5,1-11 and the point at which the name was originally changed to Peter (5,8).[1] The three texts 5,1-11, 22,31 and 24,34 are closely linked. The ἀκολουθεῖν begun in 5,11 is dealt a severe blow by Peter's denial (22,54-62), foretold in 22,31-34, and is only restored to the full with the Lord's appearance to him after the resurrection (24,34). Secondly, the universal mission which the risen Lord imparts in 24,46-48 to the disciples whom he had gathered together in Galilee recalls the words of 5,10 (ἀνθρώπους ἔσῃ ζωγρῶν) which, apart from their missionary implications,[2] have an evident universal ring.

Moreover, the Galilean period of Jesus' ministry is recalled in various ways in chs. 23-24. The Galilean women present at the crucifixion (23,49), burial (23,55) and empty tomb (24,6) are explicitly stated to have accompanied Jesus in Galilee (24,6; cf. 8,1-3). The disciples whom Jesus calls to be "witnesses" in 24,48, particularly the apostles, were gathered together by him during this period (cf. 5,1-11.27-28; 6,13). Their continual contact with Jesus, upon which Luke lays such obvious store (cf. Acts 1,21-22), begins in 5,1-11 at the commencement of his Galilean ministry and ends in 24,51 with his ascension.

The unity of 5,1–24,53 is confirmed by the unity, yet to be demonstrated, of its constituent parts, 5,1–9,50, 9,51–19,48 and 20,1–24,53. These three divisions correspond to the three stages of Jesus'

---

[1] Cf. Dietrich, *Petrusbild*, 163; Dillon, *Eye-Witnesses*, 100 n. 88.

[2] Cf. R. Pesch, *Der reiche Fischfang. Lk 5,1-11/Jo 21,1-14*, Düsseldorf 1969, 67: "... Lk 5,1-11, welche die spätere Mission der Jünger (und vorab des Simon Petrus) schon in den Blick nimmt (V.10)..."

ministry, the Galilean ministry, the travel narrative and the final events in the city of Jerusalem.[3] The principle of arrangement is geographical. It is supported, as may be seen below, by literary and thematic considerations. The unity of 5,1–24,53 provides further evidence that 1,5–4,44 functions as a preliminary narrative section in the gospel.

1. In Galilee: 5,1–9,50

1.1 Unity of 5,1–9,50

Loisy, Schürmann and Schneider treat 5,1–9,50 as a unit,[4] and not without good reason, since geographical, thematic and literary considerations may be adduced in its favour. That the specifically Galilean ministry of Jesus mentioned in Lk 23,5, Acts 10,37 and 13,31 is described in 5,1–9,50 is clear enough from the geographical indications scattered throughout:[5] the lake of Genesaret (5,1), Capernaum (7,1), Nain (7,11), Magdalene (8,2),[6] the lake (8,22), the reference in 9,7-9 to Herod, tetrarch of Galilee, and his interest in Jesus' identity. The Galilean women, witnesses of Jesus' death and burial, are explicitly shown to accompany him *in* Galilee (cf. 8,1-3; 24,6). Jesus does visit Gerasene, but, as has been noted above, Luke, unlike Matthew and Mark, expressly mentions its situation opposite Galilee (8,26), thus underlining its manifestly exceptional character.

Characteristic of this section is the theme of apostleship. Half of the gospel references to the twelve are found here (6,13; 8,1; 9,1.12; elsewhere

---

[3] Schürmann, *Lk* I, 146, divides 5,1-24,53 into two parts at 19,27/28; similarly Schneider, *Lk* I, 120; II, 383; for three part divisions of 4,14-24,53 at 9,50/51 and 19,27/28 see Knabenbauer, *Lk*, 21; Wikenhauser, *Einleitung*, 146-149; Ernst, *Lk*, 165ff.; at 9,50/51 and 21,38/22,1, Bisping, *Mk und Lk*, 145; at 9,50/51 and 19,48/20,1, Creed, *Lk*, 139.

[4] Loisy, *Lc*, 169 (part of 3,1–9,50); Schürmann, *Lk* I, 261 (part of 5,1–19,27); Schneider, *Lk* I, 120 (id.); also Wilkens, "Struktur", 1.4 (part of 1,5–9,50).

[5] Thus Loisy, *Lc*, 169. Schürmann, *Lk* I, 261, does not acknowledge such a restriction, entitling it "Jesu Volkstätigkeit landauf landab im ganzen Judenland"; similarly Schneider, *Lk* I, 120; Völkel, "Anfang", 226-228. The notices in 5,17 and 6,17 of the people streaming from all Palestine and from further afield do not indicate that Jesus has been touring these regions, as Völkel, "Anfang", 227, suggests. Their coming to Jesus is rather a consequence of the spread of his fame beyond the borders of Galilee (cf. 5,15); see Schürmann's comments on 5,17 and 6,17 in *Lk* I, 281 and 322 respectively.

[6] Magdala was on the lake of Galilee; cf. Lagrange, *Lc*, 235; Plummer, *Lk*, 215. The mention of Bethsaida in 9,10 presents a problem unless one decides with Plummer (*Lk*, 243) that there was one such place on the western and another on the north-eastern side of the lake. The context of 9,10 in Luke suggests that the evangelist saw this city as lying on the western shore, as did the writer of Jn 12,21; cf. R. E. Brown, *The Gospel According to John I-XIII*, AB 29: Garden City 1966, 82; McCown, "Gospel Geography", 17.

18,31; 22,3.30.47), and the term ἀπόστολος occurs in 6,13 and 9,10.⁷ The section contains the call of the first disciples, later apostles (5,1-11.27-28), as well as the choice and appointment of the twelve (6,13-16) and their subsequent mission (9,1-6.10), with the latter recalling Jesus' saying of 5,11b. The privileged group of three is present at the raising of the daughter of Jairus (8,51) and at the transfiguration (9,28). Peter is mentioned on other occasions (8,45: diff. Mk 5,31; 9,20.32-Luke alone; 9,33), while references to John in the context of discipleship frame the whole section (5,10-11; 9,49).⁸

The theme of the word of God is also characteristic of this section which contains frequent references to the hearing of the word or hearing Jesus (cf. 5,1.15; 6,17.27.47.49; 7,29; 8,12.13.14.15.18.21; 9,35).⁹ The expression ὁ λόγος τοῦ θεοῦ is found in 5,1, 8,11 and 8,21 (elsewhere in the gospel only in 11,21). In two strategically placed pericopes (6,46-49; 8,19-21) which conclude the two 'sermons' of Jesus (6,20-49; 8,4-21), the need for putting the word into action is stressed.¹⁰

It may also be suggested that 7,18-35 acts as something of a focal point for many of the section's themes. Recalled in this scene are the miracles of 7,1-17 (cf. v. 18: περὶ πάντων τούτων· v. 22: νεκροὶ ἐγείρονται),¹¹ 6,18-19 (cf. v. 21), 5,17-26 (cf. v. 22: χωλοὶ περιπατοῦσιν) and 5,12-16 (cf. v. 22: λεπροὶ καθαρίζονται). The description of Jesus as a φίλος... ἁμαρτωλῶν (v. 34) prepares the story of 7,36-50.¹² His healing activity, reported in summary fashion in vv. 21-22, is illustrated in 8,26-39 and 9,37-43a (expulsion of demons), in 8,42b-48 (healing of disease) and in 8,49-56 (raising from the dead). The question of Jesus' identity (vv. 18-20) is raised by Herod in 9,7-9 and by Jesus himself in 9,18-20.¹³

Support for the literary unity of 5,1–9,50 comes from three texts, 4,44, 5,1-2a and 9,51-52a. The first of these, 4,44, is eminently suitable for the conclusion of a major section of Luke's work, given that it has the character of a general summary (cf. 24,53; Acts 28,30-31) and represents a pause in the narrative. In both these respects it is instructive to compare it with concluding verses elsewhere in Luke–Acts, verses of which the periphrastic imperfect or a similar construction is a feature:

---

⁷ Elsewhere 11,49; 17,5; 22,14; 24,10.

⁸ In relation to the theme of discipleship note that five of the ten gospel occurrences of ἀκολουθεῖν are found here; in the case of μαθητής, twelve out of thirty three; note also ἐπιστάτα (5,5; 8.24.45; 9,33.49); σὺν αὐτῷ (8,1 25.28); συνεπορεύοντο αὐτῷ (7,11); συνῆσαν αὐτῷ (9,18); ὀπίσω μου ἔρχεσθαι (9,23).

⁹ Frequent also in the travel narrative; cf. 10,16.24.39; 11,21; 14,35; 15,1; 16,14; 18,23; 19,11.48; elsewhere 20,16.45; 21,38; 22,71.

¹⁰ Cf. Schürmann, Lk I, 383.471; Marshall, Lk, 330.

¹¹ Cf. Schürmann, Lk I, 407-408.

¹² Note also φαρισαῖοι (vv. 30.36.37.39); ἐσθίων... φάγος... φάγῃ (vv. 34.36).

¹³ See the schematic representation of the section in n. 53 below.

4,44: Καὶ ἦν κηρύσσων εἰς τὰς συναγωγὰς τῆς 'Ιουδαίας.

19,47 f.: Καὶ ἦν διδάσκων τὸ καθ' ἡμέραν ἐν τῷ ἱερῷ...ἐζή-
τουν...οὐχ εὕρισκον...ὁ λαὸς γὰρ ἅπας ἐξεκρέματο
αὐτοῦ ἀκούων.

21,37 f.: Ἦν δὲ τὰς ἡμέρας ἐν τῷ ἱερῷ διδάσκων, τὰς δὲ νύκτας
ἐξερχόμενος ηὐλίζετο εἰς τὸ ὄρος...καὶ πᾶς ὁ λαὸς
ὤρθριζεν πρὸς αὐτὸν...ἀκούειν αὐτοῦ.

24,53: Καὶ ἦσαν διὰ παντὸς ἐν τῷ ἱερῷ εὐλογοῦντες τὸν θεόν.

Acts 28,30 f.: 'Ενέμεινεν δὲ...καὶ ἀπεδέχετο πάντας...κηρύσσων τὴν
βασιλείαν τοῦ θεοῦ καὶ διδάσκων τὰ περὶ τοῦ κυρίου
'Ιησοῦ Χριστοῦ μετὰ πάσης παρρησίας ἀκωλύτως.

Two further observations may be made in the case of 4,44. Firstly, the mention of 'Ιουδαίας in the sense of Palestine recalls 1,5 which contains the only other use of the term in this sense in the first four chapters. The two occurrences frame the section 1,5–4,44. The second has to do with the quantity of syllables in the verse. Though it is difficult to make any affirmations on this matter in the case of prose, it is probably not without some significance that long vowels predominate in 4,44 (cf. 24,53; Acts 28,31).[14]

Both 5,1-2a and 9,51-52a exhibit elements that are typical of Lucan pericope-openings. The construction found in 5,1-2a is an elaborate one: ἐγένετο δέ followed by a time indication expressed by ἐν τῷ with the accusative and infinitive, a clause introduced by καί, a circumstantial clause introduced by καὶ αὐτός, and a connecting sentence introduced by καί. The construction in 9,51-52a is closely parallel to it, with ἐγένετο δέ followed by a time indication (ἐν τῷ + accus. and infin.), a circumstantial clause introduced by καὶ αὐτός, and a connecting sentence introduced by καί.

That Luke frequently uses ἐγένετο δέ or καὶ ἐγένετο is well known. Plummer distinguished three basic uses of this formula in the evangelist's work in which what comes to pass is expressed by a) the indicative used without a conjunction, b) the conjunction καί with the indicative, and c) the infinitive. What is important for our purpose is that all three are found in pericope openings. Indeed this position is by far the most common in the case of b (cf. 5,1.12.17; 8,1.22; 9,28.51; 14,1; 17,11; Acts 9,19-20) and c (cf. 3,21; 6,1.6.12; Acts 9,32; 14,1; 16,16; 19,1; 22,6.17; 28,17).[15] The former of these is of particular interest since 5,1-2a and 9,51-52a belong to this category.

---

[14] Cf. Quint., *Inst. Or.* IX,4.93-94; Lausberg, *Rhetorik*, 488; H.J. Hauser, *Strukturen der Abschlusserzählung der Apostelgeschichte (Apg 28,16-31)*, AnBib 86: Rome 1979, 44.

[15] Cf. Plummer, *Lk*, 45; Jeremias, *Sprache*, 25-29.129.

While the construction found in 5,1-2a has its closest parallel in 9,51-52a, close parallels are also to be found in 8,1, 14,1-2a and 17,11-12a which introduce major sections of the gospel (cf. 8,1-56; 14,1-24; 17,11-18,30).[16] Both 5,1-2a and 9,51-52a correspond to a pattern for openings of major sections in Luke's work. The uniqueness of the construction in 5,1-2a makes it suitable for its particular position at the beginning of 5,1–9,50/19,48 or 24,53.

Another element that should not be overlooked is the portrayal of Jesus in 5,1-2a. It is rare to find him described as 'standing' in the gospel. He is usually going to or coming from somewhere, or simply in movement. Only in the synagogue of Nazareth (4,16), on the occasions of the sermon on the plain (cf. 6,17), the healing of a cripple near Jericho (cf. 18,40), the appearance to his disciples as the risen Christ (cf. 24,36) and in 5,1-2a is he so described. There is a certain solemnity about such notices, and Jesus' 'majestic stance' — to borrow a phrase from Schürmann — provides a fitting and impressive note on which to open the narrative proper.[17]

1.2 *Literary Structure of 5,1–9,50*

Jesus' movements mark many pericope openings in this section (cf. 5,12.27; 6,1.6.12; 7,1.11; 8,1.22.26.40; 9,28.37), but geographical indications hold out little promise as an overall principle of arrangement here, which is not surprising, given that Jesus' ministry is confined to Galilee at this point. Proposed arrangements are quite varied. Schürmann's 'ecclesiological' two-part division, 5,1–6,49 (the new order and teaching of the Lord) and 7,1–9,50 (Israel faced with a decision for Christ that leads to division),[18] further subdivided into 5,1–6,11, 6,12-49, 7,1-50, 8,1-56 and 9,1-50,[19] exhibits elements that feature in many arrangements. Among these are the placing of the conclusion of a section at 6,11, whether it begins with 4,14, 4,31, 5,1, 5,12 or 5,17,[20] taking the sermon on the plain with the two preceding and closely linked pericopes

---

[16] For these divisions see below.

[17] Cf. Schürmann, *Lk* I, 267. The absence of Jesus' name in 5,1-5 is no insurmountable obstacle to the theory presented here. In the narrative proper of Lucian's biography of Demonax, for instance, the philosopher's name does not immediately appear, and Luke's work is not a biography (see ch. V below).

[18] *Lk* I, 261-262.386-387.

[19] This five-part division coincides with the structure of Bisping, *Mk und Lk*, 233-289, and is somewhat similar to that proposed by Schneider, *Lk* I, 120-121 (5,1–6,19; 6,20-49; 7,1-50; 8,1-56; 9,1-50).

[20] See the commentaries of Knabenbauer and J. Weiss (4,14–6,11); Ellis (4,31–6,11); Godet, Schanz, Plummer, Lagrange, Schürmann, Ernst and Evans (5,1–6,11); Hauck, Marshall and Schweizer (5,12–6,11); Schmid, Staab, Harrington and Karris (5,17–6,11); also Meynet, *Parole* I, 79 (5,17–6,11); ed. of Wescott and Hort (5,1–6,11).

to form a unit (6,12-49),[21] and taking 7,1-50, 8,1-56 and 9,1-50 to form separate units.[22] Other suggested units are 5,1–6,16,[23] 6,12–7,50,[24] 6,17–9,9[25] and 7,1–8,3.[26] Evidently despairing of finding a satisfactory structure for the section, Grundmann declined to propose any overall arrangement for it. The variety of arrangements proposed testifies to the problems created by a reliance on subject matter alone, or on a presumed Marcan *Vorlage*, or both.[27]

It is possible that the development of a specific theme may be reflected in the literary structure of a text. The theme of apostleship, which plays an important role in Luke's thought, has a prominent role throughout 5,1–9,50. An examination of the text suggests that it functions as a principle of arrangement for the section which may be divided into three parts corresponding to three successive stages in Jesus' relationship to his apostles, 5.1-6,11, 6,12–8,56 and 9,1-50. This arrangement was first put forward by Godet,[28] and later adopted by Plummer,[29] and to a lesser extent by Knabenbauer.[30] It is supported by additional evidence from the text.

1.2.1 *5,1–6,11: Gathering Disciples*[31]

Introduced in a manner typical of Luke,[32] this section shows Jesus gradually gathering around himself a group of disciples (cf. 5,1-11.27-28.30; 6,1) from whom he choses twelve (cf. 6,13). With this choice a new stage is reached in his relationship both to the disciples and to the crowds that come to hear him, and a new section begins.

The placing of a conclusion at 6,11 is supported by the fact that the opposition to Jesus which appears in 5,21, and which finds its first

---

[21] See the commentaries of Bisping, Godet, Schanz, Lagrange, Staab, Hauck, Harrington, Schürmann, Ernst and Karris; Wikenhauser, *Einleitung*, 147.

[22] See the commentaries of Bisping, Hauck and Schneider.

[23] Cf. Stuhlmueller, "Luke", 119; for 5,1–6,19 see Schneider, *Lk* I, 120; M. Theobald, "Die Anfänge der Kirche. Zur Struktur von Lk. 5.1-6.19", *NTS* 30 (1984) 91-92; Bovon, *Lk* I, 60.

[24] Cf. Ellis, *Lk*, 34.

[25] Cf. Stuhlmueller, "Luke", 119.

[26] Cf. Wikenhauser, *Einleitung*, 147; Staab, *Lk*, 50; Fitzmyer, *Lk I-IX*, 137; also Lagrange, *Lc*, xxxvi (7,1–8,21).

[27] Schürmann (*Lk* I, 261) uses what really are two principles of arrangement for his division at 6,49/7,1.

[28] *Lc* I, 287.

[29] *Lk*, xxxviiif.

[30] *Lk*, 187 (4,14–6,11 representing the only difference).

[31] See n. 20 above.

[32] Cf. Jeremias, *Sprache*, 129-130; Pesch, *Fischfang*, 66-67; L. Brun, "Die Berufung der ersten Jünger Jesu in der evangelischen Tradition", *SO* 11 (1932) 39.

outward expression in 5,30 (note ἐγόγγυζον: diff. Mt 9,11; Mk 2,16), reaches an initial climax in 6,11.[33] This motif of opposition also marks the conclusion of the travel narrative (see 19,48 and below). Indeed both 6,11 and 19,48 appear to have similar functions. By concluding their respective sections on a note of climactic opposition mingled with perplexity or the inability to act, they permit the narrative to develop along other lines, holding over for the moment the question of what will happen Jesus, and thus creating a narrative tension.

The section may be divided into two parts, 5,1-26 and 5,27–6,11. Both begin with a call to discipleship (5,1-11.27-28), contain accounts of healing and teaching activity, and conclude with verses that are parallel (cf. 5,26; 6,11: καὶ ἐπλήσθησαν φόβου... αὐτοὶ δὲ ἐπλήσθησαν ἀνοίας)[34] and that represent brief pauses in the narrative (note the imperfects ἐδόξαζον, διελάλουν).

1.2.2 6,12–8,56: Choice, Preparation of the Twelve[35]

'Εγένετο δέ followed by a general time indication (ἐν ταῖς ἡμέραις ταύταις) and the infinitive, a common Lucan pericope-opening,[36] along with a change of scene in 6,12a, mark the beginning of a new section. A night's prayer (6,12b) introduces the choice and appointment of the twelve (6,13-16) which is closely linked to the sermon on the plain both on a grammatical (cf. 6,13.17.20)[37] and a thematic level, the latter by virtue of the presence of the twelve.[38] The commonly acknowledged unit 6,12-49[39] is framed by the name Πέτρος (6,14) and the closely related term πέτρα (6,48).[40]

---

[33] For a conclusion at this point see the authors cited in n. 20 above.

[34] Morgenthaler, Geschichtsschreibung I, 142, finds the chiasmus call-miracle-miracle-call in ch. 5; also W. Wiater, Komposition als Mittel der Interpretation im lukanischen Doppelwerk, Diss. Bonn 1972, 53; Feldkämper, Betende Jesu, 56-57; but the above arrangement discounts this, and, in any case, the miracle before the call of Peter upsets the scheme.

[35] See the commentaries of Godet, Plummer, Valensin-Huby; ed. of Wescott and Hort.

[36] Cf. 3,21; 6,1.6; Acts 9,32; 28,17; Plummer, Lk, 45; Jeremias, Sprache, 26, and there n. 47.

[37] Note the relationships between vv. 13, 17 and 20: καὶ ἐκλεξάμενος ἀπ' αὐτῶν... καὶ καταβὰς μετ' αὐτῶν ἔστη... μαθητῶν αὐτοῦ... μαθητὰς αὐτοῦ· also vv. 18.27: ἀκούειν.

[38] Their presence at the sermon, which is delivered before 'all Israel' (cf. 6,17), implies that the address is meant for 'all Israel'; on the significance of the twelve see the authors listed in ch. I, n. 152; also the comments below (p. 72) on Acts 1,15-26.

[39] See n. 21 above.

[40] Cf. Dietrich, Petrusbild, 94.

A change of scene marks the beginning of ch. 7 which is a closely knit unit. The phrase περὶ πάντων τούτων of 7,18 includes the events of 7,1-17 in particular, while the spread of Jesus' fame after these events (cf. 7,17) leads directly to the delegation sent by John (7,18 ff.). There is a strong thematic link between 7,34 and the story of Jesus and the sinful woman in 7,36-50, as has been noted above, and there are thematic links also between 7,1-17 and 7,36-50 (πίστις: vv. 9.50; προφήτης: vv. 16.39). The chapter is connected to the sermon of 6,20-49 by its opening verse ('Επειδὴ ἐπλήρωσεν πάντα τὰ ῥήματα αὐτοῦ εἰς τὰς ἀκοὰς τοῦ λαοῦ), as well as by a possible reference in 7,18 (περὶ πάντων τούτων) to 6,17-49.[41]

Another change of scene marks the beginning of the third part of this section, 8,1-56, introduced by a Lucan-style pericope opening (8,1: cf. 5,12.17; 14,1; 17,11).[42] The summary of 8,1-3 presents an itinerant Jesus preaching and healing accompanied by the twelve and a number of women who serve him from their possessions. Closely linked to this summary is 8,4-21, in which Jesus' preaching is illustrated,[43] and 8,22-56, in which examples of his healing activity are given.[44] With the sending out of the twelve in 9,1-6 a new stage in Jesus' relationship to the apostles is reached and with this a new section begins.

There are other indications of the unity of 6,12–8,56. The audiences for Jesus' teaching in 6,20-49 and 8,4-21 have the same composition, the twelve, disciples and the crowd;[45] and both sermons conclude with paragraphs that stress the proper hearing of the word. The miracles reported in 8,26-56 recall Jesus' healing activity in 6,17-19, and the phrase δύναμιν ἐξεληλυθυῖαν ἀπ' ἐμοῦ of 8,46 clearly echoes δύναμις παρ' αὐτοῦ ἐξήρχετο of 6,19.[46]

A further characteristic of this section may be noted. Apart from Peter's reaction in 8,45, the question of the disciples in 8,9 and the cry for help in 8,24, the twelve take no initiative here. This apparently deliberate policy of Luke suggests that what is described in this section is a time of preparation of the twelve for their initial missionary experience. Along with the other disciples they are continually in Jesus' company, but they especially are always close at hand (cf. 8,1.45-46). They witness his

---

[41] Cf. Schürmann, *Lk* I, 407-408.

[42] Cf. Jeremias, *Sprache*, 174-176.

[43] Some commentators place the beginning of a section at this point because the so-called 'little interpolation' is held to conclude at 8,3; thus Holtzmann, *Evangelien*, 221; Staab, *Lk*, 50; Stöger, *Lk* I, 17; Fitzmyer, *Lk I-IX*, 137.

[44] Note that τῶν κατὰ πόλιν ἐπιπορευομένων πρὸς αὐτόν of 8,4 picks up διώδευεν κατὰ πόλιν of 8,1; the crowd awaiting Jesus' return from the land of the Gerasenes in 8,40 recalls the crowd listening to Jesus in 8,4-21 (cf. vv. 4.19).

[45] The concentric disposition was already noted by Bengel, *Gnomon*, 227; Godet, *Lc* I, 384; Plummer, *Lk*, 176.

[46] Note also ἰᾶτο πάντας ... ἰάθη παραχρῆμα (6,19; 8,47).

healing and teaching activity as they accompany him through the towns and villages of Galilee.

1.2.3 9,1-50: Mission of the Twelve[47]

The final part of the Galilean ministry begins with the temporary mission entrusted to the twelve (9,1-6). Composed of four units (vv. 1-17; 18-27; 28-36; 37-50), delineated by changes of scene (cf. vv. 18.28), time indications (cf. vv. 28.37) and setting (cf. 9,28-36; 37-50),[48] it is framed by references to apostles (vv. 1.49) and to power over demons (vv. 1.49).

The units are closely connected one to the other. The question of Jesus' identity (cf. 9,7-9.18-20) provides a close link between 9,1-17[49] and 9,18-27.[50] The transfiguration scene, 9,28-36, is linked to the previous one by the themes of the passion (v. 31; cf. v. 22) and glory (vv. 31-32; cf. v. 26), as well as by the phrase μετὰ τοὺς λόγους τούτους of v. 28a.[51] It is linked to 9,37-50 by the themes of the passion (cf. vv. 31.44), the hearing of Jesus' words (cf. vv. 35.44), the astonishment at Jesus' deeds (cf. vv. 43a.43b) and the incomprehension of the disciples (cf. vv. 33.45).[52]

This closely knit section, with its references to the passion, and particularly to the scene of its consummation in Jerusalem (9,31), provides a transition to the travel narrative. Indeed with its indication of the triumphant outcome of the passion it can be said to provide a transition to the rest of the gospel narrative.[53]

---

[47] A unit in the commentaries of Bisping, Godet, Plummer, Knabenbauer, Lagrange, Hauck, Staab, Valensin-Huby, Ellis, Schürmann, Schneider; eds. of Wescott and Hort, Nestle and Vogels.

[48] The mountain in the case of 9,28-36, the foot of the mount in the case of 9,37-50; the former is framed by occurrences of the noun ἡμέρα in vv. 28 and 36, while αὐτοί of v. 36 refers to Peter, John and James of v. 28; in the latter the reference to the expulsion of demons in 9,49 recalls the healing of 9,37-43a, while v. 43b is closely linked to v. 43a.

[49] Unlike Mt 14,20-21 and Mk 6,42-44, Lk 9,17 concludes the story of the miracle of the feeding of the five thousand with δώδεκα, thus forming an inclusion for 9,1-17 (cf. vv. 1.17); see the commentaries of Leaney, Schürmann, Stöger and Marshall.

[50] See the commentaries of Godet, Zahn, Knabenbauer, Grundmann, Schürmann, Stöger and Marshall.

[51] The words of the heavenly voice in 9,35 also refer to the previous section, since the call to hear Jesus is a call to accept in particular the suffering aspect of his mission (v. 22) and the demands of discipleship (vv. 23-26).

[52] Note also τῇ ἑξῆς ἡμέρᾳ κατελθόντων αὐτῶν ἀπὸ τοῦ ὄρους of v. 37a.

[53] The various literary relationships pointed out above may be schematically represented in an arrangement that offers further support for the unity of this section:

```
5,1–6,11
      6,12-19
           6,20-49
                7,1-17
                      7,18-35
                7,36-50
           8,1-21
      8,22-56
9,1-50
```

2. On the Way to Jerusalem: 9,51–19,48

2.1 *Extent of Travel Narrative*

A problem that has plagued exegetes over the years is the extent of the travel narrative. That the Lucan redacted verse 9,51[54] introduces the journey to Jerusalem and thus marks a major turning point in the gospel narrative is accepted by most, Zahn being a notable exception.[55] It is true that Jesus had already been journeying, but this had been confined, with one exception, to Galilee, and, unlike the travel narrative, did not have a specific goal. After the passion predications of 9,22 and 44 and the reference in 9,31 to Jesus' ἔξοδος about to be accomplished in Jerusalem, Jesus' journeying takes on a new tone and tension as he deliberately sets out for the city that is to reject him.[56]

The conclusion of the travel narrative is a much more contentious issue. Does it end with the parable of the pounds, with the lament over Jerusalem, in the den of thieves, or elsewhere? The choice of verse ranges from 18,14[57] to 19,48,[58] with 18,30,[59] 19,10,[60] 19,27,[61] 19,28,[62] 19,44[63]

---

[54] Cf. Jeremias, *Sprache*, 179; G. Lohfink, *Die Himmelfahrt Jesu. Untersuchungen zu den Himmelfahrts- und Erhöhungstexten bei Lukas*, SANT 26: Munich 1971, 212-217.

[55] *Lc*, 336-338.

[56] With its reference to the complex event of the death, resurrection and ascension of Jesus (cf. J. Weiss, *Evangelien*, 443; Lohfink, *Himmelfahrt*, 212-214; Schneider, *Lk* I, 229; Fitzmyer, *Lk I-IX*, 828), 9,51 can also be seen to introduce the rest of the gospel narrative.

[57] See Prologue, n. 38; also J. Blinzler, "Die literarische Eigenart des sogenannten Reiseberichts im Lukasevangelium", *Synoptische Studien*, Fs für Alfred Wikenhauser, eds. J. Schmid, A. Vögtle, Munich 1953, 20.26.

[58] Cf. Schleiermacher, *Lukas*, 158; Creed, *Lk*, 139-140; H. L. Egelkraut, *Jesus' Mission to Jerusalem: A redaction critical study of the Travel Narrative in the Gospel of Luke, Lk 9:51–19:48*, EHS XXIII.80: Frankfurt am Main 1976; K. E. Bailey, *Poet and Peasant*, Grand Rapids 1976, 79; eds. of Wescott and Hort, Nestle and Vogels. B. Rigaux, *Témoignage de l'évangile de Luc*, Bruges-Paris 1970, 268-273, takes 19,29-48 to form a transition between the travel narrative (9,51–19,28) and the following section (20,1–21,38); Grundmann, *Lk*, 365, takes 19,28-48 to form the first part of 19,28–21,38.

[59] See the commentaries of Schanz and Lagrange; also Zahn, *Lc*, 456 (11,14–18,30).

[60] Cf. Marshall, *Lk*, 401, who takes the parable of the pounds (19,11-27) to constitute a "bridge passage" between the travel narrative and the first part of the Jerusalem section (19,11–21,38).

[61] See Prologue, n. 39; also Conzelmann, *Mitte*, 53; Blinzler, "Literarische Eigenart", 20 n. 1.

[62] See Prologue, n. 40; also G. Sellin, "Komposition, Quellen und Funktion des Lukanischen Reiseberichtes (Lk. IX 51-XIX 28)", *NT* 20 (1978) 105. In this case v. 28 is taken to belong to the parable (19,11-28); thus W. C. Robinson, Jr., "The Theological Context for Interpreting Luke's Travel Narrative (9,51ff.)", *JBL* 79 (1960) 21 n. 7; de la Potterie, "Jérusalem", 66, and there n. 26.

[63] See the commentaries of Ellis, Geldenhuys, Morris and Kealy; A. Denaux, "Het lucaanse reisverhaal (Lc. 9,51–19,44)", *CBG* 15 (1969) 468-473; D. Gill, "Observations on the Lukan Travel Narrative and Some Related Passages", *HTR* 63 (1970) 199.213; P. von

and 19,46[64] in between. The first point that may be made is that the travel notices of 19,28, 29, 36 and 41, according to which Jesus is still on his way to Jerusalem, represent a major obstacle to concluding the journey at any stage prior to 19,41-44. The Lucan verb πορεύεσθαι, which is used in 9,51 to introduce the journey and later to express its continuation (cf. 9,53.56.57; 10,38; 13,33; 17,11), is found in 19,28 and 36 with Jerusalem still as the goal. The verb ἀναβαίνειν, which is used in 18,30 for the ascent to the city, has the city again as its object in 19,28.[65] And ἐγγίζειν, which appears as the final ascent to Jerusalem begins (cf. 18,35), reappears in 19,29,37 and 41 as Jesus draws gradually closer to the city.

One could, with a number of authors, conclude the journey with the lament over Jerusalem (19,41-44), arguing that the entry into the city is implied. Given Luke's brevity at times this is possible.[66] It is doubtful, though, that Luke would have concluded the travel narrative on such a negative note, and on something of an anticlimax. In any case, the aorist ἤγγισεν of 19,41, which sets the scene for the lament, does not lend itself readily to such an interpretation, since it firmly locates Jesus before, if in sight of, the city.

It is the travel notice of 19,45a (καὶ εἰσελθὼν εἰς τὸ ἱερόν) that marks the journey's final stage. The verb εἰσέρχεσθαι occurs earlier in the narrative in relation to the journey (cf. 10,38; 17,12; 19,1), and here it is used for the entry into the temple. Luke does not explicitly report Jesus' entry into the city as Matthew (21,10) and Mark (11,11) do.[67] He concentrates rather on the temple, the cultic centre of Judaism and the scene of Jesus' teaching in the following chapters. It is here that the travel narrative concludes. A pointer in this direction is given by the greeting of 19,38a (cf. 13,35) which was originally addressed to those coming to wor-

---

der Osten-Sacken, "Zur Christologie des lukanischen Reiseberichts", *EvT* 33 (1973) 476 n. 2; M. Miyoshi, *Der Anfang des Reiseberichts Lk 9,51-10,24. Eine redaktionsgeschichtliche Untersuchung*, AnBib 60: Rome 1974, 1; Talbert, *Luke*, 111-113.

[64] Cf. J. H. Davies, "The Purpose of the Central Section of St. Luke's Gospel", *SE* II, ed. F. L. Cross, TU 87: Berlin 1964, 164; de la Potterie, "Jérusalem", 63; P. Kariamadam, *The End of the Travel Narrative (18,31-19,46). A Redaction Critical Investigation*, Diss. Rome 1978; idem, "The composition and meaning of the Lucan Travel Narrative (Lk. 9,51-19,46)", *Biblebhashyam* 13 (1987) 179-198.

[65] On the meaning of 19,28 see de la Potterie, "Jérusalem", 69-70; Grimm, *Einheit*, 165.

[66] Cf. 1,56; 19,45-46.

[67] It is left implied in an account whose brevity, in comparison with the accounts of Matthew and Mark, is notable. The commentaries of Bisping, Godet (Vol. II, 1872²), Stöger, Rengstorf, Schneider, Kremer and Evans treat 19,45-48 as a unit. Schleiermacher, *Lukas*, 240, saw the travel narrative as opening in 9,51 with "einem so feierlichen Anfang" and closing in 19,47-48 with "einem so bestimmten Schluss".

ship in the temple.[68] For Luke city and temple are intimately linked (cf. 2,22-52; 4,9; 13,33-35; 24,52-53). Given that 19,45a represents the final travel notice, the journey's conclusion cannot be placed before this point. But 19,45a is linked grammatically to the notice of the traders' expulsion from the temple in 19,45b (εἰσελθὼν ... ἤρξατο ἐκβάλλειν) which is likewise linked to the composite citation of 19,46 (λέγων). The conclusion of the travel narrative cannot therefore be placed before 19,46.

Neither should it to be placed at 19,46. It is true that 19,47-48 presents Jesus teaching in the temple amidst the opposition of the Jewish leaders and the enthusiasm of the people, and as such provides an introduction to the following chapters. But this is hardly sufficient reason for placing the conclusion at 19,46, since such an introduction may also precede the section it introduces (cf. 4,44; 9,22.31; Acts 19,21; Heb 2,17-18; 5,9-10).[69] It is unlikely that a writer such as Luke would have concluded a journey that began in 9,51-52a in such impressive fashion in a 'den of thieves'. The summary of 19,47-48 provides a more obvious and indeed a more suitable conclusion. Furthermore, the composition of 19,45-48, in which the spartan account of the cleansing (19,45-46; cf. Mt 21,12-13; Mk 11,15-17) is followed immediately by the report of Jesus' daily teaching in the temple (19,47a), suggests that the cleansing is preparatory to, and intimately linked with, the teaching.[70] The decidedly negative reaction of the high priests and scribes (19,47b-48a) and the enthusiastically positive reaction of the people (19,48b) are the direct result of Jesus' teaching (19,47a). Thus 19,45-48 forms a closely knit unit. It follows that the travel narrative's conclusion should be placed at 19,48.

The opening verse of ch. 20 confirms this. Introduced by καὶ ἐγένετο, and containing a specific time indication (ἐν μιᾷ τῶν ἡμερῶν· cf. 19,47a: καθ' ἡμέραν), it has more the character of a Lucan opening than 19,45 or 47 (cf. Lk 2,1; 9,18; 11,1; 19,29), while 19,47-48 has the character of a Lucan conclusion (cf. 4,44; 21,37-38; 24,53). It should also be noted that the repetitions linking 19,47-48 and 20,1 respect their different roles. The more specific time indication of the latter, the additional information on Jesus' teaching (εὐαγγελιζομένου), and the preparation for a specific report on the activity of the high priests and scribes (21,1b) involve repetition with variation that marks the beginning of a new section.[71]

---

[68] Cf. Ps 117(8),26; also H.-J. Kraus, *Die Psalmen* II, BKAT XV.2: Neukirchen-Vluyn 1978[5], 984; A. Weiser, *The Psalms. A Commentary*, London 1971, 729.

[69] Cf. Vanhoye, *Hébreux*, 37.84-85.109-110.

[70] Cf. Conzelmann, *Mitte*, 70-71.

[71] Cf. Lausberg, *Rhetorik*, 314-317. The repetition ensures a smooth transition from the travel narrative to the gospel's final section.

Further arguments may be adduced in favour of a conclusion at 19,48. Firstly, the most characteristic aspect of the journey is Jesus' didactic and paraenetic instruction delivered in towns and villages, in houses and synagogues, and along the way, however circuitous, to Jerusalem. From this point of view his teaching in the temple, the religious centre of Judaism, marks a high point in his activity. Hence the appropriateness of concluding the journey at 19,48.

Secondly, the themes of the rejection and acceptance of Jesus run right through the travel narrative. It opens on a note of rejection (cf. 9,53), and opposition to Jesus is manifest both explicitly and implicitly on a number of occasions (cf. 10,13.25; 11,15.23.37-54; 13,14.17; 14,1; 15,2; 19,11-28.39.41-44.47). It reaches a climax in 19,47 where for the first time in the gospel (diff. Mark) the expressed desire of the Jewish leaders for his death is reported.

Apart from the disciples who accompany Jesus, instances of his acceptance by individuals, or more especially by the people, are also found throughout these chapters (cf. 9,57-62; 10,38-42; 11,27.29; 13,17; 14,25; 15,1; 17,11-19; 18,15-17.37-43; 19,1-10.48). The people's acceptance of Jesus reaches a climax in 19,48 where they are presented as hanging on to his words (ὁ λαὸς γὰρ ἅπας ἐξεκρέματο αὐτοῦ ἀκούων), so much so that they prevent the Jewish leaders for the moment from carrying out their evil design (cf. 19,47b-48a).

The fact that these two themes — the rejection of Jesus and his acceptance — reach a climax in 19,47-48 suggests a further argument on the level of the narrative plot for placing the conclusion of the travel narrative at 19,48. Opposition to Jesus has reached the point at which the Jewish leaders are seeking his death. But this is temporarily prevented by the people's acceptance of him. For the moment the Jewish leaders can do nothing (note the imperfects in 19,47-48). At this point Luke can and does begin a new section in which he treats at length Jesus' teaching in the temple. It is only in 22,3 ff., with the reappearance on the scene of Satan and the decision of Judas to betray Jesus, that the plot against him can move forward again.

A further point may be mentioned concerning the verb ἀπόλλυμι. It occurs in 13,33 where Jesus makes an important statement about his journey and his fate (οὐκ ἐνδέχεται προφήτην ἀπολέσθαι ἔξω Ἰερουσαλήμ). It is found again in 19,47 (ἐζήτουν αὐτὸν ἀπολέσαι), the only other occasion in the gospel where it is used in relation to Jesus. The repetition is scarcely fortuitous. Rather, the city has been reached, and the reader is reminded that the prediction of 13,33 can now be fulfilled.

There is sufficient reason, then, to place the conclusion of the travel narrative at 19,48. This position is further confirmed by the arrangement of the following chapters. Before taking up that point, let us look at the literary structure of 9,51–19,48.

2,2 Literary Structure of 9,51–19,48

The task of finding a literary structure for the apparently amorphous mass of material that is Luke's travel narrative is a daunting one, especially if one is to judge from the commentaries of Loisy, Lagrange and Rengstorf; they do little more than treat each pericope separately, the conviction presumably being that no overall plan is to be detected therein. Given Luke's usually careful composition, though, it is hardly likely that he would have put the material together in a haphazard fashion. Whether it is possible to trace the evangelist's mind "from sentence to sentence and from word to word"[72] is another matter, although failure to do so may lie more on the exegete's shoulders than on Luke's presumed literary deficiencies.

Various arrangements have been put forward over the years based mainly on topical, source, or a combination of chronological and geographical considerations.[73] The narrative has been taken to recount Jesus' last journey from Galilee to Jerusalem,[74] or two or even three different journeys to the city.[75] Source considerations often led to its being divided at 18,14.[76] In recent times new topical arrangements have been suggested, with the added feature in a number of cases of a chiastic structure. Yet despite all the toil and trouble there remains the problem of a satisfactory literary structure for this section of the gospel, not least because the question of a criterion or criteria for any arrangement of this material is still largely unresolved. The effort though has not been in vain. Take the historical approach, for example. While it involved chronological and geographical considerations that have long been abandoned, it did highlight the indications of Jerusalem as the journey's goal in 13,22, 17,11 and 18,31, indications that have continued to figure prominently in arrangements of the travel narrative.

The basic problem with the topical outline is that it generally lacks literary support from the text. Hence decisions as to the placing of divisions are somewhat subjective and arbitrary. Marshall, for example, has a unit entitled "The Coming of the Son of Man" (17,11–18,8). But

---

[72] With M. D. Goulder, "The Chiastic Structure of the Lucan Journey", in Cross (ed.), *SE* II, 195.

[73] Cf. L. Girard, *L'Évangile des Voyages de Jésus ou La Section 9,51–18,14 de saint Luc*, Paris 1951, 51-57; Blinzler, "Literarische Eigenart", 20-25, and there nn. 2-15; J. Schneider, "Zur Analyse des lukanischen Reiseberichtes", Schmid, Vögtle (eds.), *Synoptische Studien*, 207-229; C. L. Blomberg, "Midrash, Chiasmus, and the Outline of Luke's Central Section", *Studies in Midrash and Historiography. Gospel Perspectives* III, eds. R. T. France, D. Wenham, Sheffield 1983, 217-261.

[74] See Girard, *Voyages*, 56, and there n. 1; Blinzler, "Literarische Eigenart", 22 n. 7.

[75] See the commentaries of Knabenbauer (23-27) and Lagrange (xxxviii); also Girard, *Voyages*, 51 n. 3.

[76] See Prologue, n. 38, and n. 57 above; also Girard, *Voyages*, 65-74.

the story of the ten lepers in 17,11-19 has no reference to the Son of Man, and, as Marshall admits, it has more affinity with what precedes than with what follows.[77] Without literary support from the text chiastic arrangements are also in danger of being subjective and arbitrary. Complicating matters further in this case are the difficulties involved in evaluating the validity of a specific parallel and deciding in a particular case whether or not the parallel is significant for the chiastic arrangement.[78] In Goulder's structure, for example, 11,1 and 17,5 are parallel, being regarded as examples of "faithful prayer".[79] But a far more convincing parallel for 11,1 is available in 18,1 ff., where, unlike 17,5 ff., the verb προσεύχεσθαι is to be found.[80] Talbert's list of parallels includes the tenuously linked 10,21-24 and 18,15-17,[81] the problematic 11,37-54 and 17,1-10,[82] and the rather doubtful 10,38-42 and 18,9-14.[83]

An approach to the travel narrative that takes the travel notices to be a literary device providing a journey framework for the section represents the most promising way forward in the search for its literary arrangement.[84] The travel notices provide a principle of arrangement for Grundmann who divides the section at 13,22 and 17,11,[85] and for Ernst who makes a further division at 10,38.[86] But other travel notices at significant points throughout the narrative also appear to contribute to the journey framework, notably 11,53-54, 14,25 and 18,31 (a virtual

---

[77] *Lk*, 648. In this particular case Marshall departs from his topical arrangement of the material, placing the beginning of the section at 17,11 not because of the content of 17,11-19 but because of the nature of 17,11 as a "geographical marker".

[78] See the comments of Blomberg in "Central Section", 235-236.

[79] "Structure", 196; cf. Blomberg, "Central Section", 235.

[80] Cf. C. H. Talbert, *Literary Patterns, Theological Themes, and the Genre of Luke Acts*, SBLMS 20: Missoula 1974, 52; Bailey, *Poet*, 80-82; Blomberg, "Central Section", 235.

[81] *Literary Patterns*, 51-52; cf. νηπίοις ... βρέφη/παιδία: 10,21; 18,15-16.

[82] Jesus' attack on the pharisees and lawyers in 11,37-54 hardly matches his advice to the disciples on various matters including one's attitude towards a brother who has sinned (17,3b-4) and towards the performance of one's duties (17,7-10). The meal has very different roles in 11,37-54 and 17,7-10.

[83] The parable of the proud, disdainful pharisee and the humble, needy tax collector is scarcely a suitable parallel for the story of Mary and Martha. Moreover, the latter does not de-emphasize good works as Talbert, *Literary Patterns*, 51, suggests; it stresses the importance of hearing the word of God over the excessive provision for Jesus' physical needs (cf. πολλήν: 10,40). H. K. Farrell, "The Structure and Theology of Luke's Central Section", *TrinJ* 7 (1986) 48, appeals to the contrast in attitudes between the persons involved in both.

[84] The literary approach is of long standing; cf. Schmidt, *Rahmen*, 259-264; McCown, "Gospel Geography", 15; Girard, *Voyages*, 56 n. 4; Blinzler, "Literarische Eigenart", 34.37.

[85] *Lk*, 200; also Karris, "Luke", 677-678; Kealy, *Lk*, 266.

[86] *Lk*, 353.426.482.

travel notice).[87] Given that 9,51-19,48 describes a journey, it does not seem unreasonable to suggest that travel notices provide it with a principle of arrangement, and in particular 9,51, 10,38, 11,53-54, 13,22, 14,25, 17,11 and 18,31. The seven-part arrangement to which these give rise is supported by other literary indications from the various sections.

2.2.1 *9,51-10,37: Introduction to the Travel Narrative*

Miyoshi placed the conclusion of the journey's initial section at 10,24.[88] But καὶ ἰδού of 10,25a sets the lawyer's question, and consequently 10,25-27, in the foregoing situation.[89] Hence the narrative's 'beginning' should be seen as extending to 10,37.[90] References to the Samaritans, the first negative (9,53), the second emphatically positive (10,30-37), frame the unit.

A number of themes that recur in the travel narrative are to be found here, themes such as Jerusalem as the goal of the journey (9,51),[91] the rejection and acceptance of Jesus and his disciples (9,53.57-62; 10,5-6.10.16),[92] discipleship (9,57-62),[93] the universality of salvation (10,1.17),[94] and the preaching of the kingdom (9,60.62; 10,9.11).[95] Like the rest of the travel narrative it contains much instruction.[96] Jesus' royal status, so prominent at the conclusion of the narrative (cf. 19,11-

---

[87] With the statement of 18,31 Jesus resumes his journey (cf. 17,12). The verb ἀναβαίνειν, used of the ascent to Jerusalem in 2,42 and 18,10, is used here for the first time in the travel narrative in reference to Jesus. Its appearance at this point marks a new phase — the final phase — in the journey to Jerusalem. The notice of 18,35a, ἐν τῷ ἐγγίζειν αὐτὸν εἰς Ἰεριχώ, also suggests that 18,31 is to be regarded as a virtual travel notice.

[88] *Anfang*, 1; also Bisping, *Mk und Lk*, 291; Lagrange, *Lc*, xxxix; Marshall, *Lk*, 402; Talbert, *Lk*, 114; Farrell, "Central Section", 36; Kremer, *Lk*, 113.

[89] The expression καὶ ἰδού, which is almost always found within a pericope in Luke-Acts but which may also introduce a pericope or a larger unit (cf. Lk 2,25; 24,13), never begins a major section; it indicates a link between what is to come and what has gone before, since it places what it introduces in the foregoing situation. Cf. Brun, "Kompositionstechnik", 45; Fitzmyer, *Lk X-XXIV* (AB 28A: Garden City 1985), 877.

[90] Thus Ernst, *Lk*, 316; cf. E. LaVerdiere, *Luke*, NTM 5: Dublin 1980, 140.

[91] Cf. 13,22.33; 17,11; 18,31; 19,28.29-48.

[92] Cf. 11,23.53-54; 13,17a.34; 14,24; 19,11-28.47 (rejection); 11,23; 13,17b.18; 15,43; 19,1-10.48 (acceptance).

[93] Cf. 14,26-33; 18,22.28.43.

[94] The universal significance of Jesus' mission is implied in the sending out of the seventy (two); cf. Gen 10,2-31. The fact that their mission, like that of the twelve, is directed to Israel does not mean that its significance is restricted to Israel, but that Israel has priority in the hearing of the word. Cf. Grundmann, *Lk*, 207; Miyoshi, *Anfang*, 78.

[95] Cf. 11,2.20; 12,31.32; 13,18.20.28.29; 14,15; 16,16; 17,20.21; 18,16.17.24.25.29; 19,11.

[96] Cf. B. Reicke, "Instruction and Discussion in the Travel Narrative", *SE* I, ed. F. L. Cross, TU 73: Berlin 1959, 206-216.

28.29-38), is implied here (9,60.62; 10,1),[97] as are his prophetic (cf. 9,62)[98] and teaching roles (cf. 10,25-37).[99] This unit, therefore, may be considered as something of an introduction to the travel narrative.

2.2.2 10,38–11,54: Acceptance and Rejection

With the travel notice of 10,38, the journey, apparently at a halt in 10,1-37, is again set in motion. In having Jesus turn aside into a village the notice of 10,38 (ἐν δὲ τῷ πορεύεσθαι... αὐτὸς εἰσῆλθεν εἰς κώμην τινά) is strikingly similar to the much better known travel notice of 17,11-12a (... ἐν τῷ πορεύεσθαι... εἰσερχομένου αὐτοῦ εἴς τινα κώμην). That it performs a similar function should cause no great surprise.

The conclusion of the section is marked by a much less obvious travel notice, 11,53-54, which shows Jesus leaving the house of the pharisee (the only such notice in the gospel) and being plagued by the questioning of the pharisees and lawyers. Its summary character suggests that it does not simply inform the reader of Jesus' exit from the house. It presents him rather as leaving and going on his way plagued by his enemies constantly seeking to entrap him.[100] Travel notices act as conclusions elsewhere in Luke's gospel (cf. 2,39; 4,30; 9,56; 19,28), so that in this respect 11,53-54 is no exception.

The section is framed by two scenes, 10,38-42 and 11,37-54, which are set in a house and in the context of hospitality offered to Jesus. The two stand in sharp contrast to one another, the picture in the house of Martha being on the whole positive, that in the house of the pharisee being negative, with the pharisees and lawyers angrily rejecting his prophetic warning.[101]

Like 5,1–6,11, and the travel narrative itself, this section closes on a note of climactic opposition (cf. 6,11; 19,48). For at this point the

---

[97] Cf. I. de la Potterie, "Le titre κύριος appliqué à Jésus dans l'évangile de Luc", Descamps, de Halleux (eds.), *Mélanges Béda Rigaux*, 127-128; Miyoshi, *Anfang*, 60.76.

[98] Cf. 11,29-32 (cf. Jon 3,1-10); 13,33; 19,45-46; see Fitzmyer's comment on the latter text in *Lk X-XXIV*, 1260.

[99] Cf. 11,1.45; 13,10.22; 18,18; 19,39.47; and of course the great deal of instruction in this narrative.

[100] Note the pres. inf. ἀποστοματίζειν and the pres. ptc. ἐνεδρεύοντες; also the implication of 13,10. Cornely, *Introduction*, 164, and Knabenbauer, *Lc*, 326, place the conclusion of the travel narrative's first major section at 11,54.

[101] Apropos of 10,38 and 11,1-13 Brun, "Kompositionstechnik", 45, commented: "Der κώμη τις 10,38 tritt der τόπος τις 11,1 zur Seite; den beiden Frauen die Jesus empfangen, vor allem der Maria die das gute Teil erwählt, entspricht der Jünger der beten lernen möchte: überhaupt: das Hören des Wortes Jesu und das Beten sind wahlverwandt"; note the links between 11,1-13 and 11,14-26 provided by the theme of the kingdom (cf. 11,2.20) and οὐρανός (11,13.16), and between 11,14-26 and 11,27-54 provided by σημεῖον (11,16.29) and γενεά (11,29.50.51).

hostility towards Jesus that was simmering in 11,14-23 reaches a new level as the pharisees and lawyers not only reject Jesus' words of warning (11,29-52), but from this point onwards begin their attempts to entrap him in his speech (11,53b-54).

2.2.3 *12,1–13,21: Readiness for Judgement*

Contrasting references to leaven (ζύμη) in 12,1 and 13,21, the only occurrences of the term in Luke–Acts, frame the section 12,1–13,21 [102] which is also delineated by the travel notices of 11,53-54 and 13,22. While linking up with 11,53-54, the phrase ἐν οἷς of 12,1a also suggests that a new topic is being introduced in 12,1 ff.

There is a certain thematic unity about much of this section, as Marshall recognizes when he entitles it "Readiness for the Coming Crisis".[103] Themes relating to one's conduct in the face of the coming judgement run through ch. 12, while the theme of repentance implied there becomes explicit in 13,1-9.[104] The final part picks up from 12,31-32 the related theme of the kingdom that all are called upon to seek, conveying to the reader that this kingdom is present through the power of God working in and through Jesus (cf. 13,10-17), and giving an assurance that it will grow inexorably (cf. 13,18-21).

2.2.4 *13,22–14,24: The Universality of Salvation*

With mixed feelings Marshall places the conclusion of the section beginning with the travel notice of 13,22 at 14,35.[105] But the travel notice of 14,25 which moves the narrative from the house of a pharisee to the by-roads of Palestine and the milling crowds suggests a conclusion at 14,24.[106] It is framed by references to the theme of salvation found in 13,23 (εἰ ὀλίγοι οἱ σῳζόμενοι;) and 14,24 (οὐδεὶς ... τῶν κεκλημένων γεύσεταί μου τοῦ δείπνου).

A characteristic of this section, and one that further underlines its unity, is the presence throughout of the theme of salvation with its universal connotations and its implications for the fate of Israel. An obvious universal chord is struck in 13,29-30 with Gentiles joining the patriarchs and the prophets at the heavenly banquet, though Israel is still

---

[102] Note also κρυπτόν ... ἔκρυψεν (12,2; 13,21); ὑπόκρισις ... ὑποκριταί (12,1; 13,15).

[103] *Lk*, 508. The presence of the theme of readiness for future judgement is also evident in the incidence of terms relating to the topic in this section (ὥρᾳ: 12,12.39.40.46; τὸν καιρόν: 12,56; ταύτῃ τῇ νυκτί: 12,20).

[104] "Das schon 12,54-59 anklingende Bussmotif wird in den beiden folgende Stücken weitergeführt" (Brun, "Kompositionstechnik", 46, referring to 13,1-5.6-9).

[105] *Lk*, 562; also Bisping, *Mk und Lk*, 348.

[106] Cf. Schleiermacher, *Lukas*, 196.199, on 13,23–14,24.

not shorn of hope.[107] In 13,35 a possibility of salvation is held out to the city where Jesus is to die.[108] And Jesus' hearers are reminded in 14,15-24 that the messianic banquet is for those who respond positively to the Lord's invitation, whether they be Jews or Gentiles.[109]

The section falls readily into three parts, 13,22-30, 13,31-35 and 14,1-24. The coming of the pharisees to Jesus in 13,31 marks the beginning of the central part which is linked to the first by the phrase ἐν αὐτῇ τῇ ὥρᾳ and by the verb πορεύεσθαι (cf. 13,22.31.33.34). A change of scene in 14,1a to the house of one of the leaders of the pharisees sets the scene for the third part which sees Jesus healing (14,1-6; cf. 13,32) and teaching (14,7-24; cf. 13,22).

2.2.5 *14,25-17,10: Discipleship and Repentance*

The extent of this section which does not appear to display any significant thematic unity is determined by the travel notices of 14,25 and 17,11-12a. It opens with Jesus teaching the crowds about the requirements of discipleship (14,25-35) and closes with him giving the disciples a series of concrete rules for their life together (17,1-10; cf. μαθητής: 14,26.27.33; 17,1).[110]

Linked to the previous section by the theme of hearing Jesus (cf. ἀκούειν: 14,35; 15,1), ch. 15 forms a well-recognized unit introduced by 15,1-3 and containing three parables through which runs the theme of joy over the return of the one who was lost.[111] The following chapter is closely linked to this both grammatically, through δὲ καί of 16,1a, and thematically, through the theme of repentance (cf. 15,7.10.21.24.32; 16,30-31).

---

[107] Cf. J. Jeremias, *Jesus' Promise to the Nations*, SBT 24: London 1967², 62-63; Grundmann, *Lk*, 286-287; Wilson, *Gentiles*, 33; de la Potterie, "Jérusalem", 69; R. Fabris, "La parabola degli invitati alla cena. Analisi redazionale di Lc. 14,16-24", *La Parabola degli Invitati al Banchetto. Dagli evangelisti a Gesù*, ed. J. Dupont, TRSR 14: Brescia 1978, 139; Fitzmyer, *Lk X-XXIV*, 1023.

[108] Cf. Grundmann, *Lk*, 290; de la Potterie, "Jérusalem", 65.

[109] Cf. J. Jeremias, *The Parables of Jesus*, London 1972³, 64-65; Grundmann, *Lk*, 296-298; Wilson *Gentiles*, 34; Marshall, *Lk*, 584-587; K. E. Bailey, *Through Peasant Eyes*, Grand Rapids 1980, 88-113; J. Dupont, "La Parabola degli invitati al banchetto nel ministero di Gesù", Dupont (ed.), *Invitati al Banchetto*, 294, and there n. 24; Fitzmyer, *Lk X-XXIV*, 1053.

[110] Note the introduction συνεπορεύοντο δὲ αὐτῷ ὄχλοι πολλοί which indicates the continual presence of the crowds.

[111] Cf. E. Rasco, "Les paraboles de Luc XV. Une invitation à la joie de Dieu dans le Christ", *De Jésus aux Évangiles. Tradition et Rédaction dans les Évangiles synoptiques*, ed. I. de la Potterie, BETL 25: Gembloux 1967, 181.

2.2.6 *17,11–18,30: The Kingdom of God*

The kingdom of God is a major theme here, as is the associated theme of salvation which runs right through the section and provides a framework for it (cf. σέσωκεν: 17,19; σωθῆναι: 18,26; ζωὴν αἰώνιον: 18,30). The scenes are linked to one another in a chain of relationships that binds the whole closely together.[112] The healing of the ten lepers (17,11-19), which is a sign of the coming of the kingdom, gives rise to the question of 17,20a about the time of its coming.[113] This question in turn introduces the eschatological teaching of 17,20b-37 (cf. 17,21).

The consequence of this teaching for the Christian life is then outlined: the need for persevering prayer (18,1-8) to be made with humility (18,9-14). The note of humility is picked up in the following scene, 18,15-17, as Jesus teaches that one must be humble and receive the kingdom like a child in order to enter into it. The demands of the kingdom are presented as severe in 18,18-30, but rewarding for the one who responds to them.

2.2.7 *18,31–19,48: Conclusion of the Travel Narrative*

Jesus' words to the twelve in 18,31-34 mark a new stage on the journey to Jerusalem. Up to now Jesus has been journeying towards the city, but without making much progress. The statement ἰδοὺ ἀναβαίνομεν εἰς Ἰερουσαλήμ of 18,31 gives his journey a new urgency and an immediate goal, initiating the final ascent to the theatre of Jesus' passion, death and resurrection (cf. 18,35). References to Jesus' forthcoming death frame the section (cf. 18,32; 19,47).

The section may be divided into two parts, 18,31–19,28 and 19,29-48, with the verb ἀναβαίνειν acting as an inclusion for the first (cf. 18,31; 19,28). As in the previous section, its individual units are linked one to the other. The knowledge displayed by the blind man contrasts with the ignorance of the twelve (cf. 18,34). Jericho and the theme of Jesus as the bearer of salvation (cf. 18,42; 19,9-10) link the stories of the blind man's healing and the meeting with Zacchaeus. The cure of the blind man, the sinner's conversion and Jesus' insistence on the immediacy of salvation (cf. 19,9) seen as signs of the kingdom lead, along with the proximity of Jerusalem, to the thought of the kingdom's immediate

---

[112] Note the advice of Lucian in *Hist.* § 55 on the linking of topics like a chain (ἀλύσεως τρόπον). See G. Avenarius, *Lukians Schrift zur Geschichtsschreibung*, Meisenheim am Glan 1956, 119-120.

[113] Cf. J. Zmijewski, *Die Eschatologiereden des Lukas–Evangeliums. Eine traditions- und redaktionsgeschichtliche Untersuchung zu Lk 21,5-36 und Lk 17,20-37*, BBB 40: Bonn 1972, 48 n. 30; 330-331.

appearance (19,11).[114] The parable of the pounds (19,12-27) makes clear that this will not happen immediately. The travel notice of 19,28, which concludes the first part (cf. 11,53-54), signals the beginning of the journey's final phase. Four notices in vv. 29, 37, 41 and 45 mark Jesus' subsequent progress towards the city, and they divide the section into four parts, vv. 29-36, 37-40, 41-44 and 45-48. The whole unit 18,31–19,48, and not simply 19,47-48, may be seen as a transition to the gospel's final section, since Jesus' passion, death and resurrection are foretold in 18,31-33, and his ascension is foreshadowed in the triumphal entry of 19,37-38.[115]

2.3 Chiastic Structure

The analysis of the travel narrative carried out above reveals a seven-part structure, with 13,22–14,24 occupying the central position. The correspondences noted in the course of this analysis suggest the existence of a number of significant parallels that point towards the presence of a chiastic-type pattern.

2.3.1 9,51–10,37 and 18,31–19,48

Thematic correspondences here include Jerusalem as the goal of the journey (9,51; 18,31; 19,11.28.29-48), Jesus' preaching of the kingdom (9,57-62; 19,11-28), his rejection (9,53; 10,13.25; 19,11-28.39.41-44.47) and acceptance (9,57-62; 18,35-43; 19,1–10.48). Jesus' royal (cf. 9,60.62; 10,1; 19,11-28.29-38), prophetic (9,54.62; 19,45-46) and teaching roles (10,25; 19,39) are also indicated in both. The hospitality towards the wandering preacher enjoined in 10,1-20 is provided in 19,1-10.[116] The theme of divinely endowed vision links 10,21-24 and 18,35-43. The parable of the good Samaritan appears to be without a parallel, although one could perhaps point to correspondences, however tenuous, between references to Jerusalem in 10,30 and 18,31, and between the treatment meted out to the wayfarer in 10,30 and that facing Jesus in Jerusalem according to 18,31-33a.

2.3.2 10,38–11,54 and 17,11–18,30

The story of the rich ruler (18,18-30) hardly constitutes a good parallel for the episode involving Mary and Martha (10,38-42), but the

---

[114] A link between 19,1-10 and 19,11-28 is also forged by the introductory words of 19,11a which refer in particular to Jesus' words of 19,9-10.

[115] Cf. Davies, "Central Section", 168; de la Potterie, "Jérusalem", 66.

[116] Note δέχωνται ὑμᾶς: 10,8.10; ὑπεδέξατο αὐτὸν χαίρων: 19,6.

general theme of the proper way to follow or serve Jesus is present in both.[117] A striking parallel is to be found between 11,1-13 and 18,1-17. The two parables of 11,5-8 and 18,1-8 stress the importance of steadfast prayer in the face of difficulty,[118] while 11,1-4 and 18,9-17 broach the question of how one prays, the former answering with the Lord's prayer, the latter emphasizing the importance of child-like humility.

Correspondences between 11,14-54 and 17,11-37 are provided by earnest warnings delivered by Jesus to the pharisees in 11,37-54 and to his disciples in 17,22-37; and also by the combination of miracle (11,14; 17,11-19) and discussion touching on the coming of the kingdom and possible accompanying signs (11,15-23.29-32; 17,20-21).

2.3.3 *12,1–13,21 and 14,25–17,10*

Jesus exhorts primarily his disciples on a number of issues in 12,1-12 and 17,1-10 (cf. προσέχετε ἑαυτοῖς: 12,1; 17,3). A rather obvious parallel is constituted by 12,13-34 and 16,19-31 and particularly by the parables of the rich fool (12,16-21) and the rich man and Lazarus (16,19-31).[119] The rich men are concerned only for themselves and are altogether too intent on the treasures of this world (cf. 12,18-20; 16,19-21.25).

Readiness for the day of reckoning is a theme common to the servant parables of 12,35-38 and 16,1-9, while the reward of further authority for faithfulness to duty is common to 12,41-44 and 16,10-12. A whole series of correspondences may be pointed out between 13,1-9 and 15,1-32, as Farmer has noted, but it is the theme of repentance running right through both that provides the most important parallel.[120]

2.3.4 *13,22–14,24*

Two related Lucan themes provide significant correspondences between the first and third parts of Luke's central section, 13,22-30 and 14,1-24. The prospect of salvation for the Gentiles is held out in 13,29-30 and 14,21-23;[121] affirmed also is the offer of salvation to Israel despite the negative response of some within it (cf. 13,30; 14,15-24).

---

[117] By listening to his word rather than providing excessively for his needs, in the first, and by leaving all and following him, in the second.

[118] Cf. Blomberg, "Central Section", 239-241; Bailey, *Poet*, 80-82.

[119] Cf. Blomberg, "Central Section", 239-241; Talbert, *Literary Patterns*, 55; Farrell, "Central Section", 43.

[120] See the parallels listed in W. R. Farmer, "Notes on a Literary and Form-Critical Analysis of Some of the Synoptic Material Peculiar to Luke", *NTS* 8 (1961-62) 305-306.310-316; Blomberg, "Central Section", 241-243. On the theme of repentance see μετανοέω (13,3.5; 15,7.10); μετάνοια (15,7); ἁμαρτωλοί (13,2; 15,1.2.7.10; cf. 15,18-19).

[121] See nn. 107 and 109 above; note the correspondence ἀνακλιθήσονται ... δείπνου (13,29: 14,24).

The central verses, 13,31-35,[122] contain a number of Lucan themes that link the centre of the travel narrative to its extremes. These include Jerusalem as the goal of the journey (9,51; 13,33; 19,28.29-48), Jesus' healing activity (13,33; 18,35-43), his prophetic status (cf. 9,54.61-62; 13,33; 19,45-46), his lament over the city (13,34-35; 19,41-44), the allusion to Ps 118,26 (13,35; 19,38), the temple (13,35; 19,45-48) and Jesus' death in Jerusalem (13,33; 19,47-48). Verbal links are provided by the Lucan verb πορεύεσθαι (9,51.56; 13,31.33; 19,28.36) and by ἀπολέσθαι (13,33; 19,47).

This brief survey indicates the existence of a number of significant correspondences throughout the travel narrative. Without pressing the issue too much it does appear that the material was arranged with a chiastic order in mind, a circumstance that underlines the unity of the section.[123]

3. In Jerusalem: 20,1–24,53

3.1 Unity of 20,1–24,53

Geographical and thematic considerations point towards the unity of these five chapters. Jerusalem and its environs provide their general setting, while the Mount of Olives, which is a point of reference throughout (cf. 21,37; 22,39; 24,50 and Acts 1,12), has strong and intimate links with the temple (cf. 21,37-38; Ez 11,23; m. Par. 3,6-9; m. Midd. 2,4). Moreover, when the narrative ventures as far as Emmaus, that town is described in relation to Jerusalem (cf. 24,13), and the story associated with it is closely linked to the city (cf. 24,13.33).

The temple itself is the scene of many of the events of these chapters. References to it in 20,1 (ἐν τῷ ἱερῷ) and 24,53 (διὰ παντὸς ἐν τῷ ἱερῷ) form an inclusion for the whole section 20,1–24,53. On the thematic level the events of the passion, death, resurrection and ascension of Jesus form a characteristic unit for Luke, as may be deduced from 9,31[124] and 9,51,[125] and particularly from 18,31-33 and 24,6.

---

[122] Bailey, Poet, 81, places 13,22-35 at the centre of his chiastic structure.

[123] The various literary relationships pointed out above may be schematically represented as follows:

```
9,51–10,37
     10,38–11,54
          12,1–13,21
               13,22–14,24
          14,25–17,10
     17,11–18,30
18,31–19,48
```

[124] On the meaning of ἔξοδος see J. Mánek, "The New Exodus in the Books of Luke", NT 2 (1957-58) 8-23; Lohfink, Himmelfahrt, 213; Fitzmyer, Lk I-IX, 800.

[125] See n. 56 above.

The presence and distribution of a number of significant terms in these chapters also deserve notice. The term λαός, which occurs eleven times in the gospel's first three chapters, six in the Galilean section, and three in the travel narrative (18,43; 19,47.48), is found sixteen times in chs. 20-24 (20,1.6.9.19.26.45; 21,23.38; 22,2.66; 23,5.13.14.27.35; 24,19).[126]

The title Χριστός, which occurs four times in 1,5–4,44 and once in 5,1–9,50, is found seven times in chs. 20-24 (cf. 20,41; 22,67; 23,2.35.39; 24,26.46). The verb παραδιδόναι, which is found in reference to the passion in 9,44 and 18,32, appears in 20,20 and thereafter in 22,4.6.21.22.48, 23,25 and 24,7.20 in the same context. The frequency of the term ἀρχιερεῖς reflects the prominent role of the high priests at this stage of the gospel narrative (cf. 20,1.19; 22,2.4.50.52.54.66; 23,4.10.13; 24,20; elsewhere 3,2; 9,22; 19,47).

Finally, a number of literary relationships within the section underline its unity. The use of the name Simon in 24,34 recalls 22,31. The scene before Pilate in 23,1-5 recalls that of 20,22-26 (cf. 23,2; 20,22); the design expressed in 20,20 comes to pass in 23,1. Jesus' period in the temple is recalled in 24,53 by the disciples' continual presence there. Most significantly, perhaps, the flashback of 24,18-24 summarizes in particular the events of 20,1–24,12.

3.2 *Literary Structure of 20,1–24,53*

Schleiermacher divided these chapters into three parts at 21,38 and 23,49.[127] Others divide the material from the end of the travel narrative to the conclusion of the gospel at 21,38,[128] 23,56,[129] or both.[130] Given the setting of these chapters in and about Jerusalem a geographical principle of arrangement seems unlikely. Temporal indications, of which there are quite a few (cf. 20,1; 21,37; 22,1.7.14; 22,66; 23,12.44.54.56b; 24,1a.13), represent a more promising avenue of approach. Closer inspection of the text reveals that they mark off a three-part division of 20,1–24,53.

The time indication ἐν μιᾷ τῶν ἡμέρων of 20,1a marks the opening of this final section and gives the temporal setting for 20,1–21,36. The

---

[126] The distinction between the people and their leaders which is evident in the travel narrative is maintained throughout. The leaders of the Jews remain hostile to Jesus (cf. 20,1.19.20.26; 22,4.50.54.66; 23,35.51; 24,20), the people, with the exception of 23,18 (cf. 23,13), on his side (cf. 20,1.19.26.45; 21,38; 22,2; 23,27.35); see ch. IV, p. 144, and there n. 193.

[127] *Lukas*, 250.271.

[128] See the commentaries of Bisping, Schanz, J. Weiss, Plummer, Zahn, Valensin-Huby, Hauck, Staab, Stöger, Stuhlmueller, Marshall and Talbert.

[129] See the commentaries of Schmid and Geldenhuys; Rigaux, *Témoignage*, 268.

[130] See the commentaries of Godet, Grundmann, Morris, Schneider and Schweizer; George, "Construction", 112-117 (= *Études*, 25-30).

reference in 21,37 to Jesus' daily teaching in the temple is part of the summary 21,37-38 which rounds off the first part of the gospel's final section 20,1–21,38.

The second part of this section opens with a reference in 22,1 to the approaching feast of the Passover. Closely associated with it are two other time indications 22,7 and 22,14, likewise referring to the feast. The events of 22,7-65 are set on the day of the feast, those of 22,14-38 in the context of the 'last supper' meal, those of 22,39-65 later that evening. The temporal setting for the events of 22,66–23,56a is provided by καὶ ὡς ἐγένετο ἡμέρα of 22,66a. In noting simply the coming of day (diff. 20,1; 23,54), 22,66a gives the impression that the events of 22,66b ff. are closely associated with those of the previous night (cf. 22,39-65).[131] In so doing it provides a pointer towards the unity of 22,1-65 and 22,66 ff.

Further time indications determine the extent of this part. The general indication of 22,66a is specified by 23,54a (καὶ ἡμέρα ἦν παρασκευῆς) which in turn is specified by 23,54b (καὶ σάββατον ἐπέφωσκεν). The latter also prepares the notice καὶ τὸ μὲν σάββατον ἡσύχασαν of 23,56b which is grammatically linked to τῇ δὲ μιᾷ τῶν σαββάτων ὄρθου βαθέως of 24,1a. The time indications of 22,66a, 23,54, 23,56b and 24,1a are closely related, therefore. But the clear reference of 23,54 to 22,66a and the fact that 23,54 marks a definite pause in the narrative suggest that this verse signals the conclusion both of 22,66 ff. and of the whole unit 22,1–23,54. It also acts as a transition to the following unit 23,55–24,53, as is indicated by the relationship of 23,54b to 23,56a and 24,1a, time indications that give the unit its temporal setting.[132] The gospel's final section, then, may be divided into three parts, 20,1–21,38, 22,1–23,54 and 23,55–24,53, with time indications marking beginnings (20,1; 22,1) and conclusions (21,37; 23,54). The individual units provide confirmation of this arrangement.

---

[131] Note also the occurrences of the verb ἐμπαίζω in 22,63, 23,11 and 36; elsewhere 14,29 and 18,23.

[132] Since 23,56b marks a pause in the narrative (the first after 23,54) there is much greater justification for placing the conclusion of the burial scene and of the larger unit 22,1ff. at this point (eds. of Merk, von Soden; commentaries of Godet, Schanz, Knabenbauer, Staab, Rengstorf, Schmid, Grundmann; Huck, Lietzmann, *Synopsis*, 207; Wilkens, "Struktur", 8; F. G. Untergassmair, *Kreuzweg und Kreuzigung Jesu. Ein Beitrag zur lukanischen Redaktionsgeschichte und zur Frage nach der lukanischen "Kreuzestheologie"*, PTS 10: Paderborn 1980, 17) rather than at 23,56a (eds. of Westcott and Hort, Nestle, Vogels; commentaries of Creed, Ernst, Marshall, Talbert, Fitzmyer, Karris; Huck, Greeven, *Synopse*, 271-273). That 23,56b does not mark a conclusion is evident from the use of μέν...δέ in 23,56b and 24,1 (not μὲν οὖν...δέ as in Lk 3,18.19). This indicates that 23,56b, itself closely linked to 23,55-56a, is to be taken with 24,1 and what follows. Note the change of subject in 23,55 and the fact that this subject ("the women") is that understood in 23,56–24,3. Note also the links between 23,56a and 24,1b; 23,55c and 24,2; 23,55d and 24,3.12b; 23,55b and 24,6b.

3.2.1 20,1-21,38: Teaching in the Temple

Schanz took chs. 20 and 21 to form a unit,[133] and Nestle printed them as such in his edition of the text.[134] The temporal setting for 20,1-21,36 is a day during Jesus' period of teaching in the temple (cf. 20,1a; 21,37), and the temple is the scene of this teaching. Introduction and conclusion are clearly marked, both 20,1a and 21,37-38 conforming to Lucan patterns for such points in a narrative unit. This has been pointed out above in the case of 20,1a and to a lesser extent in that of 21,37-38.

With its description of Jesus' daily teaching in the temple, the people's positive reaction towards him, and his nightly stay on the Mount of Olives, 21,37-38 summarizes the previous narrative (20,1-21,36), while supplementing the information given there. It thus rounds off the section and forms a suitable conclusion. The repetition in 21,37-38 (ἦν δὲ τὰς ἡμέρας ἐν τῷ ἱερῷ διδάσκων ... ὁ λαὸς ... ἐν τῷ ἱερῷ ἀκούειν αὐτοῦ) of a number of terms from 20,1 (ἐν μιᾷ τῶν ἡμερῶν διδάσκοντος αὐτοῦ τὸν λαὸν ἐν τῷ ἱερῷ) forms an inclusion for the whole.

The section is composed of two parts, 20,1b-44 and 20,45-21,36, introduced by 20,1a and concluded by 21,37-38.[135] The first part is characterized by a series of questions addressed to Jesus (cf. ἐπερωτᾶν: vv. 3.21.27.40) and his replies which eventually silence the questioners (v. 40). This part concludes with Jesus himself putting a question to his hearers, a question that goes unanswered.

The notice in 20,45 that Jesus addresses himself to his disciples who have not been mentioned since the entry scene (the people are listening: v. 45a) signals the beginning of the second part which is framed by two brief exhortations (cf. προσέχετε: 20,46; 21,34).[136] The incident of the widow's offering is linked to the first exhortation by the term χήρα (20,47; 21,2). The subject of the temple is introduced in 21,5, and with it (cf. ταῦτα: vv. 6.7a) the eschatological discourse of 21,5-36.[137]

3.2.2 22,1-23,54: Passion, Death, Burial

Synoptic parallels (cf. Mt 26-27: Mk 14-15)[138] and subject matter are probably the main reasons why the unity of Lk 22-23 is affirmed from

---

[133] Lc, 472.

[134] Not retained in the 26th edition (Nestle-Aland).

[135] Note the different uses of repetition in 20,1 (cf. 19,47-48) signalling a new beginning, and in 21,37-38 signalling a conclusion; cf. Lausberg, Rhetorik, 314-321.

[136] Cf. F. Keck, Die öffentliche Abschiedsrede Jesu in Lk 20,45-21,36. Eine redaktions- und motivgeschichtliche Untersuchung, FzB 25: Stuttgart 1976, 22; ed. of Nestle.

[137] Note that ταῦτα of 21,7a recalls the words of Jesus in 21,6; see eds. of Wescott and Hort, Nestle and Vogels. Keck, Abschiedsrede, 29-31, takes the discourse to begin at 20,45; but see the criticisms voiced in J. Lambrecht's review in Bib 58 (1977) 595.

[138] Cf. Huck, Lietzmann, Synopsis, 182.

time to time.[139] But there is sufficient evidence in the text itself to enable one to broadly maintain this position with reasonable comfort.

Framed by time indications, the section opens with a reference to the approaching Passover (22,1) and closes with references to the day of preparation and the approaching Sabbath (23,54).[140] Other indications of its unity include the use of the verb παραδιδόναι in 22,4.6.21.22.48 of Judas handing Jesus over to the high priests and scribes, and again in 23,25 of Pilate handing Jesus over to their will. The theme of the kingdom is found throughout (22,16.18.29.30; 23,42.51). The prophecy of 22,37 (καὶ μετὰ ἀνόμων ἐλογίσθη) is fulfilled in 23,32-33 and 23,39-43.[141]

On the level of the plot the whole is a closely knit unit. The high priests and scribes are presented in 22,2a seeking Jesus's death but hindered by the people (22,2b). Judas, moved by Satan, provides a means of overcoming this obstacle (22,3-6a), but even for him the crowd represents a continuing problem (cf. 22,6b) thus increasing the narrative tension. With Judas constrained to await a favourable opportunity, the writer goes on to narrate the preparations for the Passover meal (22,7-13), the celebration itself (22,14-23) and Jesus' farewell address (22,24-38). A complication is introduced in 22,31-34 with the prediction of Peter's denial.

As the scene changes in 22,39 to the Mount of Olives, the narrative tension heightens. Jesus is pictured in earnest prayer before the coming ordeal. The crowd is no longer present. Judas' opportunity has arrived. The tension mounts with the arrival of the Jewish leaders led by Judas (22,47a), the subsequent act of betrayal (22,47b-48), the incident of the ear (22,49-50) and Jesus' words to those about to arrest him (22,51-53a). Jesus' acquiescence (22,53b) allows the arrest to take place (22,54). The first part of the plot against Jesus (cf. 22,5-6) is realised. The complication introduced in 22,31-34 is resolved in 22,55-62 with Peter's denial of the Lord. The scene of Jesus' mocking and beating in 22,63-65 provides a brief pause in the narrative (cf. 22,65).

The arrival of day (22,66a) sees the plot against Jesus move forward again. The early morning hearing before the Sanhedrin (22,66-71) provides the charge (cf. 22,70-71) enabling them to bring Jesus before Pilate (23,1-5). Accusations lead to questioning (23,3) and to a complication in the narrative as Pilate declares Jesus to be innocent. A further accusation (23,5) leads Pilate to send Jesus to Herod (23,6-12) who complicates matters further by agreeing with Pilate's verdict (23,9).

---

[139] See n. 130 above.
[140] The section thus has a liturgical framework.
[141] Cf. Rese, *Motive*, 156-158.

The narrative tension increases as Pilate is again faced with a decision in 23,13-25. His protestations of Jesus' innocence (23,14.15.22) and his repeatedly expressed desire to let him go (23,16.20.22) are met with repeated and vocal opposition (23,18.21.23). The final tumultuous manifestation of the will of the Jewish leaders (23,23) removes the obstacle of Pilate's conviction, and Jesus is handed over to their will (23,25). Another line of tension is resolved.

The plot now moves quickly forward to its final resolution as Jesus is led away (23,26-32) and crucified (23,33). A certain tension is created by the mocking of the Jewish leaders (23,35), the soldiers (23,36) and the 'bad' thief (23,39). But Jesus' death, foreshadowed in 23,42-43 (cf. 22,37), finally comes in 23,46.

The narrative continues with the reactions to Jesus' death of the centurion (23,47), the crowds (23,48), his acquaintances (23,49a), the women who had accompanied him from Galilee (23,49b), and Joseph of Arimathaea who buried the body (23,50-53). The double time indication of 23,54 marks a pause in the narrative and provides a suitable conclusion not only for the burial story but for the whole unit 22,1–23,54.

Lk 22,1–23,54 is composed of two parts, 22,1-65, set in the context of the Passover feast, and 22,66–23,54, set on the day after. The summary of 22,65 (καὶ ἕτερα πολλὰ βλασφημοῦντες ἔλεγον εἰς αὐτόν), which signals a pause in the narrative, brings the former to a close. The latter opens with Jesus' trial before the Sanhedrin (22,66-71) and closes with his burial by a member of that same body (23,50-53). Both parts may be further divided. A change of scene from the room of the 'last supper' to the Mount of Olives at 22,39 introduces the events surrounding Jesus' arrest (22,39-65) and marks them off from those associated with the Passover feast (22,1-38). The repetition of ἀπήγαγον αὐτόν of 22,66a in 23,26a introduces 23,26-54 which is distinguishable from 22,66–23,25 because of the latter's forensic character.[142]

3.2.3 23,55–24,53: Resurrection, Mission, Ascension

The final part of Luke's gospel forms a closely knit unit set for the most part on a single day (cf. 23,54b.56b; 24,1a) and composed of three parts. References to the tomb (τὸ μνημεῖον) in 23,55c and 24,12a provide an inclusion for the first part[143] which is closely linked to the death and

---

[142] Wescott and Hort, Nestle and Vogels print 22,66–23,25 as one paragraph.

[143] On the textual problem of 24,12 see J. Wanke, *Die Emmauserzählung. Eine Redaktionsgeschichtliche Untersuchung zu Lk 24,13-35*, EThSt 31: Leipzig 1973, 76-82; Dillon, *Eye-Witnesses*, 59-62; Metzger, *Commentary*, 184.191-193. See also 23,55c and 24,12b.

burial scenes by references to the Galilean women (cf. 23,49.55) and the body of Jesus (cf. 23,52.55; 24,3).[144]

The Emmaus narrative (24,13-35), which is framed by references to Jerusalem (ἀπὸ 'Ιερουσαλήμ: v. 13; εἰς 'Ιερουσαλήμ: v. 33),[145] is set in the context of the previous scene by its Lucan style introduction καὶ ἰδού.[146] Other close links with 23,55–24,12 are provided by δύο ἐξ αὐτῶν ἐν αὐτῇ τῇ ἡμέρᾳ of v. 13a which refers back to the disciples of 24,9 and the time indication of 24,1a, and by πάντων τῶν συμβεβηκότων τούτων of 24,14 and the flashback of 24,22-24 which refer back to the events of 23,55–24,12.

Jesus' final appearance, 24,36-53, is framed by references to his arrival (ἔστη ἐν μέσῳ αὐτῶν: v. 36) and departure (διέστη ἀπ᾽ αὐτῶν: v. 51). The introduction, ταῦτα δὲ αὐτῶν λαλούντων (v. 36a), clearly recalls καὶ αὐτοὶ ἐξηγοῦντο τὰ ἐν τῇ ὁδῷ καὶ ὡς ἐγνώσθη αὐτοῖς... of v. 35 and sets the appearance in its context.

This final appearance brings the gospel narrative to a close. But with the instructions to the disciples, the mission imparted, the promise of the Spirit and the ascension, it also provides a transition to Acts. The summary of 24,53 provides a pause in the narrative and facilitates the reader as the volume is rolled up, returned to its place and the second opened.[147]

B. Acts 1,1–28,31

Preliminary Remarks

The many attempts that have been made to find a satisfactory arrangement for the book of Acts must inevitably make one wonder about the "coherent, carefully considered plan" found there by Eduard Meyer.[148] The opening section alone, variously described as a proemium, prologue or introduction, may extend as far as v. 2,[149]

---

[144] The substantial repetition of 23,49b in 23,55ab (γυναῖκες αἱ συνακολουθοῦσαι αὐτῷ ἀπὸ τῆς Γαλιλαίας... κατακολουθήσασαι δὲ αἱ γυναῖκες, αἵτινες ἦσαν συνεληλυθυῖαι ἐκ τῆς Γαλιλαίας αὐτῷ) marks the beginning of a new section. In addition to preparing the empty tomb story, the opening sentence 23,55-56a sets the scene for the active and central role of the women in that story.

[145] Note that ἐν τῇ ὁδῷ of v. 35 recalls πορευόμενοι εἰς κώμην of v. 13.

[146] Cf. Wanke, *Emmauserzählung*, 23; also n. 89 above.

[147] See ch. V, n. 134.

[148] E. Meyer, *Ursprung und Anfänge des Christentums* III, Stuttgart-Berlin 1923, 8: "die einheitliche, sorgfältig überlegte Anlage darin".

[149] Cf. A. Loisy, *Les Actes des Apôtres*, Paris 1920, 51; L. Cerfaux, "La composition de la première partie du Livre des Actes", *ETL* 13 (1936) 670; A. Wikenhauser, *Die Apostelgeschichte*, Regensburg 1961⁴, 24; G. Stählin, *Die Apostelgeschichte*, NTD 5: Göttingen 1962, 11; H. Conzelmann, *Die Apostelgeschichte*, HNT 7: Tübingen 1972², 15;

v. 3,[150] v. 5,[151] v. 8,[152] v. 11,[153] v. 12,[154] v. 14,[155] v. 26,[156] or even further.[157] Suggestions for the narrative also vary a great deal, ranging from the two-part biographical division based on the figures of Peter (chs. 1-12)

J. Roloff, *Die Apostelgeschichte*, NTD 5: Göttingen 1981, 18-19. On the many and varied proposals for a literary structure of Acts see J. Dupont, "La question du plan des Actes des Apôtres à la lumière d'un texte de Lucien de Samosate", *NT* 21 (1979) 220-222; Schneider, *Apg* I, 65-68; F. Neirynck, "Le Livre des Actes dans les récents commentaires", *ETL* 59 (1983) 342-344; G. Betori, "Alla ricerca di un'articolazione per il libro degli Atti", *RivB* 37 (1989) 185-205.

[150] J. Knabenbauer, *Commentarius in Actus Apostolorum*, Paris 1899, 21; E. Jacquier, *Les Actes des Apôtres*, Paris 1926, 2; V. Larrañaga, "El proemio-transición de Act. 1,1-3 en los métodos literarios de la historiografía griega", *Miscellanea Biblica* II, Rome 1934, 311-374; Schneider, *Apg* I, 188; F. Mussner, *Apostelgeschichte*, Würzburg 1984, 15.

[151] Cf. K. Lake, H.J. Cadbury, *The Acts of the Apostles* IV, *The Beginnings of Christianity* I, IV, eds. F.J. Foakes Jackson, K. Lake, London 1933, 2; F.F. Bruce, *The Acts of the Apostles*, London 1951, 65; J. Munck, *The Acts of the Apostles*, AB 31: Garden City 1967, 3; I.H. Marshall, *The Acts of the Apostles*, Leicester 1980, 55.

[152] Cf. R.J. Knowling, *The Acts of the Apostles. The Expositor's Greek Testament* II.1, London 1904³, 11; Haenchen, *Acts*, 135; J.C. O'Neill, *The Theology of Acts in its Historical Setting*, London 1970², 66.72.

[153] Cf. H.J. Holtzmann, *Die Apostelgeschichte*, HCNT I,II: Tübingen-Leipzig 1901³, 23; L. Cerfaux, "Les Actes des Apôtres", Robert, Feuillet (eds.), *Introduction* II, 341; R.P.C. Hanson, *The Acts in the Revised Standard Version*, Oxford 1967, 57; R. Pesch, "Der Anfang der Apostelgeschichte: Apg 1,1-11. Kommentarstudie", *EKKV* 3 (1971) 7-35; idem, *Die Apostelgeschichte* 1, EKKNT V.1: Zürich 1986, 39.59-60; see also E. Grässer, "Acta-Forschung seit 1960", *TRu* 42 (1977) 1-2.

[154] Cf. T. Zahn, *Die Apostelgeschichte des Lucas Erste Hälfte Kap. 1-12*, Leipzig 1919¹⁻², 9.

[155] Cf. A. Bisping, *Erklärung der Apostelgeschichte*, EHNT IV: Münster 1871², 10; R. Knopf, *Die Apostelgeschichte. Die Schriften des Neuen Testaments* I, Göttingen 1907², 531; von Baer, *Heilige Geist*, 78-79; Kümmel, *Introduction*, 155; Stählin, *Apg*, 10; E. Rasco, *Actus Apostolorum. Introductio et Exempla Exegetica* I, Rome 1967, 92-99; Martini, *Atti*, 55; Dupont, "Plan des Actes", 230; D.W. Palmer, "The Literary Background of Acts 1. 1-14", *NTS* 33 (1987) 427-429; eds. of Wescott and Hort, Nestle, Vogels, etc.

[156] Cf. Bisping, *Apg*, 10; Cornely, *Introductio*, 337; Jacquier, *Actes*, 2; Loisy, *Actes*, 53; Bruce, *Acts*, 65; Wikenhauser, *Apg*, 25; Conzelmann, *Apg*, 15; Schneider, *Apg* I, 187; A. Weiser, *Die Apostelgeschichte. Kapitel 1-12*, ÖTK 5.1: Gütersloh-Würzburg 1981, 45; Roloff, *Apg*, 13 ("Prolog"); G. Schille, *Die Apostelgeschichte des Lukas*, THKNT 5: Berlin 1983, 64 ("Vorbereitung"); Dupont, "Plan des Actes", 230 (1,15-26, a development and complement of the introduction 1,1-14; cf. 230 n. 28); Pesch, *Apg* 1, 41 ("Prolog": 1,1-11.12-26); R.J. Dillon, "Acts of the Apostles", Fitzmyer, Brown (eds.), *NJBC* II, 725 ("Introduction").

[157] Cf. Munck, *Acts*, IX-XI (1,1-5,42); L. O'Reilly, *Word and Sign in the Acts of the Apostles. A Study in Lucan Theology*, AnGreg 243: Rome 1987, 213 (1-5); H. Peters, "Der Aufbau der Apostelgeschichte", *Philologus* 85 (1929) 54 (1,1-2,42).

and Paul (chs. 13-28),[158] to three,[159] four,[160] and five-part[161] divisions based on geographical and thematic considerations. An occasional author, following Jülicher's advice not to seek a carefully considered plan behind the narrative, simply takes it pericope by pericope.[162] The following analysis, despite its regrettably cursory nature, hopes to demonstrate that for Acts, at any rate, Meyer had a better feel for narrative than Jülicher.

1. 1,1-26: Proemium

Before the literary structure of the narrative can be examined, the extent of the introductory material at the beginning of the book must be determined. The task is not without its difficulties, as is evident from the variety of openings listed above. Nevertheless, an examination of the text shows that 1,1-26 forms a unit which has an introductory role in Acts.

1.1 1,1-14: Recapitulation, Repetition, Introduction

There are various reasons for treating 1,1-14 as a unit. An inclusion is formed by ὁ ᾽Ιησοῦς of v. 1 and τοῦ ᾽Ιησοῦ of v. 14, while references to

---

[158] Cf. Holtzmann, Apg, 4; Knopf, Apg, 529; G. Ricciotti, Gli Atti degli Apostoli, Tradotti e Commentati, Rome 1951, 2; Talbert, Literary Patterns, 23-26. For other two-part divisions see P.-H. Menoud, "Le plan des Actes des Apôtres", NTS 1 (1954-55) 44-51 (at 15,35); Cornely, Introductio, 337-340 (at 9,43); C. Perrot, "Les Actes des Apôtres", L'annonce de l'Évangile: Introduction Critique au Nouveau Testament II.2, eds. X. Léon-Dufour, C. Perrot, Paris 1976, 254 (at 11,26); É. Trocmé, Le "Livre des Actes" et l'Histoire, EHPR 45: Paris 1957, 88-89 (at 16,5); Schille, Apg, 64.260 (at 11,18).

[159] Bisping, Apg, 7 (at 8,3; 12,25); Knabenbauer, Actus, 25ff. (at 1,3; 12,25; 21,16); Knowling, Acts, 11 (at 2,13; 8,1; 11,18); Schneider, Apg I, 66 (at 1,26; 5,42; 15,35); see the three-part geographical scheme of J. de Zwaan, "Was the Book of Acts a Posthumous Edition?", HTR 17 (1924) 106 (at 11,18; 15,35); also Wikenhauser, Apg, 36.115 (at 2,1; 9,31; 15,35).

[160] Cf. Zahn, Apg 1-12, 9.269; 13-28 (Leipzig-Erlangen 1921), 744 (at 8,3; 12,25; 21,26); Dupont, "Plan des Actes", 231 (at 1,26; 8,3; 15,35; 19,40); E. Haenchen, "The Book of Acts as Source Material for the History of Early Christianity", Keck, Martyn (eds), Studies in Luke-Acts, 259 (at 8,3; 15,35; 21,26); Morgenthaler, Geschichtsschreibung I, 263 (at 1,3; 7,60; 21,17; 26,32); Rolland, "Actes", 83 (at 1,14; 2,4; 8,1a; 12,25; epilogue: 28,16-31); the twelve-part arrangement of Pesch (Apg 1-12, 36-42) is based on a four-part division (at 1,26; 15,33; 28,16).

[161] Cf. Cerfaux, "Actes", 341-345 (at 1,11; 5,42; 12,25; 15,35; 19,20); Kümmel, Introduction, 154-156 (at 1,14; 8,3; 11,18; 15,35; 19,20); Munck, Acts, IX-XI (at 5,42; 11,18; 15,33; 18,28); O'Neill, Theology, 72 (at 1,8; 8,3; 11,18; 15,35; 19,20); Roloff, Apg, 12-14 (at 1,26; 5,42; 9,31; 15,35; 19,20); for six-part divisions based on the summaries (see n. 186 below) or chronological criteria see Betori, "Articolazione", 200-202.

[162] Cf. A. Jülicher, Einleitung in das Neue Testament, Tübingen 1906[5-6], 394, who advises that a "fein überlegten Plan darf man in dem Buche, das lediglich nach der Reihenfolge die Begebenheiten vorträgt, nicht suchen."

the apostles in vv. 2 and 13 are also indicative of its unity. Jesus' command of v. 4 is represented as fulfilled in vv. 12-14, a fulfilment that is also expressed in verbal contacts between the texts (vv. 4.12-13: ἀπὸ Ἱεροσολύμων μὴ χωρίζεσθαι... περιμένειν· ὑπέστρεψαν εἰς Ἰερουσαλήμ... καταμένοντες). The list of apostles in v. 13, with its reminder of the one that has fallen by the wayside, prepares the account of Judas' substitution in 1,15-26. Together with the summary of v. 14 it provides a transition to the following unit.

To those who place the conclusion of the book's initial unit at v. 11[163] it may be pointed out that the notice of the disciples' return to Jerusalem in v. 12 is closely linked to the ascension scene, so much so, in fact, that only in v. 12 is the event's location given. Moreover, τότε (v. 12a) is never used in Luke–Acts to introduce a major section (diff. Mt).[164] Much more suitable than v. 11 for a conclusion is v. 14. This summary which features the periphrastic imperfect (ἦσαν προσκαρτεροῦντες) marks a pause in the account (cf. Lk 4,44; 5,16; 19,47-48; 22,65). With its general time indication καὶ ἐν ταῖς ἡμέραις ταύταις, v. 15 represents a more obvious Lucan opening than v. 12 (cf. Lk 1,5.39; 2,1; 6,12; Acts 6,1).

It is true that ὁ Ἰησοῦς ὁ ἀναλημφθείς of v. 11 recalls ὁ Ἰησοῦς... ἀνελήμφθη of vv. 1-2. But this repetition marks the end of an internal development begun in v. 3 and it need not and does not mark the conclusion of the book's initial unit. The gospel does not furnish a contrary argument, since it does not actually close with the ascension. Two important events follow Jesus' taking up in Lk 24,51, the return of the disciples to the city (24,52) and their stay there in obedience to Jesus' command (24,53). These two events, with additional details, are again recounted in 1,12-14. Together with v. 13, which reminds the reader of the gospel theme of Judas' betrayal, they form part of the recapitulation and repetition that mark the opening unit of Acts.

The presence of recapitulation and repetition in 1,1-14 is indeed striking. The first two verses summarize the gospel's narrative proper, that is, from the beginning of Jesus' ministry to his ascension. In 1,3-14 there is extensive repetition with a good deal of variation, as the author recounts post-resurrectional appearances, the injunction to await the coming of the Spirit in Jerusalem, the ascension, the return of the disciples to the city and their activity there. Of those present in the 'upper room' the eleven remaining apostles (cf. Lk 6,14-16) and Mary are named.

---

[163] See n. 153 above.
[164] It is used frequently by Matthew at the beginning of pericopes and larger sections; cf. 2,16; 3,13; 4,1; 9,14; 11,20; etc.

Such extensive repetition at the beginning of the second volume of an ancient literary work is unusual. It is not unknown, though,[165] and is not without reason here. In the gospel the author was anxious to provide an effective conclusion for his first volume; at the beginning of Acts he is concerned to prepare the reader for the narrative that follows.[166] Given that recapitulation, repetition and introductory elements are characteristic of the proemium of a second or successive volume of a literary work, their presence in 1,1-14 suggests that these verses form a unit which may be classified as, or as part of, a secondary proemium.[167]

1.2 *1,15-26: Recomposition of the Twelve*

The account of Matthias' election is a self-contained unit, framed by references to Judas (vv. 16.25), in which the betrayer's replacement is first of all advocated (vv. 16-22) and then chosen (vv. 23-26). It is closely lin-

---

[165] Josephus begins Bk V of his *Jewish War* (§ 1) with a brief recapitulation of the final verses of Bk IV (cf. §§ 659-663) and a repetition with a slight variation of that book's final phrase. In the rest of the secondary proemium (V,2-20) he repeats in summary form the account he had given in Bk IV of the strife occasioned by the Zealots (cf. §§ 128ff.); for repetition in a secondary proemium see also Char., *De Chaer. et Call.* V,1.1-2; VIII,1.1-5a; *Corpus Hermeticum* XIII,1. In Jos., *Ant.* XVIII,1 and XX,1, repetition is part of the narrative proper (see the conclusions of XVII and XIX).

[166] In Lk 24 the evangelist is anxious to highlight the bringing to faith of the disciples, the recomposition of the group of disciples in Jerusalem (24,33-35), the imparting of a universal mission (24,47-48) and the injunction to await the coming of the Spirit in the city (24,49). The events of the chapter are telescoped into one day in order to provide a culminating point for the final section and a fitting conclusion for the gospel (see C. B. R. Pelling, "Plutarch's adaptation of his source-material", *JHS* 100 (1980) 127-128, on chronological compression in Plutarch). At the beginning of Acts the evangelist avails himself of the recapitulatory possibilities of the secondary proemium to include material omitted in Lk 24. Cf. M.C. Parsons, *The Departure of Jesus in Luke-Acts. The Ascension Narratives in Context*, JSNTSS 21: Sheffield 1987, 192-198; Palmer, "Acts 1. 1-14", 427-438.

[167] Recapitulation of a previous volume and the indication of the theme or a summary of the contents of the volume being introduced, if often brief, are common features of a secondary or transitional proemium; see, for instance, the secondary proemia of Polybius (*Hist.* II,1.1-4; III,1.1-11; IV,1.1-2.11), Diodorus (*Hist.* II,1.1; III,1.1), Philo (*De Spec. Leg.* I,1; II,1; III,7; *De Ebr.* § 1; *Quod Omnis Probus Liber* § 1), Dioscorides, *De Mat. Med.* II Pr.) and Artemidorus (*Oneirocritica* II Pr.); cf. Larrañaga, "Proemio-Transición", 350-359. In noting that Acts 1,8 contained the programme of Acts, Overbeck (in W. M. L. de Wette, *Kurze Erklärung der Apostelgeschichte*, ed. F. Overbeck, KEHNT I.IV: Leipzig 1870⁴, XXI) and later Adolf Harnack (*Die Apostelgeschichte*, BENT III: Leipzig 1908, 207) removed the need for adventurous reconstructions of hypothetical introductions corresponding to classical models (e.g. Norden, *Agnostos Theos*, 315-316). Of importance, too, the work of Cadbury (*Making*, 198-199) and Haenchen (*Acts*, 139-140 nn. 7-8; 141 n. 2) who pointed out the Lucan style of Acts 1,3. For repetition in a secondary proemium see n. 165 above. For examples of recapitulation followed directly by the narrative see Larrañaga, "Proemio-Transición", 340-349.356-364.

ked to 1,1-14, particularly the transitional vv. 13-14. The introductory time indication of v. 15a and the repetition of the term ἀδελφοί of v. 14 in v. 15[168] set the election in the context of vv. 13-14, a summary that is recalled also by the figure of Peter, the indication of the number of disciples present (v. 15b) and the actual theme of 1,15-26.[169]

It is also closely associated with what follows. The presence of the newly reconstituted group of twelve at Peter's Pentecost sermon has an important symbolic content. For it implies that 'all Israel' is being addressed here; that the new people of God now being formed stands in continuity with Israel; and that Israel itself has the primacy in the hearing of the word.[170] The restoration of the original number, therefore, is a necessary preliminary to the preaching of the word at Pentecost.

But 1,15-26 forms part of the unit 1,1-26. Its close verbal links with 1,1-14 suggest as much, but even more so its final phrase, μετὰ τῶν ἕνδεκα ἀποστόλων. This is the only occasion in Luke-Acts where both a number, whether eleven or twelve (cf. 2,14), and the term ἀπόστολος appear together in reference to the apostles. Normally one suffices to identify the group. The pleonastic ἀποστόλων of v. 26 is a deliberate insertion to form with ἀποστόλοις of v. 2 an inclusion for the unit 1,1-26.[171]

A survey of secondary or transitional proemia reveals how individual and complex they can be. In *Contra Apion*, Josephus, having summarized the previous volume and having indicated the theme of the present one (II,1-2a), goes on to introduce in II,2b-7 the person and writings of Apion about whom much will be written in the narrative proper beginning in II,8. In *De Vita Mosis*, Philo recapitulates Bk I and indicates the theme of Bk II in II,1-3a, while the rest of the proemium (II,3b-11) is occupied with remarks on Moses' qualifications as law-giver, high priest and prophet, remarks that are preliminary to the narrative proper beginning in II,12.[172]

---

[168] For this anaphoric type repetition see Lausberg, *Rhetorik*, 314-315.

[169] Note also μάρτυς: vv. 8.22; ἐκλέγομαι: vv. 2.24.

[170] See ch. I n. 152.

[171] Note how Tacitus marks the conclusion of the complex proemium of his *Histories* with a repetition: I,1: Initium mihi operis Servius Galba iterum Titus Vinius consules erunt ... dum res populi Romani; I,11: Hic fuit rerum Romanarum status, cum Servius Galba iterum Titus Vinius consules..., rei publicae prope supremum (cf. Leeman, "Prologues", 174); other examples are to be found in Jos., *JB* V,1-20 (στάσις: vv. 2.20); *C. Ap.* I,1-59 (τὴν ἀρχαιολογίαν συγγραφῆς (1) ... βλασφημίαις (2) ... περὶ τῆς ἡμετέρας ἀρχαιότητος ... μάρτυσι (4) ... συγγραφεῦσιν (58) ... τὰς μαρτυρίας τῆς ἀρχαιότητος ... τοὺς ... βλασφημοῦντας (59); Thuc., *War* I,1.1-23.6 (τὸν πόλεμον: I,1.1; 23.6).

[172] Recapitulation in VIII,1 of Char., *De Chaer. et Call.*, is followed by additional information on the situation that arose at the end of Bk VII and a comment on its possible outcome (VIII,2), indications of Aphrodite's dissatisfaction with this situation

In addition to the usual recapitulation and indication of theme, then, a secondary or transitional proemium may have one or more sections that are in various ways preliminary or preparatory to the narrative proper.[173] In the light of this, 1,1-26 may be classified as a secondary or transitional proemium containing a recapitulation of the previous volume (1,1-2), an indication of the theme of the present one (1,8), a certain amount of repetition, and a preliminary narrative unit (1,15-26) preparatory to the narrative proper that begins in 2,1.

2. *Literary Structure of 2,1–28,31*

The narrative proper of Acts opens in a style not untypical of Luke (cf. Lk 2,1; 9,51), while its closing summary in 28,30-31 is likewise couched in Lucan style (cf. Lk 4,44; 19,47-48; 21,37-38; 24,53). References to the nations (2,5; 28,28) and the Holy Spirit (2,4; 28,25) frame the narrative, as do instances of the term παρρησία (2,29; 28,31)[174] and Old Testament citations from Joel and Isaiah (2,17-21; 28,26-27). Peter's initial Pentecost appeal to the people of Israel (cf. 2,14.22) contrasts with Paul's words of 28,26-28 which are likewise intended for Israel, though in a somewhat different spirit.[175]

There is little consensus about the literary structure of this narrative.[176] Biographical, thematic and geographical criteria, or some combination of these, have been used to determine the structure. The two-part biographical scheme based on the figures of Peter (1-12) and Paul (13-28) and recently reproposed by Talbert[177] is open to major objections. Peter is not mentioned at all in chs. 6 and 7, where Stephen is the principal figure, but he does play a significant role in ch. 15. Paul, on the other hand, appears already in chs. 7 (v. 58) and 8 (vv. 1a.1b-3). Indeed the persecution in which he plays a prominent part has a vital role in the spread of the word of God beyond Jerusalem (cf. 8,1b-3.4; 11,19).

---

and of her desire to intervene (VIII,3) — two elements that are preparatory to the narrative proper — and an introduction (VIII,4-5a) to the narrative proper that begins in VIII,5b.

[173] See, for example, Jos., *C. Ap.* I,1-59; Philo, *De Abr.* §§ 1-60; Tac., *Hist.* I,2-3.4-11; Sall., *Cat.* 5,1–16,4. In some cases general considerations having little if anything to do with the narrative proper may precede the recapitulation and indication of content; see, for instance, the proemia of Diodorus in *Hist.* XII,1.1-5, XIV,1.1-2.3, XV,1.1-5, XVIII,1.1-4, and XIX,1.1-9, or Philo, *De Spec. Leg.* III,1-6.

[174] The only other occurrences of the term in Acts are 4,13.29.31 (elsewhere: Mt 0; Mk 1; Lk 0; Jn 9; Rest 16).

[175] See below.

[176] Cf. Neirynck, "Livre des Actes", 342-344; Betori, "Articolazione", 185-205.

[177] *Literary Patterns*, 23-26. For criticisms of two-part biographical arrangements of Acts see Menoud, "Plan des Actes", 44-45; Schneider, *Apg* I, 65.

His conversion and initial preaching are narrated in 9,1-31, and he is found preaching in Antioch in 11,26 (cf. 11,25) and carrying out an important mission of mercy for the community there in 11,27-30 and 12,25.

Geographical considerations have influenced most literary arrangements. Taking 1,8 to indicate the exact plan of the narrative, Knowling divided it into three parts at 8,1/2 and 11,18/19.[178] O'Neill adjusted this slightly and added divisions at 15,35/36 and 19,20/21 to leave him with a five-fold division at 8,3/4, 11,18/19, 15,35/36 and 19,20/21.[179] Divisions based on such considerations have also been put forward by Bisping and Jacquier (at 8,3/4; 12,25/13,1), de Zwaan (11,18/19; 15,35/36), Wikenhauser (9,31/32; 15,35/36), Kümmel (8,3/4; 11,18/19; 15,35/36; 19,20/21), Dupont (8,3/4; 15,35/36; 19,40/20,1) and Weiser (8,3/4; 15,35/36).[180] Thematic considerations led C.H. Turner to take five summaries describing the spread and growth of the word of God (6,7; 9,31; 12,24; 16,5; 19,20) to divide Acts into six panels and two roughly equal divisions corresponding to the figures of Peter and Paul.[181] These summaries could represent a principle of arrangement for the narrative, given the prominence of this theme. But closer inspection discounts this, as it does a number of other suggested points of division.

The placing of a major point of division at 5,42 owes much to its nature as a summary and the presence of a new topic in 6,1-6 (the appointment of deacons) which is closely related to what follows in 6,7–8,3.[182] Jerusalem, however, is still the setting for the events of 6,1–8,3. And while it is true that these events ultimately lead to the spread of the word far beyond the city (cf. 8,1b-3.4; 11,19), it seems more advisable to take 6,1–8,3 as a transitional unit concluding the section 2,1–8,3 (see below).[183] In this case the summary 6,7 does not initiate a new section. In any event, apart from the obvious thematic link between the appointment of Stephen and his subsequent brief ministry, trial and death, there are close verbal links between 6,5 and 6,8 and 10.[184]

The summary of 9,32 introduces Peter into the narrative and marks the beginning of a unit which, however, extends only to 11,18 where Peter disappears from the scene for a time. The initial reference to Peter's

---

[178] *Acts*, 11.

[179] *Theology*, 70-72.

[180] Cited in nn. 149, 150, 155, 156 and 159 above.

[181] C.H. Turner, "Chronology of the New Testament", *A Dictionary of the Bible* I, ed. J. Hastings, Edinburgh 1906, 421.

[182] For a new beginning at 6,1 see Cerfaux, "Actes", 341; Schneider, *Apg* I, 69; Roloff, *Apg*, 106; Munck, *Acts*, XI.

[183] Schille, *Apg*, 64, takes 1,1–8,1a to form a unit.

[184] 6,5: Στέφανον, ἄνδρα πλήρης πίστεως καὶ πνεύματος ἁγίου·
6,8: Στέφανος δὲ πλήρης χάριτος καὶ δυνάμεως· 6,10: τῷ πνεύματι ᾧ ἐλάλει.

activity in 9,32 is set in the context of the summary of 9,31 whose reference to peace recalls the hostile activities of Saul that followed Stephen's death (cf. 8,1b-3.4; 9,1-2).[185] The two summaries mark a point of division within the section 8,4–11,18 (see below).

The summary of 12,24 is overshadowed by 12,25 which, with its references to Barnabas and Saul and their διακονία, recalls 11,29-30 and brings the unit 11,19–12,25 (cf. 11,22.25) to a close.[186] The commissioning of Paul and Barnabas in 13,1-3 initiates Paul's first missionary journey (13,1–14,28). The summary of 16,5 is part of a section that begins in 15,36. The repetition involved between 16,5 and 15,41 marks the conclusions of two smaller units within the section 15,36–18,22.[187]

Lake and Cadbury take 19,21 to mark the real beginning of Paul's last journey to Jerusalem, thus placing a major point of division at Turner's final summary (19,20).[188] This verse does contain geographical indications, though different from 8,4 and 15,1, for example. A problem facing this point of division is that Paul does not leave Ephesus until 20,1, and even then he heads for Macedonia and Greece, not for Jerusalem. The verse has an important function in the rest of the narrative but only in the sense that it prepares the reader for Paul's final journey to the city and for his subsequent transfer to Rome.[189] There are other summaries dotted around the narrative (e.g. 2,47; 11,21; 13,49), but none suggest, nor did Turner, that the author used them as a principle of arrangement for his material.[190]

The general geographical thrust of Acts, with its account of the preaching and spread of the word in Jerusalem, throughout Palestine and the Greek speaking world, and as far afield as Rome, points towards the possible use of a geographical principle of arrangement here. The mission charge of 1,8b to be witnesses in Jerusalem and in all Judea and Samaria and to the end of the earth suggests a three-part arrangement of the

---

[185] Note the personal nature of the notice in 9,32 when compared with 8,4 or 11,19.

[186] Cf. O'Neill, *Theology*, 64: "12,24 marks no more than a stage in the story, a general formula expressing optimism at what has just happened, before the work of Barnabas and Paul is taken up again." Cf. Lausberg, *Rhetorik*, 320-321.

[187] Ἐπιστηρίζων τὰς ἐκκλησίας ... αἱ μὲν οὖν ἐκκλησίαι ἐστηροῦντο · cf. Lausberg, *Rhetorik*, 320-321.

[188] Lake, Cadbury, *Acts* IV, 243; Kümmel, *Introduction*, 156; O'Neill, *Theology*, 72; see also Roloff, *Apg*, 13; Weiser, *Apg* (*Kapitel 13-28*, ÖTK 5.2: Gütersloh 1985), 387.

[189] Other instances of Luke preparing events beforehand are to be found in Acts 9,16 where Paul's missionary journeys are prepared, 20,22-23 which prepares Paul's imprisonment in Jerusalem, and 23,11 which prepares the trip to Rome; in the gospel see, for example, 4,13 and 22,3.53, 20,20 and 23,1-5. Since Paul really only begins to retrace his steps towards Jerusalem in 20,3-4, 20,1 (Dupont, "Plan des Actes", 229; Schille, *Apg*, 394) seems excluded as the opening verse of Acts' final section.

[190] See the comments of H. J. Cadbury, "The Summaries of Acts", Foakes Jackson, Lake (eds.), *Beginnings* I.V, 392-402; also O'Neill, *Theology*, 64.

narrative along geographical lines. An analysis of the text confirms the existence of such an arrangement, though not an exact reproduction of the pattern of 1,8b (cf. 8,5-40). Major points of division are to be found at 8,3/4 and 21,17/18, with 11,18/19, 14,28/15,1, 15,35/36 and 18,22/23 representing points of division within the lengthy central section. Various literary indications in the text support this arrangement.

2.1 In Jerusalem: 2,1-8,3

The geographical setting of Jerusalem lends a unity to 2,1-8,3 which opens with the coming of the Spirit at Pentecost (2,1-4; cf. 11,15) and closes with the persecution following Stephen's death.[191] Throughout this section the preaching of the word is directed only to Israel (cf. 2,36; 3,26; 4,10; 5,31) whose primacy in hearing it is thus respected. There is no movement of preachers outside the city. They are present there continually, whether in the temple (3,1-4,2; 5,12.20-21.25.42) or in houses (cf. 5,42). This is reflected in the use of ἐν (εἰς) Ἰερουσαλήμ/Ἱεροσολύμοις throughout (cf. 2,5; 4,5; 6,7; 8,1)[192] and in frequent references to the temple.[193] With the death of Stephen ἔξω τῆς πόλεως (7,58) the end of the Jerusalem stage is foreshadowed. The subsequent persecution leads to the spread of the word beyond the city (cf. 8,4; 11,19).

The section is composed of three units, 2,1-4,31, 4,32-5,42 and 6,1-8,3, with summaries which refer to the preaching of the word in 4,31 and 5,42 marking the points of division.[194] The first unit is framed by references to the Holy Spirit (2,4; 4,31),[195] the second by references to the apostles (prominent figures in 4,32-5,42) and their witness (4,33; 5,40-42),[196] and the third by time indications (6,2; 8,1b), as well as by references to the twelve (6,2; 8,1c) and to Stephen (6,5; 8,2).

---

[191] For a conclusion at 8,3 see the commentaries of Bisping, Zahn, Jacquier, Wikenhauser, Mussner, Weiser; O'Neill, *Theology*, 72; Kümmel, *Introduction*, 155; Dupont, "Plan des Actes", 226; ed. of Nestle. G. Betori, *Perseguitati a causa del Nome. Strutture dei racconti di persecuzione in Atti 1,12-8,4*, AnBib 97: Rome 1981, extends the first part of the narrative to 8,4, Schille, *Apg*, 64, to 8,1a.

[192] See also 4,27; 5,28. Note the reference in 5,16 to those coming into the city from the towns around to be healed.

[193] Ἱερόν: fourteen times between 2,46 and 5,42; τόπος: 6,13.14; οἶκος: 7,47. The Sanhedrin is also prominent here; cf. 4,15; 5,21.27.34.41; 6,12.15.

[194] Καὶ ἐλάλουν τὸν λόγον τοῦ θεοῦ μετὰ παρρησίας ... οὐκ ἐπαύοντο διδάσκοντες καὶ εὐαγγελιζόμενοι τὸν Χριστόν, Ἰησοῦν (4,31; 5,42).

[195] Καὶ ἐπλήσθησαν πάντες πνεύματος ἁγίου ... καὶ ἐπλήσθησαν ἅπαντες τοῦ ἁγίου πνεύματος (2,4; 4,31).

[196] 4,33: ἀπεδίδουν τὸ μαρτύριον οἱ ἀπόστολοι τῆς ἀναστάσεως τοῦ κυρίου Ἰησοῦ · 5,40-42: ... τοὺς ἀποστόλους ... οὐκ ἐπαύοντο διδάσκοντες καὶ εὐαγγελιζόμενοι τὸν Χριστόν, Ἰησοῦν.

The third unit, 6,1–8,3, provides a smooth transition to the narrative's central section; for recounted here is a chain of events that leads to the flight of "all except the apostles" from the city and the spread of the word throughout Palestine and further afield (cf. 8,1b.4; 11,19).[197]

2.2 Missionary Preaching: 8,4–21,17

a) Extent

A summary report in 8,4 of the spread of the word of God by those fleeing from Jerusalem introduces a new section. It picks up the report of 8,1c, repeating the verb διασπείρω, but unlike 8,1c it does not specify geographical areas. This lack of specificity suggests that what is being introduced in 8,4 is not simply the spread of the word to Judea and Samaria (cf. 8,1b) but its diffusion over a much wider area.

The subsequent narrative confirms this, for already by 9,19 the word of God has reached Damascus, and in 9,20 Paul is preaching Christ in the synagogues of that city. Furthermore, the spread of the word to Phoenecia, Cyprus and Antioch, reported in 11,19, is presented as another aspect of the missionary activity resulting from the persecution that followed Stephen's death. This suggests that the section beginning in 8,4 extends beyond 11,19. Where does it end?

Weiser places its conclusion at 15,35,[198] making a distinction between the missionary activity of 8,4–15,35, which sees the word preached in Samaria, Judea, Antioch and Asia Minor, and that of 15,36–28,31, in which the word reaches Rome. But it is difficult to see why one should distinguish between the missionary activity of 8,4–15,35 and 15,36 ff. The distinction should rather be made between the whole missionary movement which sees the word of God preached throughout Palestine and far beyond its borders in the Greek speaking world and the events that lead to Paul's ministry in Rome. Paul's detention by the Jews (cf. 21,18-30), his arrest by the Roman authorities (21,31-36), and the accusations, hearings and defence speeches that follow represent a very different phase in the narrative from his missionary journeys. His arrest in the temple actually sets in motion a chain of events that eventually brings him to Rome on appeal to Caesar (cf. 25,11-12).

---

[197] Acts 8,1b-3 represents a good example of the overlapping, ἀνακεκρᾶσθαι κατὰ τὰ ἄκρα, recommended by Lucian (Hist. § 55): 8,2 concludes the story of Stephen; 8,1bc anticipates that of Philip in 8,4-40; 8,3 anticipates 9,1-2 on Saul; the writer thus achieves a certain interweaving of matter, συμπεριπλοκὴ τῶν πραγμάτων, in keeping with Lucian's advice (Hist. § 55); cf. Dupont, "Plan des Actes", 224-226; Avenarius, Geschichts-schreibung, 119-120.

[198] Apg 1-12, 27.

Independent literary support for concluding this section with Paul's third missionary journey is present in the shape of a number of terms that are characteristic of this missionary section. The Lucan verb διέρχεσθαι (Mt 2; Mk 2; Lk 10; Jn 3; Acts 20; Rest 6), used to describe the movements of the preachers of the word and found throughout this section (8,4.40; ... 20,2.25), occurs only here in Acts. Another verb of movement, κατέρχεσθαι, (Lk 2; Acts 13; Jn 1) is, with the exception of 27,5, likewise confined to this section (8,5; 9,32; 11,27; ... 19,1; 21,3.10). The case is similar with εὐαγγελίζεσθαι and its related nouns. Apart from 5,42, occurrences of the verb which is found here on fourteen occasions (8,4.12; ... 17,18) and of the nouns εὐαγγέλιον (15,7; 20,24) and εὐαγγελιστῆς (21,8) are to be found only here. The verb κηρύσσειν is, with the exception of 28,31, also confined to these chapters (8,5; 9,20; 13,37.42; 15,21; 19,13; 20,25).

The most striking evidence in favour of the unity of this central section, though, is that provided by the figure of Philip. Paul's final port of call as he comes to the end of his third missionary journey is the home of the 'evangelist' of Samaria (cf. 21,8-14). It is surely significant that as the description of Paul's missionary journeys draws to a close the initial journey outside Jerusalem is so explicitly recalled (8,5-40). The section is framed in fact by references to Philip and his mission (... εὐαγγελιζόμενοι ... Φίλιππος ... ἐκήρυσσεν ... τὸν Χριστόν ... Φιλίππῳ εὐαγγελιζομένῳ: 8,4-5.12; Φιλίππου τοῦ εὐαγγελιστοῦ: 21,8) and to Caesarea (8,40; 21,8.14).[199]

The problem remains of establishing where exactly the section ends, since the conclusion of Paul's third missionary journey is variously placed at vv. 14, 15, 16, 17, 18 and 26 of ch. 21.[200] The destination of this journey is first given in 19,21. It is mentioned on two occasions in ch. 20 (vv. 16.22), and more frequently as Paul draws closer to Jerusalem (21,4.11.12.13.15.17).

References to Paul's arrival in Caesarea in 21,8 and to his departure therefrom in 21,16 suggest that the conclusion should not be placed before the latter point. Indeed Paul and his companions are only beginning the final stage of their journey to Jerusalem in 21,15 (ἐπισκευασάμενοι

---

[199] Note also πνεῦμα ἅγιον (8,15); τὸ πνεῦμα τὸ ἅγιον (21,11).

[200] For the conclusion of this journey at 21,14 see Knopf, *Apg*, 529; Peters, "Aufbau", 54; Schille, *Apg*, 394; Schneider, *Apg* I, 68; at 21,15, Cornely, *Introductio*, 340; at 21,16, Bisping, *Apg*, 301; Knabenbauer, *Actus*, 361; at 21,17, A.C. Winn, "Elusive Mystery. The Purpose of Acts", *Int* 13 (1959) 149; Morgenthaler, *Geschichtsschreibung* I, 163; A.J. Mattill, Jr., "The Purpose of Acts. Schneckenburger Reconsidered", *Apostolic History and the Gospel*, Biblical and Historical Essays presented to F.F. Bruce, eds. W.W. Gasque, R.P. Martin, Exeter 1970, 118; E. Plümacher, "Apostelgeschichte", *TRE* III, 485; at 21,18, Holtzmann, *Apg*, 4; at 21,26, Zahn, *Apg 13-28*, 395; Conzelmann, *Apg*, 15. Stählin, *Apg*, 272, considers 21,1-17 to form a unit.

ἀνεβαίνομεν εἰς Ἱεροσόλυμα). The analogy of the gospel's travel narrative which concludes in 19,48 with Jesus' arrival in the temple points towards 21,17 as the conclusion of this missionary journey and consequently of the whole central section.

Contrasting references to the city of Jerusalem frame 8,4–21,17. It opens with disciples fleeing the city to escape the persecution in which Paul plays a central role (cf. 8,3) and it closes with the voluntary arrival in the city of Paul and his companions. The hostile note of 8,4a contrasts with the joy of 21,17. But the latter only masks for the moment the hostility predicted in 21,11. The city in reality has changed little. The development of the narrative plot also points in this direction, since Paul's resolve to go to Jerusalem (19,21), which encounters mounting opposition as the goal draws nearer (cf. 21,4.12-13) but which survives nonetheless (cf. 21,13-14), is only realized in 21,17.

b) *Arrangement*

Given the underlying geographical thrust of this section one would expect journey indications, departures, arrivals, etc., to play an important role in its arrangement. Such indeed is the case. Geographical indications suggest a division of the narrative into five parts (8,4–11,18; 11,19–14,28; 15,1-35; 15,36–18,22; 18,23–21,17) closely linked one to the other (cf. 8,4; 11,19; 14,28 f.; 15,23 ff.41; 18,19-23), with 15,1-35 forming the pivotal point of the whole.

2.2.1 *8,4–11,18: From Samaritans to Gentiles*

The repetition of a number of significant terms from 8,4 (οἱ μὲν οὖν διασπαρέντες διῆλθον εὐαγγελιζόμενοι τὸν λόγον) in 11,19 (οἱ μὲν οὖν διασπαρέντες... διῆλθον... λαλοῦντες τὸν λόγον) delimits the first part, 8,4–11,18.[201] This opening section, which may be divided into three parts, each with its own protagonist and marked by the summaries 8,40 and 9,31 (8,4-40; 9,1-31; 9,32–11,18), shows the word preached first to Samaritans (8,5-25; cf. 1,8), then to a worshipper of the Lord from Ethiopia (8,26-40) and finally to the first Gentile (10,1–11,18). With Peter's conversion of Cornelius the spread of the word among the Gentiles is prepared. But it is prepared also by Paul's conversion in ch. 9, and particularly by the Lord's statement in 9,15 that Paul is to be a chosen instrument of his to carry his name before the Gentiles as well as the sons of Israel. The approving comment on the events of 10,1-48 of the church in Jerusalem (11,18) which brings the section to a fitting conclusion highlights the Gentile mission. Thus 8,4–11,18 acts as an

---

[201] Cf. Lausberg, *Rhetorik*, 318-320.

introduction to the whole missionary section which sees the word being preached especially among the Gentiles.

2.2.2 *11,19-14,28: 'Turning to the Gentiles'*

The almost exact repetition of 8,4 in 11,19 marks the beginning of a section that extends to the narrative pause of 14,28.[202] It is framed by references to Antioch (11,19; 14,26) which plays a central role in the narrative from this point until 18,22-23. Of note also is the thematic parallel between 14,27 and 11,18, both of which comment on the pagan mission.[203]

The section is composed of two main parts, 11,19-12,25 and 13,1-14,28.[204] The first opens in Antioch (11,19-30) and continues with what in reality are two digressions, the accounts of Peter's imprisonment and deliverance (12,1-17) and the death of Herod (12,18-23). The second recounts the commissioning of Barnabas and Saul and their first missionary journey during which Paul delivers a stern warning to the Jews (13,40-41) and initiates his Gentile mission (13,46-48). It concludes with the return of the missionaries to their point of departure (cf. 13,1-3; 14,21-28).

2.2.3 *15,1-35: Council of Jerusalem*

With the arrival in Antioch of people from Judea preaching the necessity of circumcision for salvation (15,1) a disturbing problem is introduced into the narrative, one which leads directly to the Council of Jerusalem. This section, for which the Council provides a thematic unity, is framed by the journeys of Paul and Barnabas to and from the city (cf. 15,1-5.30-35) and by contrasting references to false and true teaching, a fundamental point in the narrative at this stage (cf. vv. 1.35).[205]

Acts 15,1-35 forms the centre and the pivotal point of the missionary section as a whole.[206] The Council, called to deal with the question raised

---

[202] *Διέτριβον* δὲ χρόνον οὐκ ὀλίγον σὺν τοῖς μαθηταῖς.

[203] Cf. 11,18: Ἄρα καὶ τοῖς ἔθνεσιν ὁ θεὸς τὴν μετάνοιαν εἰς ζωὴν ἔδωκεν· 14,27: ἀνήγγελλον ὅσα ἐποίησεν ὁ θεὸς μετ' αὐτῶν καὶ ὅτι ἤνοιξεν τοῖς ἔθνεσιν θύραν πίστεως.

[204] Cf. Schille, *Apg*, 260.279.

[205] Cf. S. Panimolle, *Il discorso di Pietro all'assemblea apostolica* I, SB 1: Bologna 1976, 176-177; the section 15,1-35 may be divided into five units, 15,1-5, 6-12, 13-21, 22-29 and 30-35.

[206] Cf. Menoud, "Plan des Actes", 51: "...l'effort missionnaire des débuts aboutit naturellement à la conférence de Jérusalem... Si la conférence est un point d'aboutissement, elle est en même temps un point de départ"; also E. Rasco, "Spirito e istituzione nell'opera lucana", *RivB* 30 (1982) 306-307.

in Antioch (15,3), is the inevitable outcome of the missionary activities of Peter (10,1–11,18; cf. 15,7-8.14) and especially of Paul and Barnabas (cf. 9,15; 13,44–14,28; 15,12). Its resolution of that question paves the way for the further spread of the word (cf. 16,5.31; 19,10.20; 20,20-21) and provides a reassurance for those already converted to the faith (cf. 15,36; 16,4-5; 18,23).

2.2.4 *15,36–18,22: The Greek World*

The first stage of Paul's post-conciliar activity is closely linked to 15,1-35 by the geographical references of 15,41 (cf. 15,23), the figures of Silas (cf. 15,40; 15,22) and Barnabas (cf. 15,36-39; 15,2-35), and the remark of 16,4 which echoes 15,23-29.[207] Initially Paul revisits cities where he and Barnabas had already preached, but divine guidance (cf. 16,6-7.10) soon leads him further afield to the cities of Macedonia and Greece. This new phase of the mission concludes in 18,22 with Paul's return to Antioch whence he had departed.

Schneider places a break at 18,22,[208] as does Nestle-Aland,[209] but Wescott and Hort and the *Greek New Testament* place it at 18,23.[210] As we have seen above, geographical indications have been used to delineate Paul's first missionary journey (13,1–14,28), the section 11,19–14,28 and the Council of Jerusalem. In the light of this, and given the geographical thrust of the whole central section, it is not surprising to find references to the city of Antioch, the focal point of Paul's missionary labours between 11,19 and 18,22, delineating the section 15,36–18,22 (cf. 15,35.40-41; 18,22).[211]

2.2.5 *18,23–21,17: Reassurance and Farewell*

The anaphoric type repetition ἐξῆλθεν... διήρχετο... ἐπιστηρίζων - ἐξῆλθεν, διερχόμενος... ἐπιστηρίζων (15,40 f.; 18,23) signals a new beginning in 18,23 (cf. 11,19 and 8,4) and justifies the arrangement of the text found in Nestle-Aland. The verse also has a number of characteristics not untypical of Lucan openings such as an indefinite time

---

[207] Schille, *Apg*, 329, takes 15,36–18,23 to form a unit.

[208] *Apg* II, 193; also Mussner, *Apg*, 96.

[209] Not so Nestle (e.g. 7th ed., 1908). For the conclusion of this missionary journey at 18,22 see Holtzmann, *Apg*, 4; Jacquier, *Actes*, 469; Knabenbauer, *Actus*, 273; Knopf, *Apg*, 599; Wikenhauser, *Einleitung*, 182; Winn, "Elusive Mystery", 149; the codices A and D have a break/full stop at 18,22; B does not.

[210] Also eds. of Tischendorf, Nestle, von Soden; cf. Schille, *Apg*, 329; Neirynck, *Actes*, 344.

[211] References to Syria (cf. 15,41; 18,18) and occurrences of the term ἐκκλησία in 15,41 and 18,22 should also be noted.

indication, καὶ ποιήσας χρόνον τινά (cf. Acts 15,36; Lk 5,27; 10,1; Acts 6,1; 28,17),[212] a change of scene expressed by the verb ἐξέρχεσθαι (cf. Lk [2,1]; 5,27; 6,12; Acts 20,1), and a summary statement of missionary activity containing the verb διέρχεσθαι (cf. Lk 17,11; Acts 8,4; 11,19). In addition, 19,1a links up with 18,24-28 through its reference to Apollo, while the geographical indication διελθόντα τὰ ἀνωτερικὰ μέρη of 19,1b picks up, indeed presupposes, the notice διερχόμενος... τὴν Γαλατικὴν χώραν καὶ Φρυγίαν of 18,23.

Geographical indications abound throughout this section (cf. 18,23; 19,1.21; 20,1-2.6.13-15; 21,1-3.7-8.15-17) which is framed by two such indications, 18,23 and 21,17. The city of Ephesus links this journey to the previous one, the present visit (19,1-40) having been prepared by that of 18,19-21. This final journey opens with a picture of Paul strengthening disciples (18,23; cf. 20,1-2.7-11), while his farewell speech to the elders of Ephesus at Miletus (20,18-35) indicates that this phase of his life is drawing to a close. The following verses, 21,1-17, describe the journey to Jerusalem in accordance with the inspired decision of 19,21.

2.3 To Rome: 21,18–28,31

The advice given by James and the elders in Jerusalem to Paul (cf. 21,18.23-24) sets in motion a chain of events that eventually leads him to Rome. Framed by references to God's salvific activity among the Gentiles (cf. 21,19; 28,28),[213] the section has a marked geographical character moving from Jerusalem through Caesarea to Rome.[214] An examination of the text suggests a three-part arrangement associated with these cities.

The repetition of τῇ δὲ ἐπιούσῃ of 21,18 in 23,11 forms an inclusion for the first part, 21,18–23,11,[215] set in Jerusalem. The events subsequent to Paul's seizure in the temple by the Jews (21,27-30), his arrest by the Romans (21,31-33), and his first defence speeches (21,37–22,31; 23,1-8) come to an initial conclusion in 23,10-11 with Paul under Roman arrest (23,10) but assured that he will bear witness in Rome (23,11; cf. 19,21).

---

[212] Cf. Acts 15,36: μετὰ δέ τινας ἡμέρας. A participle at the beginning of a major section is also found in Acts 8,4; 11,19; 15,1; for smaller units see Lk 4,38; 6,20; 9,1.10; 19,1.11; Acts 4,23; 13,13; 14,21; etc.

[213] 21,19: ὧν ἐποίησεν ὁ θεὸς ἐν τοῖν ἔθνεσιν διὰ τῆς διακονίας αὐτοῦ · 28,28: τοῖς ἔθνεσιν ἀπεστάλη τοῦτο τὸ σωτήριον τοῦ θεοῦ.

[214] Compare the passage from Acts 21,17 to 21,18ff. and that from Lk 19,47-48 to 20,1ff. Holtzmann, Apg, 4, took 21,19–28,31 to form a unit, Zahn, Apg 13-28, 744, 21,27b-28,31, Conzelmann, Apg, 16, 21,27-28,31.

[215] Many commentators take 22,30–23,11 to form a unit; see, for example, the commentaries of Schneider (Vol. II, Freiburg 1982), Wikenhauser, Haenchen, Conzelmann, Weiser; diff. Marshall, Acts, 366 (22,30–23,10).

A plot against Paul's life (23,12) leads to his transfer to Caesarea which is the scene of most of the second part, 23,12–26,32 (cf. 23,12-35).[216] This part is framed by references to Paul's possible demise (cf. 23,12; 26,31). It is his appeal to Caesar that prepares the final part of this section, for although his innocence is accepted by the Romans, the appeal necessitates his dispatch to Rome (cf. 25,10-12.21.25; 26,31-32).

The concluding unit, 27,1–28,31,[217] opens with Paul's departure for Rome in 27,1-2. The notice of his arrival in the city in 28,16 has a transitional character, marking as it does the conclusion of the voyage (27,1–28,16; cf. Lk 1,56; 2,39; 19,45-48; Acts 21,17) and introducing his witness in Rome (28,17-31). With ἐγένετο δέ and a time indication, 28,17 rather than 28,16a[218] has the Lucan credentials for an introduction to the finale of Acts (cf. Lk 2,1; 6,1.6.12; also 5,1; 9,51). In Rome the word of God has not reached the end of the earth.[219] But with its unhindered preaching to all, Jews and Gentiles alike,[220] in the capital and centre of the οἰκουμένη, it is well on the way.

Conclusion

The unity of Lk 5,1–24,53 further confirms the existence of a major break in the gospel narrative at 4,44. It suggests also that 1,5–4,44

---

[216] For a conclusion at 26,32 see Bisping, *Apg*, 370; Knabenbauer, *Actus*, 391; Peters, "Aufbau", 54; Mattill, Jr., "Purpose", 118.

[217] Cf. Bisping, *Apg*, 400; Knopf, *Apg*, 656; Morgenthaler, *Geschichtsschreibung* I, 163; Mattill, Jr., "Purpose", 118.

[218] J. Dupont, "La conclusion des Actes et son rapport à l'ensemble de l'ouvrage de Luc", *Les Actes des Apôtres. Traditions, rédaction, théologie*, ed. J. Kremer, BETL 48: Gembloux-Louvain 1979, 362-363; Hauser, *Abschlusserzählung*, 11-17; also B. Prete, "L'arrivo di Paolo a Roma e il suo significato secondo Atti 28,16-31", *RevB* 31 (1983) 147-187; Bisping, *Apg*, 422; Cornely, *Introductio*, 340. The correspondence noted by Dupont between vv. 16 and 31 may equally well, and in this case more reasonably, be explained as a correspondence between two conclusions (cf. Lk 19,47-48 and 21,37-38; Acts 11,18 and 14,28). Note also the progression between 28,14 and 16 (ἤλθαμεν ... εἰσήλθομεν). Cf. Knabenbauer, *Actus*, 149; Marshall, *Acts*, 420; Pesch, *Apg 1-12*, 41 (28,17-31: "Epilog"); Schille, *Apg*, 476.

[219] There is no reason to equate Rome with τὸ ἔσχατον τῆς γῆς, as W. C. van Unnik has demonstrated in "Der Ausdruck ἕως ἐσχάτου τῆς γῆς (Apostelgeschichte i,8) und sein alttestamentlicher Hintergrund", *Studia Biblica et Semitica*, Fs für T.C. Vriezen, Leiden 1966, 335-349 (= *Sparsa Collecta. The Collected Essays of W.C. van Unnik* I, Suppl. NT 29: Leiden 1973, 386-401); also Samain, "APXH", 302-303 n. 13; diff. Dupont, "Salut", 140-141.

[220] As the Western text understood and made explicit: ἀπεδέχετο πάντας ... Ἰουδαίους τε καὶ Ἕλληνας: 614, 2147 pc (gig p) vg^mss sy^h; diff. Haenchen, *Acts*, 726; J. Gnilka, *Die Verstockung Israels. Isaias 6,9-10 in der Theologie der Synoptiker*, SANT 3: Munich 1961, 130, and there n. 2; but see Stählin, *Apg*, 329; Dupont, "Conclusion", 377-378; V. Stolle, *Der Zeuge als Angeklagter. Untersuchungen zum Paulus Bild des Lukas*, BWANT 102: Stuttgart 1973, 86-87 n. 108.

functions as a preliminary narrative section in the gospel. Additional evidence in favour of 1,5–4,44 having such a function comes from the existence of a preliminary or preparatory narrative section at the beginning of Acts.

Luke and Acts have remarkably similar literary structures. Each has a proemium, a preliminary narrative section, which in the case of Acts is part of the proemium, and a narrative proper that is arranged in three parts according to geographical considerations.[221] A lengthy central section is a prominent feature of both volumes, likewise with a geographical principle of arrangement, and the theme of the universality of salvation is strikingly present in their central units (cf. Lk 13,22–14,24; Acts 15,1-35). The first and third sections of the narrative proper of both are divided into three parts, with the proportion of the central section to the initial and concluding sections being roughly the same in each case.

Meyer's judgement is certainly vindicated in the case of Acts, and the striking similarities between the literary structures of the two volumes add further support to the overall arrangements of the gospel outlined above and to arguments in favour of the unity of the two-volume work.

---

[221] Ancient historians were no strangers to geographical methods of arrangement (κατὰ τόπους), as is clear from Dion. Hal., *De Thuc.* §9. Polybius used a geographical principle of arrangement within a chronological framework (cf. P. Pédech, *Polybe, Histoires* I, Paris 1969, XVI).

CHAPTER III

THE ROLE OF LK 1,1-4 IN LUKE–ACTS

Introduction

The literary analysis conducted in the first two chapters revealed a structure of Luke's gospel containing a major break after 4,44. It also revealed the unity of 1,5–4,44 which, it suggested, functions as a preliminary narrative unit in the gospel. The relationship between Luke's proemium and 1,5–4,44 and between the proemium and 5,1 ff. will now be further explored, as will the role of 1,1-4 in the work as a whole. Before this latter point is taken up the relationship between Luke and Acts is examined both from the point of view of the proemium and from that of the rest of the work, and further evidence is offered for their unity.

1. Lk 1,1-4 and 1,5–4,44

The phrase παρηκολουθηκότι ἄνωθεν πᾶσιν, and the adverb ἄνωθεν, in particular, is of crucial importance for determining the relationship between 1,1-4 and 1,5–4,44. Since each of the terms that go to make up this phrase is capable of multiple interpretations, it has not surprisingly been the object of much debate and the cause of no little difference of opinion. In the light of this it seems advisable to take a fresh look at each term in turn in the hope of clarifying the meaning of the phrase and establishing, if possible, the exact relationship between 1,1-4 and what follows.

1.1 *Παρακολουθεῖν*

The verb παρακολουθεῖν literally means "to follow" or "to accompany". In a metaphorical sense it has been translated "to follow", "to keep in touch with", "to get acquainted with information" and "to investigate", the latter, it should be said, not without Cadbury's fervent protests over half a century ago.[1] Examples of the use of the verb from

---

[1] H.J. Cadbury, "Commentary on the Preface of Luke", Foakes Jackson, Lake (eds.), *Beginnings* I.II, 502; idem, "The Knowledge Claimed in Luke's Preface", *Exp* 24

classical texts, from the writings of Josephus and Philo, and from papyri suggest that it can refer to following events at first hand, that is, as an eyewitness, or to following them at second hand through oral or written reports, or to both. Let us examine the evidence.

The use of παρακολουθεῖν in reference to following events at first hand may be illustrated from Jos., C. Ap. I,53. In this text the evident contrast between παρηκολουθηκότα τοῖς γεγονόσιν and παρὰ τῶν εἰδότων πυνθανόμενον suggests that two methods of gathering exact information about actual facts are referred to here, namely, following or keeping in touch with events as an eyewitness, inquiring from eyewitnesses or consulting their reports.

This is confirmed by the context. Two methods of gathering information are already mentioned in C. Ap. I,45-50 where Josephus criticizes Greek writers for venturing to describe events in which they took no part without seeking information from those who knew the facts (cf. I,45).[2] Josephus claims to have used both methods in gathering information for his history of the war (cf. §§ 48-49).[3] His credentials for writing the history are that he had been an actor (αὐτουργός) in many, and an eyewitness (αὐτόπτης) of most, of the events (§ 55).[4]

Other examples of the use of παρακολουθεῖν of following events as an eyewitness are not lacking. In Pol., Hist. I,67.12 the generals who were acquainted with the performance of the Carthaginians in Sicily, and who had made promises of bounties (cf. I,45.3), are contrasted with the general who had not been present on any of these occasions (τὸν δὲ μηδενὶ τούτων παρηκολουθηκότα τοῦτον). In Lucian's Symposium (§ 1), Lycinus expresses his surprise that Charinus, who had brought a report about a quarrel, could give a clear account of it since he had not witnessed (followed) the events leading up to it (μὴ παρακολουθήσας ἐκείνοις). In P. Mich. Zeno 36,7-10 Zeno is told to order his agent to check all the accounts of the beer shop and follow or supervise all the

---

(1922) 403-409; more recently in "'We' and 'I' Passages in Luke-Acts", NTS 3 (1956-57) 130-131; cf. W. C. van Unnik, "Once More St. Luke's Prologue", Neot 7 (1973) 17; J. J. Wettstein, Novum Testamentum Graecum I, Amsterdam 1751, 644-645; also W. Grimm, "Das Proömium des Lucasevangelium", Jahrbücher für Deutsche Theologie 16 (1871) 46-49.

[2] C. Ap. I,45: οἷς μήτ'αὐτοὶ παρεγένοντο μήτε πυθέσθαι παρὰ τῶν εἰδότων ἐφιλοτιμήθησαν.

[3] Josephus points out that he was in command of the Galileans while resistance was possible. In prison he kept a careful record of all that went on under his eyes and he kept abreast of what was happening in the city through the reports of deserters; indeed he was the only one, he avers, in a position to understand the information they gave.

[4] Justus, he maintains in Vita § 358, could not have written an accurate account of the events in Jerusalem since he was neither a combatant there nor had he read Caesar's Commentaries; see also Jos., C. Ap. I,56; Vita §§ 342.348.

operations of the brewery (καὶ παρακολουθεῖν πᾶσι τοῖς κατὰ τὸ ἐργαστήριον).[5]

This sense is most likely included in the use of the verb by Philo when he declares (*De Decal.* §88) that it would be madness to ask a man to testify that he had seen and heard, had been in touch throughout with, things which he had not seen nor heard (ἃ μήτ᾽ εἶδες μήτ᾽ ἤκουσας, ὡς ἰδών, ὡς ἀκούσας, ὡς παρηκολουθηκὼς ἅπασιν). It can hardly be excluded from the use of the verb by Demosthenes in two speeches, *Contra Olymp.* §40[6] and *De Falsa Leg.* §257,[7] and in his *Letter to the Athenians*,[8] although in these cases the verb may also refer to information obtained at second-hand. Indeed in the second speech this seems necessarily the case in order that Demosthenes be acquainted with all the villainies of Jimarcus.[9]

The texts of Philo and Demosthenes cited in the previous paragraph provide examples of the verb's use for following or keeping in touch with events at second-hand either through oral reports (or questioning) of eyewitnesses or through written reports ultimately stemming from eyewitnesses.[10] This meaning may be illustrated from the well known and oft quoted text of Demosthenes, *De Cor.* §172, where the Greek orator affirms that he has been in touch with events from the beginning (παρηκολουθηκότα τοῖς πράγμασιν ἐξ ἀρχῆς) so that he is able to fathom correctly the purposes and desires of Philip. The messenger mentioned in *De Cor.* §169 certainly brought him an oral report. But keeping in touch with events in the north must also have necessitated written reports.

Further examples are to be found in the papyri. An instance from the Zenon archives, which refers to keeping in touch with (keeping an eye on) prices through an intermediary (*P. Mich. Zeno* 28,26: ὅπως παρακολουθήσωμεν ταῖς τιμαῖς),[11] may be added to the letters cited by Cadbury which were written to keep the recipient in touch with events happening elsewhere (*PSI* 411,3-4; *P. Lond.* 23,53-56).[12]

---

[5] (254 B.C.); published in *Zenon Papyri in the University of Michigan Collection* (*Michigan Papyri* I), ed. C.C. Edgar, Ann Arbor 1931, 103.

[6] Τοῖς εἰδόσιν ἀκριβῶς ἕκαστα ταῦτα τὰ πράγματα ὡς ἔχει καὶ παρηκολουθηκόσιν ἐξ ἀρχῆς.

[7] Ἵν᾽ ὡς μετὰ πλείστης συγγνώμης παρ᾽ ὑμῶν ὁ τὰ τούτου πονηρεύματ᾽ ἀκριβέσ- τατ᾽ εἰδὼς ἐγὼ καὶ παρηκολουθηκὼς ἅπασι κατηγορῶ.

[8] *Ep.* I,4.1463: ἀλλ᾽ ὅσα τυγχάνω δι᾽ ἐμπειρίαν καὶ τὸ παρηκολουθηκέναι τοῖς πράγμασιν εἰδώς.

[9] One could also cite Plut., *Aem.* 31,6, and a scholion to Thuc., *War* V,26, both listed by Wettstein. These two modes of gathering information are also mentioned in Thuc., *War* I,22.1-2.

[10] Cf. Jos., *C. Ap.* I,56; *Vita* §§342.358.

[11] Edgar, *Zenon Papyri* I, 88-89 (256 B.C.).

[12] *PSI* 411,3-4 (iii B.C.): ὅπως οὖν παρακολουθῶν καὶ σὺ πρὸς ταῦτα ἐξαγάγῃς τοὺς λόγους, γέγραφά σοι (*Papiri Greci e Latini* IV, Florence 1917, 139); *P. Lond.* 23,53-56 (158-157 B.C.): τῆς...ἐπιστολῆς τὸ ἀντίγραμμον ὑποτετάχαμεν ὅπως παρακολλούθῃς (*Greek Papyri in the British Museum* I, ed. F.G. Kenyon, London 1893, 39-40).

The examples from the speeches of Demosthenes and from the papyri all refer to keeping in touch with or following contemporary events, and Cadbury makes much of this in his interpretation of the term.[13] But παρακολουθεῖν is also used of following events that are not contemporary. An instance of this usage is provided by Polybius in *Hist.* III,32.2. He saw his forty-volume history as enabling the reader to follow (παρακολουθῆσαι) clearly events that go from 264 to 146 B.C., that is, events that are both contemporary and non-contemporary. In the long run the verb acquires for the reader only the sense of following non-contemporary events.

Josephus provides another pertinent example. In *Vita* § 357 he reprimands Justus for not acquainting himself (παρακολουθήσας) with all that the Romans endured or inflicted upon the Jews at the siege of Jotapata at which Justus was not present.[14] This Justus should presumably have done through inquiry from eyewitnesses or through consulting the written reports contained in the *Commentaries* of Caesar (cf. *Vita* § 358).

In some instances παρακολουθεῖν may refer to following a course of events as an eyewitness of some and with the aid of second-hand reports for others. Such is the case in the speeches of Demosthenes cited above (*De Falsa Leg.* § 257; *Contra Olymp.* § 40), and in his *Letter to the Athenians* (I,4.1463). It may also be true of the use of the verb in his speech *De Cor.* § 172 and in Philo, *De Decal.* § 88.

The verb παρακολουθεῖν, then, can signify to follow or keep in touch with events at first hand as an eyewitness, or to follow or get acquainted with events at second-hand through reports of eyewitnesses whether oral or written, or through reports, oral or written, ultimately stemming from eyewitnesses. It can signify to follow or get acquainted with events whether contemporary or not. And it can also be used of following a course of events as an eyewitness of some and with the aid of second-hand reports for others. That it has this range of meanings in Lk 1,3 cannot *a priori* be ruled out, given the general nature and the brevity of Luke's statement. This statement, therefore, can include the narratives of Luke's predecessors, other written and/or oral sources whether anterior or posterior to these narratives, and eyewitness reports of the author himself (e.g. the "we" sections in Acts). Internal evidence may indicate the limits of implied claims.

It should also be noted that following a course of events can hardly exclude the notion of investigation, however primitive. Questioning eyewitnesses or other informants, comparing their reports, visiting the

---

[13] "Commentary", 501-502; idem, "Knowledge", 403-409.
[14] *Vita* §§ 353-358.

scene of the action, acquainting oneself with past events, however recent (cf. Jos., *Vita* § 357), all imply some measure of investigation. Cadbury's strenuous and repeated objection that no example of the use of the verb in this sense is to be found[15] may be met with an example from the Zenon archives: *P. Zeno* 56 B 4-5 (SB 5 8244 10-11).[16] Referring to irregularities in Heraclides' barley returns, Zeno writes to his agent Cleitarchus expressing his surprise that he had not investigated the matter (θαυμάζω οὖν, εἰ μὴ παρηκολουθήκεις).[17]

1.2 Ἄνωθεν

The most common rendering for the adverb ἄνωθεν which literally means "from above", "from on high", is "from the beginning". The older commentaries translated it "from the beginning" and so do most modern commentaries.[18] But Lagrange, citing Origen, suggested that its correct sense was "depuis longtemps".[19] Origen's "ab initio", however, refers to the beginning of Luke's acquaintance with Christianity so that it does not really support Lagrange's case. The adverb may indeed indicate a long period, but it need not; in any case this is deduced not from the actual expression but from other considerations.

Influenced by his interpretation of παρακολουθεῖν as referring to contemporary events, Cadbury saw ἄνωθεν as carrying back not from the ministry of John to Luke's birth stories, but from the time of writing back over a considerable period of the author's own association with the movement he is describing.[20] He later offered the translation "from a good while back",[21] a rendering with which Dupont's "depuis un temps

---

[15] "Commentary", 502; idem, "Knowledge", 403-409; idem, "Passages", 131-132.

[16] (251 B.C.); published in *Greek and Demotic Texts from the Zenon Archives*, ed. P. W. Pestman, P. L. Bat. 20A: Leiden 1980, 210.

[17] In Pestman, *Zenon Archives*, 211, J. K. Winnicki translates the text: "Ich wundere mich doch, dass Du der Sache nicht nachgegangen bist"; Zenon is complaining here to Cleitarchus that he would have known certain facts about a missing quantity of barley had he investigated the matter.

[18] See, for example, Bisping, *Mk und Lk*, 149; Schanz, *Lk*, 53-54; Zahn, *Lk*, 55 ("bis in ihre ersten Anfänge hinauf"); Plummer, *Lk*, 4; Schmid, *Lk*, 30; Schürmann, *Lk* I, 4; also G. Klein, "Lukas 1,1-4 als theologisches Programm", *Zeit und Geschichte*, Dankesgabe an R. Bultmann, ed. E. Dinkler, Tübingen 1964, 207ff.; Samain, "APXH", 323 ("depuis les origines").

[19] *Lc*, 6 (*PG* 13,1804); followed by Loisy, *Lc*, 74: "dès longtemps"; see also M. Dibelius, "Die Herkunft der Sonderstücke des Lukasevangeliums", *ZNW* 12 (1911) 338.

[20] Cadbury, *Making*, 347. In "Knowledge", 409, he had written that it must be understood not of the point in history to which the author carried back his researches, but rather of "that early time in his own life at which his touch with events began and from which it has continued."

[21] "Passages", 130, where ἄνωθεν is taken to be different from ἀπ᾽ ἀρχῆς.

considérable"[22] accords. The English edition of Walter Bauer's dictionary takes "for a long time" to be a possible meaning for ἄνωθεν in Lk 1,3;[23] not so the German original which renders the adverb with "von Anfang an", and does not list "for a long time" as a possible meaning.[24]

Bauer cites Dem. 44,6 (*Contra Leoch.*), Ditt., *Syll.*³ 1104,11 (37/6 B.C.), *P. Oxy.* 237,VIII.31 (89 A.D.), En 98,5 and Philo, *De Vita Mosis* II,48 to illustrate the use of ἄνωθεν with the meaning "from the beginning".[25] The *Lexicon* of Liddell, Scott and Jones includes two texts from Plato (*Phlb.* 44d; *Lg.* 781d) to which the meanings "from the beginning" or "from farther back" may be attributed,[26] and to these Renehan, in his *Supplement* to the *Lexicon*, adds Hippocr., *VM* 3,10.[27] The examples from Plato and Hippocrates are of particular note since the context is one of inquiry. In these cases the adverb signifies "from the beginning" or "from farther back".[28]

The second set of texts cited by Bauer, and for which he gives the meanings "from of old" and "from earlier" ("von alters", "von früher her"), is: Ditt., *Syll.*³ 685,81.91; 748,2; *P. Tebt.* 59,7.10; Jos., *Ant.* XV,250; Acts 26,5; Ael. Arist. 50,78K. For these the English edition of the dictionary gives the meaning "for a long time", and it includes Lk 1,3 in the list of illustrative examples. A closer look at the texts cited by Bauer reveals that the adverb does not primarily have this meaning in any of these texts.

---

[22] J. Dupont, *Les sources du Livre des Actes. État de la question*, Bruges 1960, 105, and there n. 1.

[23] Arndt, Gingrich, *Lexicon*, 76; it also includes Lk 1,3 among the texts in which the adverb could signify "from the beginning".

[24] *Wörterbuch*, 140.

[25] See also F. Zorell, *Lexicon Graecum Novi Testamenti*, Rome 1978³, 130; F. Büchsel, "ἄνω κτλ.", *TDNT* I, 378; J. Beutler, "ἄνωθεν", *EWNT* I, 270. The text from Demosthenes refers to tracing a family line back to the beginning. Philo refers to the beginning of Moses' writings — the creation story; *P. Oxy.* 237,VIII.31, to keeping records from the beginning; Ditt., *Syll.*³ 1104,11, to the beginning of an assembly or conference (παραίτιος τῆς ἄνωθεν συλλογῆς). Other examples are to be found in Jos., *Ant.* XVI,161.174, where the reference is to the beginning of Roman rule in Palestine, although in these cases the meanings "from farther back" or "former" are also possible; in Jos., *C. Ap.* II,125, the reference is to the beginning of the Egyptian people.

[26] H. G. Liddell, R. Scott, H. S. Jones, *A Greek-English Lexicon*, Oxford 1977, 169; the two texts from Plato are both found in the context of inquiry and can signify taking up the subject from farther back or from the beginning.

[27] R. Renehan, *Greek Lexicographical Notes. A Critical Supplement to the Greek-English Lexicon of Liddell-Scott-Jones*, Hypomnemata 45: Göttingen 1975, 35.

[28] For "from farther back" see also Dem., 44,6 (*Contra Leoch.*): μικρῷ ἄνωθεν τὰ περὶ τοῦ γένους ὑμῖν διεξελθεῖν· Plato, *Tim.* 18d: τοὺς δ᾽ ἔμπροσθεν καὶ ἄνωθεν γονέας τε καὶ γονέων προγόνους· idem, Phaedo 101d: ἥτις τῶν ἄνωθεν βελτίστη φαίνοιτο (higher principles); Jos., *C. Ap.* I,28: ἐκ μακροτάτων ἄνωθεν χρόνων.

The reference to hereditary friendship (ἄνωθεν πατρικὴν φίλιαν) in *P. Tebt.* 59,7-8 (c. 99 B.C.) suggests the meaning "from of old", or better "from the beginning". The latter meaning fits *P. Tebt.* 59,10,[29] Ael. Arist. 50,78K,[30] Jos., *Ant.* XV,250, where the context is again one of friendship,[31] and possibly also the later texts Ditt., *Syll.*³ 685,81.91 (139 A.D.) and 748,2 (171 A.D.).[32] Indeed when a long period is explicitly indicated. in *P. Oxy.* 237,VIII.31 and Hippocr., *VM* 3,20-21, the expression ἐκ(ἐν) πολλῶν(ῷ) χρόνων(ῳ) is used. Side by side with it (VIII.29; 3,10), and clearly distinguished from it, is ἄνωθεν which signifies "from the beginning" or "from farther back" and which in these cases refers to an earlier point. Whether it signifies 'from the beginning' or simply 'from farther back' is deduced from the context. Whether the time-span in question is long, as in the example from Hippocrates, or short is also deduced from the context.

The occurrence of ἄνωθεν in Acts 26,4-5 merits closer consideration not only because of its Lucan context but also because of the presence in the same sentence of the term ἀρχή, a circumstance that provides a point of comparison with Lk 1,2-3. In the text from Acts Paul claims to have lived as a true pharisee from his youth (ἐκ νεότητος). The Jews can support his claim firstly because his life from the beginning was spent among his own people and in Jerusalem (v. 4b),[33] and secondly because of their comprehensive knowledge of his life (προγινώσκοντές με ἄνωθεν· v. 5a). Ἄνωθεν adds more to the preposition πρό of the participle than simply "from farther back", since such a meaning would hardly make v. 5a comprehensive enough to justify Paul's claim in v. 5b. It is because Jewish testimony goes back to the beginning of Paul's life, thus covering his whole life to date, that he can make the statement of v. 5b without fear of contradiction. Lack of comprehensiveness makes the rendering "for a long time" unlikely, and the same is true for the position of Cadbury and Dupont who take the adverb to represent a point in time

---

[29] The claim in this text is really that the writer has always revered and worshipped the temple (διὰ τὸ ἄνωθεν φοβεῖσθαι καὶ σέβεσθαι τὸ ἱερόν).

[30] Ἄνωθεν Ἀριστείδην γιγνώσκω.

[31] Φίλοι γὰρ ἄνωθεν ἦσαν· the implication seems to be that the two mentioned were always friends of Herod; one was his cousin; see also *Ant.* XVI,242-243.

[32] In Ditt., *Syll.*³ 685,81, the reference is to preserving with sacred laws etc. the holy place of Zeus "from the beginning"; in 685,91 the adverb refers to the beginning of the disputes; in 748,2 to the Romans who have done what is right from the beginning. In Jos., *Ant.* XVI,161.174, the author refers to the favourable treatment meted out to the Jews by the Romans since their arrival; in *C. Ap.* I,237 he refers to the city of Avaris which, according to theological tradition, was dedicated "from the beginning" to Typhon (κατὰ τὴν θεολογίαν ἄνωθεν Τυφώνιος).

[33] Cf. Klein, "Lukas 1,1-4", 208-209; Samain, "ΑΡΧΗ", 323.

later than that indicated by ἀρχή.[34] The context suggests that ἄνωθεν and ἀπ' ἀρχῆς refer to the same point in time, namely, the beginning of Paul's life, so that ἄνωθεν, in this particular case, may be rendered "from the beginning".

It is important to remember that in the context of inquiry, whether ἄνωθεν has the sense of "from the beginning" or "from farther back", the reference is usually to the point at which the inquiry begins, never, it seems, to the length of time it takes. Examples may be cited from the writings of Plato, Hippocrates, Demosthenes and Philo,[35] and from the historians Thucydides, Diodorus, Dionysius of Halicarnassus and Josephus.[36] The duration of one's investigations is expressed with different terminology,[37] and Cassius Dio, Dionysius and Diodorus actually give the length of time spent in the preparation of their works.[38] With this in mind let us turn to Lk 1,3.

The presence of the term ἀρχή (beginning), the fact that some notion of inquiry can hardly be excluded from the verb παρακολουθεῖν, and the parallels discussed above all suggest that ἄνωθεν in this verse signifies either "from the beginning" or "from farther back". This is also suggested by Luke's characterization of his own work in Lk 1,3. While putting himself into the same category as his predecessors (ἔδοξε κἀμοί), he also distinguishes his work from theirs. Their narratives are presented as being faithful (καθώς) to the accounts, written or oral, stemming ultimately from those who were eyewitnesses from the 'beginning' of Jesus' ministry.[39] With the phrase παρηκολουθηκότι ἄνωθεν Luke implies that his inquiry goes beyond the information supplied by his predecessors' narratives, beginning at an earlier point.

It is possible to translate ἄνωθεν with "from farther back" and to understand from the wider context that Luke began following or getting acquainted with events at a point farther back than that indicated by ἀρχή of 1,2. Given the general nature of ἄνωθεν, it is arguable that the

---

[34] Cadbury, "Passages", 130; Dupont, *Sources*, 104; but see the criticisms of Haenchen, *Acts*, 682 and 683 n. 1, and of Klein, "Lukas 1,1-4", 208.

[35] Plato, *Phlb.* 44d; *Lg.* 781d; Hippocr., *VM* 3,10; Dem., 44,5.6 (*Contra Leoch.*); Philo, *De Vita Mos.* II,48. In the context of friendship the examples appear to stress the fact of its existence from of old or always; cf. *P. Tebt.* 59,7-8; Jos, *Ant.* XV,250.

[36] Cf. Thuc., *War* I,1.1; Diod., *Hist.* I,4.1; Dion. Hal., *Ant. Rom.* I,7.2; Jos., *Ant.* I,26.

[37] Cf. ἐκ(ἐν) πολλῶν(ῷ) χρόνων(ῳ): *P. Oxy.* 237,VIII.29; Hippocr., *VM* 3,20-21; Theophr., *Char.* Dedic. Letter 2.

[38] Dio Cassius' investigations took ten years; Dionysius of Halicarnassus spent twenty two years preparing his work; Diodorus, thirty for preparation and composition. Whenever reference is made to the scope of the investigations, which is by far the more important and more frequently mentioned aspect, the starting point is given; see the examples listed in n. 36 above.

[39] On the sense of ἀρχή here see n. 41 below.

material right back to the annunciation of John's birth is included.[40] It is more likely, though, that the adverb signifies "from the beginning". Examples of its use particularly in the context of inquiry and of the use of παρακολουθεῖν in texts such as Pol., *Hist.* III,32.2, and Dem., *De Cor.* § 170, suggest that ἄνωθεν in Lk 1,3 refers to a definite point, more precisely, to the beginning of something.

The general context identifies this beginning. The section that immediately follows 1,1-4, namely 1,5-25, narrates the beginning of the 'good news' (cf. 1,19: εὐαγγελίσασθαι),[41] for the announcement of John's birth signals the dawn of the time of fulfilment.[42] It is to the beginning of this new epoch in salvation history that ἄνωθεν refers.[43] The adverb thus forges a direct link between the proemium and the immediately following narrative.

1.3 Πᾶσιν

As has been frequently pointed out, the adjective πᾶσιν may be masculine or neuter, referring to the eyewitnesses and ministers of the word, in the former case, to the πράγματα of 1,1, in the latter. Cadbury suggested that it could be used without antecedent but in much the same sense as if neuter.[44] Some early Christian writers understood παρακολουθεῖν of literal accompaniment and took πᾶσιν to refer to the "eyewitnesses and ministers of the word".[45] The sense of παρηκολουθηκότι ἄνωθεν adopted above suggests that it refers to πραγμάτων.

An additional implication contained in the term πᾶσιν is that Luke's investigations, which began at an earlier point than that covered by the

---

[40] That it includes the infancy narrative is suggested, for example, by Schanz, *Lc*, 53-54; B. Weiss, *Die Evangelien des Markus und Lukas*, Göttingen 1901³, 216-217; J. Weiss, *Evangelien*, 396; Schürmann, *Lk* I, 11; Klein, "Lukas 1,1-4", 209; Samain, "ΑΡΧΗ", 323; Schneider, *Lk* I, 39; S. Brown, "The Role of the Prologues in Determining the Purpose of Luke-Acts", *Perspectives on Luke-Acts*, ed. C.H. Talbert, Edinburgh 1978, 104. Grundmann, *Lk*, 44, takes it to refer to the birth of Jesus.

[41] Mark identifies the beginning of the 'good news' (ἀρχὴ τοῦ εὐαγγελίου) with the preaching of the Baptist and Jesus' initial preaching (1,1-15; cf. Hos 1,2). For the beginning of the 'good news' Luke uses ἄνωθεν: cf. Grimm, "Proömium", 42 (... a primis rei evangelicae initiis), in reference to this term. The term ἀρχή is used by Luke to refer to the Galilean beginning of Jesus' ministry (1,2; cf. 3,23; 23,5), the Pentecost event (Acts 11,15) and the beginning of Paul's life (Acts 26,4), by Mark for the 'good news' (1,1), creation (10,6; 13,19) and the beginning of sufferings (13,8).

[42] Cf. Bisping, *Mk und Lk*, 149: "Auch die Morgenröthe des kommenden Tages will er in sein Gemälde aufnehmen".

[43] Note that Polybius' main reason for beginning his work where he did was because it marked the beginning of a new epoch in history (cf. *Hist.* I,3.3-5; IV,2.4-11).

[44] "Commentary", 503.

[45] Cf. Papias in Eus., *Hist. Eccl.* III,39; Justin, *Dial. Tryph.* 103; Iren., *Adv. Haer.* III,14.1-2.

narratives of his predecessors, are also more complete than theirs. Implied here, too, is the greater scope of his written work.

The phrase παρηκολουθηκότι ἄνωθεν πᾶσιν, then, gives us in very general terms the scope and perhaps something of the method of Luke in his two-volume work (see below). While being sufficiently general to include within its compass the whole of Luke–Acts, it furnishes a direct link with 1,5 ff. and hence with the preliminary narrative unit 1,5–4,44.

2. Lk 1,1-4 and the beginning of the narrative proper

The beginning of the narrative proper of an ancient literary work was usually carefully chosen. An author's choice might not meet with universal approval (cf. Dion. Hal., *De Thuc.* § 10), and one might still feel obliged to justify it (cf. Pol., *Hist.* I,3.1-6; III,1.1.5.9; IV,1.9-2.10), but its importance in any literary work was clearly recognized. The proemium generally contained some indication of where this point was to be found. Not infrequently this took the form of an explicit reference, as in the historical writings of Herodotus (*Hist.* I,5), Polybius (*Hist.* I,3.1-6; etc.), Dionysius of Halicarnassus (*Ant. Rom.* I,5.3; 8.1.4), Josephus (*BJ* I,18.30), Diodorus (*Hist.* I,4.5), Tacitus (*Hist.* I,1) and Sallust (*Cat.* 4,5; *Jug.* 5,3), the works of Isocrates (*Helen* § 16; *Pan.* §§ 15.19), Theophrastus (*Char.* Pr. 5) and Philo (*De Spec. Leg.* I,1), *Rhet. ad Her.* I,1.1 and 2 Macc 2,32. In all of these ἀρχή and ἄρχομαι or their Latin equivalents are used to indicate this point.[46] In these cases, too, the proemium's reference to the work's subject matter provides an additional pointer to the beginning of the narrative proper. In the absence of an explicit indication of this initial point such a reference is particularly useful, as is evident, for example, from the *Letter of Aristeas* (§ 1), or the works of Arrian (*An.* I Pr. 1), Philostratus (*Apoll.* I,2), Livy (*Ab Urbe* Pr. 1) and Cicero (*De Inv.* I,1.1; 4.5).

Luke's proemium contains no explicit reference to the starting point of the narrative proper, but it does contain some possible pointers to it. The reference to the narratives of Luke's predecessors represents one such pointer. The subject matter of these narratives is specified as "the things that have come to completion (pass) among us" (τῶν πεπληροφορη-μένων ἐν ἡμῖν πραγμάτων). It is further specified that it ultimately stems from the group of 'eyewitnesses and ministers of the word' and represents a faithful reproduction of their accounts (καθώς). The subject matter of Luke's work is similar (ἔδοξε κἀμοί), even if it has a wider scope. Luke's insistence on the ultimately eyewitness-character of the information

---

[46] It is referred to by the term πρότερον in Jos., *Ant.* I,26 and *C. Ap.* I,58, and by πρῶτον in Thuc., *War* I,23.5, and Diog. Laert., *Lives* I,21.

covering at least the whole of Jesus' ministry (cf. Acts 1,21-22; 10,37-39) and his emphatic use of ἀσφάλεια, the term upon which the whole proemium converges, have implications for the beginning of his narrative proper.

It is worth recalling at this juncture the example of Polybius. One of the reasons why he chose to begin his narrative proper with the events in Greece from the 140th Olympiad onwards (220-216 B.C.) was that this period coincided with his own and the preceding generation so that he had been present at some events and had the testimony of eyewitnesses for others. Had he begun at an earlier date, he writes, repeating mere hearsay evidence, neither his estimates nor his assertions would be safe (ἀσφαλεῖς · cf. Hist. IV,2.1-3). Similar reasoning may have moved Luke to choose an initial point for his narrative proper. The evangelist is clearly anxious to show Theophilus the reliability or certainty of what he had been taught. Beginning his narrative proper at the point where the eyewitness evidence of the group of 'eyewitnesses and ministers of the word' begins would certainly contribute to the reliability of his own work and thus to his overall objective. The point at which this eyewitness-ship begins is Lk 5,1-11.

The term λόγος in 1,2 may also point towards the beginning of the narrative proper in 5,1. Occurrences of the term in the gospel (8,12.13.15; cf. 8,11.21) and in Acts (4,4; 6,4; 8,4; 10,36.44; 11,19; 14,25; 16,6; 17,11; 18,5) make clear that it is equivalent to ὁ λόγος τοῦ θεοῦ/κυρίου[47] and signifies above all the Christian message. The first use of the expression ὁ λόγος τοῦ θεοῦ in the gospel is found in 5,1. The repetition of the term λόγος of 1,2 in the equivalent expression of 5,1 may be purely coincidental, but this literary relationship could point towards a new beginning, namely, the beginning of the narrative proper, particularly since the subject matter of the work being introduced is related to this term (cf. 1,2). Similar repetitions characterizing the beginning of the narrative proper are to be found, for instance, in the book of Sirach and in Josephus' Contra Apion.[48]

The phrase ἀπ᾽ ἀρχῆς in Lk 1,2 adds its weight to the arguments in favour of 5,1. The other occurrences of ἀρχή in Luke–Acts with the meaning "beginning" (Acts 11,15; 26,4) are not of much assistance in determining its significance in Lk 1,2. But the verb ἄρχομαι, which

---

[47] Cf. Acts 4,31; 6,2.7; 8,14.25; 11,1; 16,32; 17,13; 18,11: ὁ λόγος τοῦ θεοῦ/κυρίου: also 12,24; 13,5.7.44.46.48; 15,35; 19,10; 20,35; see Grimm, "Proömium", 42; R. Glöckner, Die Verkündigung des Heils beim Evangelisten Lukas, WS TR 9: Mainz 1975, 32-34. Origen (In Luc. Hom. I,4; PG 13,1804) and Ambrose (Exp. Ev. Sec. Lucam I,5ff.) took λόγος in Lk 1,2 to refer to the eternal word.

[48] σοφίας...πᾶσα σοφία (Sir Pr. 1; 1,1); χώραν...κατῴκησεν...χώραν οἰκοῦμεν (Jos., C. Ap. I,1.60); cf. Lausberg, Rhetorik, 318-320.

occurs frequently in Luke–Acts with the meaning "to begin",[49] is of considerable assistance, especially its occurrences in Lk 3,23, 23,5, Acts 1,22 and 10,37, all of which refer to the beginning of Jesus' ministry. Two points in particular emerge from them: the initial period of Jesus' ministry is set in Galilee (cf. Lk 23,5b; Acts 10,37) after the baptism of John (cf. Acts 10,37), and this period is covered by continuous αὐτοψία (cf. Acts 1,21-22). It has already been pointed out above that such a period is described in Lk 5,1–9,50, and it has also been noted that only in 5,1-11 does this continuous αὐτοψία begin. The association in Lk 1,2 between ἀρχή and the eyewitness-ship of the group of 'eyewitnesses and ministers of the word', a group that is clearly associated with Jesus' ministry, suggests that ἀρχή should be taken to refer to the beginning of Jesus' ministry in Galilee, and in particular to 5,1 ff.[50]

Acts 1,1-2 provides general support for the indications of Lk 1,1-4. The secondary proemium of an ancient literary work which contains a résumé of the previous volume summarizes its narrative proper and does not include in this its proemium or other introductory sections. The example of Jos., C. Ap. II,1, which refers to I,60 ff., may be cited; so also Cic., De Inv. II,3.11, which refers to I,5.6 ff., and Rhet. ad Her. II,1.1, which refers to I,2.1 ff. Since the summary of Luke's first volume in Acts 1,1-2 is a summary of Jesus' ministry, then the beginning of the gospel's narrative proper should not be placed prior to the beginning of this ministry.[51]

Luke's proemium, then, provides some support for the literary analysis conducted in the previous chapters. Moreover, in providing an indication of where the narrative proper of the work begins it fulfils a role common to the proemium of many an ancient literary work.

3. Lk 1,1-4: Proemium to Luke–Acts

For Schürmann Lk 1,1-4 is the proemium of the gospel alone; the evangelist did not have Acts in mind at this point.[52] The more prevalent

---

[49] The verb is found both with (27x) and without the infinitive (Lk 3,23; 23,5; 24,27.47; Acts 1,22; 8,35; 10,37; 11,4); cf. J. W. Hunkin, "Pleonastic ἄρχομαι in the New Testament", JTS 25 (1924) 393-394.

[50] Ancient writers used ἀρχή in a variety of ways. Historians like Thucydides, Polybius, Diodorus, Appian and others endeavoured to establish the ἀρχή of the wars they so often describe. The beginning of a new phase of life is often marked in biographical writing, whether it be boyhood (Plut., Philop. 1,2), public life (Plut., Them. 3,1), public office (Suet., Galba 6,1) or kingship (Xen., Ages. 1,5; Suet., Dom. 3,1; Tib. 7,1; Claud. 7,1).

[51] It is equally clear that one cannot deduce from Acts 1,1 that Luke's infancy narrative did not form part of the original work, as Conzelmann, Mitte, 9 n. 2, and Glöckner, Verkündigung, 24-25, do.

[52] Lk I, 4 — a point of view not without support; cf. Grimm, "Proömium", 54-55; Conzelmann, Mitte, 7 n. 1; Haenchen, Acts, 119 and 136 n. 3.

opinion is that these verses introduce the whole of Luke–Acts.[53] It has been shown above that Lk 1,1-4 links up with 1,5–4,44 and with the beginning of the narrative proper (5,1 ff.). A number of arguments may be adduced to show that Lk 1,1-4 was composed as a proemium for the whole of Luke–Acts which was conceived as a two-volume work.

The proemium itself already indicates in various ways that such is the case. The subject matter of Luke's narrative proper is given not as the life of Jesus, nor as all that he did and taught from the beginning up to his ascension (cf. Acts 1,1-2), but as "the things that have come to completion (pass) among us". It is more extensive, therefore, than the ministry of Jesus.

The qualification ἐν ἡμῖν seems well suited to include the events of Acts. Indeed Cadbury felt it better suited to "the more recent events" of that volume,[54] and Dillon would hardly disagree.[55] But the phrase is general enough to include both the events and the tradition concerning them.[56] It is much like καθ᾽ ἡμᾶς of Pol., *Hist.* I,4.5,[57] which covers a lengthy period, including events that predate the writer's birth.[58] Similarly, ἐν ἡμῖν of Lk 1,1 can be taken to cover the ministries of Jesus and his disciples, as well as events of Luke's own time.[59]

---

[53] Cf. Zahn, *Lk*, 50; Meyer, *Ursprung* I (Stuttgart-Berlin 1921), 5ff.; Klostermann, *Lk*, 1; Cadbury, "Commentary", 492; Schmid, *Lk*, 28-29; Grundmann, *Lk*, 43; E. Lohse, "Lukas als Theologe der Heilsgeschichte", *EvT* 14 (1954) 257; Kümmel, *Introduction*, 128, and there n. 5; see also Minear, "Birth Stories", 118-119.

[54] "Commentary", 496; see his discussion in "Knowledge", 412-413. Plummer, *Lk*, 3, suggests that it probably means "among us Christians", a view shared by Lohse, "Lukas", 257 n. 3, Haenchen, *Acts*, 119, and Klein, "Lukas 1,1-4", 197. Toynbee, in *Historical Thought*, 59, translates it "in our society".

[55] *Eye-Witnesses*, 271, and there n. 115.

[56] There is no reason why the *Gleichzeitigkeit* (cf. Glöckner, *Verkündigung*, 19-20) of events and tradition, even if the tradition be a twofold one, should cause difficulties, as it does for Dillon (*Eye-Witnesses*, 271, and there n. 115). Josephus certainly had no difficulty in using παραδιδόναι for the tradition he handed on to the reader of his *Jewish War* (VII,454) where no appreciable time span need exist. Neither had Dioscorides when referring to the information handed on in the books of his predecessors (cf. *De Mat. Med.* I Pr.) which may be of an earlier generation, though not necessarily so. Dioscorides also used the verb when referring to the information he was handing on in his own work (cf. *De Mat. Med.* II Pr.; III Pr.; IV Pr.).

[57] Rendered "in our own times" by W. R. Paton in his edition (LCL) of Polybius' *Histories*.

[58] Polybius' dates are 208-126 B. C., while the main part of his historical work covers the years 264-146 B. C. The narrative proper begins with the 140th Olympiad (220-216 B. C.).

[59] This need not imply a long period of time in the case of the commonly accepted date of Luke's gospel (late 60's, early 70's), and certainly not if the date put forward in J. A. T. Robinson, *Redating the New Testament*, London 1976, 92 (c. 62 A. D.) were accepted. In any case, the ministries of Jesus' disciples were contemporary with Luke's life, and probably that of Jesus also.

The double characterization of the main ultimate sources of Luke's account as a group of "eyewitnesses from the beginning" and "ministers of the word" could be taken to point towards a narrative that goes beyond the gospel narrative, since the listing of sources carries with it the implication of at least a co-extensive narrative. From the point of view of the ultimately eyewitness nature of the listed sources the double characterization strongly suggests that Luke was anxious to highlight this aspect not only in the case of Jesus' ministry — for that the second characterization was not necessary — but also in the case of the ministries of the disciples.

One could object that Lk 1,4 (ἵνα ἐπιγνῷς περὶ ὧν κατηχήθης λόγων) concerns only τὰ περὶ τοῦ 'Ιησοῦ and does not include the events of Acts. But Acts is very much concerned with "the things concerning Jesus". For it shows how the promise of Lk 24,49 is fulfilled in the coming of the Spirit and how the word of God is preached to the nations, beginning from Jerusalem, in keeping with Jesus' command of Lk 24,47. It shows, too, how the 'witnesses' fulfilled their appointed role (cf. Lk 24,48). And the Pentecost speech of Peter, for example, is surely an integral part of preaching τὰ περὶ τοῦ κυρίου 'Ιησοῦ Χριστοῦ (cf. Acts 28,31).

There are a number of indications in the rest of the gospel and in Acts that the former was written with the latter in mind. The use of Is 6,9-10 provides one such indication. The brevity of its citation in Lk 8,10 (cf. Mt 13,14-15; Mk 4,12) may well be due to the fact that Luke wished to cite it at length in Acts 28 in order to provide an effective conclusion for his work. Another indication may be represented by the reference in the trial of Stephen to the accusation made by false witnesses against Jesus concerning the temple (cf. Acts 6,13-14). The accusation is found in Mt 26,59-61 and Mk 14,55-58 (cf. Jn 2,19-21), but not in Luke's account of the Jewish trial of Jesus (22,66-71). Having no role for it there, since false witnesses play no part in that trial scene, Luke held it over for use in the trial of Stephen.

Indications found towards the gospel's conclusion are even more significant. The nature of "the power from on high" (Lk 24,49) is only specified in Acts 1,5 and 8. The exact site of the ascension is only given in Acts 1,12. And the parousia is associated with the ascension only in Acts 1,10-11, an association that would have motivated well the reference in Lk 24,52 to the great joy of the disciples returning from the scene of the ascension. Lk 24,47-49, with its promise of the Spirit and its commands, clearly looks forward to Acts and their fulfilment. On the level of the narrative the promise of the Spirit, the commands to be witnesses and missionaries and to await the coming of the Spirit in Jerusalem, all create narrative tensions that are resolved only in Acts and that hold the reader's or hearer's attention as one moves from the first to the second volume.[60]

It is true that neither the remarkable resemblances in literary structure pointed out in the previous chapter nor the many thematic correspondences that are to be found between Luke and Acts prove conclusively their structural unity or simultaneous preparation. They do, however, point quite firmly in their direction. The theme of the word of God certainly does.[61] Two aspects of the content of this word are highlighted in Acts, the kingdom of God and "the things concerning the Lord Jesus Christ" (cf. 28,31).[62] Both these aspects are present in the gospel. The kingdom is the central element of the preaching of Jesus. But since the kingdom is present in and through his person (cf. Lk 11,20), this preaching of Jesus is also about himself. These aspects are also characteristic of the preaching of the disciples (cf. Lk 9,2.7-9.18-20; 10,9.11.17).[63]

The use of the expression ὁ λόγος τοῦ θεοῦ in the gospel, and in particular in 5,1 where the first disciples/apostles are present, brings out the fact that the Christian message has its beginnings in the preaching of Jesus, or better still, that it is the continuation of Jesus' preaching.[64] It is hardly coincidental that the narrative proper of Luke's work opens with an explicit reference to the word of God (5,1) and closes with a description of Paul's preaching in terms of the two main aspects of the content of this word.

It is also noteworthy that the verb εὐαγγελίζεσθαι is used not only of the preaching of Jesus (cf. 4,43; 7,22; 8,1; 20,1; Acts 10,36), but also of the preaching of John (3,18; cf. Acts 10,37; 13,24), the apostles (9,6; Acts 5,42) and disciples (Acts 8,4.12.25.35.40; 11,20), Paul and Barnabas (Acts 13,32; 14,7.15.21; 15,35) and of Paul himself in Athens (Acts 17,18). The 'good news' firmly links Luke and Acts.

The salvation of the Gentiles is another theme that gives rise to significant correspondences between the two volumes. It is present in Lk

[60] Cf. T. Birt, *Das Antike Buchwesen in seinem Verhältnis zur Literatur*, Aalen 1974 (repr. Berlin 1882²), 132; also W. Schubart, *Das Buch bei den Griechen und Römern*, Berlin-Leipzig 1921², 54-55; F. G. Kenyon, *Books and Readers in Ancient Greece and Rome*, Chicago 1980 (repr. Oxford 1932), 61-65.

[61] Cf. Lk 1,2.4; 4,22.(32); 5,1; 8,11.12,13.15.21; 11,28; Acts 2,41; 4,4.29.31; 6,2.4.7; 8,4.14.25; 10,36.44; 11,1.19; 12,24; 13,5.7.44.46.48; 15,35.36; 16,6.32; 17,11.13; 18,11; 19,10; 20,32; also Bovon, *Luc*, 281: "La notion de parole de Dieu garantit donc la continuité entre l'Evangile et les Actes"; Haenchen, *Acts*, 98; W. C. van Unnik, "The 'Book of Acts' the Confirmation of the Gospel", *NT* 4 (1960) 58; O. Betz, "The Kerygma of Luke", *Int* 22 (1968) 133; Fitzmyer, *Lk I-IX*, 157-158.

[62] Cf. Acts 8,12; 19,8; 28,23.

[63] Cf. I. H. Marshall, *Luke: Historian and Theologian*, Exeter 1970, 160.

[64] Cf. Schürmann, *Lk* I, 267.

2,32 and Acts 13,47 under the form of an allusion to Is 49,6 in the former and a citation of that text in the latter. Another text from Isaiah, 40,5 LXX, is used in Lk 3,6 and Acts 28,28, the latter indicating that by then the prophecy associated with John's appearance in Lk 3 is being fulfilled. The Gentile question is to be found at the centre of the lengthy central sections of both volumes (cf. Lk 13,22–14,24; Acts 15,1-35), and the universal mission imparted to the disciples by Jesus forms a connecting link between the gospel's conclusion (24,47) and the proemium of Acts (1,8).

The divinely ordained aspect of the Gentile mission is made clear in the gospel through the prophecy of Simeon (2,30-32), the citation of Is 40,5 LXX (3,6) and the words of Jesus (24,47), and in Acts through the story of the conversion of Cornelius (10,1–11,18), the citation of Is 49,6 (13,47) and various interventions at the Council of Jerusalem (cf. 15,7-18).

The theme of Israel is treated similarly in both. The primacy of Israel in the hearing of the word is implied through the presence of the twelve and of 'all Israel' at the sermon on the plain (cf. 6,12-49) and at Peter's Pentecost speech (cf. 1,15-26; 2,14.37). This primacy is respected right through, and the promise transparent in the words of the angel in Lk 1,32-33 is never rescinded, not even at the conclusion of Acts.[65]

Significant correspondences between the two volumes are represented by the activity of the Spirit in the infancy narrative (cf. 1,15.35.41-43.67-79; 2,25-32), in Jesus' ministry (cf. 4,18-21; Acts 10,38) and in the ministry of his disciples (cf. Acts 2,4.17-18). Jesus' promise of the guidance of the Holy Spirit at the moment of need (Lk 12,12) is fulfilled, for example, in Acts 4,8. Indeed the former could be said to prepare the latter. This manner of preparing events to be narrated in Acts may be even more strikingly illustrated from Lk 21,12-15, for the predictions made by Jesus there are fulfilled in detail in Acts.[66]

There are significant parallels between the passion of Jesus and the martyrdom of Stephen (cf. Lk 22,69; 23,46.(34); Acts 7,56.59.[60]),[67] and, as has often been noted, between the passion of Jesus and the suffering of Paul.[68] The latter parallels are of particular note. They include, for

---

[65] See ch. IV, pp. 142-143; also R. Maddox, *The Purpose of Luke-Acts*, FRLANT 126: Göttingen 1982, 180.

[66] Cf. Acts 4,3.8-12.15-18; 5,18.27.32.40-41; 6,9-10; 8,3; 9,1-2; 12,1-5; etc.; for further examples see J. Neyrey, *The Passion According to Luke. A Redaction Study of Luke's Soteriology*, New York-Mahwah 1985, 87-88.

[67] Cf. J. Bihler, *Die Stephanusgeschichte im Zusammenhang der Apostelgeschichte*, MTS I.16: Munich 1963, 16-19; Radl, *Paulus und Jesus*, 40.

[68] Cf. R.B. Rackham, *The Acts of the Apostles*, London 1912[6], 401-402.404.477-478; Grundmann, *Lk*, 455; Radl, *Paulus und Jesus*, 159-265; Stolle, *Zeuge*, 215-220; A.J. Mattill, Jr., "The Jesus-Paul Parallels and the Purpose of Luke-Acts: H.H. Evans Reconsidered",

instance, their declared readiness to suffer (Lk 13,33; Acts 21,13; Lk 18,31-32; Acts 21,11), arrest by the Jews (Lk 22,47-54; Acts 21,30), hearings before the Sanhedrin (Lk 22,66-71; Acts 22,30–23,10), the Roman authorities (Lk 23,1-5.13-25; Acts 23,12–25,12) and the Jewish king (Lk 23,6-12; Acts 25,23–26,32), the repeated declarations of innocence by the Roman authorities (Lk 23,4.14.15.22; Acts 23,29; 25,25) and the Jewish king (Lk 23,15; Acts 26,31-32), in neither case leading to release, and a striking use of the verb αἴρω of taking life (cf. Lk 23,18; Acts 8,33; 21,36; 22,22), a use that is proper to Luke in the New Testament.

There are many other correspondences between the two volumes, as a careful reading of Nestle's marginal notes and the writings of Rackham, Morgenthaler, Radl and others demonstrate.[69] The sheer number and quality of the correspondences, highlighted at times by verbal similarities,[70] suggest the simultaneous preparation of both volumes and their completion one immediately after the other.[71]

The existence of Acts as a separate volume does not militate against this. Because of the limitations imposed by the use of the roll in antiquity,

---

NT 17 (1975) 32-37; S. F. Praeder, "Jesus-Paul, Peter-Paul, and Jesus-Peter Parallelisms in Luke-Acts: A History of Reader Response", *Society of Biblical Literature 1984 Seminar Papers*, ed. K. H. Richards, Chico 1984, 37.

[69] Cf. Rackham, *Acts*, xlvii-xlix; Morgenthaler, *Geschichtsschreibung*, 178-186; Radl, *Paulus und Jesus*, 39-265; Mattill, Jr., "Parallels", 15-46; G. Muhlack, *Die Parallelen von Lukas-Evangelium und Apostelgeschichte*, TW 8: Frankfurt am Main 1979; R. F. O'Toole, "Parallels between Jesus and His Disciples in Luke-Acts: A Further Study", *BZ* 27 (1983) 195-212; Praeder, "Parallelisms", 23-39; I. H. Marshall, "Luke and his 'Gospel'", *Das Evangelium und die Evangelien*, Vorträge vom Tübinger Symposium 1982, ed. P. Stuhlmacher, WUNT 28: Tübingen 1983, 300-304; Neyrey, *Passion*, 89-107.

[70] See, for example, ἄτοπος in Lk 23,41; Acts 25,5; 28,6 (elsewhere in the NT in 2 Thess 3,2); ἀπολογέομαι in Lk 12,11; 21,14; Acts 19,33; 24,10; 25,8; 26,1.2.24 (elsewhere in the NT in Rom 2,15; 2 Cor 12,19); κατηγορεῖν in Lk 23,2.10.14; Acts 22,30; 24,2.8.13.19; 23,5.11.16; 28,19; see also Lk 24,26 and Acts 14,22; Lk 18,32 and Acts 21,11; Lk 22,42 and Acts 21,14; Lk 23,14-22 and Acts 28,18; cf. Radl, *Paulus und Jesus*, 349-350.

[71] For the argument in favour of an interval between them see, for example, Schneider, *Apg* I, 120, and his acceptance (69 n. 25) of J. C. Hawkins' position (*Horae Synopticae. Contributions to the Study of the Synoptic Problem*, Oxford 1899, 143-146). Hawkins' lists are not as impressive as they might seem at first sight: the frequency of ἀνήρ, ὀνόματι, and ἀπολογέομαι in the second half of Acts, κατέρχομαι in the missionary section and πνεῦμα ἅγιον throughout, just to cite from his first list, is readily explicable on the basis of subject matter. Luke's use of the temple saying attributed to Jesus (cf. Mt 26,59-61; Mk 14,56-58; Jn 2,19.21) in Stephen's trial (Acts 6,13-14) and of Is 6,9-10 in Lk 8,10 and Acts 28,26-27 may be cited in favour of simultaneous preparation; so too the conclusion of the gospel and the beginning of Acts. See the comments of J. B. Tyson, *The Death of Jesus in Luke-Acts*, Columbia 1986, 4, and R. C. Tannehill, *The Narrative Unity of Luke-Acts. A Literary Interpretation* I, Philadelphia 1986, 2-3, on the unity of Luke-Acts; also the problems associated with it raised by J. Dawsey, "The Literary Unity of Luke-Acts: Questions of Style – A Task for Literary Critics", *NTS* 35 (1989) 48-66.

any author of that time who wrote with pretensions to be read and who wished to write a lengthy work had to divide it into two or more volumes for the reader's convenience. "A big book", Callimachus used to say, "is a big nuisance",[72] and the maximum length of a roll containing a literary work appears to have been about 35 feet.[73] Having gathered his material together,[74] Luke most likely made a rough draft of the whole, dividing it into two main parts and arranging it, before writing or dictating the final version.[75] As in the case of such multi-volume works, the proemium to the first volume is the proemium to the whole work.

4. Lk 1,3: Καθεξῆς

The adverb καθεξῆς has long been recognized as a vehicle of Luke's intentions for his narrative. But its exact significance has been, and remains, a matter of much debate. That it refers to an order of some kind is generally accepted. But the nature of this order is far from being agreed.

Proposals as varied as "non confusa" (Maldonatus),[76] "in uninter-rupted sequence" (Schegg),[77] "continua serie" (Völkel),[78] "well thought-out order" (Klostermann),[79] and "ordered sequence" (Schürmann)[80] are to be found. The older commentaries such as those of Maldonatus, Grotius and Bengel, mindful of the difficulties in Luke's chronology when compared with the other synoptics, took the adverb to refer more to a systematic than a chronological order.[81] The later commentaries of Bisping, B. Weiss and others, showed a marked preference for the latter.[82]

---

[72] Ath., *Deiph.* III,72a.

[73] Cf. Kenyon, *Books*, 52; also pp. 172-173 below.

[74] Note the perfect παρηκολουθηκότι.

[75] Cf. Jos., *C. Ap.* I,50; Lucian, *Hist.* §§ 47-48; Avenarius, *Geschichtsschreibung*, 71-104; C. B. R. Pelling, "Plutarch's method of work in the Roman Lives", *JHS* 99 (1979) 92-95.

[76] J. de Maldonado, *Commentarii in Quatuor Evangelistas* II, Mainz 1611, 11.

[77] P. Schegg, *Evangelium nach Lukas* I, Munich 1861, 20; see A. Hilgenfeld, "Das Vorwort des dritten Evangeliums (Luc. I,1-4)", *ZWT* 44 (1901) 3: "ununterbrochen".

[78] M. Völkel, "Exegetische Erwägungen zum Verständnis des Begriffs ΚΑΘΕΞΗΣ im Lukanischen Prolog", *NTS* 20 (1973-74) 298; see authors listed in Grimm, "Proö-mium", 50.

[79] *Lk*, 3.

[80] *Lk* I, 12 (chronological).

[81] Maldonado, *Commentarii* II, 11; H. Grotius, *Annotationes in Novum Testamentum* I, Halle 1769², 676; Bengel, *Gnomon*, 200; see also Schegg, *Lk* I, 20; Schanz, *Lc*, 54.

[82] Bisping, *Mk und Lk*, 149; Godet, *Lc* I, 76; B. Weiss, *Mk und Lk*, 267; cf. Knaben-bauer, *Lc*, 39-40; B. S. Easton, *The Gospel According to St. Luke: A Critical and Exegeti-cal Commentary*, New York 1926, 2; see also Grimm, "Proömium", 50; Cornely, *Introduc-tio*, 150.

While recognizing that a chronological arrangement was not necessarily implied in the adverb, but merely an arrangement of some kind, Plummer felt that Luke had chronological order chiefly in view.[83] Rengstorf and Schürmann display an even greater insistence on the chronological aspect.[84] Recent articles by Völkel, Kürzinger, Mussner and Schneider reveal that the question is far from settled.[85]

Καθεξῆς is formed from ἐξῆς which signifies "one after another", "in order", or "in a row".[86] It is usually equated with the more common ἐφεξῆς for which the meanings "in order", "one after another", "continuously" and "successively" are given.[87] For καθεξῆς the dictionaries list the meanings "in order", "in a row", "one after another" (in logical or temporal sequence: Bauer), "successively", "continuously", "as follows" and "the following".[88] Even though the latter two scarcely merit serious consideration in a proemium where every word is weighed and evaluated,[89] the choice remains large and the interpretations varied.

Let us look first of all at extra-biblical examples of the adverb's use. In Plut., Mor. 615B two methods of passing a myrtle spray from one guest to another at a party are described, one simple, to which ἐφεξῆς is applied, the other intricate and described as οὐ καθεξῆς.[90] Völkel suggests the sense of "uninterrupted" for καθεξῆς here.[91] But the continuous nature of both sequences demands that one look elsewhere for the particular point expressed by the adverb. This is to be found in the contrast between the two sequences, that is, between the normal or

---

[83] Lk, 5.

[84] Rengstorf, Lk, 15; Schürmann, Lk I, 12.

[85] Völkel, "Erwägungen", 289-299; J. Kürzinger, "Lk 1,3: ... ἀκριβῶς καθεξῆς σοι γράψαι", BZ 18 (1974) 249-255; F. Mussner, "Καθεξῆς im Lukasprolog", Jesus und Paulus, Fs für W. G. Kümmel, eds. E. E. Ellis, E. Grässer, Göttingen 1975, 253-255; G. Schneider, "Zur Bedeutung von καθεξῆς im lukanischen Doppelwerk", ZNW 68 (1977) 128-131; see also J. Drury, Tradition and Design in Luke's Gospel. A Study in Early Christian Historiography, London 1976, 82; Fitzmyer, Lk I-IX, 298-299.

[86] Cf. Liddell-Scott-Jones, Lexicon, 594.

[87] Cf. Liddell-Scott-Jones, Lexicon, 742.

[88] Cf. Liddell-Scott-Jones, Lexicon, 852; Bauer, Wörterbuch, 704; Zorell, Lexicon Graecum, 633, who translates it with continuo ordine for Lk 1,3 and Acts 11,4, noting that the order need not be chronological.

[89] But see I. I. du Plessis, "Once more: the purpose of Luke's Prologue (Lk I 1-4)", NT 16 (1974) 269, who takes it to signify "as follows"; similarly Kürzinger, "Lk 1,3", 253. Klein, "Lukas 1,1-4", 211, sees it as chronologically structured, linking different phases, and in particular, reflecting the intended continuation of the gospel in Acts; cf. Brown, "Prologues", 106.

[90] Plut., Mor. 615B: ... δεύτερον δ'ἐφεξῆς ἑκάστῳ μυρσίνης παραδιδομένης... ἄλλοι δέ φασι τὴν μυρσίνην οὐ καθεξῆς βαδίζειν, ἀλλὰ καθ'ἕκαστον ἀπὸ κλίνης ἐπὶ κλίνην διαφέρεσθαι (LCL); ἐφεξῆς and καθεξῆς appear as synonyms here.

[91] "Erwägungen", 296.

natural order of going from person to person in each row and the unusual or peculiar order of going back and forth between the rows.

In *Test. Juda* 25,1 of the *Testaments of the Twelve Patriarchs* καθεξῆς is used in reference to the order in which the sons of Jacob will be rulers over the tribes of Israel: "first Levi, second Judah, ... sixth Issachar, καὶ οὕτως καθεξῆς πάντες.[92] This final phrase suggests that the particular sequence in view, which is clearly not chronological, corresponds to some known or traditional order. The adverb does not imply an exhaustive list, as Völkel holds.[93] This aspect is indicated by πάντες.

The case of Schol. Aristoph., *Nub.* 616 is somewhat similar. Here a festival day was assigned to each god in order, Zeus on the first day, Poseidon on the second, καὶ τοὺς ἄλλους θεοὺς καθεξῆς.[94] Completeness is indicated by τοὺς ἄλλους. As the scholion makes clear, καθεξῆς refers to a definite calendrical order which the gods were unable to follow.[95] In the three cases mentioned up to now the sequence is also continuous. In two other texts cited by Völkel[96] the adverb signifies "continuously" or "successively" (Aelian, *Var. Hist.* 8,7)[97] and "one after another" (*IGRR* IV,1432.9).[98]

In the Greek bible καθεξῆς is confined to Luke–Acts, and then only occurs in Lk 1,3, 8,1, Acts 3,24, 11,4, and 18,23. In Lk 8,1 and Acts 3,24 it has the meaning "following", while in Acts 18,23 it signifies "successively" or "one after another".[99] The use of the adverb in Acts 11,4, where it refers to Peter's speech (Πέτρος ἐξετίθετο αὐτοῖς καθεξῆς λέγων), is much more difficult to describe, but it is also more important than the others because of the similarity of its context to that of Lk 1,3.

---

[92] Cf. *The Testaments of the Twelve Patriarchs. A Critical Edition of the Greek Text*, ed. M. de Jonge, PVTG I.2: Leiden 1978, 77.

[93] "Erwägungen", 297.

[94] Καὶ γὰρ ἐν τῇ πρώτῃ ἡμέρᾳ τεταγμένον ἦν τὸν Δία τιμᾶν, ἐν τῇ δευτέρᾳ τὸν Ποσειδῶνα, καὶ τοὺς ἄλλους θεοὺς καθεξῆς. οὗτοι δέ, ὅτε ἔδει τῷ Δίϊ θύειν, τῷ Ποσειδῶνι ἔθυον,... (*Aristophanis Nubes graece et latine una cum scholiis graecis*, ed. T. C. Harles, Leipzig 1788, 334).

[95] Since the gods followed astronomical order they never knew when their festivals were due and consequently were deprived of their festal suppers (cf. 1.618); cf. W. J. M. Starkie, *The Clouds of Aristophanes*, London 1911, 328.

[96] "Erwägungen", 295-296.

[97] Πέντε δὲ ἡμέρας καθεξῆς τοὺς γάμους ἔθυεν· cited from *Claudii Aeliani Varia Historia*, ed. M. R. Dilts, Leipzig 1974, which does not include ἐξῆς (cf. Völkel, "Erwägungen", 296).

[98] ...τοὺς ὑπογεγραμμένους ἀγῶνας· Σμύρναν Ὀλύμπια...Ἀδριάνια Ῥώμην ... πάντας καθεξῆς· here again it is πάντας that indicates completeness.

[99] Cf. Cadbury, "Commentary", 504-505.

A comparison between the story of the conversion of Cornelius in Acts 10,1-48 and its retelling in Peter's speech of 11,5-17 brings out a number of characteristics of the latter and helps to clarify the adverb's meaning. Though the events narrated by Peter in his speech follow one another in chronological order, no real interest in chronological accuracy is evident. The speech begins not at the beginning of the course of events surrounding the conversion of Cornelius as recounted in ch. 10, but with Peter's vision (10,9 ff.). Time indications are omitted (cf. 10,23-24.30), and the chronology is compressed for effect (cf. 11,12).

Since Peter concentrates on the events that are relevant to his case, many details are omitted, especially from Acts 10,17-33, although a couple are added (cf. 11,14.16). His account, therefore, is not 'complete',[100] and it does not represent an 'uninterrupted sequence' of the events of Acts 10 (cf. 10,24-29; 11,12). The sequence of events in 11,5-16 is continuous, however, and the guiding hand of God is visible throughout. But where does v. 17 fit into this sequence? To answer this let us turn to the rhetorical treatises and to their teaching on defence speeches, since Peter's speech may be classified as such.

Although a division of the defence speech in five parts is given by Quintilian (*Inst. Or.* III,9.1) and in six parts by Cicero (*De Inv.* I,14.19) and the author of *Rhetorica ad Herennium* (I,3.4), the basic division of such a speech was the four-part division consisting of proemium, narrative or statement of facts, proof and epilogue.[101] Since both the proemium and epilogue could be readily omitted,[102] the necessary parts of a defence speech were, in general, the narrative or statement of facts and the proof,[103] although in certain cases the former could also be dispensed with or summarized.[104]

Peter's speech contains no proemium. It did not need one since the subject matter of the speech was clear and the attention of the hearers

---

[100] Cf. Schneider, "Bedeutung", 130; Völkel, "Erwägungen", 293-294.

[101] See tables in Lausberg, *Rhetorik*, 148-149; L. Calboli Montefusco (ed.), *Consulti Fortunatiani. Ars Rhetorica*, ESUFC 24: Bologna 1979, 364; also R. Volkmann, *Die Rhetorik der Griechen und Römer in systematischer Übersicht*, Leipzig 1885², 123ff.; Lausberg, *Rhetorik*, 146-247; Martin, *Rhetorik*, 52-166; Kennedy, *Persuasion*, 119-123; Calboli Montefusco, *Fortunatiani*, 362-424; Quint., *Inst. Or.* IV Pr. 6; Diog. Laert., *Lives* VII,43; Fort., *Rhet.* II,12. Although the four-part division given by Aristotle in *Rhet.* III,13.4.1414b mentions the πρόθεσις instead of the διήγησις, the following discussion describes a narration (the two were related, in any case, the one being a brief summary of the other).

[102] On the omission of the proemium see Anaxim., *Rhet.* 29.7.1436b.19ff.; Arist., *Rhet.* III,14.6.1415a; Cic., *De Or.* II,79.320; *De Inv.* I,15.21; Quint., *Inst. Or.* II,13.5; IV,1.25.72; Thuc., *War* III,30.1; on the epilogue see Arist., *Rhet.* III,13.3.1414b; Quint., *Inst. Or.* VI,1.1ff.

[103] Cf. Arist., *Rhet.* III,13.1.4.1414ab.

[104] Cf. Quint., *Inst. Or.* IV,2.4-6; Volkmann, *Rhetorik*, 149.

was already rivetted on the speaker to hear his defence.[105] He begins with the statement of facts, narrating what happened.[106] He does not begin at the very beginning with the vision of Cornelius, but with his own vision, and he recounts what happened in a continuous sequence of events showing how each successive step was motivated by God. His line of defence, in fact, is that God directed his every step so that what he did was not done on his own initiative but in obedience to the divine will. This statement of facts concludes with a saying of Jesus which is directly relevant to Peter's case: "John baptised with water, but you shall be baptised with the Holy Spirit".

The next part of the speech, the proof, is thus well prepared, and the argument of v. 17, introduced by εἰ οὖν, follows on naturally. The case must be judged on whether or not Peter could prevent God's will being carried out.[107] The verdict is inescapable (v. 18). There is no need for an epilogue in such a short speech. It is composed simply of a statement of facts, or a narrative, and a proof.[108]

It should be remembered too that from a rhetorical point of view order seems to have meant good order.[109] An important part of this was the beginning and end of the various parts of the speech. In the case of the narrative or statement of facts, for example, one need not begin at the

---

[105] On the purpose of the proemium see below (pp. 110-112).

[106] Quintilian (*Inst. Or.* IV,2.31) describes the statement of facts as consisting in the persuasive exposition (ad persuadendum expositio) of that which either has been done, or is supposed to have been done, or (according to Apollodorus) a speech instructing the audience on the nature of the case in dispute; it prepares the proof (cf. III,9.7: Expositio enim probationum est praeparatio).

[107] Cf. Quint., *Inst. Or.* III,11.4; also *Rhet. ad Her.* I,16.26; the rejection of responsibility for what one is charged by transferring it to another is mentioned in *Rhet. ad Her.* I,15.25 as a possible line of defence.

[108] J. Dupont, "La structure oratoire du discours d'Étienne (Actes 7)", *Bib* 66 (1985) 153-167, argues that Stephen's speech in Acts 7,2-53 contains an *exordium* (v. 2a), *narratio* (vv. 2b-34), transition (v. 35), *argumentatio* (vv. 36-50) and a *peroratio* (vv. 51-53). But it is more likely that Stephen's *narratio* or statement of facts extends as far as v. 50. It prepares what in effect is an accusation (vv. 51-53) in which Stephen addresses himself in strongly polemical tones to his hearers, speaking directly to them for the first time since the proemium (note change to 2nd pers.). The speech does not have an epilogue. See the proposal by M. Dumais, *Le Langage de L'Évangélisation. L'annonce missionaire en milieu juif (Actes 13,16-41)*, Rech. 16: Tournai-Montreal 1976, 320-323, of a rhetorical disposition for Acts 13,16-41. For a look at Paul's defence speeches in Acts 22-26 from a rhetorical point of view see W. R. Long, "The Paulusbild in the Trial of Paul in Acts", *Society of Biblical Literature 1983 Seminar Papers*, ed. K. H. Richards, Chico 1983, 87-105; J. Neyrey, "The Forensic Defense Speech and Paul's Trial Speeches in Acts 22-26: Form and Function", *Luke-Acts. New Perspectives from the Society of Biblical Literature Seminar*, ed. C. H. Talbert, New York 1984, 210-224.

[109] Cf. Quint., *Inst. Or.* III,3.8 who defines arrangement (dispositio) as the marshalling of arguments in the best possible order (quasi aliud sit dispositio quam rerum ordine quam optimo collocatio).

beginning of things or conclude at the end, but at points which suit the speaker's purpose.[110] The narrative of Peter's speech does not begin at the beginning of the events related in ch. 10, as we have seen above, but at the most effective point for Peter's defence, namely, his heavenly vision. It concludes also on a strong note, not with the last of the events of ch. 10, but with a saying of Jesus.

In Acts 11,4, then, καθεξῆς may be used as a term of broad application and not without rhetorical overtones. Taking into account its inherent note of continuity,[111] the context of Peter's speech, particularly its narrative, and the extra-biblical examples cited above, it is arguable that the adverb carries the implications of a traditionally arranged (narrative-proof)[112] and well ordered speech, with suitable beginning and end, whose narrative[113] recounts a continuous sequence of events relevant to Peter's defence, related broadly speaking in the order in which they happened,[114] and with the guiding hand of God everywhere visible. It resembles to a certain extent the terms τάξις and οἰκονομία which the rhetorical treatises use, though not always in the same way,[115] for the arrangement of a speech and its parts. The specific contribution of καθεξῆς may be its implication of continuity.

Before turning to Luke's proemium a further point should be noted. If the question of order is important for the speech, it is no less so for the historical work. Dionysius of Halicarnassus took Thucydides to task for the arrangement of his narrative. He criticized its division according to winters and summers, since this destroyed the continuity of the narrative and made it unclear and difficult to follow.[116] And he added his voice to those critics who found fault with the order (τάξις) of the work, complaining that he chose neither the right beginning nor a fitting place

---

[110] Cf. *Rhet. ad Her.* I,9.14.

[111] Note that ἐφεξῆς is used in Arist., *Rhet.* III,16.1.1416b, in reference to a continuous narrative (οὐκ ἐφεξῆς ἀλλὰ κατὰ μέρος): see also 16.2.1416b.

[112] Cf. Quint., *Inst. Or.* IV,3.1; *Rhet. ad Her.* III,9.17. A distinction was made between natural and artificial order, with the latter indicating any departure from the usual order of narrative-proof; cf. Quint., *Inst. Or.* IV,3.1; *Rhet. ad Her.* III,9.17; Lausberg, *Rhetorik*, 245-247.

[113] In *Rhet. ad Her.* III,9.17 it is stated that the *dispositio* refers both to the whole speech and its individual parts; cf. Quint., *Inst. Or.* III,9.2.

[114] See the advice of Lucian, *Hist.* §49; Cic., *De Inv.* I,20.29; *Rhet. ad Her.* I,9.15.

[115] Dionysius of Halicarnassus uses both οἰκονομικός and οἰκονομία in a general sense for arrangement (*De Thuc.* §§9.10), with διαίρεσις, τάξις and ἐξεργασία designating subdivisions; similarly Hermagoras with οἰκονομία (cf. Quint., *Inst. Or.* III,3.9). But Lucian, *Hist.* §§6.48 uses τάξις in a general sense as does Diog. Laert., *Lives* VII,43; see also Arist., *Rhet.* III,1.1.1403b; 12.6.1414a; cf. F. H. Colson, "Τάξει in Papias (The Gospels and the Rhetorical Schools)", *JTS* 14 (1913) 62-69.

[116] *De Thuc.* §9; *Ep. ad Pomp.* §3. On the desirability of continuity in a narrative see Dion. Hal., *De Thuc.* §9; Quint., *Inst. Or.* IX,4.129; but see Arist., *Rhet.* III,16.1.1416b.

to end it.[117] The importance of the beginning and end of the narrative emerges clearly from the proemia of historical works such as those of Thucydides, Josephus, Diodorus and Polybius where one or both points are mentioned.[118]

In the light of the above remarks a number of possibilities may be mentioned for the use of καθεξῆς in Lk 1,3. First of all, it could express Luke's intention of writing a continuous narrative. This could imply that the events are recounted in something of a chronological order, an order which the rhetorical treatises recommended to speakers for clarity's sake and one which historians were urged to use as far as they could, and did use.[119] But it need not. If some chronological order is intended here, then it can only be a very general one, since Luke shows little interest in strict chronology.[120]

It is more likely that Luke's claim refers to the continuity of the narrative itself. The geographical outline of the whole and the frequent 'travel notices' scattered throughout give a strong sense of movement and continuity to the narrative which progresses from Galilee to Jerusalem to Rome in two volumes, with the second following on directly from the first. This note of continuity is strengthened by transitions from one major section to the next and from one volume to the next,[121] by the way particular scenes are linked together[122] or set in the narrative,[123] by the

---

[117] *De Thuc.* § 10; *Ep. ad Pomp.* § 3.

[118] Cf. Thuc., *War* I,23.5 (cf. I,1.1), and criticisms of his beginning and end in Dion. Hal., *De Thuc.* §§ 10-12; Jos., *Ant.* I,7, referring to his work on the Jewish war; Diod., *Hist.* I,3.6; 4.5; Pol., *Hist.* I,3.1-6; III,1.1-11; IV,2.1-11; Dion. Hal., *Ant. Rom.* I,8.1-2; also Colson's comments on Mark's order (τάξις) in "Papias", 65-67.

[119] See n. 110 above; Dion. Hal., *De Thuc.* §9; Cic., *De Or.* II,15.63; Avenarius, *Geschichtsschreibung*, 124.

[120] See, for example, the Galilean ministry (cf. 5,1.17; 6,1.6; 8,22; 9,18), the travel narrative (cf. 10,38; 11,1.14; 13,10.22; 14,1.25) or Acts (cf. 6,1; 9,28-31.32; 11,19-30; 12,1).

[121] Note the transitional elements in 9,1-50 for the travel narrative (cf. 9,31), in 18,31–19,48 for the final section (cf. 18,31-33; 19,37-38.47-48), in ch. 24 for Acts (cf. 24,36-53), in Acts 6,1–8,3 for the missionary section 8,4–21,17 (esp. 8,1b-3), in 18,23–21,17 for the final section (cf. 19,21); see comments in ch. II above in the course of the literary analysis.

[122] See remarks in ch. II above (pp. 45-46.48 and nn. 112 and 197) on the links between Lk 7,11-17 and 7,18ff.; 17,11-19 and 17,20a; Acts 8,1b-3, 8,4ff. and 11.19ff.; also Lk 6,12–7,50, 9,51–10,37 and Acts 10,1–11,18; see the comments of Lohse, "Heilsge-schichte", 259-261.

[123] Cf. Lk 11,37-52; 13,34-35 (diff. Mt 23,1-39). Both Lk 11,37-52 and 13,34-35 contribute to the development of the narrative; Jesus' harsh words in the former provoke the reaction of the scribes and the pharisees who from this point onwards endeavour to entrap him in his speech (cf. 12,1; 14,1; 20,1ff.); the latter text occupies a significant place at the centre of the travel narrative where it implies that Jesus' journey is of crucial importance for Jerusalem. Acts 15, as has been noted above, results from the missionary work of Peter, Paul and Barnabas in the preceding chapters, and removes difficulties for the Gentile mission. Note the associations between Acts 4,32-37 and 5,1-11; 14,28 and 15,1ff.

preparation of later events, whether through predictions[124] or anticipations,[125] by flashbacks,[126] by the many summaries dotted throughout both volumes,[127] and by such things as the explicit mention of the Galilean women in 8,1-3 (cf. 23,49.55; 24,6) and the promise of the Spirit in 24,49 (cf. Acts 2,1-4). On a thematic level Luke emphasizes, for example, the continuity between the ministries of Jesus and the disciples[128] and between Israel and the Church or the new people of God.[129] The account does not always flow in a continuous line, it is true (cf. Lk 3,2-20.21; Acts 8,1c; 8,4–11,18; 11,19 ff.).[130] But in general Luke appears to strive for continuity, and in large measure has succeeded.

Secondly, in conveying the sense "in order", καθεξῆς probably also signifies good order. Luke could justifiably claim to have chosen a suitable beginning and a fitting conclusion for his narrative. He begins at a point where αὐτοψία begins (Lk 5,1) so that the whole narrative proper is covered by eyewitness reports, the latter stages perhaps even in part by personal eyewitness-ship ("we" sections). A guarantee of reliability is thus provided for the narrative. Concluding on a positive note, with the unhindered preaching of the word of God to all at the centre and capital of the known world, he leaves the reader with an indication of his continuing hope that this word will eventually reach the ends of the earth and that 'all flesh' will see the salvation of God (cf. Acts 28,28; Lk 3,6).

Thirdly, the adverb may imply showing the presence of a divine guiding hand in the course of events narrated (cf. Acts 11,4-18). Such guidance is a prominent feature of the spread of the word in Acts,[131] but

---

[124] See, for example, Jesus' prediction in 5,10c and its fulfilment in 9,1-6, 10,1-12.17 and Acts; the passion predictions of 9,22.31.44 and 18,31-33 and their fulfilment; see also 13,35 and 19,38; 22,31-34 and 22,56-61; 24,49 and Acts 2,1-4.

[125] Cf. Lk 5,10c; 9,1-6; 10,11-12.17; 20,20; Acts 9,15-16; 19,21; 23,11; also such notices as Lk 9,9b (cf. 23,8) and 20,20 (cf. 23,1-5); cf. 4,13 and 22,3.53.

[126] Cf. Lk 24,18-22; Acts 2,22-33; 3,13-18; 10,36-42; 11,5-16; 13,23-31; 15,7-8.12; 22,1-21; 26,2-23.

[127] Cf. Lk 5,15-16; 6,11; 7,17; 8,1; 13,22; 15,1-2; 19,47-48; 21,37-38; 24,53; Acts 1,14; 2,42-47; 4,32-35; 5,12-16.42; 6,7; 8,4; 9,31; 11,19; 12,24; 16,5; 19,20 (cf. Lk 1,80; 2,40.52; 3,18; 4,14-15.44); see Cadbury, "Summaries", 393; H. Steichele, *Vergleich der Apostelgeschichte mit der antiken Geschichtsschreibung. Eine Studie zur Erzählkunst in der Apostelgeschichte*, Diss. Munich 1971, 63-64.

[128] See above pp. 99-101; also R. F. O'Toole, *The Unity of Luke's Theology. An Analysis of Luke-Acts*, GNS 9: Wilmington 1984, 62-94.

[129] The latter emerges from, and stands in continuity with, Israel (cf. Lk 1,16-17; 3,3-18; 6,13.17; 7,29-30; 12,32; Acts 1,15; 5,11; 8,1.3; 11,26; 15,14-18; 18,10; 20,28). Luke is also anxious to show that the Gentiles participate in the promise made to Israel (cf. Lk 2,30-32; 3,4-6; 24,47; Acts 3,25; 13,47; 26,22-23).

[130] See also Lk 1,57-80; 2,1ff.; Acts 8,3.4-40; 9,1-2.

[131] Cf. Acts 2,22-36; 3,13-18.26; 8,26-29; 9,4-19; 10,1-11.18; 13,30.33.37; 14,27; 15,7-8.14; 16,6-10; 19,21; 21,19; 22,18-21; 23,11; also O'Toole, *Unity*, 26.

it is also present in the gospel, as is evident from the infancy narrative, the baptism account, and such statements as Lk 10,21 and 22,42. The adverb may also imply showing how the course of events narrated corresponds to the plan of God enunciated in the scriptures — a prominent Lucan theme[132] — or fulfils prophecies and predictions of Jesus.[133]

The importance for Luke's purpose of the two elements eyewitness-ship and conformity to the will of God is brought home by Acts 2,23-36. There Peter calls on his hearers to believe with certainty (ἀσφαλῶς) that God has made Jesus both Lord and Messiah. The basis for his call is their αὐτοψία (βλέπετε καὶ ἀκούετε · 2,33) and the conformity of this event to the will of God expressed in the scriptures (cf. 2,34-35).[134]

Finally, the adverb's use in Acts 11,4 and in the extra-biblical examples discussed above suggests that Luke may intend broadly following a 'traditional' arrangement of the material that he has assembled, presumably that found in his predecessors' narratives, and that material is included on the basis of its relevance to his theme and purpose.[135]

5. Lk 1,1-4: Purpose

The beginning and end of any literary work are of obvious importance, and in ancient times, when rolls were the order of the day and when reading was a slow and arduous process, the beginning was doubly so. To enable one to ascertain quickly what a work was about it was helpful to have indicated at the beginning the subject matter and literary genre of the work so that the reader or an unfortunate servant did not have to wind through feet of papyrus to discover this information.

---

[132] Cf. Lk 3,6; 4,18-21; 18,31-33; 24,26-27.46-47; Acts 2,22-36; 3,18-26; 8,32-35; 10,43; 13,27-28.47; 15,14-17; 17,2-3; 26,22-23; 28,25-27.

[133] See n. 124 above.

[134] Parallels are not lacking for the certainty following from eyewitness-ship and conformity to the will of God expressed in the scriptures or in the words of Jesus or those of the heavenly messengers. Jesus' miracles before John's messengers and his allusions to the prophecies of Is 35,5 and 61,1 should lead to the realization of his identity (cf. 7,22); it is only Jesus' explanation of the scriptures about himself to the Emmaus disciples (24,25-27) and the opening of their eyes (24,31) that enable them to report that he is truly (ὄντως) risen; the Galilean women come to faith through their eyewitness-ship of the empty tomb, the words of the two heavenly figures (cf. 24,6-7.23) and their remembrance of those of Jesus (24,6-8); the certainty of the parousia is based on the eyewitness-ship of the departing Jesus and the words of the heavenly figures (Acts 1,9-11).

[135] A narrative composed with these various concerns in mind should convey to Theophilus the reliability or certainty of the λόγοι in which he has been instructed, assuring him that what remains to be fulfilled (cf. Lk 3,6; 24,47; Acts 1,8.11; 3,20-21) will indeed find fulfilment; cf. Schneider, "Bedeutung", 130-131.

What was far more important than this practical consideration, though, was the need to prepare the reader or hearer at the very beginning of a literary work or speech for what was to come.[136] Aristotle described the proemium as a "paving of the way" (ὁδοποίησις) for what follows,[137] and the term proemium itself, whether derived from προ-οἴμη or προ-οἶμος, indicates its nature as such.[138]

Rhetorical treatises devoted great attention to the proemium of the speech and how its purpose of preparing the hearer could be achieved.[139] Three ways were advocated for accomplishing this: making the hearer well-disposed, attentive and ready to learn (benevolum, attentum, docilem).[140] The treatises dwelt at length upon how each of these could be effected. Though intended for the orator, the advice was applicable to the proemia of ancient literary works in general. This is evident from Lucian's treatise on the writing of history (§ 53) and more importantly from a consideration of such proemia.[141] Lucian, it is true, advised the historian to omit from his proemium the first of the orator's aims, namely, making the hearer well-disposed.[142] But how the first could be separated from the other two is not specified, and in practice it does not appear to have been (cf. Dion. Hal., Ant. Rom. I,1.1; Diod., Hist. I,1.1; 5.2).[143]

Catching the attention of the reader or hearer and making him well-disposed and ready to learn were achieved in a variety of ways in the proemia of ancient literary works. A favourite means was to stress the

---

[136] Cf. Rhet. ad Alex. 29.1436a33ff. (ἀκροατῶν παρασκευή); Rhet. ad Her. I,3.4 (per quod animus auditoris constituitur ad audiendum); Quint., Inst. Or. IV,1.5 (ut auditorem, quo sit nobis in ceteris partibus accommodatior, praeparemus); Dion. Hal., De Lys. § 17 (ἀκροατὴν παρασκευάσας).

[137] Rhet. III,14.1.1414b: Τὸ μὲν οὖν προοίμιόν ἐστιν ἀρχὴ λόγου, ὅπερ ἐν ποιήσει πρόλογος καὶ ἐν αὐλήσει προαύλιον· πάντα γὰρ ἀρχαὶ ταῦτ' εἰσί, καὶ οἷον ὁδοποίησις τῷ ἐπιόντι· he goes on to say that in speeches and epic poems the proemia provide a sample of the subject in order that the hearers may know beforehand what it is about, and he adds that he who puts the beginning into the hearer's hand enables him, if he holds fast to it, to follow the story (14,6.1415a).

[138] See the discussion in Quint., Inst. Or. IV,1.1-3; also A. Aloni, "Prooimia, Hymnoi, Elio Aristide e i cugini bastardi", QUCC 33 (1980) 30-34; Volkmann, Rhetorik, 127-128; Martin, Rhetorik, 60-61.

[139] Cf. Rhet. ad Alex. 29.1436a33-1438a2; Arist., Rhet. III,14.1.1414b-15.10.1416b; Quint., Inst. Or. IV,1.1-79; Rhet. ad Her. I,4.1-7.11; Cic, De Inv. I,15.20-18.26; Fort., Rhet. II,13-15; Volkmann, Rhetorik, 128-148; Lausberg, Rhetorik, 150-163; Martin, Rhetorik, 63-72.

[140] Cf. Arist., Rhet. III,14.7.1415a (εὔνουν, προσεκτικόν, εὐμάθειαν): Quint., Inst. Or. IV,1.5 (benevolum, attentum, docilem); in similar order, Cic., De Inv. I,15.20; Rhet. ad Her. I,4.6 (attentum, docilem, benevolum).

[141] For the historical proemia see Lieberich, Proömien; also Janson, Prefaces, 64-72.

[142] Hist. § 53; also § 14; cf. Avenarius, Geschichtsschreibung, 115-116 and 116 n. 33.

[143] See the remarks of Janson, Prefaces, 65-66; also Lieberich, Proömien, 22.30.36-37; Avenarius, Geschichtsschreibung, 116 n. 33.

value of the work in comparison with its predecessors in the same field.[144] Other means included indicating the subject matter of the work,[145] its purpose,[146] its importance[147] and its usefulness.[148] The reliability of one's sources might be emphasized, especially if these were eyewitness sources.[149] The writer might indicate the lengths to which he went to obtain accurate information, noting the time devoted to it,[150] the eyewitness-ship of the 'field of action',[151] the care taken in comparing eyewitness accounts.[152] He might also note the scope and accuracy of his investigations[153] and the care with which the actual narrative was composed.[154] The reader or hearer was doubtless grateful for the outline or plan of the work sometimes given[155] and for the occasional summary of events (*Vorgeschichte*) which helped one to follow better the events recounted in the narrative proper.[156] Lucian advised that the attention of the audience could be gained by showing that what was to come was important, essential, personal or useful.[157]

Luke's brief and well-written proemium was undoubtedly calculated to impress. But its very brevity, together with the general nature and consequent ambiguity of its language, does not make it easy to decipher. Though quite familiar with the ways and means of making an audience well-disposed in the proemium of a speech (cf. Acts 10,34b-35; 17,22b;

---

[144] See, for example, Dion. Hal., *Ant. Rom.* I,1.1 (referring to the proemia of Anaximenes and Theopompus which contain attacks on their fellow historians); I,5.4-6.3; Jos., *BJ* I,1-2.6-8; Diod., *Hist.* I,3.1-8; Arrian, *An.* I Pr. 1-3; Diosc., *De Mat. Med.* I Pr.; *Rhet. ad Her.* I,1.1.

[145] See the many examples given by D. Earl, "Prologue-form in Ancient Historiography", *ANRW* I.2, ed. H. Temporini, Berlin-New York 1972, 842-856; also ch. I, n. 21.

[146] See, for instance, Herod., *Hist.* I,1; Thuc., *War* I,1.1; Pol., *Hist.* I,1.1-2.5; Dion. Hal., *Ant. Rom.* I,5.1-3; also ch. I, n. 27. For Aristotle the most essential function of the exordium is to make clear the end or purpose of a speech (cf. *Rhet.* III,14.6.1415a).

[147] Cf. Herod., *Hist.* I,1; Thuc., *War* I,1.1-2; 23.1-3; Dion. Hal., *Ant. Rom.* I,2.1-3.6; Diod., *Hist.* I,1.1-5; Jos., *Ant.* I,4.

[148] Cf. Pol., *Hist.* I,1.2; 2.8; Diod., *Hist.* I,1.1-2.8; Dion. Hal., *Ant. Rom.* I,5.3; 6.3-4; Jos., *BJ* I,30; *Ant.* I,14; Livy, *Ab Urbe* Pr. 9-10.

[149] Cf. Thuc., *War* I,22.3; Pol., *Hist.* III,4.13; IV,2.2-3; Jos., *BJ* I,3.6; Dion. Hal., *Ant. Rom.* I,6.2; Diosc., *De Mat. Med.* I Pr.

[150] Cf. Dion. Hal., *Ant. Rom.* I,7.2; Diod., *Hist.* I,4.1.

[151] Cf. Diod., *Hist.* I,4.1; Jos., *C. Ap.* I,47-49.53-54; Diosc., *De Mat Med.* I Pr.

[152] Cf. Thuc., *War* I,22.3; Pol., *Hist.* IV,2.2-3.

[153] Cf. Thuc., *War* I,22.1-3; Diod., *Hist.* I,4.1-5; Dion. Hal., *Ant. Rom.* I,7.1-3; also ch. I, n. 25.

[154] Cf. Dion. Hal., *Ant. Rom.* I,6.2 (apropos of Q. Fabius and L. Cincius); also I,6.3; Jos., *BJ* I,9.

[155] Cf. Diod., *Hist.* I,4.6-7; Dion. Hal., *Ant. Rom.* I,5.1-2; 8.1-2; Pol., *Hist.* III,1.9-3.9; see also Thuc., *War* I,23.5.

[156] Cf. Herod., *Hist.* I,2-5; Thuc., *War* I,2.1-19.1; Tac., *Hist.* I,4-11.

[157] *Hist.* §53.

24,2b-4.10; 26,2-3), Luke, apart from the dedication to Theophilus, does not overtly resort to that here. But there are elements which are intended to gain the goodwill and attention of the reader and make one ready to learn. A number of these have already been pointed out in ch. I — the indications of subject matter and of the ultimately eyewitness nature of the sources listed, the care taken in the composition of the work, the completeness and accuracy of the investigations, the promise of an 'ordered' account and the purpose of the work.[158]

For an instructed Theophilus (cf. Lk 1,4),[159] the proemium clearly conveys the importance of what is to come. If read with the sensibility of Schürmann, the phrase τῶν πεπληροφορημένων ἐν ἡμῖν πραγμάτων already carries an implication that the work's subject matter is related to the teaching he has received.[160] But the references to the "ministers of the word" and the λόγοι in which Theophilus has been instructed[161] make this relationship abundantly clear. It is a relationship which conveys to the instructed reader that what is to come is important, personal, useful, and indeed essential.

For the non-instructed reader, likely nonetheless to have been familiar with a number of the terms in Lk 1,1-4,[162] the promise of a well-ordered, reliable, accurately researched account would certainly make a good impression. The reference to Luke's predecessors' narratives would probably have suggested an historical work,[163] although the unusual phrase ὑπηρέται ... τοῦ λόγου would probably have caused some

---

[158] See ch. I, p. 11, and there nn. 21-27.

[159] Whether baptized or not (cf. Acts 18,25) is not a problem in the light of v. 4; see the comments of Grundmann, *Lk*, 45; Schürmann, *Lk* I, 13-14, and there nn. 86-87; Marshall, *Lk*, 43; Fitzmyer, *Lk I-IX*, 300.

[160] *Lk* I, 5.7; cf. Lohse, "Heilsgeschichte", 261; U. Luck, "Kerygma, Tradition und Geschichte Jesu bei Lukas", *ZTK* 57 (1960) 60; Fitzmyer, *Lk I-IX*, 293.

[161] Zigabenus (*Commentarius in Quatuor Evangelia* II, ed. C. F. Matthaei, Berlin-London 1845, 205) took λόγων to refer to words of faith (λόγοι τῆς πίστεως): B. Weiss, *Mk und Lk*, 267, Holtzmann, *Synoptiker*, 304, and Fitzmyer, *Lk I-IX*, 301, to Christian teaching or instruction. Λόγοι appears to be related to λόγος of v. 2 (cf. Lk 4,32.36; 10,39; 21,33; 24,19), but it can hardly be equated with it, as Glöckner, *Verkündigung*, 34, suggests. The term appears to refer rather to aspects of the Christian message, aspects that may be transparent in the preoccupations manifested by the evangelist throughout his work.

[162] Many of the terms appear in the proemia to historical, medical and scientific works, as is to be expected given the common purpose shared by such proemia; cf. Wettstein, *Novum Testamentum* I, 644-645; Grimm, "Proömium", 35-53; Klostermann, *Lk*, 1-3; W. K. Hobart, *The Medical Language of St. Luke*, Dublin-London 1882, 86-90; Cadbury, "Commentary", 492-509; Plummer, *Lk*, 5-6; van Unnik, "Luke's Prologue", 12-26; T. Callan, "The Preface of Luke-Acts and Historiography", *NTS* 31 (1985) 577-580; L. Alexander, "Luke's Preface in the Context of Greek Preface-Writing", *NT* 28 (1986) 72-74.

[163] See ch. V, pp. 165-168.

puzzlement, conjuring up thoughts perhaps of a medical, philosophical, or even a religious work.[164] The mixture of the familiar and the decidedly unfamiliar, though, should at least have moved one to read further.

Finally, an aspect of Luke's proemium that would have impressed the reader is its attitude towards previous narratives of a similar kind and subject matter. While Luke places himself alongside his predecessors in his undertaking (cf. Lk 1,3), he gives the distinct impression through his claims for the accuracy and completeness of his investigations[165] that his work is meant to mark an improvement on their narratives.[166] This impression is conveyed even more strongly by the adverb καθεξῆς, since it is the 'order' of the narrative in particular that allows Theophilus to ascertain the reliability or certainty of the λόγοι.

Luke's attitude towards tradition is not a negative one, though.[167] The anonymous nature of his work alone suggests as much.[168] So too does the description of the narratives of Luke's predecessors as faithful accounts (καθώς) of the tradition handed on by those who from the beginning were eyewitnesses and who were also ministers of the word. Luke's positive attitude emerges above all from the programme of his work. This programme is at once literary, historical, and, for the instructed, theological. It is reflected in the terms ἀρχή... ἄνωθεν... καθεξῆς... λόγων... ἀσφάλεια. While opening his work at the dawning of a new epoch (ἄνωθεν), Luke only begins his narrative proper with the ἀρχή of Jesus' ministry in Galilee, an ἀρχή that is covered by eyewitness reports handed on faithfully by the tradition. Furthermore, is it not the ἀσφάλεια of the λόγοι which form part and parcel of this tradition that he is anxious to show? In Luke's case tradition acts as the faithful mediator of events which he narrates in an order that respects this tradition, while modifying its presentation.[169]

---

[164] On the use of ὑπηρέτης in medical and religious contexts see K. H. Rengstorf, "ὑπηρέτης κτλ.", *TDNT* VIII, 543; Hobart, *Medical Language*, 88-89; on the use of λόγος in the Greek and Hellenistic world see H. Kleinknecht, "λέγω κτλ.", *TDNT* IV, 77-91.

[165] See the combination of motifs in Thuc., *War* I,22.2-3: Diod., *Hist.* I,3.6-8; 4.1-5; Dion. Hal., *Ant. Rom.* I,6.1; 7.1-8.2; Jos., *C. Ap.* I,53-55; on the question of grammar see Cadbury, "Commentary", 504.

[166] Proemial references to predecessors are usually critical. Diodorus is surprisingly positive in this respect (cf. *Hist.* I,1.1; 3.1), though not without a critical note (cf. I,3.1-5); but see Cic., *De Or.* I,6.22.

[167] As Klein, "Lukas 1,1-4", 206, feels.

[168] The writer is prepared to retreat behind the tradition. See the remarks of H.-W. Bartsch, *Wachet aber zu jeder Zeit! Entwurf einer Auslegung des Lukasevangeliums*, Hamburg-Bergstedt 1963, 13.

[169] Accurate research and eyewitness-ship are important for the reliability of the narrative. But Luke's emphasis lies on the actual presentation of the whole. The question of the rhetorical influence on history arises here. A problem of long standing (cf. H. Peter,

Conclusion

Various aspects of the relationship between Lk 1,1-4 and the remainder of Luke–Acts have emerged. The phrase παρηκολουθηκότι ἄνωθεν πᾶσιν of Lk 1,3 is sufficiently specific and at the same time sufficiently general to link Lk 1,1-4 to 1,5ff. and to cover the events of Acts, thus including within its compass the whole of Luke-Acts. Luke's proemium points towards Lk 5,1 as the beginning of the gospel's narrative proper, thus confirming the literary analysis above. It also conveys in a number of ways the evangelist's intention of composing a two-part work covering the ministries of Jesus and his 'witnesses'. The body of the work contains a number of indications that Luke–Acts was planned and executed as a two-volume work.[170]

While the influence of Hellenistic theory and practice on Lk 1,1-4 is evident in the proemial motifs used and in the manner of their use, Luke's own personal contribution comes to the fore. Although his work is meant to mark an improvement on those of his predecessors, he nevertheless displays a positive attitude towards the tradition he has received. In addition to the literary and historical dimensions of the programme set

---

Wahrheit und Kunst. Geschichtsschreibung und Plagiat im klassischen Altertum, Leipzig-Berlin, 1911; E. Norden, *Die Antike Kunstprosa* I, Leipzig-Berlin 1909, 81-95; F. H. Colson, "Some Considerations as to the Influence of Rhetoric upon History", *PCA* 14 (1917) 149-173; idem, "Notes on St Luke's Preface" *JTS* 24 (1923) 304-309; Cadbury, "Commentary", 498-500; M. L. W. Laistner, *The Greater Roman Historians* I, SCL 21: London 1947, 29-35; A. D. Leeman, *Orationis Ratio. The Stylistic Theories and Practice of the Roman Orators, Historians and Philosophers*, Amsterdam 1963, 171-174; P. A. Brunt, "Cicero and Historiography", *Φιλίας χάριν. Miscellanea di Studi Classici in onore di E. Manni* I, eds. M. J. Fontana, M. T. Piraino, F. P. Rizzo, Rome 1980, 309-340), it has recently been raised by E. Güttgemanns in "In welchem Sinne ist Lukas "Historiker"? Die Beziehungen von Luk 1,1-4 und Papias zur antiken Rhetorik", *LingBibl* 54 (1983) 9-26, and F. Siegert in "Lukas – ein Historiker, d.h. ein Rhetor? Freundschaftliche Entgegnung auf Erhardt Güttgemanns", *LingBibl* 55 (1984) 57-60. The question is much too complex to treat in the compass of a note. But it should be noted in reply to Güttgemanns that rhetoricians made an important distinction between the narrative of a speech which aimed at credibility (cf. Cic., *De Or.* II,80.326; *Or.* 36.124) and the historical narrative which aimed at truth (cf. Thuc., *War* I,20.3; 22.2-4; Diod., *Hist.* I,2.2; Dion. Hal., *De Thuc.* §8; Lucian, *Hist.* §§7-9; Cic., *De Or.* II,15.62; also the comments of H. Homeyer (ed.), *Lukian. Wie man Geschichte schreiben soll*, Munich 1965, 266-267). The striking aspect of Luke's proemium is the modesty of its claims. He says little about his sources, makes only a possible implicit claim for eyewitness-ship of some events (the "we" sections of Acts), and says nothing about eyewitness-ship of the 'field of action' (cf. Diod., *Hist.* I,4.1; Pol., *Hist.* III,48.12; X,11.4), although Haenchen, *Acts*, 86, mentions this as a real possibility. Too much should not be made of historians' criticisms of one another, criticisms that neither Thucydides (cf. Jos., *C. Ap.* I,18) nor Polybius (cf. Dion. Hal., *Ant. Rom.* I,6.1) managed to escape.

[170] Further support for the unity of Luke-Acts is provided in chs. IV and V.

out in his proemium, he includes a vital theological dimension. His use of traditional proemial motifs reflects, in the final analysis, the particular nature of his work as a whole. Before examining its contribution in that respect (see ch. V below), it is necessary to look at the role and situation of Lk 1,5–4,44 in Luke–Acts.

CHAPTER IV

THE ROLE OF LK 1,5–4,44 IN LUKE-ACTS

Preliminary Remarks

Many studies on the infancy narrative and on the following two chapters indicate the existence of a relationship between various parts of 1,5–4,44 and the remainder of Luke–Acts.[1] Given that the two-volume work was conceived and executed as a whole, as has been suggested above, the presence of such a relationship is perfectly understandable and hardly unexpected. Determining its extent and nature is another matter. By examining these early chapters from different perspectives, taking account also of the remainder of Luke–Acts, one should be in a position to be more specific about this relationship. Since the person and mission of Jesus are accorded such prominence in 1,5–4,44 attention will be focussed on each in turn. Before that another important aspect of these chapters will be examined, namely, their view of salvation history, a view that has been the subject of much debate ever since the appearance of Conzelmann's *Die Mitte der Zeit*.

1. Time of Fulfilment

A point that these chapters make, and make repeatedly, is that the time in which the events narrated in Luke–Acts take place is the time of fulfilment. The verb πληροφορέω in Lk 1,1 may already indicate as much.[2] But there is no lack of indications in 1,5–4,44. Even if one were to ignore the infancy narrative, as Conzelmann does to a great extent, there would still be sufficient material to show that the particular periodic division of salvation history proposed by him does not lie on very solid foundations. Before examining the various indications in 1,5–4,44 of the time of fulfilment, it may be helpful to consider Conzelmann's position.

---

[1] See Prologue, pp. 2-5 above.
[2] Cf. Schürmann, *Lk* I, 5; Maddox, *Luke-Acts*, 141-142.

1.1 *Critique of Conzelmann's Theory*

To offer a proper critique of Conzelmann's position, it is necessary first of all to look at the division of salvation history put forward by Heinrich von Baer, a division to which Conzelmann is much indebted.[3]

On the basis of his study of the Holy Spirit in the writings of Luke, von Baer concluded that the evangelist had divided salvation history (a term taken over from Eduard Meyer)[4] into three epochs, that of the Old Testament, that of the Son of God, and that of the Spirit.[5] He based his distinction on what he saw as three different levels of the Spirit's manifestation in salvation history. The first of these, the Spirit of prophecy, he regarded as characteristic of the Old Testament epoch, and as linking John, Elizabeth, Zachary and Simeon to this epoch.[6] He took John to be the representative of this epoch of salvation history, as well as its conclusion and culmination.[7] With the conception of Jesus by the Spirit (1,35) and his 'new-begetting' as Messiah at his baptism,[8] the new epoch of the Son of God begins.[9] In this epoch the Spirit of God is present in a new way as the Spirit of God's son, and its possession is unique to him in this period.[10] The epoch comes to a close with Jesus' ascension and corresponds to his time on earth.[11] Between the ascension and the beginning of the third epoch lies an interim period characterized by the absence of the Spirit (cf. Acts 1,15-26).[12] The coming of the Spirit at Pentecost marks the beginning of the third epoch in which the Spirit of the exalted Lord is at work in the community of disciples.[13] So much for von Baer's position which is reflected to a large degree also in the works of Hauck[14] and Lampe.[15]

---

[3] *Heilige Geist*, 43-112.

[4] *Ursprung* I, 2. Meyer used the term in pointing out that Luke, unlike the other evangelists, considered the spread of the gospel as "einen wesentlichen Teil der Heilsgeschichte".

[5] On von Baer's study see M. B. Turner, "Jesus and the Spirit in Lucan Perspective", *TB* 32 (1981) 4-7.

[6] *Heilige Geist*, 47: "Johannes... erscheint als der Träger einer veralteten Stufe der Gottesoffenbarung"; 49: "... die Geistesträger der alten Zeit".

[7] *Heilige Geist*, 46-47.

[8] *Heilige Geist*, 59; von Baer accepted the Western reading for 3,21 (cf. 58 n. 18).

[9] *Heilige Geist*, 59: "... sowohl in der Verkündigung wie in der Jordantaufe das Anbrechen ein und derselben Heilsepoche, der des Sohnes, geschildert wird... die beide ausdrücklich als Zeugung des Gottessohnes bezeichnet werden".

[10] *Heilige Geist*, 48-49.71.

[11] *Heilige Geist*, 78.

[12] *Heilige Geist*, 79-85.

[13] *Heilige Geist*, 85.45.

[14] *Lk*, 55-56.

[15] G. W. H. Lampe, "The Holy Spirit in the Writings of St. Luke", *Studies in the Gospels*, Essays in Memory of R. H. Lightfoot, ed. D. E. Nineham, Oxford 1955, 159-200, a position he substantially modified in *God as Spirit*, Oxford 1977, 62-72.

Conzelmann sought to refine von Baer's division of salvation history and to put it on a more solid foundation.[16] Undoubtedly aware of the weaknesses of von Baer's theory, especially his delineation of the period of the Old Testament, Conzelmann proposed new criteria for the division of salvation history. It is here that his problems begin. Whereas von Baer used one basic criterion for his division, Conzelmann uses at least three: Lk 16,16 to delineate the epoch of Israel;[17] 4,13.16 ff. and Acts 10,38 for the epoch of Jesus;[18] the Spirit for the epoch of the church.[19] The use of non-complementary or non-convergent criteria to divide what is essentially a continuous period of time inevitably leads to difficulties. In the final analysis these turn out to be insurmountable.[20]

Although Conzelmann's division between the period of Israel and that of Jesus on the basis of Lk 16,16 gave rise to much controversy, his interpretation of the verse was not without support at the time. Von Baer had cited it in support of his theory.[21] Schrenk and Hauck had argued from it that John belonged to the era of the law and the prophets in contrast to the new era characterized by the 'good news'.[22] Friedrich had interpreted it to indicate John as the boundary between the old and the new, while still belonging to the law and the prophets.[23] But 16,16 does not bear up well under the weight placed on it by Conzelmann.[24] For one thing, it may be interpreted either as excluding John from the period beginning "from then" (ἀπὸ τότε),[25] or as including

---

[16] *Mitte*; see also his "Zur Lukasanalyse", *ZTK* 49 (1952) 16-33.

[17] *Mitte*, 9.16-17.

[18] *Mitte*, 9.22, and 22 n. 2.

[19] *Mitte*, 9.22.171-172.

[20] See the criticisms of Conzelmann's epochal structure in Robinson, Jr., *Way of the Lord*, 24-30, criticisms that are attenuated somewhat in the German version (Hamburg 1964, 23ff.); also Fitzmyer, *Lk I-IX*, 182-187.

[21] *Heilige Geist*, 47 n. 1.

[22] G. Schrenk, "βιάζομαι κτλ.", *TDNT* I, 612; Hauck, *Lk*, 207.

[23] G. Friedrich, "εὐαγγελίζομαι κτλ.", *TDNT* II, 719; this he did despite taking the announcement of John's birth to constitute an intimation of messianic salvation, and the message he preached to represent 'good news'. For E. Lohmeyer, *Das Urchristentum I. Johannes der Täufer*, Göttingen 1932, 20, John the Baptist marks "die Scheide und Wende der Zeiten", his reception of the Spirit in the womb fulfils an ancient eschatological hope (p. 23), the announcement of his birth is 'good news' (p. 46).

[24] Cf. W. G. Kümmel, " 'Das Gesetz und die Propheten gehen bis Johannes' – Lukas 16,16 im Zusammenhang der heilsgeschichtlichen Theologie der Lukasschriften", *Verborum Veritatis*, Fs für G. Stählin, eds. O. Böcher, K. Haacker, Wuppertal 1970, 94-102; M. Bachmann, "Johannes der Täufer bei Lukas: Nachzügler oder Vorläufer?", *Wort in der Zeit. Neutestamentliche Studien*, Festgabe für K.H. Rengstorf, eds. W. Haubeck, M. Bachmann, Leiden 1980, 140-150; S.G. Wilson, *Luke and the Law*, SNTSMS 50: Cambridge 1983, 43-51; also Minear, "Birth Stories", 122; Wink, *Baptist*, 51-57; Dillon, *Eye-Witnesses*, 272-273 n. 117; Fitzmyer, *Lk I-IX*, 183-184; M. Klinghardt, *Gesetz und Volk Gottes*, WUNT 2.32: Tübingen 1988, 60-82.

[25] Cf. *Mitte*, 17-18; S. Schulz, *Q. Die Spruchquelle der Evangelisten*, Zürich 1972, 264-265.

him as its beginning.[26] For another, the use of the verb εὐαγγελίζεσθαι in 1,19 and 3,18 in relation to John favours his assignment to the era of the 'good news'.[27] The evidence from 16,16 is far too fragile and ambiguous to be used as a basis for a division of salvation history, and especially so, since support for such a division is significantly lacking elsewhere in Luke–Acts.[28]

If Conzelmann had used 16,16 to define the epoch of Jesus, one would have expected it to begin with 4,16 ff., 4,14 f., or 4,43 (the first explicit mention of the kingdom of God in his preaching), and to end with his ascension (cf. Acts 1,3). He used Lk 4,13 instead, taking Satan's departure from Jesus ("having completed every temptation") to mark the beginning of the epoch. His description of it as a "Satan-free age"[29] presumably conveys the notion that Jesus is no longer tempted by Satan, since it cannot indicate Satan's absence from the scene. He may be very much on the defensive, but he is certainly not absent (cf. 8,12; 10,17-18; 11,14-22; 13,11-17; Acts 5,3; 10,38).[30] Conzelmann also regarded Lk 4,16 ff. or 4,18-21 and Acts 10,38 as characterizing this age.[31]

On the basis of the first criterion and indeed on the basis of the other two also, this epoch can hardly be said to end before the ascension, since Jesus is never again tempted by Satan.[32] Haenchen, in fact, places the end of the epoch of Jesus at the ascension.[33] Conzelmann places it at Lk 22,35/36,[34] taking the view that the new set of instructions given by Jesus to his disciples marks the end of the 'age of salvation'; the disciples are again in danger of temptation (22,36).[35] At this point Conzelmann has changed perspective. It is no longer Satan's direct relationship to Jesus that is the determining factor, but Satan's relationship to the disciples, an element that had no bearing on the choice of 4,13 as the beginning of the epoch. As for Jesus, Satan returns to the attack in 22,3. But his efforts to

---

[26] Cf. Kümmel, "Gesetz", 94-102; Bachmann, "Johannes", 141-149; Wink, Baptist, 51-55; Marshall, Historian, 146; also Haenchen, Acts, 96.

[27] Cf. Schürmann, Lk I, 178-179, and there nn. 120 and 124; Schweizer, Lk, 50; Wink, Baptist, 52-53; also Friedrich, "εὐαγγελίζομαι", 719, for whom John as precursor of the Messiah is an "evangelist" whose message is "good news" and whose story is the "beginning of the Gospel"; Marshall, Historian, 146.

[28] Cf. Kümmel, "Gesetz", 99-101; Wink, Baptist, 52.55; A. N. Wilder, Eschatology and Ethics in the Teaching of Jesus, New York-London 1939, 175 n. 5.

[29] Mitte, 22.

[30] Cf. S. Brown, Apostasy and Perseverance in the Theology of Luke, AnBib 36: Rome 1969, 6-7; also J.-W. Taeger, Der Mensch und sein Heil. Studien zum Bild des Menschen und zur Sicht der Bekehrung bei Lukas, SNT 14: Gütersloh 1982, 73, and there n. 284.

[31] Mitte, 9.22 n. 2; idem, "Lukasanalyse", 32.

[32] Cf. Brown, Apostasy, 9-10.

[33] Acts, 96.

[34] Mitte, 9.74.

[35] Mitte, 9.22.74.

frustrate God's plan take on a form entirely different from that of 4,1-13. He comes not to tempt Jesus, but to facilitate the design of the Jewish leaders already intent on his life (cf. 19,47; 22,2).[36]

It is in moving from the epoch of Jesus to that of the church that the complications for Conzelmann's theory become most serious. The beginning of the latter epoch is variously placed at 22,36,[37] the passion,[38] the complex resurrection-ascension-Pentecost,[39] the ascension,[40] the exaltation[41] and Pentecost.[42] This confusion is a direct result of the lack of a clear criterion for the final epoch, but even more so of the non-convergent criteria used to delineate the various epochs of salvation history.

In the light of all this, a number of questions arise. To what epoch does the agony in the garden belong? Where does Jesus' death on the cross fit in? If the age of Jesus is the 'age of salvation', how can one justify omitting from this age the portrayal of the positive salvific value of Jesus' death in 23,39-43[43] or the resurrection and ascension?[44] Is it not an unjustifiable impoverishment to reduce the salvific aspect of the epoch of Jesus to the absence of Satan, as Conzelmann appears to do,[45] since Jesus' salvation, as Fitzmyer points out, brings defeat of evil in all its forms, whether physical, psychic or satanic?[46] True, Conzelmann also regards 4,18-19 and Acts 10,38 as characterizing the age of Jesus. But precisely for this reason the omission from the age of salvation of Lk 23,39-43, for example, is difficult to understand.

Conzelmann's position, in reality not far removed from that of von Baer, leaves itself open to further criticisms. The beginning proposed by him for the epoch of Jesus coincides with the first manifestation of the power of the Spirit in Jesus' public life. It is, in fact, the gift of the Spirit that enables Jesus to defeat Satan (cf. 4,1; Acts 10,38) and bring about

---

[36] The thrust of 4,13 which has Satan leave of his own accord, not dismissed as in Mt 4,10, is that he is free to return when the propitious moment arrives to attempt once more to thwart God's plan. Jesus' presence as such does not eliminate the danger of temptation for his disciples (cf. 8,12; 11,4c; 22,46).

[37] *Mitte*, 9; idem, "Lukasanalyse", 32.

[38] *Mitte*, 9.

[39] *Mitte*, 167.

[40] *Mitte*, 9.190; cf. Haenchen, *Acts*, 96.

[41] *Mitte*, 167.

[42] Cf. *Mitte*, 9.22.190-191.195, and 195 n. 1.

[43] On Lk 23,39-43 see A. Vanhoye, "Structure et théologie des récits de la Passion dans les évangiles synoptiques", *NRT* 89 (1967) 161; Rasco, *Lucas*, 133-134; Rese, *Motive*, 157-158; S. A. Panimolle, "Il valore salvifico della morte di Gesù negli scritti di Luca", *Sangue e Antropologia Biblica* 1.11, ed. F. Vattioni, CSSC 1.II: Rome 1981, 669-671.

[44] Panimolle, *Discorso* (Vol. III, Bologna 1978), 130-132; idem, "Morte di Gesù", 661-664; A. George, "Le sens de la mort de Jésus pour Luc", *RB* 80 (1973) 213-215.

[45] *Mitte*, 9.168; idem, "Lukasanalyse", 21.

[46] *Lk I-IX*, 187. Cf. Lk 4,18-21; Acts 10,36-38.

the 'salvific Satan-free age' of Conzelmann.[47] An age defined in these terms should include the rest of Jesus' life on earth. And since the Spirit equips the disciples for their role as witnesses to Jesus and his message in Acts, should not their situation vis-à-vis Satan in the 'time of the church' be somewhat similar, as indeed Lk 10,17-19 suggests?[48]

Conzelmann, like von Baer, takes the Spirit to determine Jesus' unique position in salvation history by virtue of the fact that it rests on him alone in this central period.[49] But if the Spirit does determine this situation, then one would expect the period of Jesus to begin with his conception through the Spirit, or at least with the epiphany at the baptism,[50] and to conclude with the ascension. Conzelmann more or less ignores 1,35, making do with a brief reference,[51] while he does not discuss 3,22 from this point of view.[52] One may well inquire as to which epoch the baptism and the events surrounding it belong, particularly since the baptism is regarded by Conzelmann as a stage in Jesus' ministry[53] and one which is fundamental for Jesus' messianic consciousness.[54]

Finally, the epoch of the church for Conzelmann is really that of the Spirit and begins at Pentecost, though even then this epoch is not to be regarded as an eschatological epoch.[55] It is true that the manifestation of the Spirit at Pentecost is communitarian and as such to be distinguished from its manifestations in the infancy narrative. But the individual manifestations of the Spirit in the latter are so frequent and so characteristic of this point in time that a relationship between the two is difficult to deny.[56] Von Baer resolved the problem of the Spirit's manifestation in the infancy narrative in his own way, but Conzelmann avoided the issue, content to dismiss the references to the Spirit in 1,17 and 35 as special cases.[57]

---

[47] Cf. *Mitte*, 168: "Die Geistbegabung realisiert sich in der Begegnung mit dem Satan. Dieser muss weichen. Damit ist der Heilscharakter der anbrechenden, satansfreien Zeit konstituiert; also 181.

[48] Cf. G. Baumbach, *Das Verständnis des Bösen in den synoptischen Evangelien*, TA 19: Berlin 1963, 183: "denn die Satansaussagen der Apostelgeschichte dienen — ähnlich wie die zwischen Luk. 4,13 und 22,3 — dazu, den Sieg des in den Missionaren und der Gemeinde wirksamen Heiligen Geistes über den Satan zu demonstrieren"; see Maddox, *Luke-Acts*, 143.

[49] Cf. von Baer, *Heilige Geist*, 45.71; Conzelmann, *Mitte*, 167.171-172.

[50] Von Baer, *Heilige Geist*, 48-49 and 59, takes both events to mark the beginning of the epoch of Jesus.

[51] *Mitte*, 171 n. 2.

[52] Cf. *Mitte*, 167.

[53] *Mitte*, 180-181.

[54] *Mitte*, 50-51.

[55] Cf. *Mitte*, 87.167.

[56] See pp. 125-126 below.

[57] *Mitte*, 171 n. 2.

1.2 *Modifications of Conzelmann's Theory*

Attempts have been made to refine Conzelmann's structure in the light of difficulties that have been noted from time to time. Tatum endeavoured to show that the three-part division, and particularly the epoch of Israel, obtains even when account is taken of the infancy narrative's theology.[58] Like von Baer he distinguished between the prophetic Spirit operative in the case of John, Zachary, Elizabeth and Simeon and the creative Spirit operative in the conception of Jesus (1,35).[59] He took the former to recall the nature and work of the Spirit in old Israel, and to characterize the period in salvation history before the beginning of Jesus' ministry as the epoch of Israel.[60]

Haenchen preferred to see the whole of Jesus' ministry on earth as constituting the 'middle of time' between the periods of the law and the prophets and that of the church.[61] Wink proposed the three-part division of the period of the promise (the law and the prophets), the period of fulfilment, to which John belongs, and the period of the church.[62] Arguing along the same lines as von Baer, Dunn took John's ministry to belong entirely to the old covenant, the epoch of Israel, and the new age to begin with the descent of the Spirit at Jesus' baptism.[63] Fitzmyer proposes a three-part division comprising the periods of Israel (from creation to the appearance of the Baptist: 1,5–3,1), Jesus (from the baptism of John to the ascension: 3,2–24,51) and the church (from the ascension to the parousia: 24,52–Acts 1,3–28,31).[64]

1.3 *The Problem*

None of the modifications of Conzelmann's theory succeeds in removing the real problem which is that of the three-epoch structure of salvation history itself, particularly the epoch of Israel or the Old Testament. This is not surprising since all these modifications were made within Conzelmann's framework, and consequently within the framework originally proposed by von Baer. Herein lies the kernel of the problem.

Von Baer based his three-epoch structure of salvation history on his view of the Spirit's role in Luke's writings. He argued that since the Spirit which is manifested in the case of John, Zachary, Elizabeth and Simeon is the Spirit of prophecy, it links these figures to the epoch of the Old

---

[58] "Luke I-II", 184-195.
[59] "Luke I-II", 187.
[60] "Luke I-II", 186-190.
[61] *Acts*, 96.
[62] *Baptist*, 55.
[63] J. D. G. Dunn, *Baptism in the Holy Spirit*, SBT II.15: London 1970, 31-32.
[64] *Lk I-IX*, 185.

Testament of which it is characteristic. But von Baer overlooked the fact that the Spirit in Luke–Acts, whether in the case of John, Zachary, Elizabeth, Simeon, Jesus (cf. Lk 4,18 f.), the disciples at Pentecost (cf. Acts 2,17), or other cases in Acts, is primarily the Spirit of prophecy.[65] His division of salvation history on the basis of the different levels of the manifestation of the Spirit is without foundation, particularly the proposed epoch of the Old Testament. There is no reason why the Spirit of prophecy should be taken to link John, Zachary and others to the epoch of the Old Testament or Israel, not even by virtue of its individual manifestations.[66] If anything, this renewed activity of the Spirit, as we shall see below, signals the arrival of the eschatological age, the age of fulfilment.

1.4 The Spirit: Eschatological Sign

A number of Old Testament texts, notably Is 32,15, 44,3-5, Ez 36,26-27 and Joel 2,28-32 (3,1-5 LXX), present the general gift of the Spirit to the people of God as characteristic of the eschatological age.[67] The expectation of a Spirit-endowed eschatological figure, be it royal or prophetic (cf. Is 11,2; 42,1; 61,1), is also to be found in the Old Testament.[68] So too is that of a Spirit-endowed eschatological precursor in the shape of a returning Elijah (cf. Mal 3,23; Sir 48,10.12; 2 Kgs 2,9-14), an expectation attested also by the gospels (cf. Mt 11,14; Mk 9,11-13; Lk 9,8.19).

In the light of these expectations it may be claimed that the outpouring of the Spirit on 'all flesh', proleptically realised at Pentecost, represents a clear eschatological event. The phenomena accompanying this event,[69] possible allusions in the narrative to the new covenant offered again to 'all Israel',[70] the insertion in Joel's prophecy of the

---

[65] Cf. de la Potterie, "L'onction", 229-235; Lampe, God as Spirit, 65.

[66] As against the communal manifestation prophesied in Joel 2,28-29 (cf. Acts 2,17-18).

[67] Cf. R. Albertz, C. Westermann, "rūaḥ", THAT II, eds. E. Jenni, C. Westermann, Munich 1976, 750-752; W. Bieder, "πνεῦμα κτλ.", TDNT VI, 370; E. Sjöberg, "πνεῦμα κτλ.", TDNT VI, 384-385; Lampe, God as Spirit, 63; Lentzen-Deis, Taufe Jesu, 140-170; Schubert, "Luke 24", 178.

[68] Cf. Lentzen-Deis, Taufe Jesu, 144-146.

[69] Cf. Acts 2,2-4: ... ἄφνω ἐκ τοῦ οὐρανοῦ ἦχος ... πνοῆς βιαίας ... γλῶσσαι ὡσεὶ πυρός, ... ἤρξαντο λαλεῖν ἑτέραις γλώσσαις. On their OT background see Weiser, Apg 1-12, 83-84; Schneider, Apg I, 246-247, and there nn. 33-36; J. Dupont, "La nouvelle Pentecôte: Ac 2,1-11", ASeign 30 (1970) 30-34.

[70] Cf. J.A. Fitzmyer, "The Ascension of Christ and Pentecost", TS 45 (1984) 432-434; R. Le Déaut, "Pentecôte et tradition juive", ASeign 51 (1963) 22-38, esp. 33-38; Bovon, Luc, 239; but see J. Kremer, Pfingstbericht und Pfingstgeschehen. Eine exegetische Untersuchung zu Apg 2,1-13, SBS 63-64: Stuttgart 1973, 264.

phrase ἐν ταῖς ἐσχάταις ἡμέραις,[71] and the continuation of the citation as far as Joel 2,32a (3,5a LXX), a verse that is echoed in the preaching of Acts 9,14.21 and 22,16, all point towards the eschatological nature of the age that is present.

It may be further claimed that the generalized gift of Acts 2,4 (καὶ ἐπλήσθησαν πάντες πνεύματος ἁγίου) and the fulfilment of Joel's prophecy (cf. Acts 2,18: ... ἐπὶ τοὺς δούλους μου ... τὰς δούλας μου ... ἐκχεῶ ἀπὸ τοῦ πνεύματός μου, καὶ προφητεύσουσιν) are anticipated in the infancy narrative. Attention is drawn to this linguistically in the case of Elizabeth and John (καὶ ἐπλήσθη πνεύματος ἁγίου ἡ Ἐλισάβετ: 1,41; cf. 1,15),[72] Simeon (καὶ πνεῦμα ἦν ἅγιον ἐπ᾽ αὐτόν: 2,25; δοῦλον: 2,29) and Zachary (ἐπλήσθη πνεύματος ἁγίου καὶ ἐπροφήτευσεν: 1,67). Moreover, Simeon's inspired announcement of the presence of salvation in the person of Jesus (cf. 2,25-32) anticipates Jesus' own message in 4,16-21 and that of Peter and Paul in Acts (cf. 2,21; 4,12; 13,46-47; 28,28).[73] Simeon anticipates them also in his announcement of the universal aspect of this salvation (2,30-32).[74] In praising God for raising up 'a horn of salvation in the house of David' (1,69) and for fulfilling the words of the prophets (1,70), the inspired utterances of Zachary likewise anticipate apostolic preaching (cf. Acts 2,30; 3,18.21; 13,23; 15,14-17).

On the individual level Lk 3,22 and especially 4,18-21 (cf. 7,22) represent Jesus as the expected Spirit-endowed eschatological figure of Is 42,1 and 61,1. The description of John's role in terms of the eschatological role of the returning Elijah (cf. Lk 1,17) and the fact that he is equipped by the Spirit for his role suggest that John, too, is a Spirit-endowed eschatological figure. In the light of all this it is difficult to escape the conclusion that the activity of the Spirit which is so characteristic of Luke's infancy narrative marks the advent of the eschatological age.

---

[71] Haenchen's view of the non-eschatological nature of the third epoch, similar to that of Conzelmann, leads him to prefer the reading from B (μετὰ ταῦτα); see his "Schriftzitate und Textüberlieferung in der Apostelgeschichte", ZTK 51 (1954) 162, and Acts, 179. Conzelmann himself is more cautious (cf. Mitte, 87, and there n. 2); cf. Schneider, Apg I, 268 n. 35.

[72] Note the similarity between the Spirit's activity in the case of John and at Pentecost. John is equipped with the Spirit from his mother's womb for the mission of precursor for which he was destined (cf. Lk 1,15-17). The group of disciples, and especially the twelve, are equipped with the Spirit at Pentecost for the mission entrusted to them by the risen Christ (cf. Lk 24,47-48; Acts 1,8). Both John and the disciples preach Jesus, albeit from different perspectives, and both begin their missions on receipt of the Spirit (cf. Lk 1,41-44; Acts 2,14ff.).

[73] Cf. Schürmann, Lk I, 124: "er gehört somit schon in die Reihe der "christlichen" Propheten (vgl. 1,41-45.67-79; 2,36.38), deren Aufgabe es ist, im Geiste Gottes den Christus zu erkennen und zu verkünden"; also Schubert, "Luke 24", 178.

[74] Cf. Fitzmyer, Lk I-IX, 422.

The theme of the Spirit in Luke-Acts does indicate a structure of salvation history, but not that of von Baer or Conzelmann. It indicates rather the two-part scheme of promise and fulfilment. This fulfilment is celebrated in the canticles of Mary (cf. 1,54-55), Zachary (cf. 1,69-70. 72-73) and Simeon (cf. 2,30-32),[75] and it encompasses the 'times' of John (cf. 1,17; 3,4-6; 7,27),[76] Jesus (cf. 4,18-21; 18,31-33; 22,37; 24,26-27.44-46),[77] and the disciples or the church (cf. Lk 24,47; Acts 2,17-21; 10,43; 13,46-47; 15,14-17).[78] The Spirit itself is a part and a sign of this time.[79]

Within this time of fulfilment a further structure is visible. John is equipped with the Spirit from the womb for his prophesied eschatological role of precursor, a role that begins in the womb (cf. Lk 1,15-17.41-44) and that ends with his imprisonment and violent death (3,20; 9,9). Through his conception by the Spirit Jesus is equipped for his prophesied mission as the bearer of the good news of salvation, indeed of salvation itself (4,18-21). As the Christ, the one anointed by the Spirit in a unique way (cf. 4,18.41), his path to glory is destined to be through suffering and death in accordance with the divine plan enunciated in the scriptures (cf. 24,26-27.46; Acts 2,23-36; 3,13-18).

Endowed with the Spirit, poured forth by the exalted Christ (Acts 2,33), the disciples are equipped to carry out their role of proclaiming the kingdom of God and 'the things concerning the Lord Jesus', to heal and cast out demons, to preach repentance in Jesus' name to all the nations in fulfilment of the scriptures (cf. Lk 24,46-47; Acts 13,47). They too are ready to face imprisonment (cf. 4,3-21; 5,18.28-32.40-41; 20,22-24; 21,11.13) and even death (6,8-7,60; 21,13) in their ministries.[80]

---

[75] Recalled in the canticles are the promises to Abraham (1,54-55.72-73; cf. Gen 17,7; 18,18; 22,16-17; 26,3; Ex 2,24; Ps 105,8-11; 106,45; Mic 7,20) and to David (1,69-70; cf. 2 Sam 7,9-16; Ps 132,17); cf. Brown, *Birth*, 358-359.386-387.

[76] He belongs to the time of fulfilment insofar as he is the Lord's forerunner; cf. Mal 3,1.23-24; also Laurentin, *Luc I-II*, 34-36; Wink, *Baptist*, 54-55; Brown, *Birth*, 276-279; Schürmann, *Lk* I, 34-36.

[77] See also 1,32-33 (cf. 2 Sam 7,9-16; Is 9,5-6); 7,22; Acts 2,22-35; 3,18; 8,32-35; 13,23; cf. Laurentin, *Luc I-II*, 71-72; Brown, *Birth*, 310-311; Fitzmyer, *Lk I-IX*, 338-339; Legrand, *L'Annonce*, 156.

[78] See also Lk 2,30-32 and the allusions there to Is 49,6, 52,10 and 40,5 LXX; Lk 3,6; Acts 28,30.

[79] The activity of the Spirit in equipping John, Jesus and the disciples for their respective roles in salvation history, provides a strong unifying link between Luke and Acts.

[80] Controversy surrounds Luke's view of the duration of the third period, that of the Spirit. It has been discussed at length in the recent work of Maddox, *Luke-Acts*, 100-157; cf. Kümmel, *Introduction*, 144-145; E. Rasco, "Hans Conzelmann y la 'Historia Salutis'. A propósito de 'Die Mitte der Zeit' y 'Die Apostelgeschichte'", *Greg* 46 (1965) 308-309.

The time of fulfilment, therefore, comprises the 'times' of John, Jesus and the disciples or the church, and the Spirit equips each for his or their particular role in salvation history. It is not John who forms a bridge or stands as a transitional figure between the old and the new, the time of the promise and its fulfilment. This role is filled by the figures of Zachary and Elizabeth, Mary and Joseph, the shepherds, Simeon and Anna — the faithful ones in Israel. They have lived with the promise. Now, inspired by the Spirit, they witness the beginning of its fulfilment and celebrate the σήμερον, the νῦν of salvation.

1.5 *The New Age*

There are other indications in the infancy narrative of the arrival of the time of fulfilment. The marvellous nature of the events surrounding the conceptions and births of John and Jesus — the signs, the angelic appearances, the messages, the canticles of praise, the sheer amount of space devoted to their description, all suggest a new intervention of God in salvation history. A mosaic of identifiable reminiscences of Old Testament figures and events, particularly in the first two scenes, recalls the familiar pattern of God's interventions in the past on behalf of his people.[81] In so doing it characterizes the present intervention not only as greater than these, but also as the decisive one inaugurating the eschatological age.[82] This is confirmed by the name of the heavenly messenger (cf. Dan 8-10), by other striking reminiscences of the text of Daniel (cf. 1,10-11: Dan 9,20-21; 1,19: Dan 10,11)[83] and especially by the manifestation in the inspired utterances of Elizabeth, Zachary and Simeon of the long promised gift of prophecy (cf. Acts 2,17-18; Joel 2,28-29).

---

[81] These allusions recall not just miraculous conceptions such as that of Isaac but divine interventions involving other individuals such as Noah (cf. 1,6; Gen 7,1), Abraham (cf. 1,7b.18; Gen 16,11; 15,8), Gideon, Moses and Jeremiah (cf. 1,26-38; Judg 6,11-24; Ex 3,1-4,17; Jer 1,4-10), Samson (cf. 1,15bd; Judg 13,4-5; 16,17), Elisha (cf. 1,15c; Sir 48,12), and so on; cf. F. Ó Fearghail, "The Imitation of the Septuagint in Luke's Infancy Narrative", *PIBA* 12 (1989) 57-78.

[82] The imitation of the language and style of the Septuagint intensifies the recall of God's past salvific interventions by recreating the language and style, the atmosphere and colouring of the bible that recounts them. On the much debated 'biblical' atmosphere and colouring in the infancy narrative see Cadbury, *Making*, 122-123.221-225; E. Plümacher, *Lukas als hellenistischer Schriftsteller. Studien zur Apostelgeschichte*, SUNT 9: Göttingen 1972, 28-72; Brown, *Birth*, 245-247; P. Winter, "The Cultural Background of the Narrative in Luke I and II", *JQR* 45 (1954-55) 238-242; Schmid, *Lk*, 85; Lohfink, *Sammlung*, 21; Fitzmyer, *Lk I-IX*, 312; Ó Fearghail, "Imitation", 58-60.70-75.

[83] Cf. Brown, *Birth*, 270-271, where these and other possible parallels are given; also Fitzmyer, *Lk I-IX*, 315-316.

The dawning of this age is greeted by what Bultmann called "eschatological joy".[84] Through the agency of Zachary, Elizabeth and their neighbours, this joy greets the birth of John (cf. 1,14.58.64) who himself rejoices at the presence of the one whose way he is to prepare (cf. 1,44). But it is on Jesus that this "eschatological joy" is really concentrated. Elizabeth (1,42-45), Mary (1,28.47-55), Zachary (1,68-79), Simeon (2,28) and Anna (2,38) all participate in it, as do the shepherds. Indeed 'all the people' (cf. 2,10) are destined to participate in the cosmic joy that greets Jesus' birth (cf. 2,14).[85] The atmosphere of joy and peace (cf. 2,14) that pervades the infancy narrative is a fitting setting for the dawn of the messianic age.[86]

The two terms νῦν and σήμερον highlight the advent of the eschatological age. Because Mary has become the mother of the Lord, from now (νῦν) on all generations will call her blessed.[87] Since Simeon has seen the salvation of God, the glory of Israel, the light of the Gentiles, he can now (νῦν) die in peace.[88] For the shepherds who hear the 'good news' of Jesus' birth, that day (σήμερον) marks the realization for them of their warmest hopes and expectations.[89] At Nazareth, the congregation in the synagogue hears that the promise of Isaiah is fulfilled in the person and message of Jesus 'today' (σήμερον), a 'today' that is programmatic for the new eschatological age.[90]

---

[84] R. Bultmann, "ἀγαλλιάομαι κτλ.", *TDNT* I, 20. Cf. P. J. Bernadicou, "The Lucan Theology of Joy", *ScEs* 25 (1973) 79-81; A. Weiser, "ἀγαλλιάω κτλ.", *EWNT* I, 18; J. P. Martin, "Luke 1:39-47", *Int* 36 (1982) 396-397.

[85] Thus anticipating the joy of the believers of Acts 2,46-47; see also Acts 8,39; 13,48; 16,34.

[86] Cf. Fitzmyer, *Lk I-IX*, 409; also Schürmann, *Lk* I, 93; Rengstorf, *Lk*, 41-42.

[87] The phrase ἀπὸ τοῦ νῦν in 1,48 refers to the present moment or the immediate future (cf. Lk 2,23; 5,10; 12,52; 22.18.69; Acts 18,6), not "the coming inauguration of a new age of salvation", as Fitzmyer, *Lk I-IX*, 367, holds. Elizabeth is the first of a long line to ring Mary's praises (1,42-45).

[88] On the use of νῦν in the rest of Luke, and especially in the passion, see G. Ferraro, "Il Termine 'ora' nei vangeli sinottici", *RivB* 21 (1973) 383-400.

[89] Cf. Brown, *Birth*, 402: "*sēmeron* catches Luke's sense of realised eschatology"; L. Legrand, "L'Évangile aux Bergers. Essai sur le genre littéraire de Luc, II,8-20", *RB* 75 (1968) 167-168; Grundmann, *Lk*, 83.

[90] Given that it is part of the programmatic Nazareth scene. The 'today' of Lk 4,21 indicates the presence of salvation, just as it does in the case of Zacchaeus (19,5.9) and the good thief (23,43). The occurrences of the adverb in association with the theme of salvation in 2,11 and especially in 23,43 pose a major problem for a 'period of salvation' going from 4,13 to 22,3.35. Cf. B. Prete, "Prospettive messianiche nell'espressione *sēmeron* del Vangelo di Luca", *Il Messianismo*, Atti della XVIII Settimana Biblica, Brescia 1966, 272-275; Schürmann, *Lk* I, 233; Untergassmair, *Kreuzweg*, 203.

1.6 *Passing of the Temple Cult*

Another aspect of the infancy narrative that suggests the dawning of a new age is its attitude towards the temple cult. It is well recognized that the temple and its cult are portrayed in a positive light in Lk 1-2 which is framed by temple scenes. The announcement of John's birth is made in the context of the temple cult. Jesus is presented to God in the temple, the decreed purificatory offering is made, and Jesus is brought there as a youth of twelve on the feast of the Passover. Nevertheless there are elements in the narrative that foreshadow the passing of the old cultic order.

The extraordinary events surrounding the announcement of John's conception and birth — the appearance of the angel Gabriel in the sanctuary of the temple at the solemn moment of the incense offering, the ominous delay of Zachary in the sanctuary (1,21),[91] his dumbness on leaving there and his consequent inability to pronounce the priestly blessing over the waiting and astonished people[92] — all point in this direction.

The implied comparison between the first two scenes noted above supports this view. The cultic centre of Judaism is relativized as a place of contact with God, as the announcement of Jesus' birth, in contrast to that of John, takes place far removed from Jerusalem. And Zachary's blessing of peace (cf. Num 6,24-26) gives way to the peace that comes through the Christ-event (cf. Lk 2,14; 24,50-51).[93]

The presentation in the temple may provide another element foreshadowing the passing of the old cultic order. For whatever about Luke's lack of clarity in 2,22-24,[94] he does appear to have a purpose in mind. According to Ex 13,2 the dedication of the first-born was enjoined on the Israelites by God, and it was the first-born that performed the

---

[91] Cf. *m.Yom.* 5,1, with regard to the high priest on the Day of Atonement: "... in the outer space he prayed a short prayer. But he did not prolong his prayer lest he put Israel in terror"; tr. by H. Danby, *The Mishnah*, London 167; cf. *b.Yom.* 53b.

[92] Cf. *m.Tam.* 7,2; Sir 50,20. A 'priestly blessing', however, is imparted at the gospel's conclusion (24,50-51); see n. 93.

[93] Note that Jesus is portrayed in Lk 24,50-51 in a typically priestly stance with arms upraised "to bless" (cf. P. van Stempvoort, "The Interpretation of the Ascension in Luke and Acts", *NTS* 5 (1958-59) 34-35; Grundmann, *Lk*, 453-454; J. Coppens, "Le Messianisme sacerdotal dans les écrits du Nouveau Testament", *La Venue du Messie. Messianisme et Eschatologie*, ed. É. Massaux, RB VI: Louvain 1962, 109; A. Vanhoye, *Prêtres anciens, prêtre nouveau selon le Nouveau Testament*, Paris 1980, 75-76, and 75 n. 52). Only on two occasions in the OT does a person "lift his hands" to bless, and each time it is the high priest at the conclusion of a sacrifice (Lev 9,22; Sir 50,20; cf. Vanhoye, *Prêtres*, 76). Here it is Sir 50,20 that is recalled (cf. Lk 24,52-53 and Sir 50,21-22).

[94] See the attempts at clarification in Brown, *Birth*, 447-451, and Fitzmyer, *Lk I-IX*, 420-421.

cultic service before it was taken over by the Aaronites and Levites (cf. Num 3,11-13; 8,15-19).[95] Even after this they were considered to belong to God and had to be redeemed (cf. Num 18,15-16). Samuel was not redeemed but was presented to the Lord for service in the temple and was eventually left there (cf. 1 Sam 1,22.24-28; 2,11.18; 3,1).[96]

As in the case of Samuel, Jesus is presented to the Lord in the temple and there is no mention of a redemption. Unlike Samuel he never returns there in any cultic capacity. There is, however, a deliberate citation of Ex 13,2 in Lk 2,23. In the light of the equally deliberate, and for the reader somewhat pleonastic, reference to Jesus' first-born status in 2,7, it is not inconceivable that in 2,22-24 Luke recalls the situation prior to the Levitical priesthood in order to foreshadow its passing. The priestly blessing of this first-born on the Mount of Olives (cf. 24,50-52), opposite and in sight of the temple sanctuary, may be interpreted in a similar vein, particularly since it contrasts with the lack of a blessing on Zachary's part in the gospel's opening scene.[97]

It is true the temple and its cult are presented in a mainly positive light throughout both volumes,[98] although those most intimately associated with them are certainly not (cf. 19,47; 20,19; 22,2.4.50-54.66; 23,13-18; 24,20; Acts 4,1-21; 5,17-40; 7,51-53; 9,1-2; 22,5; 23,2; 24,1; 26,10.12). However, Jesus' sayings in Lk 13,35[99] and 21,5-7.20-24, Stephen's strong words before the Sanhedrin (cf. Acts 7,47-50.55-56),[100]

---

[95] Cf. Philo, *De Sacr.* §§ 118-120; *Tg. Ps.-Jon.* Ex 24,5. On the tradition associated with Reuben's loss of this privilege of the first-born see *Gen R* 98,4; 99,6; *Tg.* 1 Chr 5,1-2; *Tg. Neof.* 1 Gen 49,3; Add. 27031 Gen 49,3 (cf. R. Le Déaut, *Targum du Pentateuque* I, SC 256: Paris 1978, 434-435).

[96] Samuel is given a Levitical ancestry in 1 Chr 6,12-13. In 1 Sam 2,11 and 18 he is presented as carrying out a priestly activity, the verb λειτουργέω being used for it in the LXX; cf. P. Kyle McCarter, Jr., *1 Samuel*, AB 8: Garden City 1980, 82. The first-born sons of priests and Levites did not have to be redeemed according to *m.Bekh.* 2,1.

[97] On the priestly blessing of Lk 24,50-51 see n. 93 above. Apropos of the scene of the blessing and its relationship to the temple it should be noted that the ceremony of the red heifer took place on the Mount of Olives, in the sight of the temple sanctuary. The eastern wall of the temple was lower than the others so that the priest carrying out the rite should be able to look directly into the entrance of the sanctuary when sprinkling the blood in the direction of the Holy of Holies; cf. *m.Par.* 3,6-9; 4,2; *m.Midd.* 2,4.

[98] The temple is the goal of Jesus' journey to Jerusalem (cf. 19,45a), and he teaches there at length after cleansing it (19,45b-21,38). The disciples, after the ascension, are shown continually in the temple praising God (24,53). Again in Acts there is a positive attitude towards the temple (cf. 2,46; 3,1.11; 5,12.20-21.25; 21,26-27; 25,8). Cf. F.D. Weinert, "Luke, Stephen, and the Temple in Luke-Acts", *BTB* 17 (1987) 88-90.

[99] Cf. Schulz, *Spruchquelle*, 356 n. 230; Grundmann, *Lk*, 289; Ernst, *Lk*, 434.

[100] Cf. Weiser, *Apg 1-12*, 187; M. H. Scharlemann, *Stephen: A Singular Saint*, AnBib 34: Rome 1968, 104-107. Like the temple, with which it is intimately linked (cf. Lk 2,22-52; 4,9; 24,52-53), Jerusalem also loses its central position in Jewish expectation (cf. Is 2,2-3; 60,1–62,12; 66,18-20), a loss that is foreshadowed in Lk 19,41-44, 21,20-24, 24,47

the splitting of the temple veil before Jesus' death[101] and the breaking of bread in the houses (cf. Acts 2,42.46; 20,7) [102] represent elements which together appear to foreshadow the eventual demise of temple and cult. The note sounded in Lk 1,5-4,44 continues to sound, if somewhat faintly at times, in the rest of Luke's work.

Throughout Luke-Acts the evangelist works with the scheme of promise and fulfilment. Again and again in 1,5-4,44 he underlines this fulfilment and portrays in various ways how God's decisive intervention in salvation history ushers in the new, eschatological age. From this point of view 1,5-4,44 can be seen to have an introductory role in the work as a whole.

2. Person of Jesus

Many of the elements that go to make up the portrait of Jesus which is found in 1,5-4,44 play a part in the rest of Luke-Acts.[103] This is true of the titles that are introduced here[104] and of much of the information concerning Jesus' identity and mission found in angelic communications, inspired prophecies and in the words of John and Jesus. By examining the portrait of Jesus found in these chapters and noting how it relates to that of the remainder of the work one should be in a position to describe more clearly the role of these chapters in Luke-Acts. Let us look first of all at various aspects of the presentation of the person of Jesus here.

2.1 Jesus as King

In the announcements of his birth in 1,26-38 and 2,1-21 Jesus is presented above all as a royal figure. Davidic associations range from the throne of David that is to be his for ever (1,32-33)[105] to the city of his birth (2,4.11), to the lineage of Joseph, Mary's betrothed (1,27; 2,4; 3,31), to the shepherds who recall the shepherd-figure of the youthful David (cf. 1 Sam 16,11; 17,15.28.34).[106]

---

and Acts 1,8. It may already be foreshadowed in the contrast and implicit comparison between Lk 1,5-25 and 1,26-38.

[101] Cf. Godet, *Lc* II, 423; Plummer, *Lk*, 538 n. 1; A. Casalegno, *Gesù e il Tempio. Studio redazionale su Luca – Atti*, Brescia 1984, 131.

[102] Cf. Casalegno, *Tempio*, 204-205.

[103] There are personal details here that do not play a part in the narrative proper, as for instance the names of Mary and Joseph, Jesus' circumcision, his kinship with John.

[104] On the titles of Jesus in Luke-Acts see Fitzmyer, *Lk I-IX*, 197-219; George, *Études*, 215-282.

[105] Cf. A. George, "La royauté de Jésus", *Études*, 264; K. Berger, "Die königlichen Messiastraditionen des Neuen Testaments", *NTS* 20 (1973-74) 38.

[106]. Cf. Schürmann, *Lk* I, 108; Fitzmyer, *Lk I-IX*, 395.

The implicit contrast drawn in Lk 2,1-21 between the child wrapped in swaddling clothes and laid in a manger (2,6) and the ruler of the 'world', Caesar Augustus (2,1), points to Jesus' kingship being of a different order.[107] On the one hand there is the political saviour[108] who brings peace to a world[109] for which his birthday is the beginning of the 'good news';[110] on the other, Jesus, whose birth represents good news of great joy for all the people (2,10), the true saviour (2,11)[111] who truly brings peace to the world (2,14).

The title Χριστός, the most important of the titles attributed to Jesus,[112] may also indicate royal status.[113] In the Old Testament anointing is associated with royal (cf. 1 Sam 24,7),[114] prophetic (cf. 1 Kgs 19,16)[115] and priestly figures (cf. Ex 29,7),[116] and likewise in Qumran (cf. 11QMelch 18;[117] 1QS 9,11[118]), if 1QSa 2,14.20 refers to a royal figure.[119]

---

[107] Cf. Wis 7,4-5; Is 1,3; Jer 14,8; also C. H. Giblin, "Reflections on the Sign of the Manger", *CBQ* 29 (1967) 100; Brown, *Birth*, 418-420; Fitzmyer, *Lk I-IX*, 395.

[108] In the Myra inscription Augustus was hailed as God, ruler of the earth and sea, benefactor and saviour of the whole world (τὸν εὐεργέτην καὶ σωτῆρα τοῦ σύνπαντος κόσμου· *IGRR* III,719; III,721 speaks in similar terms of Tiberius Caesar).

[109] On the Pax Augusta see *Res Gestae Divi Augustae* 11,12-45 (*IGRR* II,719); tr. in C. K. Barrett, *The New Testament Background: Selected Documents*, London 1956, 2-4; see also Philo, *Leg. ad Gaium* § 309.

[110] Cf. Ditt., *OGIS* II,458, II,40-41: ἦρξεν δὲ τῶι κόσμωι τῶν δι' αὐτὸν εὐαγγελίων ἡ γενέθλιος τοῦ θεοῦ... (9 B.C.) — the Priene inscription.

[111] On σωτήρ see Fitzmyer, *Lk I-IX*, 197.

[112] Cf. *Lk I-IX*, 197.

[113] Derived from the verb "to anoint" (χρίειν: mšḥ), the term signifies "the anointed one"; Acts 4,27, 10,38, Lk 4,18 and 4,41 testify to its etymological force for Luke; cf. Grundmann, "χρίω κτλ.", *TDNT* IX, 494-495; W. C. van Unnik, "Jesus the Christ", *NTS* 8 (1961-62) 104-105; A. S. van der Woude, "χρίω κτλ.", *TDNT* IX, 509-510 (on Qumran, 517-520); M. de Jonge, "χρίω κτλ.", *TDNT* IX, 511-517.

[114] Also 1 Sam 26,9; 2 Sam 1,14.16; 19,21; Is 45,1; Sir 48,8a; cf. F. Hesse, "χρίω κτλ.", *TDNT* IX, 498-501.

[115] Also Is 61,1; Sir 48,8b. The prophet Elisha was installed not by anointing but by Elijah handing him his mantle (cf. 1 Kgs 19,20) so that Sir 48,8b is to be understood in a metaphorical sense; likewise the anointing of Is 61,1; see M. de Jonge, "The use of the word "anointed" in the time of Jesus", *NT* 8 (1966) 135 n. 3; de la Potterie, "L'onction", 225.

[116] Also 40,13; Lev 4,5; 8,12; 10,7; Num 3,3; Sir 45,15; cf. Hesse, "χρίω", 498-501.

[117] Cf. M. de Jonge, A.S. van der Woude, "11Q Melchizedek and the New Testament", *NTS* 12 (1965-66) 306-307. Note that the prophets are called "the anointed of his holy spirit" in CD 2,12, and "the anointed" in CD 6,1 and 1QM 11,7.

[118] Cf. K. G. Kuhn, "The Two Messiahs of Aaron and Israel", *The Scrolls and the New Testament*, ed. K. Stendahl, New York 1957, 55-57; I. Moraldi, *I Manoscritti di Qumran*, Turin 1971, 188-189 (note). Kuhn also points to the expectation of royal and priestly messiahs in the *Testaments of the Twelve Patriarchs*, and the association of 'anointing' and the priestly figure in *Test. Levi* 17,2-3 (pp. 57-58).

[119] Cf. van der Woude, "χρίω", 518; Moraldi, *Qumran*, 189 (note). It is found on a number of occasions in the Psalms of Solomon (17,32; 18: title; 18,5.7) and particularly in

In a number of Qumran texts the anointed one may exhibit characteristics of more than one of these.[120] In all these cases, however, it is the context that determines the nature of the anointed figure.[121]

In Lk 1,5-4,44 the term Χριστός is found in 2,11.26, 3,15 and 4,41, while its cognate verb is found in 4,18. The latter text along with Acts 4,27 and 10,38 speaks of an anointing with the Spirit.[122] This event is usually taken to have occurred at Jesus' baptism.[123] It seems more likely that the anointing of the Spirit which equips Jesus for his mission, and which is referred to in Lk 4,18 and Acts 10,38, takes place at the moment of Jesus' conception (cf. Lk 1,35),[124] although a further, metaphorical aspect of this anointing (cf. 1 Kgs 19,20; 19,16) appears to be expressed in the epiphany of Lk 3,22 which has an initiating function with respect to Jesus' mission.[125] Both 1,35 and 3,22, however, need to be included in any consideraton of the term Χριστός in 1,5-4,44.

The royal context of 1,35 and 2,11 has been noted above (cf. 1,32-33; 2,1-21). In 3,22 the variant of D, which clearly recalls Ps 2,7,[126]

17,21-32 which refers to a king who will be an "anointed of the Lord"; cf. de Jonge, "Anointed", 134-137.

[120] Cf. CD 12,23–13,1; 14,19; 19,10.

[121] Cf. de Jonge, "Anointed", 147; de la Potterie, "L'onction". 226-234.

[122] See especially Acts 10,38: Ἰησοῦν... ὡς ἔχρισεν αὐτὸν ὁ θεὸς πνεύματι ἁγίῳ καὶ δυνάμει: also Lk 4,18: πνεῦμα κυρίου ἐπ᾽ ἐμέ, οὗ εἵνεκεν ἔχρισέν με. The association of 'anointing' and 'spirit' is already found in 1 Sam 16,13 in the case of David; later in Is 61,1.

[123] See, for example, Godet, Lc I, 291-292; Schanz, Lc, 185; von Baer, Heilige Geist, 65; de la Potterie, "L'onction", 226 ff.; Schürmann, Lk I, 229-230; Fitzmyer, Lk I-IX, 532; Grundmann, "χρίω", 534.

[124] The parallel between John and Jesus that runs through 1,5–4,44, and that is weighed heavily in Jesus' favour, suggests that while John is equipped with the Spirit already in his mother's womb for his mission (cf. 1,15.41.44), Jesus, who is conceived by the Spirit, is at that moment equipped for his mission. Thus the angel can announce to the shepherds in 2,11 the birth of the Χριστός, and the epiphany at the baptism can present him to John and "all the people" as the one anointed with the Spirit whom they await (cf. 3,15). Note that Acts 10,38, which refers to Jesus' anointing πνεύματι ἁγίῳ καὶ δυνάμει, has closer links with Lk 1,35 (πνεῦμα ἅγιον... καὶ δύναμις ὑψίστου) than with 3,22 through its reference to the divine δύναμις (cf. W. Grundmann, "δύναμαι κτλ.", TDNT II, 300-301; G. Voss, Die Christologie der lukanischen Schriften in Grundzügen, SN 2: Paris-Bruges 1965, 75-76) and its anarthrous πνεῦμα ἅγιον. Given this use of πνεῦμα ἅγιον in Acts 2,4 for the Pentecost Spirit's outpouring and in the infancy narrative for its anticipation on an individual level (cf. Lk 1,41.67; 2,29; also p. 125 above), it is likely that the article in 3,22 adds a personifying rather than an eschatological dimension (cf. Blass, Debrunner, Grammar, 134 (257.2); diff. de la Potterie, "L'onction", 235).

[125] See ch. I, nn. 86 and 129. Maldonatus (Commentarii II, 146-147) distinguished between the gift of the Spirit at Jesus' conception and a metaphorical anointing at his baptism.

[126] Cf. F. Lentzen-Deis, "Ps 2,7, ein Motiv früher "hellenistischer" Christologie? Der Psalmvers in der Lectio varians von Lk 3,22, im Ebionäerevangelium und bei Justinus Martyr", TP 44 (1969) 342-362; idem, Taufe Jesu, 186.

has certainly a royal sense. But σὺ εἶ ὁ υἱός μου alone may recall υἱός μου εἶ σύ of Ps 2,7b (cf. Acts 13,33).[127] If the servant-figure of Is 42,1, which combines both royal and prophetic characteristics,[128] is recalled in the phrase ἐν σοὶ εὐδόκησα, then the figure represented in Lk 3,22 has a prophetic as well as a royal aspect. Both, in any case, are suggested by the public and private aspects of 3,21-22, typical of a royal designation and a prophetic call respectively.[129]

Jesus' royal status is conveyed with other titles. Σωτήρ in 2,11 may be mentioned, given its royal context, and especially the implied contrast with Caesar Augustus, 'saviour'.[130] Κύριος may also convey this status.[131] If Elizabeth's inspired words in 1,43 echo Ps 110,1[132] or 2 Sam 24,21,[133] then the title has a royal connotation here.[134] The context of Lk 2,11 is, as has already been noted, a royal one. Given the Davidic reference in 1,69, the reference in 1,76 may also be to a royal figure (cf. 1,69a.77).[135]

The title υἱὸς (τοῦ) θεοῦ appears first in 1,35 where it recalls the equivalent expression υἱὸς ὑψίστου of 1,32[136] which is found in a royal context (cf. 1,32-33). The presentation of the king as son of God in Davidic texts such as 2 Sam 7,14, Ps 2,7 and 89,27-28 suggests a royal aspect for the title's use in Lk 1,35.[137] The genealogy, as we have seen, traces Jesus' lineage through David (cf. 3,31), while royal connotations may also be present in the use of the title in 3,22, if allusions to Ps 2,7 or Is 42,1 are present. The refusal of Satan's offer of universal domination in the second of Jesus' temptations as Son of God (Lk 4,5-8) suggests a royal power that does not come from Satan and is not political, but comes from the Father and is of a kind that gives him power and dominion over demons (cf. 4,41; Acts 10,38).

---

[127] Cf. Schürmann, Lk I, 192-193; Marshall, Lk, 155; but see Lentzen-Deis, Taufe Jesu, 185-186, and there n. 416; Fitzmyer, Lk I-IX, 485.

[128] Cf. Lentzen-Deis, Taufe Jesu, 157-158, and there n. 260.

[129] Cf. C. Westermann, Isaiah 40-66. A Commentary, tr. by D.M.G. Stalker, London 1969, 94-95. One cannot speak of a prophetic call here; at most the epiphany can be said to be something in the nature of a signal to begin one's ministry (see ch. I, n. 86).

[130] See inscription cited in n. 108 above.

[131] Cf. A. George, "Jésus Fils de Dieu dans l'Évangile selon saint Luc", RB 72 (1965) 186-188 (= Études, 216-217); Lentzen-Deis, Taufe Jesu, 186, and there n. 415.

[132] Cf. de la Potterie, "Titre", 119-120. The verse is cited in Acts 2,34.

[133] As seems more likely; cf. D. M. Stanley, "The Mother of My Lord", Worship 34 (1959-60) 330; Schürmann, Lk I, 68 n. 184.

[134] Cf. L. Cerfaux, "Le titre Kyrios et la dignité royale de Jésus", Recueil Lucien Cerfaux I, BETL 6: Gembloux 1954, 49-50; de la Potterie, "Titre", 120.

[135] See also possible allusions in 1,69 to 1 Sam 2,10 and Ps 132,17; cf. Fitzmyer, Lk I-IX, 383; Brown, Birth, 386; Schürmann, Lk I, 86 n. 33.

[136] Cf. J. A. Fitzmyer, "The Contribution of Qumran Aramaic to the Study of the New Testament", NTS 20 (1973-74) 391-394; Legrand, L'Annonce, 190.

[137] Cf. E. Lövestam, Son and Saviour. A Study of Acts 13,32-37. With an Appendix 'Son of God' in the Synoptic Gospels, ConNT 18: Lund 1961, 93.

As has been shown by Cerfaux, de la Potterie, George and others, Jesus appears elsewhere in the gospel as a royal figure.[138] He is presented as such at the beginning of the travel narrative, sending forth the seventy (two) disciples (Lk 10,1),[139] and at its conclusion, in the parable of the pounds (19,11-28) and particularly in the description of his entry into Jerusalem (cf. 19,38).[140] Jesus' royal status is repeatedly referred to during the passion, sometimes in a political sense (cf. 23,2.3.37.38), but also with a far deeper meaning (cf. 22,29-30; 23,42-43).[141] The theme is found on a number of occasions in Acts (cf. 2,25-36; 13,23.32-37; 15,16-18; 17,7).

2.2 *Jesus as Prophet*

Jesus' prophetic status is clearly indicated in Lk 1,5-4,44. The association of Χριστός with the figure of John in 3,15 shows that the title may indicate a prophetic figure (cf. 3,2b.3.7-18).[142] As we have seen above, the 'anointed one' pointed out by the epiphany of 3,22 may have a prophetic as well as a royal aspect. But it is in the Nazareth scene that Jesus' prophetic status is most evident. Jesus' own description of his mission in 4,18-19 suggests that the anointing referred to there has a prophetic character, and he confirms this with explicit and implicit references later in the scene to his prophetic status (cf. 4,24.25-27).[143]

The parallel that runs through 1,5-4,44 underlines this status. John is an eschatological prophet, the precursor (cf. Is 40,3-5; Lk 3,4-6), whose conception and birth represent 'good news' of the coming salvation (cf. 1,19.69.76), and whose ministry prepares the people for the coming of Jesus, the one greater than he (cf. 3,15-18).[144] Jesus is the anointed eschatological prophet who proclaims the presence of salvation in and through his person (cf. 4,18-21). That he should suffer the fate of the prophets may be suggested by the parallel with John (cf. 3,20). With his rejection as the eschatological prophet of Isaiah by his own in Nazareth and their subsequent attempt on his life the shadow of the cross certainly appears.

---

[138] Cerfaux, "Dignité Royale", 35-63; de la Potterie, "Titre", 126-129.141-146; George, "Royauté", 257-282; Fitzmyer, *Lk I-IX*, 215-216.

[139] Cf. de la Potterie, "Titre", 126-128; Grundmann, *Lk*, 208; Miyoshi, *Anfang*, 60.76.

[140] Cf. Grundmann, *Lk*, 366-367; George, "Royauté", 274-276.

[141] The verb κυριεύω, which comes from the noun, is used with reference to kings in Lk 22,25 — the only occurrence of this verb in the gospels and Acts.

[142] John is presented as a prophetic figure by his 'call' (3,2b), his prophetic preaching (3,7-18), his fearless opposition to Herod (3,19), and also by his imprisonment which foreshadows his ultimate fate (3,20).

[143] Cf. de la Potterie, "L'onction", 227-234.

[144] This is the picture of John found in the rest of Luke-Acts; cf. Lk 7,26-30; 16,16; Acts 10,37; 13,24-25.

Jesus' prophetic status emerges in the rest of the narrative proper in a variety of ways.[145] During the Galilean ministry one can point to reminiscences (cf. 7,12.15 and 1 Kgs 17,17.23; 7,22 and Is 61,1), the reaction to Jesus' miracle at Nain (cf. 7,16), the rumours concerning his identity (cf. 9,8.19) and the symbolism of the transfiguration scene (cf. 9,30-31.35). Jesus' journey to Jerusalem is depicted as the deliberate journey of a prophet moving inexorably towards his destined fate (cf. 9,51.54.62; 11,49-50; 13,33-34), a fate foreshadowed by John's violent death (cf. 3,20; 9,9) and accomplished in Jerusalem (cf. 22,64; 24,19-20). Peter presents Jesus as such in Acts 3,22-23. Those who continue Jesus' mission in Acts are portrayed in a similar light (cf. 2,18; 4,29-31; 6,8-7,60; 9,3-17; 13,1; 26,16-18).[146]

2.3 Jesus as Priest

Gerhard Friedrich found many traces in the synoptics of Jesus' presentation as the messianic high priest,[147] but few were convinced of his thesis and it met with severe criticism.[148] Undeterred, Mahnke has reproposed his theory on the basis of the temptation on the pinnacle of the temple.[149] Like Friedrich. he takes Ps 91,11-12 to recall *Test. Levi* 5,3 and the role of the angels in the temptation scene to parallel their role in guiding the high priest Levi to earth in this latter text.[150] The parallel is

---

[145] Cf. Busse, *Wunder,* 381-414; Fitzmyer, *Lk I-IX,* 213-215; J. Navone, *Themes of St. Luke,* Rome 1970, 132-141; R.J. Miller, "Elijah, John, and Jesus in the Gospel of Luke", *NTS* 34 (1988) 611-622; D.S. Ravens, "Luke 9. 7-62 and the Prophetic Role of Jesus", *NTS* 36 (1990) 119-129.

[146] Cf. P.S. Minear, *To Heal and to Reveal. The Prophetic Vocation According to Luke,* New York 1976, 122-147.

[147] "Beobachtungen zur messianischen Hohepriestererwartung in den Synoptikern", *ZTK* 53 (1956) 265-311; these included Jesus' description as ὁ ἅγιος τοῦ θεοῦ (pp. 275-278; cf. W. Grundmann, "Sohn Gottes (ein Diskussionsbeitrag)", *ZNW* 47 (1956) 125-126), his exorcisms (pp. 278-279, with references to *Test. Levi* 18,12; *Test. Dan* 5,19-20), his baptism, which he took to be Jesus' consecration as high priest (pp. 280-286), his blessing of the children (pp. 294-297), his cleansing of the temple (pp. 297-299) and his temptation on its pinnacle (pp. 300-301).

[148] In support, O. Cullmann, *The Christology of the New Testament,* tr. by S.C. Guthrie, C.A.M. Hall, London 1963, 104-105 n. 1; H. Mahnke, *Die Versuchungsge-schichte im Rahmen der synoptischen Evangelien. Ein Beitrag zur frühen Christologie,* BET 9: Frankfurt am Main 1978, 118-124; sharply critical, J. Gnilka, "Die Erwartung des messianischen Hohenpriesters in den Schriften von Qumran und im Neuen Testament", *RevQ* 2 (1959-60) 395-426; F. Hahn, *Christologische Hoheitstitel. Ihre Geschichte im frühen Christentum,* Göttingen 1964², 231.235-241; H. Braun, "Qumran und das Neue Testament. Ein Bericht über 10 Jahre Forschung (1950-1959)", *TRu* 28 (1962) 107-108.138.158-159.

[149] *Versuchungsgeschichte,* 113-124.297-316.

[150] *Versuchungsgeschichte,* 122-123; see the comment of E. Lohmeyer on the corresponding temptation in Mt 4,5-7 in *Das Evangelium des Matthäus,* ed. W. Schmauch, Göttingen 1967⁴, 57-58.

difficult to sustain, since the context of the temptation is quite different. It is Jesus' trust in God that is being tested by Satan, whereas no such motif is present in *Test. Levi* 2-5. The latter presents a figure being conducted to earth and armed by the angel who offers him protection while he is avenging on the Shechemites the rape of Dinah; the protection offered by the angels according to Ps 91,11-12 is very different.[151] A 'confirmatory' miracle is sought by Satan,[152] not a messianic display of miraculous power before a non-existent audience.[153]

Is there any suggestion in Lk 1,5-4,44 of Jesus as a priestly figure? From the point of view of his lineage Mary's relationship to Elizabeth (cf. 1,36), described in 1,5 as a daughter of Aaron, must be considered. But since this need not imply that Mary belonged to a priestly family, a relationship due to marriage being quite possible,[154] it does not necessarily imply a priestly lineage for Jesus. The parallel between John and Jesus in 1,5-4,44 may be of greater significance. John, who is of perfect priestly descent, is never himself associated with temple or synagogue, whereas his kinsman Jesus, who does not appear to be of priestly descent, is associated very much with both (cf. 2,22-52; 4,9.14-44).

In support of his thesis, Friedrich cited Sir 45,6 and Ps 105 (106),16 in which the term ἅγιος is applied to Aaron.[155] But little can be deduced from this since the adjective is also applied to Elisha (2 Kgs 4,9) and its cognate verb to Jeremiah (Jer 1,5) in the Old Testament.[156] Nevertheless, Luke's use of the adjective in relation to Jesus may not be without some significance.

In the Old Testament both adjective and verb are used among others for priests (Lev 21,6.7.8; 22,9), Nazarites (Num 6,5.8; Judg 16,17) and the first-born (Ex 13,2.12).[157] In the Qumran documents their equivalents are used in relation to the Qumran community (1QSb 1,5; 1QM 6,6). In Luke–Acts ἅγιος is applied to prophets (Lk 1,70; Acts 3,21), Christians (Acts 9,32), the first-born (Lk 2,23) and Jesus (Lk 1,35; 4,34; Acts 4,27.30). The occurrence of the term itself, therefore, is not sufficient to determine the nature of the figure to which it refers. Context is again of vital importance.

---

[151] There it refers to Yahweh's protection of the faithful one, the one who has made the Lord his refuge.

[152] To prove that God protects Jesus; cf. Schürmann, *Lk* I, 213.

[153] Cf. Schürmann, *Lk* I, 213, and there n. 195; Marshall, *Lk*, 173; Godet, *Lc* I, 273-274.

[154] Cf. Plummer, *Lk*, 25.

[155] "Beobachtungen", 276.

[156] Cf. Gnilka, "Erwartung", 410.

[157] Also Israel (Deut 7,6; 14,2.21; 26,19), the remnant (Is 4,3), the elect of Yahweh (Dan 7,21; Tob 8,15; 12,15).

The first two occurrences of the term ἅγιος in reference to Jesus, Lk 1,35 and 4,34, tell us little. The third is found in 2,23 in an adapted citation from Ex 13,2. The context is a cultic one, the presentation of Jesus in the temple (Lk 2,22) and the purification of Mary (2,24). It has been suggested above that in 2,22-24 Luke may be recalling the situation prior to the establishing of the Levitical priesthood in order to foreshadow this priesthood's passing. Implied here may be the notion that with the coming of Jesus a new situation has arisen in which a new mediation outside and apart from the temple cult is possible.[158]

This portrayal of Jesus may find confirmation in 24,50-52 where he is presented in a typically priestly stance reminiscent of Lev 9,22 and of Sir 50,20 in particular.[159] The priestly blessing had a central role in the daily cultic life of Judaism, being imparted twice daily in the temple. It was not confined to the temple, though, for it was imparted also in the synagogue (cf. *m.Sot.* 7,6-7). It was, however, rigorously restricted to the priests from the time of the monarchy. While the picture of Jesus imparting a 'priestly blessing' on the Mount of Olives, outside temple and synagogue, opposite and most likely in sight of the sanctuary,[160] may foreshadow the passing of the Levitical priesthood,[161] it may also point towards a new priestly mediator who is about to ascend to his Father.[162]

2.4 *Jesus as Teacher*

Jesus also appears in the role of teacher in Lk 1,5-4,44. The well known portrayal of him sitting among the teachers in the temple illustrates the child's precocious wisdom and understanding (2,46-47).

---

[158] The association of ἅγιος and the conception of Jesus through the Spirit in 1,35 may, if Jesus' 'anointing' with the Spirit is to be identified with this moment (see above), be regarded as preparing him for a priestly role (cf. Lev 8,12), though not necessarily so (cf. Jer 1,5).

[159] See n. 93 above.

[160] See n. 97 above.

[161] See p. 130 above; also van Stempvoort, "Ascension", 35, on the "ominous aspect" of the blessing of Lk 24,50-53.

[162] Abundant evidence of the expectation of an eschatological priestly figure or Messiah is to be found in the Qumran documents (cf. 1QS 9,11; 1QSa 2,11-12; CD 12,23-24; 14,19; 19,10-11) and *The Testaments of the Twelve Patriarchs* (*Reub.* 6,8-12; *Sim.* 7,1-2; *Levi* 8,11-14; 18,1-14; *Jud.* 21,2). This expectation is generally linked to the figures of Aaron and Levi. One text, *Test. Levi* 18,1-14, speaks of the failure of the old wicked priesthood (v.1) and the raising up by the Lord of a new priest (v.2: ἱερέα καινόν) who does not belong to the Levitical priesthood. Cf. M. de Jonge, "Christian influence in the Testaments of the Twelve Patriarchs", *Studies on the Testaments of the Twelve Patriarchs. Text and Interpretation,* ed. M. de Jonge, SVTP 3: Leiden 1975, 193-246; K. G. Kuhn, "Die beiden Messias Aarons und Israels", *NTS* 1 (1954-55) 168-173; G. R. Beasley-Murray, "The Two Messiahs in the Testaments of the Twelve Patriarchs", *JTS* 48 (1947) 1-12; Vanhoye, *Prêtres,* 59-64.

But it does more than that, for his answers and the accompanying admiration of his hearers foreshadow his future role as a teacher.[163] There is probably also here the implication that Jesus is one who will be a greater teacher than any of those among whom he finds himself.[164]

Both John and Jesus are portrayed as teachers in 3,1–4,44, although the title διδάσκαλος is used only of John (3,12). The terms διδάσκειν and διδαχή are used of Jesus' teaching (4,15.31.32). The parallel between them is again weighed heavily in Jesus' favours, as his teaching evokes praise (cf. 4,15) and astonishment (cf. 4,32), and most important of all is a teaching with authority (4,32: ἐν ἐξουσίᾳ· cf. 4,36).

Jesus is presented as a teacher throughout the narrative proper. The Galilean ministry opens with the call of the first disciples/apostles set in the context of his teaching (cf. 5,3), and it continues in that vein with two major teaching sections, 6,20-49 and 8,4-21. The travel narrative's most characteristic feature is Jesus' didactic and paraenetic instruction delivered along the way, in towns and villages, in houses and synagogues (cf. 11,1; 13,10.22), while his lengthy period of teaching activity in the temple is a prominent feature of the gospel's final section (cf. 19,47; 21,37).

Jesus is accepted as a teacher by non-disciples who address him as διδάσκαλος (cf 7,40; 8,49; 9,38). These include lawyers (cf. 10,25; 11,45; 18,18), pharisees (cf. 19,39), scribes (cf. 20,39), sadduccees (cf. 20,28) and the Jewish authorities in general (cf. 20,21.28.39).[165] Not surprisingly it is this aspect of his ministry that is mentioned in the summary of the contents of Luke's first volume in Acts 1,1-2 (cf. Lk 24,19).

The authoritative aspect of Jesus' teaching is conveyed in the use of the term ἐπιστάτης, a term that was used to render 'rabbi' and 'rabban' in Christian Palestine,[166] and that usually indicates some form of

---

[163] Cf. Fitzmyer, *Lk I-IX,* 218; J.J. Kilgallen, "Luke 2,41-50: Foreshadowing of Jesus, Teacher", *Bib* 66 (1985) 558.

[164] The foreshadowing of future greatness in an infancy narrative is a common theme of ancient biographical writing. It is to be found, for example, in Plutarch's *Lives* of Alexander (cf. 5,1-3) and Alcibiades (cf. 2,1), Philo's *Life* of Moses (cf. *De Vita Mos.* I,21) and Philostratus' *Life* of Apollonius (cf. I,7). It is also present in Josephus' autobiography (*Vita* §§ 8-9). Cf. Talbert, "Prophecies of Future Greatness", 136-137.

[165] Jesus uses the term διδάσκαλος of himself in 22,11, but in that case he is speaking in terms understandable to the innkeeper; implicit, though, is his authority (cf. 22,11-13).

[166] Cf. G. Dalman, *Die Worte Jesu,* Leipzig 1930², 400. The term may have a variety of meanings including that of teacher; cf. H. Stephanus, *Thesaurus Graecae Linguae* III, eds. C.B. Hase, G. and L. Dindorf, Paris 1835, 1795-1796; A. Oepke, "ἐπιστάτης", *TDNT* II, 622-623; Bauer, *Wörterbuch,* 543; F. Preisigke, *Fachwörter des öffentlichen Verwaltungsdienstes Ägyptens in den griechischen Papyrusurkunden der ptolemäisch-römischen Zeit,* Göttingen 1915, 89-90; Liddell, Scott, Jones, *Lexicon,* 659; Grimm, "ἐπιστάτης", 93-94; R. Riesner, *Jesus als Lehrer. Eine Untersuchung zum Ursprung der Evangelien-Überlieferung,* WUNT 2.7: Tübingen 1981, 248; O. Glombitza, "Die Titel διδάσκαλος und ἐπιστάτης für Jesus bei Lukas", *ZNW* 49 (1958) 276-277.

authority.[167] The term, which is found only in Luke's gospel in the New Testament, is confined almost exclusively to the disciples and apostles (cf. 5,5; 8,24.45; 9,33.49)[168] and points towards their acceptance of Jesus' authoritative position as teacher within their group.[169] That this relationship continues with the risen Lord is suggested by the use of the phrase μαθητὰς τοῦ κυρίου in Acts 9,1.[170]

It is evident from this examination of royal, prophetic, priestly and teaching aspects of the portrait of Jesus present in Lk 1,5-4,44 that already in these chapters one is given a fairly complete composite picture of Jesus' identity, and one that is consonant with the picture found in the remainder of Luke-Acts.

3. Mission of Jesus

As Lk 1,5–4,44 has much light to throw on the identity of Jesus, so it has on his mission. John's mission has its importance here where it is described at greater length than in Matthew and Mark. He is after all an 'end time' figure for Luke with an eschatological message and mission. But he is subordinate to Jesus on whom these chapters really focus. The implied comparison between the two serves to throw the unique features of Jesus' mission into sharper relief.

3.1 *Universal Significance*

John's mission is presented as restricted to Israel. He is to turn the sons of Israel to the Lord their God, and thus to make ready for the Lord Jesus a people prepared. His commission is for Israel,[171] and the ministy described in 3,2b-20 corresponds to this limitation (cf. Acts 13,24: προκηρύξαντος... παντὶ τῷ λαῷ Ἰσραήλ). The comparison that runs through Lk 1,5-4,44 suggests that for Jesus the prospect is different.

---

[167] In so doing it respects its semantic thrust; cf. Liddell, Scott, Jones, *Lexicon,* 659 (ἐπιστάτης II,1-III,3); Stephanus, *Thesaurus* III, 1795-1796; Grimm, "ἐπιστάτης", 94; Glombitza, "Titel", 276-277.

[168] The use of the title by the lepers in 17,13 suggests that they accept Jesus' authority; cf. Grimm, "ἐπιστάτης", 94; Glombitza, "Titel", 278.

[169] Note the context of the initial use of the term in 5.5 (cf. 5,3) and the extent of the disciples' exposure to Jesus' teaching in the Galilean section where all but one of the occurrences of the title are to be found (cf. 5,17; 6,6.20-49; 7,24-35; 8,4-21; 9,21-27.43b-50); one of the characteristic aspects of the travel narrative, the general context of 17,13, is its presentation of Jesus as a teacher throughout. Cf. Grimm, "ἐπιστάτης", 94.

[170] The term μαθητής, which is only introduced in the gospel in 5,30, is used frequently in Acts, though not always of the Lord's disciples (cf. 9,25; 19,1); cf. Fitzmyer, *Lk I-IX,* 218.

[171] Cf. Lk 1,17b.80b; also ch. I, n. 61.

As the angel's message of 1,32-33 indicates, Jesus' mission is also directed to Israel.[172] But the universal tones of 2,1-14 already point towards a mission that transcends Israel (e.g. 2,14b: ἐπὶ γῆς εἰρήνη ἐν ἀνθρώποις εὐδοκίας),[173] even if λαός in 2,10 refers to Israel.[174] It is the inspired words of Simeon in 2,30-32 that bring out most clearly the child's universal significance, presenting the salvation which Jesus represents as destined for all, Jew and Gentile alike.[175]

A clear reference to the universality of salvation is to be found in 3,6 where the citation from Isaiah is continued on to Is 40,5b LXX (καὶ ὄψεται πᾶσα σὰρξ τὸ σωτήριον τοῦ θεοῦ). Although the citation is associated with the beginning of John's ministry, it is to Jesus, through whom salvation comes, that the reference really is, for John and Jesus are indissolubly linked.[176] The genealogy of 3,23-38, which traces back Jesus' lineage not merely to David and Abraham but to Adam and God, shows that his mission relates not just to Israel but to all mankind.[177] The examples from the ministries of Elijah and Elisha of divine favour shown through them to non-Israelites (4,25-27) give further indications of a mission whose significance goes beyond Israel.[178]

This does not mean that Israel loses its special place in God's plan. The angel's words in 1,32-33 suggest its permanent inclusion therein, as indeed does 3,6, while the canticles celebrate the fulfilment of the promises made to Israel. Its primacy in the hearing of the word, indicated in Simeon's canticle, is respected in John's ministry and in the anticipation of Jesus' ministry in 4,14-44.

But Jesus' mission is not to gather a new or a true Israel, as Lohfink suggests.[179] The indications of the universal significance of his mission (cf. 2,14.30-32; 3,23-38; 4,25-27), the crucial importance accorded to response to the word of God rather than to heritage (cf. 3,8), the foreshadowing of the Jewish cult's passing, and the possible representation of Jesus as a priest of a new order (see above), point towards a new people of God that

---

[172] The "house of Jacob" is a synonym for Israel as the people of God (cf. Is 2,6; 8,17; 14,1; etc); diff. Lohfink, *Sammlung*, 25 ("das endzeitliche Gottesvolk").

[173] Cf. Schürmann, *Lk* I, 110; Wilson, *Gentiles*, 34-35; Lohfink, *Sammlung*, 28; Brown, *Birth*, 402; Fitzmyer, *Lk I-IX*, 409.

[174] See ch. I, p. 18, and there nn. 63 and 64.

[175] Cf. Wilson, *Gentiles*, 36-38; Fitzmyer, *Lk I-IX*, 428; Marshall, *Lk*, 120-121; Creed, *Lk*, 41.

[176] Just as the announcement of John's birth and its coming to pass indicate the proximate birth of Jesus (cf. 1,15-17.69.76-77), so too the beginning of John's ministry signals that the ministry of Jesus is soon to follow.

[177] Cf. Schürmann, *Lk* I, 201; Wilson, *Gentiles*, 39-40.

[178] Cf. Schürmann, *Lk* I, 238.

[179] *Sammlung*, 23.30.31.33, etc; see criticisms of Hauser, *Abschlusserzählung*, 90-91, and there n. 88.

is formed of Israelite and non-Israelite alike. It is a people that stands in continuity with Israel (cf. 1,16.17.32-33.54.73; 2,14.32; 3,18; 4,14-44), but is not to be identified as a new or a true Israel.

In the narrative proper, the Gentile mission is foreshadowed at various times during Jesus' ministry not only in the oft quoted mission of the 70(2),[180] the sayings of 13,29-30 and the parable of the great banquet (14,16-24), but also in the accounts of the healing of the centurion's servant (7,1-10) and of the Gerasene demoniac (8,26-39), the sayings of 10,13-15 and 11,29-32,[181] and perhaps even the parable of the mustard seed (13,18-19).[182] It is explicitly commanded by the risen Lord in 24,47 and in Acts 1,8. It begins under divine direction in Acts 10 with Peter's conversion of Cornelius (cf. 10,1-11,18; 15,7), but it is primarily Paul who carries it forward. Though his initial 'turning' to the Gentiles is occasioned by Jewish rejection of his preaching in Antioch of Pisidia (cf. 13,45-51), his work among them is shown to be an integral part of God's plan as enunciated in the scriptures (cf. 13,47; 15,14-17).

Israel's continuing role in God's plan is evident in the choice of the twelve and their presence at Jesus' first major sermon delivered before an audience representative of 'all Israel' (cf. 6,17), and in the recomposition of the group of twelve to ensure their presence at Peter's Pentecost address to 'all Israel' (cf. Acts 1,15-26; 2,5-37). The primacy of Israel in the hearing of the word is respected in Jesus' ministry, in the universal mission he imparts, in the preaching of the early church (Acts 1,15-26; 2,1-8,3), and in the missionary movement even after the Gentile mission commences (cf. 11,19; 13,5.14; 14,2; 17,1-2.10.17; 18,5.19; 19,8; 28,17).

The story of Israel in Luke-Acts is a tragic one,[183] but despite division in the face of the word of God and repeated Jewish opposition, Israel is not left bereft of hope, not even at the conclusion of Luke's work.[184] The harsh tones of the Old Testament citation in 28,26-27 (Is 6,9-10) with its earnest warning to Israel on the consequences of its

---

[180] Cf. Rengstorf, Lk, 133; H. Flender, Heil und Geschichte in der Theologie des Lukas, BET 41: Munich 1965, 26; but note the caveat of Wilson, Gentiles, 45-47.

[181] Cf. Fitzmyer, Lk X-XXV, 853.934; Wilson, Gentiles, 4-5.

[182] Cf. Jeremias, Promise, 68-69; idem, Parables, 147.149.

[183] Cf. R. C. Tannehill, "Israel in Luke-Acts: A Tragic Story", JBL 104 (1985) 69-85; see below.

[184] For the contrary opinion see Haenchen, Acts, 102; Gnilka, Verstockung, 153-154; J. T. Sanders, "The Salvation of the Jews in Luke-Acts", Society of Biblical Literature 1982 Seminar Papers, ed. K. H. Richards, Chico 1982, 472; idem, The Jews in Luke-Acts, London 1987, 53; Schille, Apg, 479; Roloff, Apg, 374-375; Weiser, Apg 13-28, 683; etc. Many suggest that Luke sees individual Jews repenting and coming to faith; see, for example, A. George, "Israël dans l'œuvre de Luc", RB 75 (1968) 524; Dupont, "Conclusion", 377-380; Hauser, Abschlusserzählung, 109; Schneider, Apg II, 419; Roloff, Apg, 375; Weiser, Apg 13-28, 683.

rejection of the word,[185] and the clear statement in 28,28 of the divine favour shown to the Gentiles whose response to the word of salvation will be positive, together represent a final double edged attempt to spur Israel on to repentance so that "all flesh" will see the salvation of God (cf. Lk 3,6).[186] The universal promise of Is 40,5 LXX (cf. Lk 3,6; Acts 28,28) is not abrogated in the finale of Acts. The final glimpse of Paul preaching openly and unhindered in Rome to Jews and Gentiles alike (28,30-31) suggests that hope for Israel has still not been abandoned.[187]

Jesus' mission is not to gather a new or a true Israel. The group of Jesus' followers gathered together initially in Galilee stands in continuity with Israel, as is underlined by its central core of the twelve and the hundred and twenty disciples present at Pentecost (cf. Acts 1,15). The divine plan envisages a new people of God open to all peoples (cf. Lk 2,30-32; 3,6; Acts 1,6-8; 15,14-18; 18,10; 28,28-31), formed on the basis of a positive response to the word of God (cf. Lk 3,8; 6,46-49; 8,19-21; Acts 2,38-40; 3,23; 13,46.48; 15,7; 26,20; 28,23.31), and obtained through the sacrifice of his son (cf. Acts 20,28) with whose blood a new covenant is established (cf. Lk 22,20).[188]

3.2 Rejection – Acceptance

Simeon's 'oracle' to Mary in 2,34-35 presents her child as set for the fall and the rise of many in Israel and for a sign that is to be contradicted. Rejection and acceptance in Israel are to be his lot.[189] These two themes are also found in 4,14-44.

The Nazareth scene portrays the rejection of Jesus and his message by his own townspeople. With the attempt on his life in 4,29 Calvary

---

[185] Cf. Wikenhauser, *Apg*, 289: "...eine ernste Warnung und Mahnung". For previous warnings see Lk 3,8; 11,37-52; 13,34-35; 19,11-28.41-44; 20,9-19; Acts 2,40; 3,23; 13,40-41. It is important to note the particular context of Is 6,9f. here. In 28,23-25 the reaction to Paul's preaching is mixed — belief and unbelief. But the disruptive, often violent opposition that Paul experienced earlier (cf. 13,45.50; 14,2.19; 17,5.13; 18,6.12-13; 19,9; 20,3; 21,27-36; 22,22; 23,12-15) is absent. Instead discord reigns, and no opposition follows in 28,30-31 (see also 19,10). In this situation the use of Is 6,9f. seems somewhat harsh and out of place unless its purpose as a warning is recognized.

[186] For the paraenetic use of the Gentiles to reproach Israel see Lk 4,25-27; 7,9; 11,29-32; 13,28-30; 14,23-24; Acts 13,40-41. Cf. P. D. Meyer, "The Gentile Mission in Q", *JBL* 89 (1970) 405-417; F. Ó Fearghail, "Israel in Luke-Acts", *PIBA* 11 (1988) 26-35.40-43.

[187] Texts such as Acts 1,6-8 and 3,19-21.25-26 reinforce this view; see Mussner, *Apg*, 16-17.30-31; Tannehill, "Israel", 76-77.83-84; R. L. Brawley, *Luke-Acts and the Jews. Conflict, Apology, and Conciliation*, SBLMS 33: Atlanta 1987, 155-159; J. T. Carroll, *Response to the End of History. Eschatology and Situation in Luke-Acts*, SBLDS 92: 1988, 161 n.191; also O'Neill, *Acts*, 87 n.1.

[188] See further Ó Fearghail, "Israel", 36-37.43.

[189] Cf. Brown, *Birth*, 460-462; Fitzmyer, *Lk I-IX*, 422-423; Schneider, *Lk* I, 72.

already looms on the horizon. While provoking the total rejection of his own people, the polemical examples cited from the ministries of Elijah and Elisha set the scene for the acceptance by non-Israelites of Jesus during his ministry and of his word afterwards. The picture found in 4,31-43 stands in sharp contrast as the inhabitants of Capernaum give Jesus a favourable reception. He is received in the house of Simon's mother-in-law, whom he cures, and by whom he and others are served. Many who were sick and possessed by demons are brought to him and healed (4,40-41). Reaction is so favourable that the people try to prevent his departure from their midst (4,42-43).

The pattern of rejection and acceptance found in 1,5–4,44 is reproduced throughout Luke–Acts. During the Galilean ministry the negative attitude of the scribes and pharisees (cf. 5,21.30; 6,7.11) contrasts with the positive attitude of the disciples, ordinary Jews and even Gentiles (cf. 5,1.15.26.28; 6,17; 7,1-10; 8,1-3.26-39). A similar pattern is present in the travel narrative[190] where a clear distinction between the Jewish leaders and the people eventually emerges (cf. 19,47-48).[191] This distinction is present for much of the Jerusalem section,[192] but is blurred at the moment of Pilate's final decision against Jesus (cf. 23,13.18; Acts 3,17),[193] a decision that leads to the cross and the culmination of Jesus' rejection.

The pattern of acceptance and rejection is also a characteristic of the mission of Jesus' witnesses, whether in Jerusalem (2,1–8,3),[194] in the missionary section (8,4–21,17),[195] or in the final chapters of Acts

---

[190] Rejection: 9,53; 11,53; 13,17a.34; 14,24; 19,11-28.47; acceptance: 9,57.61; 10,38-42; 11,27; 13,17b; 17,16-18; 18,15.43; 19,1-10.48.

[191] Opposition becomes more radical after Jesus' denunciation of the scribes and pharisees in 11,37-52 (cf. 11,53-54), but the crowds come to accept him more and more (cf. 12,1; 14,25; 18,43 — note the change from ὄχλος in 18,36 to λαός in 18,43; 19,37-39.

[192] Rejection: 20,2.19.20.26; 22,2-6.47-71; 23,2.10.35; acceptance: 20,19.26; 21,38; 23,27.35.42.48.

[193] Cf. Lohfink, *Sammlung*, 42-43. But this attitude (cf. 23,18 ff.) is temporary and exceptional; the people are soon again shown in a positive light (cf. 23,27.35.48), and their attitude after Jesus' death bespeaks their sorrow for what has happened (cf. 23,48).

[194] The immediate impact of the apostolic preaching is evident in the numerous conversions of Jews (cf. 2,41-42.44-47; 4,4; 5,13), including priests (6,7). But the Sanhedrin still rejects this preaching and seeks to suppress it (cf. 4,1-21; 5,17-18.28.33.40; 6,12–7,60), while specific groups of Jews are found to actively oppose it (cf. 6,9-12).

[195] The spread of the word among Jews is repeatedly noted here (cf. 9,31.35.42; 12,24; 14,1; 16,5; 17,4.11-12; 18,8; 19,20), as is its acceptance by non-Jews (cf. 8,5-25.26-40; 10,1-11.18; 11,20-21; 13,48-49; 14,1.27; 15,7; 16,14-15.33; 17,4.34; 19,10.20). Jewish opposition is constantly present (cf. 9,1.23; 12,1-3; 13,45.50; 14,2.19; 17,5.11.13; 18,6.12-13; 20,3.19) and even inspires Gentile opposition (cf. 14,2.5).

(21,18–28,31).[196] Many Jews and Gentiles accept the word, while many Jews oppose it, at times even violently.[197]

3.3 *Word and Deed*

Conzelmann's view that Luke ranks deed above word, seeing above hearing,[198] has received its share of criticism, and not without reason.[199] Lk 4,14-44 helps to clarify the issue. Just as its pattern of rejection and acceptance is programmatic for the ministries of Jesus and his disciples, so also is its presentation of the relationship between word and deed.

The introductory and concluding verses of 4,14-44 focus on the word (4,14–15.44), although deeds may be alluded to in 4,14b.[200] No deeds are performed during Jesus' visit to Nazareth. Yet his ministry is characterized there in deed (4,18.23.25-27) as well as word (4,18-19.21-27). Jesus' miraculous activity is more pronounced in 4,31-43 (cf. 4,33-35.38-41), although it is framed by general references to Jesus' teaching (4,31-32a) and preaching (4,43). Deed is effected through word 4,32.35-36.39), thus demonstrating the power and authority of that word, and it is interpreted by word (4,43). Deed illustrates and validates word (cf. 4,18-19.32.36.43), and serves to spread its knowledge and Jesus' fame (4,36-37) so that many more come to hear him and to be healed (4,40-43).[201] The kingdom that Jesus preaches (4,43) is present in word and deed (cf. 4,18-21.32-36.38-41).[202] These two aspects of his activity are presented as complementary in 4,14-44. They are vital for Luke's portrait of Jesus (cf. Acts 1,1; Lk 24,19).[203] He strives to balance them in this anticipatory section, and he does likewise in the narrative proper.

---

[196] Acceptance by Jews (cf. 21,20; 28,24a.30) and Gentiles (cf. 28,28-31); rejection by Jews, particularly their leaders (cf. 21,27-36; 22,22-23; 23,12-13; 24,1; 25,2; 28,24b).

[197] That the Jews who oppose the preaching of the word are not representative of Israel is suggested by the fact that the provenance and partial nature of the opposition is repeatedly specified (cf. 6,9; 14,1-5.19; 17,4.5.13; 18,6; 19,9; 21,27; 23,12-13; 24,19).

[198] *Mitte*, 177-179.

[199] Cf. Schürmann, *Lk* I, 232 n. 74; Rese, *Motive*, 152 n. 39; Dillon, *Eye-Witnesses*, 127, and 127-128 n. 172. The opposite has also been claimed; cf. A. George, "Le miracle dans l'œuvre de Luc", *Les miracles de Jésus selon le Nouveau Testament*, ed. X. Léon-Dufour, Paris 1977, 268.

[200] Cf. Schürmann, *Lk* I, 222; Marshall, *Lk*, 176.

[201] Note the implication in Jesus' reply of v. 43 as to the aspect of the word. See the redactional argument of P. J. Achtemeier, "The Lucan Perspective on the Miracles of Jesus: A Preliminary Sketch", *JBL* 94 (1975) 550-551, for a Lucan balance between Jesus' miraculous activity and his teaching.

[202] Cf. Prast, *Presbyter*, 276-77; Völkel, "Deutung", 63; O. Merk, "Das Reich Gottes in den lukanischen Schriften", Ellis, Grässer (eds.), *Jesus und Paulus*, 208; Busse, *Nazareth-Manifest*, 81; Agua Pérez, "Cumplimiento", 278.

[203] See Dillon's comments (*Eye-Witnesses*, 127 n. 172) on Conzelmann's treatment of such 'traditional' expressions as 'see and hear', 'do and teach', 'work and word' (*Mitte*, 178-179, and 178 n. 2).

Word (5,1-3) and deed (5,4-7) precede the call of the first disciples. But the miracle does not form the basis of their call, as has been suggested.[204] Simon, James and John become disciples of Jesus not only because of his wondrous power but also in response to his compelling invitation to follow him (cf. 5,10-11).[205] The healing of the leper leads to the spread of Jesus' fame so that people come to him in greater numbers 'to hear' him and 'to be healed' (5,15). The balance between word and deed is maintained in the accounts of the healing of the paralytic (cf. 5,17) and of the man with the withered hand (cf. 6,6), and again on the occasion of the sermon on the plain (cf. 6,17-49).[206] Jesus' deeds (cf. 7,1-17.21-22) and words (cf. 6,20-49; 7,22) show the disciples of John that he is 'the one who is to come'.[207] Teaching (cf. 8,1.4-21) and miracle (cf. 8,2-3.22-56) are balanced in 8,1-56, as they are in 9,1-50, whether in the case of Jesus (cf. 9,11.35.37-43a.43b-45) or the twelve (cf. 9,2.6).

There are indications that Luke strives for a certain balance between the two in the travel narrative, despite its greater concentration on teaching and fewer miracle accounts. Both aspects are found in Jesus' instruction to the seventy (two) disciples (10,9), in his words of rejoicing on their return (10,23-24), and in the controversy over Jesus and Beelzebul (11,14-23). The kingdom parables of 13,18-21 represent a comment on the healing of the woman crippled for eighteen years (13,10-16),[208] while word (13,22-30; 14,7-24) frames deed (cf. 13,32; 14,1-6) in the central unit (13,22–14,24).[209]

The cleansing of the leper in 17,11-19 is seen as a sign of the kingdom and leads to Jesus' preaching on the kingdom (cf. 17,20-37).[210] Deed and word convey the need for humility to enter the kingdom in 18,15-17, while in 18,31-19,28 deeds (cf. 18,35-43; 19,1-8) and words (cf. 19,9-10) lead to the question about the kingdom in 19,11 and to the parable of the pounds in 19,12-28. The Jerusalem section is characterized mainly by Jesus' teaching. But Jesus' ministry is summarized in 24,19 in terms of word and deed. And both are required to bring the apostles to faith in the risen Christ.[211]

---

[204] Cf. Conzelmann, *Mitte,* 178.

[205] Likewise Levi (cf. 5,27-28). The miracle in 5,1-11 is really an 'acted sign' that indicates the future for these first disciples. The word of Jesus interprets this sign (cf. 5,10c).

[206] Note the chiastic structure word — deed — deed — word in 6,17-49.

[207] The phrase περὶ πάντων τούτων of 7,18a refers not only to 7,1-17 but also to the preceding sermon, 6,20-49; πτωχοὶ εὐαγγελίζονται of 7,22 echoes μακάριοι οἱ πτωχοί, ὅτι ὑμετέρα ἐστὶν ἡ βασιλεία τοῦ θεοῦ of 6,20.

[208] Note οὖν in v. 18a; cf. Marshall, *Lk,* 560.

[209] Jesus' reply of Lk 13,32 is couched in terms of Herod's expectations (cf. 9,7-9; 23,8).

[210] See ch. II, p. 58, and there n. 113.

[211] Cf. Dillon, *Eye-Witnesses,* 127.

Acts also preserves a certain balance between word and deed. Peter's words at Pentecost (2,14-40) follow the miracle of the tongues (2,1-13) and bring many to the faith (cf. 2,41). Teaching, signs and wonders are features of the apostles' work (cf. 2,42-43).[212] The healing of the lame man (3,1-10) brings many people to the scene and leads to the sermon of 3,12-26 (cf. 4,8-12). In the prayer of 4,29-30, the miracle and teaching of 5,12-42, and the ministry of Stephen (cf. 6,8-10), a balance between words and deeds is maintained. This is true also of descriptions of the work of Philip (cf. 8,5-40), Barnabas and Saul (cf. 13,5-12; 14,3.8-10), Paul and Timothy (cf. 16,13-34), and Paul himself (cf. 19,8-12; 20,7-12).[213]

Luke, then, preserves a certain balance between word and deed throughout his account. In many cases word precedes deed,[214] in others, the reverse.[215] Sometimes the word is accentuated,[216] sometimes the deed.[217] Deeds illustrate, demonstrate and lead on to words, while words complement, interpret and validate deeds. Moreover, deeds are often effected by words.[218] Both are important, indeed essential, for the adequate description of the ministries of Jesus and his disciples.

3.4 Programmatic Victory over Satan

The relationship between Jesus and Satan that is delineated in Lk 1,5-4,44 is also programmatic for the rest of Luke–Acts. Jesus, equipped with the power of the Spirit (cf. 4,1.18; Acts 10,38), is shown to triumph over Satan in the temptations of Lk 4,1-13, while in the exorcisms of 4,33-35 and 4,41 he is seen as the 'stronger one' freeing others from Satan's bondage.

In his ministry Jesus is portrayed as the 'stronger one' who overcomes Satan (cf. 11,14-22) and who frees a daughter of Abraham from her bondage of many years (13,16). His power over demons is frequently demonstrated (cf. 6,18; 8,2.26-39; 9,37-43; 11,14; 13,16.32). He bestows it on the twelve and the seventy (two) for their temporary missions (9,1; 10,17-20), foreshadowing the permanent gift of Pentecost.

---

[212] On the unity of 2,42-47 see Weiser, *Apg 1-12,* 101-106.

[213] On closer examination Conzelmann's list of texts supporting his position (cf. *Mitte,* 179 n. 3) is less impressive than it seems at first sight: Lk 7,22 (cf. 4,18-19); 10,23 (cf. 10,24); 19,37 (cf. 19,11-28.47-48; 20,1-21,38); Acts 8,13 (cf. 8,6.12); 14,11 (cf. 14,9-10); 26,16 (cf. 26,20).

[214] Cf. Lk 5,1-11.15b.17-26; 6,6-11.18; 8,1-3; 9,2.6.11; 13,10-16; Acts 4,29-30; 8,5-6; 10,36-38; 13,5-12; 14,3.

[215] Cf. Lk 5,12-15a; 7,1-17.21-22; 10,9.23-24; 11,14-23; 14,1-24; 17,11-37; 24,19; Acts 1,1; 2,1-40; 3,1-26; 5,12-42; 6,8-10.

[216] Cf. Lk 9,35; 10,16.39; 11,28; 13,22; 15,1; 19,47-48; 21,37-38; Acts 4,4; 13,13-52; 15,7.

[217] Cf. Lk 7,18-23; 13,32; 19,37; Acts 2,22b; 9,32-43; 15,12.

[218] Cf. Lk 5,23-24; 7,11; 8,24.29.55; 9,42; 18,42; Acts 3,6; 9,40.

Jesus is not tempted by Satan in the course of his ministry.[219] But Satan does return to the offensive in the passion narrative striving to destroy Jesus by facilitating the desire of the Jewish leaders for his life (cf. 22,2-6). His apparent triumph is momentary, however, as Jesus' resurrection turns apparent defeat into renewed victory, a victory already foreshadowed before his death in the incident of the good thief (cf. 23,40-43) and after it by the reactions of those present (cf. 23,47-48).

Equipped by the Spirit at Pentecost, the disciples have power over demons and can free others from their bondage, as they could during their earlier temporary missions (cf. Acts 5,16). The Spirit equips Philip (8,7) and Paul (16,18) with this power.[220] The incident involving the sons of Sceva (19,13-16) shows the powerlessness of those without the Spirit.

3.5 *Faithful to Father's Plan*

The enigmatic statement of Lk 2,49 shows Jesus already conscious of the necessity (δεῖ) to fulfil his Father's plan for him. The composite citation in 4,18-21 presents this plan as including above all a mission in favour of the poor, an aspect underlined by its jubilary (cf. Is 61,1-2) and sabbatical background (cf. Is 58,6).[221] It is a mission also in favour of captives, including, in the Lucan context, those bound by Satan (cf. Lk 4,33-36.41; 13,16), and in favour of the bruised and the downtrodden among whom one may number the sick, the lame, the destitute, and so on (cf. 4,38-40; 7,22; 14,13). The glimpse afforded us of Jesus' activity in 4,31-43 already shows his commitment in this direction. That his mission as presented here includes sinners can hardly be excluded from the twice mentioned ἄφεσις of 4,18, particularly the second case.[222]

Jesus' consciousness of the Gentile component of his mission (cf. 2,30-32) is conveyed by the examples given in 4,25-27, while his perception of the divine constraint on him to preach the kingdom throughout Palestine is expressed in 4,43 (cf. 4,44). The temptation account had already seen Jesus prove himself the obedient, faithful Son of God. His faithfulness to his mission is also shown in 4,14-44 in the face of rejection by his own (cf. 4,22.29.30.31.43).

In the narrative proper Jesus' commitment to the poor is repeatedly made clear from the inaugural and programmatic sermon on the plain

---

[219] Cf. Brown, *Apostasy*, 9-10.15-16; Fitzmyer, *Lk X-XXIV*, 1441.

[220] Cf. Acts 6,3; 9,17.

[221] Cf. R. B. Sloan, Jr., *The Favorable Year of the Lord. A Study of Jubilary Theology in the Gospel of Luke*, Austin 1977, 28-44. The poor may also be understood in a general way to include not just the poor in the strict sense but captives, the blind, the bruised and the downtrodden.

[222] Cf. R. Bultmann, "ἀφίημι κτλ.", *TDNT* I, 511. The theme contributes to the image of the compassionate Jesus present in 4,14-44 (cf. 4,18-19.33-36.38-41).

(cf. 6,20) to the story of the widow's offering (21,1-4). It is expressed in sayings (cf. 7,22; 14,13; 18,22), parables (cf. 14,21; 16,25) and stories (cf. 19,8-9). It is a commitment to which the early Christians subscribe (cf. Acts 2,44-45; 4,32-37; 6,1-3; 20,35), so much so that Acts 4,34 suggests by allusion the fulfilment of the sabbatical ideal expressed in Dt 15,4 LXX.

The programme of Lk 4,14-44 is reflected in the many exorcisms in which Jesus and his disciples free those held in bondage by demons (cf. 6,18; 8,26-39; 9,1-6.37-42; 10,17-20; 11,14-22; 13,16; Acts 5,16; 8,7; 10,38; 19,12), the frequent miracles of healing (cf. Lk 6,18; 7,22; 8,42b-48; 14,2-5; 17,11-19; Acts 3,1-8; 5,16; 8,7; 14,8-10; 19,12; 28,8-9), the restoration of sight to the blind (cf. Lk 7,21-22; 18,35-43), the relief given to sinners and the compassion shown them throughout (cf. 5,20.29-32; 7,34.36-50; 15,1-32; 18,9-14; 19,10; 23,43; 24,47; Acts 2,38; 5,31; 8,22; 11,18; 17,30; 20,21; 26,20).[223]

In keeping with the programmatic anticipation of Lk 4,14-44 the kingdom is preached by Jesus throughout Palestine, beginning from Galilee (cf. 8,1; 9,2; 10,9.11; 11,14-20; 17,11-19.20-21; 19,9-11). His disciples carry out temporary missions in Galilee and along the way to Jerusalem (cf. 9,6; 10,9.11) before preaching the kingdom far beyond Palestine's borders (Acts 8,12; 14,22; 19,8; 20,25; 28,31) in obedience to the risen Christ's command. The Gentile component of Jesus' mission, foreshadowed at various times during his ministry (cf. Lk 13,29-30; 14,11-24), finds clear expression in this mission command (cf. 24,47; Acts 1,8). The book of Acts describes how this command is put into effect.

Jesus faithfulness to his mission is shown particularly by his acceptance of the inevitable fate of the prophets. Indeed he goes to meet it (cf. Lk 9,22.31.44.51; 13,33; 18,31-33; 22,42.53b; 23,46), and his disciples are prepared to follow his example (cf. Acts 4,19-20; 5,29-32.41; 7,2-60; 21,11-14).

4. Preparatory Role of Lk 1,5-4,44 in Luke–Acts

The foregoing analysis has given us an indication of the role of 1,5-4,44 in Luke–Acts. The decisive nature of the divine intervention in salvation history that initiates the new, eschatological age is highlighted in various ways, particularly in the infancy narrative. Allusions to and reminiscences of Old Testament texts, the canticles of praise that celebrate the fulfilment of the promise, and the use of Old Testament citations in 3,1-4,44 make abundantly clear that Luke is working with the scheme of promise and fulfilment. The view of salvation history conveyed in these chapters is programmatic for the remainder of the work.

---

[223] These reflect the presence of salvation in and through the person of Jesus, a presence that is explicitly noted throughout Luke-Acts; cf. 7,50; 8,48.50; 17,19; 19,9-10; 23,43; Acts 2,40; 4,12; 5,31.

A striking feature of 1,5-4,44 is the number of themes introduced here that run through the two-volume work. In this respect 1,5-4,44 may be readily compared to a musical overture. Some themes have been mentioned already, themes such as the Spirit, salvation, joy, repentance, the fulfilment of the promise, the kingdom of God, the divine 'must', Israel and its divided response, the Gentiles and their paraenetic use in warning Israel, the poor, the temple. Other themes such as prayer (cf. 1,10; 2,36-38; 3,21), peace (cf. 1,79; 2,14.29), compassion (cf. 4,33-36.38-41), social justice (cf. 3,10-14), Jerusalem (cf. 1,5-2,52; 4,12), and the way (cf. 4,30) are also found in these chapters.[224]

Many of the elements of the portrait of Jesus that are scattered throughout the narrative proper are in large measure anticipated or foreshadowed here in its composite picture of Jesus as king, prophet, priest and teacher. The same is true of Jesus' mission. Its universal significance with its Jewish and Gentile components is expressed in these chapters, as is the prospect of the formation of a new people of God emerging from and in continuity with Israel, but open to all peoples. Programmatic notes are sounded in the depiction of Jesus' triumph over Satan and in showing his faithfulness to his divine mission. The rejection and acceptance that are to meet him and his message and be encountered also by his witnesses are anticipated here.

There are other points of view from which 1,5-4,44 may be considered preparatory to the narrative proper. Since the main lines of the portrait of Jesus both with respect to his person and his mission are already drawn in 1,5-4,44, the reader or hearer at this point has knowledge that the characters of the narrative proper do not have. This creates various possibilities for the narrative proper.[225]

It creates an additional interest in the development of the narrative as one can observe from one's privileged position the crowds grappling with the question of Jesus' identity (cf. 5,26; 7,16-17; 9,7-9.19.43a; 11,15-16; 13,17; 18,15.43; 19,11.48; 23,48); Herod endeavouring to satisfy his curiosity (cf. 9,7-9; 23,8-11.15); John and his disciples apparently coming to an appreciation of Jesus' status (cf. 7,18-20); the apostles and disciples gradually making their way along a path paved with misunderstanding and denial (cf. 8,25; 9,20.45; 18,15.34; 22,31-34.54-62), scepticism (cf. 24,9-12) and despair (cf. 24,16-21), to a knowledge that comes only with the appearances and interpretative words of the risen

---

[224] See above; also Fitzmyer, *Lk I-IX*, 143-251; Navone, *Themes*; Bovon, *Luc*; O'Toole, *Luke's Theology*; A. A. Trites, "The Prayer Motif in Luke-Acts", Talbert (ed.), *Perspectives*, 168-186; W. E. Pilgrim, *Good News to the Poor. Wealth and Poverty in Luke-Acts*, Minneapolis 1981.

[225] Cf. R. A. Culpepper, *Anatomy of the Fourth Gospel. A Study in Literary Design*, Philadelphia 1983, 89.

Christ and the gift of the Spirit (cf. Acts 2,14-36). A statement such as that of Lk 5,10c takes on a deeper meaning in the light of the universal significance of Jesus' mission indicated in 1,5–4,44.

Another aspect of the knowledge given in 1,5–4,44 is the capacity for irony that it creates in the subsequent narrative.[226] The address of the centurion in 7,6-8, the reaction of the crowds to the miracle at Nain (cf. 7,16), the confessions of Peter (9,20) and the centurion at the cross (23,47), or Jesus' remarks in 11,29-32 to the effect that one greater than Solomon or Jonah is present, all these mean much more to the omniscient reader or hearer. The reaction of the scribes and pharisees to Jesus' forgiveness of sins in 5,21 strikes one as ironic in the light of his identity and mission as communicated in 1,5–4,44; tragically so the questions of the high priests and Pilate during the passion (cf. 22,66.70; 23,3), the insults to which Jesus is submitted on the cross (cf. 23,35-38.39), the affixed inscription (23,38).

The great irony of the account is of course the rejection of Jesus by many of those who had eagerly awaited his coming and particularly the Jewish leaders. Foreshadowed in 2,34-35 and 4,16-30, Jesus' rejection is played out in the narrative proper as the Jewish leaders, unmindful of the scriptures (cf. Lk 11,52; Acts 13,27), gradually grow more hostile towards him (cf. Lk 6,11; 11,53-54) and eventually plot his death (cf. 19,47; 22,2). With the decisive help of one of Jesus' apostles (cf. 22,3-4), their opposition to Jesus leads to the crucifixion of one whom they failed to recognize as the Christ (cf. 22,66), the Son of God (22,70), their king (23,2). Pilate's submission to the Jewish demands portrays him in a pathetic light, since he is convinced, like the reader, of Jesus' innocence. The tragic irony of the Jewish action is underlined again and again in the speeches of Acts (cf. 2,22-23; 3,13-15.17; 7,51-53; 13,26-29).

On the level of plot development the gospel's initial chapters create narrative tensions in various ways, tensions that serve to give the whole a dramatic unity. In the light of 2,30-32, 3,6 and 4,25-27, one is anxious to see how the universality of salvation will be achieved. This anxiety grows as Jesus preaches almost exclusively in Palestine, although alluding occasionally to the Gentile mission (cf. 13,29-30; 14,15-24). Jesus' command of 24,47 and Acts 1,8 partly releases the tension, but only partly, since the preaching in Acts 2,1-8,3 is confined to Jerusalem.

Peter's conversion of Cornelius, the missionary work of Paul and Barnabas and the historic decision of the Council of Jerusalem point towards the accomplishment of the divine design. But it is only with the arrival of Paul in Rome and the concluding statements of 28,28-31 that the tension is released and one is reassured that the prophecies of Lk 2,30-32 and 3,6 will be fulfilled.

---

[226] Cf. Culpepper, *Anatomy,* 165-180.

The destiny of Israel is another strand of tension that runs through Luke–Acts. With statements such as those of Lk 1,32-33 and 2,34, and the scene at Nazareth, the question of Israel's fate is a live one. In the narrative proper a division within Israel soon appears (cf. 6,6-11), and it gradually becomes more apparent as Jesus meets rejection and acceptance. These conflicting reactions reach an initial climax at the conclusion of the travel narrative (19,47-48) where Jewish opposition to Jesus becomes a murderous plot (cf. 19,47), but where the enthusiasm of the people for his teaching temporarily prevents its realisation (cf. 19,48). The plot eventually achieves its goal, only to be followed by the resurrection and Jesus' command to his disciples to pursue a universal mission. Whither Israel now?

The apostolic preaching in Jerusalem represents a renewed offer of salvation to 'all Israel' (cf. Acts 2,14-40; 3,19-21.25-26). It meets with acceptance and rejection, the latter leading to persecution and to the spread of the word beyond Jerusalem (cf. 8,4; 11,19). The missionary section of Acts sees the word accepted by Samaritans and Gentiles, while Jewish reaction is, as before, divided. Jewish hostility, which is vehement at times, leads Paul to the Gentile mission, but not to the abandonment of Israel despite the ominous words of 13,46. As has been suggested above, the conclusion of Acts represents a double edged attempt to spur Israel on to repentance (cf. 28,26-28).[227] This strand of tension remains unresolved at the conclusion of Luke–Acts.[228]

Lk 1,5–4,44, then, prepares the reader or hearer in various ways for the narrative that follows by indicating the coming of the eschatological age and the use by Luke of the scheme of promise and fulfilment, introducing themes that run through the two-volume work, presenting various aspects of the person and mission of Jesus, creating narrative tensions and giving the narrative proper an enhanced capacity for irony. It acts, in effect, as a preparatory unit for the narrative proper of Luke's work.[229]

Examples of introductory or preparatory narrative units are not uncommon in ancient literary works.[230] Such units might form part of the

---

[227] See above pp. 142-143, and 143 nn. 185 and 187.

[228] Likewise that of the temple cult (see pp. 130-131 above). Its passing appears to be foreshadowed in 1,5–2,52, here and there in the gospel narrative (cf. 13,35; 21,5-7.20-24; 23,45; 24,50-52), and in Acts (cf. 2,46; 20,7; 7,47-50.55-56). But the disciples are still praying in the temple at the conclusion of the gospel (24,53) and the beginning of Acts (cf. 2,46; 3,1-8; 5,20.25.42), and Paul is to be found there in Acts 21.

[229] The themes of discipleship and eyewitness-ship which are lacking in 1,5–4,44 have already been introduced in Luke's proemium in the reference to the group of 'eyewitnesses and ministers of the word'.

[230] Cf. K. Lorenz, *Untersuchungen zum Geschichtswerk des Polybios*, Stuttgart 1931, 87-88 n. 93, who cites examples from Thucydides, Ephorus, Duris, Anaximenes, Strabo,

proemium, as in the works of Herodotus (*Hist.* I,2-5), Thucydides (*War* I,2.1-19.1), Sallust (*Hist.* fr. 7-18),[231] Appian (*Hist.* I Pr.) or Tacitus (*Hist.* I,4-11),[232] or they might be placed between the proemium and the narrative proper, as in the works of Thucydides (*War* I,89.1-118.2), Sallust (*Cat.* 5,1-16,4),[233] or Polybius. The latter prefixed two books to the narrative proper of his *History,* describing them with the terms προκατασκευή (I,3.10; 13.1.7.8; II,71.7) and κατασκευή (I,13.5). Their purpose was to render the narrative proper more intelligible and easy to follow (cf. I,3.8-10; 13.9-10).[234]

Dionysius of Halicarnassus used the verb προκατασκευάζω in relation to material presented before the narrative and anticipating events recounted there with the purpose of rendering the narrative more credible and effective.[235] The term προκατάστασις was also used for a narrative unit preliminary to the narrative proper; Hermogenes used προδιήγησις as its equivalent.[236] The terms used by Polybius, Dionysius and Hermogenes refer to narrative units that belong neither to the proemium nor the narrative proper. The terms themselves convey the idea of a preliminary or introductory narrative unit that has a preparatory role with respect to the narrative proper.

Lk 1,5-4,44 lies between the proemium and the narrative proper of Luke's gospel, and, as we have seen, is closely linked to both. In addition to the characteristics of this unit pointed out above, it may be noted that it contains a summary of events surrounding the births and childhood of John and Jesus (1,5-2,52), a summary of John's ministry (3,1-20), a

---

Josephus, Arrian and Sallust. See the discussion of introductory units associated with secondary proemia in ch. II, pp. 71-73 above.

[231] On Sallust's introductory unit contained in the proemium of his *Histories,* see P. Klingner, "Über die Einleitung der Historien Sallusts", *Hermes* 63 (1928) 165-192; A. La Penna, *Sallustio e la "rivoluzione" romana,* Milan 1969², 332-333.

[232] Cf. Leeman, "Prologues", 175; G.E.F. Chilver, *A Historical Commentary on Tacitus' Histories I and II,* Oxford 1979, 33.

[233] Between the proemium of his *Catiline Conspiracy* (1-4) and the beginning of the narrative proper in 17,1 Sallust has a portrait of Catiline (5,1-8), an excursus putting Catiline's decadence into the context of the general decline of morals in Rome (6,1-13,5), a development of the portrait of 5,1-8 and a more immediate preparation for the conspiracy (14,1-16,4). In 4,5 Sallust himself presents his portrait of Catiline as preceding the beginning of the narrative proper (... *prius explananda sunt, quam initium narrandi faciam*).

[234] Thucydides' so called Pentekontaëtie (*War* I,89.1-118.2) acted, according to Pédech (*Polybe,* 33 n. 1), as a model for Polybius' introductory volumes.

[235] *Is.* 15,1: Τότε δὲ προκατασκευάζεταί τινα πρὸ τῶν διηγήσεων πράγματα καὶ προλαμβάνει τὰ μέλλοντα πιστοτέρας αὐτὰς ἢ κατ' ἄλλο τι χρησιμωτέρας ποιήσειν οἰόμενος (cf. 15,3).

[236] *Περὶ Εὑρ* II,1; cf. I.C.T. Ernesti, *Lexicon Technologiae Graecorum Rhetoricae,* Leipzig 1795, 292: "Προκατάστασις, est veluti *aditus narrationis,* eiusque *praeparatio,* quae et προδιήγησις dicitur Hermogeni ... *narratio antecedens, et antecurrens.*"

genealogy and a number of events preliminary to Jesus' ministry including a programmatic meeting with Satan (3,21–4,13), and an anticipated portrait of that ministry (4,14-44). It contains, therefore, elements of the summary-type introductory narrative unit exemplified in the proemia of Herodotus or Thucydides, as well as biographical elements of the type exemplified in the introductory narrative units of Sallust's *Catiline Conspiracy*. Its literary role is similar to that of the classical parallels mentioned above, its uniqueness quite evident, even though all such introductory units have their own individual characteristics. Of the terms used to describe such units in classical literature – προκατασκευή, κατασκευή, προκατάστασις and προδιήγησις – Hermogenes' προδιήγησις is perhaps the most suitable to describe the role of 1,5–4,44 in Luke–Acts, being broad enough to embrace its various facets as set out above. In any event, the role of this unit within Luke–Acts is clearly a preparatory one. This circumstance has important repercussions for the discussion that follows in ch. V.

Conclusion

Lk 1,5–4,44 represents a preparatory narrative unit not without parallel in ancient literary writings. Situated between the proemium and the narrative proper, it prepares the reader or hearer in a variety of ways for the narrative that follows. It does so with the aid of inspired prophecies, angelic communications, reminiscences and citations of Old Testament texts, the foreshadowing and anticipation of future events, programmatic scenes, composite units and statements.

It makes clear the eschatological nature of the age ushered in by the announcement of the forerunner's birth, and shows that Luke is working with the scheme of promise and fulfilment. It introduces the person and mission of Jesus, indicating his significance both for Israel and the Gentiles. The portrait of Jesus drawn in this preparatory section lends an added interest to various aspects of the development of the narrative, creates narrative tensions that help to bind the various episodes of the two-volume work together, and bestows on it an additional capacity for irony.

Lk 1,5–4,44 differs in method, style and presentation from the proemium of Luke's work, and in purpose for the most part. But it does share one aim with Lk 1,1-4, namely, that of preparing the hearer or reader for the narrative that follows.

CHAPTER V

THE LITERARY FORM OF LUKE–ACTS

Introduction

Lk 1,1-4, as we have seen in ch III, indicates a programme for Luke's two-volume work that is at once literary, theological and historical. Accurate research and eyewitness-ship represent important features of this programme in which the main emphasis lies on the actual presentation of the material. The evident interest of Luke's proemium in the reliability of the narrative and in methods of research and presentation that are common to ancient historians led Conzelmann to argue that the evangelist's presentation of the relationship between the object of faith and the gospel narrative at this point differs radically from that of Mark. Whereas Mark's narrative provides a broad unfolding of the kerygma, Luke's is not itself kerygma, but functions as the kerygma's historical foundation, being added a secondary factor.[1] Klein takes the 'profane' style of Luke's proemium and the consequent rejection of a *lingua christiana* to indicate the objective verifiability of the content of faith.[2] In his opinion Luke puts historical certainty before the certainty of salvation and presents the object of faith as a succession of historical events.[3] In the light of the critical positions of Conzelmann and Klein it seems advisable to take a closer look at the literary form of Luke's work, particularly from the point of view of its proemium.

Surprisingly enough, few have attempted to define the literary form of this two-volume work, possibly because of Overbeck's apparently harsh opinion of Luke's decision to follow his gospel with Acts.[4] Most of the attention has been devoted to the gospels which are frequently seen as an original Christian creation — the only original form, in Overbeck's view, with which Christianity enriched literature.[5] The search for parallels

---

[1] *Mitte*, 3.

[2] Cf. Klein, "Lk 1,1-4", 214.

[3] Cf. Klein, "Lk 1,1-4", 216.

[4] F. Overbeck, *Christentum und Kultur*, Basle 1919, 78; see the comment of J.-C. Emmelius, *Tendenzkritik und Formengeschichte. Der Beitrag Franz Overbecks zur Auslegung der Apostelgeschichte im 19. Jahrhundert*, FKDG 27: Göttingen 1975, 182-186.

[5] F. Overbeck, "Über die Anfänge der patristischen Literatur", *HZ* 48 (1882) 443; see also R. Bultmann, *Die Geschichte der Synoptischen Tradition*, FRLANT 29: Göttingen

in contemporary literature has led to their being placed most notably in the categories of ancient biography[6] and ancient aretalogical writing.[7] A prominent and influential feature in the debate has been the distinction made by Schmidt between *Hochliteratur* and *Kleinliteratur*, with the gospels usually assigned to the latter category.[8] Acts has been described among other things as an apologetic work of various shades,[9] a religious

---

1921, 227-229; N. Perrin, "The Literary *Gattung* 'Gospel' — Some Observations", *ET* 82 (1970-71) 4; Kümmel, *Introduction*, 35-37; P. Vielhauer, *Geschichte der urchristlichen Literatur. Einleitung in das Neue Testament, die Apokryphen und die Apostolischen Väter*, Berlin-New York 1978, 282-283.350.354; Pesch, *Markusevangelium* I, 1; R. Guelich, "The Gospel Genre", Stuhlmacher (ed.), *Evangelium*, 211-217.

   [6] Cf. C. M. Votaw, "The Gospels and Contemporary Biographies", *AJPh* 19 (1915) 45-73.217-249; repr. as *The Gospels and Contemporary Biographies in the Greco-Roman World*, ed. J. Reumann, BS 27: Philadelphia 1970; C. H. Talbert, *What is a Gospel? The Genre of the Canonical Gospels*, Philadelphia 1977; idem, *Literary Patterns*, 125-140; D. Lührmann, "Biographie des Gerechten als Evangelium. Vorstellungen zu einem Markus-Kommentar", *WuD* NF 14 (1977) 39.43; P. L. Shuler, *A Genre for the Gospels. The Biographical Character of Matthew*, Philadelphia 1982, 43-45. A. Dihle, "Die Evangelien und die griechische Biographie", Stuhlmacher (ed.), *Evangelium*, 402-411, recognizes the gospels as biographies of Jesus but insists that they are not comparable to Greek biographies; W. Marxsen, "Bemerkungen zur "Form" der sogenannten synoptischen Evangelien", *TLZ* 81 (1956) 347, describes Mark as a "kerygmatic biography", a description which M. Hengel, "Probleme des Markusevangeliums", Stuhlmacher (ed.), *Evangelium*, 260, applies to all four gospels; see the discussion of D. E. Aune in *The New Testament in Its Literary Environment*, Philadelphia 1989, 27-76; also V. Fusco, "Tradizione evangelica e modelli letterari. Riflessoni su due libri recenti", *BibOr* 144 (1985) 78-90; G. N. Stanton, *The Gospels and Jesus*, Oxford 1989, 14-33; C. J. Hemer, *The Book of Acts in the Setting of Hellenistic History*, ed. C. H. Gempf, WUNT 49: Tübingen 1989, 33-43.91-100.

   [7] Cf. M. Smith, "Prolegomena to a discussion of Aretalogies, Divine Men, the Gospels and Jesus", *JBL* 90 (1971) 174-199; see also J. M. Robinson, H. Koester, *Trajectories through Early Christianity*, Philadelphia 1971; H. Koester, "Überlieferung und Geschichte der frühchristlichen Evangelienliteratur", *ANRW* II.25.2, ed. W. Haase, Berlin-New York 1984, 1509-1512; R. H. Gundry, "Recent Investigations into the Literary Genre 'Gospel'", *New Dimensions in New Testament Study*, eds. R. N. Longenecker, M. C. Tenney, Grand Rapids 1974, 102-107; W. Schmithals, *Das Evangelium nach Markus* I, ÖTK 2.1: Gütersloh-Würzburg 1979, 45-46; H. C. Kee, "Aretalogy and the Gospel", *JBL* 92 (1973) 402-411.

   [8] K. L. Schmidt, "Die Stellung der Evangelien in der allgemeinen Literaturgeschichte", *EYXAPIΣTHPION. Studien zur Religion und Literatur des Alten und Neuen Testaments* II, Fs für H. Gunkel, ed. H. Schmidt, FRLANT NF 19.2: Göttingen 1923, 50-134. For Cadbury, *Making*, 131, the difference between "formal literature" and the gospels "is perhaps in degree rather than in kind". See also Tyson, *Death of Jesus*, 9-16.

   [9] Cf. A. G. McGiffert, "The Historical Criticism of Acts in Germany", Foakes Jackson, Lake (eds.), *Beginnings* I.II, 363-395; de Wette, Overbeck, *Kurze Erklärung der Apostelgeschichte* LXIVf.; J. Weiss, *Ueber die Absicht und den literarischen Charakter der Apostelgeschichte*, Göttingen 1897, 56.

history,[10] an historical work,[11] and an historical monograph.[12] It has also been regarded as related to, if quite different from, the *praxeis* literature of the Hellenistic world.[13]

Meyer had no hesitation in declaring Luke–Acts a two-volume historical work, as Bisping had done before him.[14] Plümacher views the work in terms of two Sallustian-type historical monographs.[15] Hengel prefers to compare it to Jewish Hellenistic historiographical writing,[16] while Talbert seeks a biographical-type model in Diogenes Laertius' *Lives of the Philosophers*.[17] Other suggested analogies include didactic biography[18] and the novel, both in its historical[19] and Christian forms.[20]

Given that opinions on the literary form or genre of the canonical gospels, Acts and Luke-Acts are so varied, a fresh look at the question from the point of view of Luke–Acts may prove useful. Before undertaking this a few preliminary remarks are necessary on the role sometimes attributed to anonymity in this debate, on the use made in the debate of the term 'gospel', and on the importance of literary structure for the determination of literary form or genre.

---

[10] Cf. Perrot, "Actes" 255-262.

[11] Cf. Meyer, *Ursprung* III, 5-7; Jacquier, *Actes*, XLIX; M. Dibelius, *Studies in the Acts of the Apostles*, ed. H. Greeven, London 1973, 123-124. Kümmel, *Introduction*, 161-162, dismisses this description, pointing out the lack of many of the marks of real historical writing such as completeness of material, exactitude of historical detail, consistent chronology and biographical interest.

[12] Cf. Conzelmann, *Apg*, 7; E. Plümacher, "Die Apostelgeschichte als historische Monographie", Kremer (ed.), *Les Actes des Apôtres*, 457-466; M. Hengel, *Zur urchristlichen Geschichtsschreibung*, Stuttgart 1979, 37.48-49; Weiser, *Apg 1-12*, 29-31; Schneider, *Apg* I, 122-125; W.W. Gasque, "A Fruitful Field. Recent Studies of the Acts of the Apostles", *Int* 42 (1988) 129.

[13] Cf. A. Wikenhauser, *Die Apostelgeschichte und ihr Geschichtswert*, NA 8.3-5: Münster 1921, 94-107; also P. Wendland, *Die Urchristliche Literaturformen*, HNT I.3: Tübingen 1912²⁻³, 314-335.

[14] Cf. Meyer, *Ursprung* III, 5-7; earlier Bisping, *Mk und Lk*, 146.

[15] E. Plümacher, "Neues Testament und hellenistische Form. Zur literarischen Gattung der lukanischen Schriften", *ThViat* 14 (1979) 109-123.

[16] *Geschichtsschreibung*, 48-49.

[17] *Gospel*, 95-96; idem. *Literary Patterns*, 125-140; see also K. Berger, "Hellenistische Gattungen im Neuen Testament", Haase (ed.), *ANRW* II.25.2, 1231-1264. According to this analogy the gospel is seen as the biography of the philosopher-founder and Acts as the narrative of the disciples and followers and their school.

[18] Cf. V. Robbins, "Prefaces in Greco-Roman Biography and Luke-Acts", *PerspRelStud* 6 (1979) 107-108.

[19] Cf. R.J. Karris, "Widows and Minors: Literary Criticism and Luke's Sitz im Leben", *Society of Biblical Literature 1978 Seminar Papers* I, ed. P.J. Achtemeier, Missoula 1978, 53. R.I. Pervo, *Profit with Delight. The Literary Genre of the Acts of the Apostles*, Philadelphia 1987, 115-138, designates Acts as such.

[20] Cf. S.F. Praeder, "Luke-Acts and the Ancient Novel", *Society of Biblical Literature 1981 Seminar Papers* I, ed. K.H. Richards, Chico 1981, 288-289; for recent work on the ancient novel see G. Anderson, *Ancient Fiction. The Novel in the Graeco-Roman World*, Totowa 1984; Pervo, *Profit with Delight*, 86-114.169-177.

1. Anonymity

Anonymity has been used as a criterion to distinguish literature from non-literature,[21] 'popular' from 'artistic' or 'high' literature,[22] but such a use is difficult to justify. How, for example, is one to classify the book of Job, regarded as a work of "high literary quality",[23] or the heroic poems of the *Iliad* and *Odyssey*?[24]

Anonymity is a prominent feature of ancient literature, being found in Old Testament historiography,[25] Jewish literature,[26] the New Testament,[27] early Christian writings,[28] and to a lesser extent in classical literature.[29] In the context of works situated in a living tradition it can certainly imply the writer's respect for that tradition and his probable concept of himself as a faithful transmitter thereof (cf. Lk 1,1-4; 1 Jn 1,5). But whether he appends his name to his work or not, the writer is the one who ultimately selects and arranges the material and gives it its final overall literary structure.[30] His literary product must be judged for what it is, and not on the basis of a particular literary convention.

---

[21] Cf. H. R. Balz, "Anonymität und Pseudepigraphie im Urchristentum. Überlegungen zum literarischen und theologischen Problem der urchristlichen und gemeinantiken Pseudepigraphie", *ZTK* 66 (1969) 418-419.428-429.

[22] See the comments of G. Bornkamm, "Evangelien, formgeschichtlich", *RGG*³ II, ed. K. Galling, Tübingen 1958³, 750; Kümmel, *Introduction,* 37. One wonders what Flaubert would have thought of Kümmel's position given his view that the author, in his work, should be like God in the universe, everywhere present, but nowhere visible; cf. R. Scholes, R. Kellogg, *The Nature of Narrative,* New York 1966, 268.

[23] Cf. M. H. Pope, "Book of Job", *The Interpreter's Dictionary of the Bible* II, ed. G. A. Buttrick, Nashville-New York 1962, 914; also R.A.F. McKenzie, "Job", *JBC* I (ed. R. E. Murphy), 512.

[24] Commenting on the fact that Homer never refers to himself in his poetry, although others such as Hecataeus, Herodotus and Thucydides do in their works, Dio Chrysostom (*Or.* 53,9-10) suggests that "like the prophets of the gods, he speaks, as it were, from the invisible, from somewhere in the inmost sanctuary".

[25] Almost all the books of the OT appeared anonymously. Talmudic tradition listed authors for some of these (cf. *b. B. B.* 14b-15a).

[26] Cf. *Book of Jubilees, Testaments of the Twelve Patriarchs, Liber Antiquitatum Biblicarum.*

[27] Cf. Matthew; Mark; Luke-Acts; John; 1 John; Hebrews; also M. Wolter, "Die anonymen Schriften des Neuen Testaments. Annäherungsversuch an ein literarisches Phänomen", *ZNW* 79 (1988) 1.

[28] Cf. *1 Clement, Didache, Epistle of Barnabas, Gospel of Truth.*

[29] The rhetorical treatises *Rhet. ad Alex.* (cf. ed. of H. Rackham, LCL, 258-260), *Rhet. ad Her.* (cf. ed. of H. Caplan, LCL, vii-xiv) and 'Longinus', *De Subl.* (cf. *OCD,* 743) are also anonymous works. In antiquity anonymous works were not infrequently attributed to well known authors of works of a similar genre (cf. *OCD,* 90.743).

[30] Moreover, a work that is largely a 'community product' need not have a 'non-literary' character. Much of the material in the *Iliad* and the *Odyssey* appears to have had an existence in the community long before it was put into written form (cf. C. M. Bowra, *Homer,* London 1979, 2; idem, *Tradition and Design in the Iliad,* Oxford

2. Gospel

When used as an indication of literary form or genre the term 'gospel' clearly conveys the uniqueness of the gospels.[31] But it is doubtful whether it should be used in this way at all. It is well recognised that the term εὐαγγέλιον in the New Testament does not indicate literary genre. It occurs generally in the singular and denotes the Christian message and its proclamation.[32]

It is generally accepted that the term became a designation of literary genre in second century writings of the Apostolic Fathers, but this is doubtful.[33] As in the New Testament the term may denote the Christian message of salvation (cf. *Ep. of Barn.* 5,9; 1 *Cl.* 47,2; *Did.* 8,2) or the content of written works (cf. *Did.* 15,3-4; 2 *Cl.* 8,5). It is used in the plural in reference to the individual gospels by Justin (*Apol.* I,66.3), the *Muratorian Canon* (vv.9.17), Clement of Alexandria (*Strom.* III,13) and Irenaeus (*Adv. Haer.* III,1.1; 11.8),[34] while the *Muratorian Canon* (v.2) and Irenaeus (*Adv. Haer.* III,1.1; 11.8) still use the singular to indicate the one message of salvation contained in these books.[35] It is hardly

---

1930, 1; G. S. Kirk, *Homer and the Oral Tradition,* Cambridge 1976, 201-217). In the final analysis an individual took it upon himself to organize the material, give it written form and a final literary framework (cf. Kirk, *Homer,* 204).

[31] For its use as an indication of literary genre see, for example, W. Schneemelcher in E. Hennecke, W. Schneemelcher, *New Testament Apocrypha* I, London 1963, 76.79; Perrin, "Gattung", 4; H. Frankemölle, "Evangelium als theologischer Begriff und sein Bezug zur literarischen Gattung 'Evangelium'", in D. Dormeyer, H. Frankemölle, "Evangelium als literarische Gattung und als theologischer Begriff. Tendenzen und Aufgaben der Evangelienforschung im 20. Jahrhundert, mit einer Untersuchung des Markusevangeliums in seinem Verhältnis zur antiken Biographie", Haase (ed.), *ANRW* II.25.2, 1983.

[32] On this term see J. Schniewind, *Euangelion. Ursprung und erste Gestalt des Begriffs Evangelium* I, BFCT 2.13: Gütersloh 1927; Friedrich, "εὐαγγελίζεσθαι", 727-735; Schneemelcher in Hennecke, Schneemelcher, *Apocrypha* I, 71-75; G. Strecker, "Literarkritische Überlegungen zum εὐαγγέλιον-Begriff im Markusevangelium", *Neues Testament und Geschichte. Historisches Geschehen und Deutung im Neuen Testament,* Fs für O. Cullmann, eds. H. Baltensweiler, B. Reicke, Zürich-Tübingen 1972, 91-104; idem, "εὐαγγέλιον", *EWNT* II, 176-186; Vielhauer, *Geschichte,* 252-258; M. Erbetta, *Gli Apocrifi del Nuovo Testamento* I.1, Turin 1975, 55-63; Kümmel, *Introduction,* 35-36; Frankemölle, "Evangelium", 1635-1694; Koester, "Frühchristlichen Evangelienliteratur", 1464-1465; idem, "From the Kerygma-Gospel to Written Gospels", *NTS* 35 (1989) 361-370. In the much discussed text of Mk 1,1 it indicates the subject matter of the work; cf. E. Lohmeyer, *Das Evangelium des Markus,* Göttingen 1967⁸, 10; W. Marxsen, *Mark the Evangelist. Studies on the Redaction History of the Gospel,* tr. by J. Boyce et al., Nashville-New York 1969, 91.

[33] Cf. Koester, "Kerygma-Gospel", 370-381.

[34] See texts in Aland, *Synopsis,* 533-538.

[35] Cf. Iren., *Adv. Haer.* III,11.8: καὶ τὰ εὐαγγέλια... Τὸ δὲ κατὰ Λουκᾶν... τετράμορφον καὶ τὸ εὐαγγέλιον. The gospel titles exhibit this latter use. On these titles and their dates see N.B. Stonehouse, *Origins of the Synoptic Gospels. Some Basic*

without significance that Justin (*Apol.* I,66.3) used not this term but the term "memoirs" (ἀπομνημονεύματα) to describe the canonical gospels (ἃ καλόνται εὐαγγέλια). The term 'gospel' denotes the content of these early Christian writings, not their literary form or genre.

Significantly, the designation 'gospel' was used in relation to writings different in literary form or genre from the canonical gospels. Irenaeus, for example, used it for the homiletic type *Gospel of Truth* which, he wrote, agreed in nothing with the gospels of the apostles.[36] When the term was applied to such writings as the *Gospels* of Thomas and Philip, both collections of logia,[37] or to the *Gospels* of Judas[38] and Eve,[39] or the *Gospel of Perfection,*[40] it became even less suitable for the role of distinguishing literary form or genre. In reality, in the cases cited above from the *Gospel of Truth* to the *Gospel of Perfection,* the term 'gospel' indicates a book that announces a message of joy which is soteriological for the most part. It is not an indication of literary form or genre. The early Christian writers do not appear to have seen it as such, and Luke did not use the term when referring to his predecessors' writings (cf. Lk 1,1). The preached gospel's outline may have given rise to a new literary genre, but the term itself is hardly a suitable one with which to indicate the literary form or genre of a written work.

Questions, London 1964, 15-18; D. E. Aune, "The Problem of the Genre of the Gospels: A Critique of C. H. Talbert's *What is a Gospel?*", *Studies of History and Tradition in the Four Gospels, Gospel Perspectives* II, eds. R. T. France, D. Wenham, Sheffield 1981, 44.

[36] *Adv. Haer.* III,11.8. The work contains no account of the life, works or words of Jesus, and according to H.-C. Puech in Hennecke, Schneemelcher, *Apocrypha* I, 238, has "the character of a public address, a lecture, interrupted by admonitions to the audience, present or imagined"; cf. Erbetta, *Apocrifi* I.1, 519. Clement of Alexandria (*Strom.* III,9.63; 13.93) uses the term in reference to the "gospel of the Egyptians", but its literary form or genre is not known.

[37] Cf. Puech in Hennecke, Schneemelcher, *Apocrypha* I, 271-307; also Erbetta, *Apocrifi* I.1, 213-243.253-282.

[38] Puech, in Hennecke, Schneemelcher, *Apocrypha* I, 314, suggests that the work "was probably in substance an exposition of the secret doctrine (licentious and violently antinomian in character) ostensibly revealed by Judas." Irenaeus (*Adv. Haer.* I,31.1) described it as a "fictitious history".

[39] A second century gnostic work which, Puech suggests (Hennecke, Schneemelcher, *Apocrypha* I, 241-243), may have set forth the gnostic doctrine of salvation; cf. Erbetta, *Apocrifi* I.1, 537-538.

[40] Puech speculates (Hennecke, Schneemelcher, *Apocrypha* I, 232-233) that this 'gospel', described as gnostic by Epiphanius (*Pan.* XXVI,2.5), may have taught the ideal of perfection and the means of attaining it, or it may have been a gospel destined for the perfect, or may have been considered perfect in itself, containing the sum total of revelation or of gnosis.

3. Literary Structure

Since it is the work as a whole, which is more than the sum of its parts, that is crucial for literary form or genre,[41] the arrangement or literary structure of a work is a decisive factor in its determination.[42] Moreover, such parts as the proemium and epilogue, the beginning and end of the narrative proper, preparatory units and disgressions, represent invaluable sources of information on the author's intention and its realisation, and on the particular nature of the work.[43]

3.1 Proemium

The proemium is undoubtedly a privileged part of the literary structure, introducing as it does the work as a whole and conveying the intention which underlies it.[44] Its opening words frequently indicate literary form or genre, as may be readily demonstrated from the historical works of Herodotus,[45] Thucydides[46] and Josephus,[47] the biographical writings of Xenophon[48] and Tacitus,[49] or the rhetorical treatise of Quintilian.[50]

---

[41] Cf. E. Güttgemanns, *Offene Fragen zur Formgeschichte des Evangeliums. Eine methodologische Skizze der Grundlagenproblematik der Form- und Redaktionsgeschichte*, BET 54: Munich 1971², 184-185.

[42] Cf. R. Wellek, A. Warren, *Theory of Literature*, London 1956, 216; W. Doty, "The Concept of Genre in Literary Analysis", *Seminar of Biblical Literature Proceedings 1972*, ed. L. C. McGaughy, Missoula 1972, 422.

[43] Cf. F. Lentzen-Deis, "Methodische Überlegungen zur Bestimmung literarischer Gattungen im Neuen Testament", *Bib* 62 (1981) 14-15.

[44] On the function of the proemium in a literary work see ch. III, pp. 110-112; also Earl, "Prologue-form", 842-856. If, as could undoubtedly happen, and indeed frequently did, the proemium was written after the rest of the work's outline or even the work itself was completed, then the author's intention should be even more evident at this point. The epilogue, coming at the end of the work and offering in recapitulatory fashion an overview of the whole, should also be invaluable in determining literary form or genre; on the function of the epilogue see Quint., *Inst. Or.* IV,1.5.27-28; VI,1.9-12.

[45] In his opening words he informs the reader (*Hist.* I,1) that his work (ἱστορίης ἀπόδεξις) sets out to preserve the memory of the past by putting on record the astonishing deeds both of Greeks and Barbarians, and more particularly by showing how they came into conflict (τά τε ἄλλα καὶ δι' ἥν αἰτίην ἐπολέμησαν ἀλλήλοισι).

[46] *War* I,1.1: ... ξυνέγραψε τὸν πόλεμον τῶν Πελοποννησίων καὶ 'Αθηναίων ὡς ἐπολέμησαν πρὸς ἀλλήλους.

[47] *BJ* I,1: 'Επειδὴ τὸν 'Ιουδαίων πρὸς 'Ρωμαίους πόλεμον ...· see also Appian, *Hist. Rom.* Pr. 1: Τὴν 'Ρωμαϊκὴν ἱστορίαν ἀρχόμενος συγγράφειν ...

[48] The encomiastic nature of Xenophon's *Agesilaus* is made clear from the beginning (1,1): Οἶδα μέν, ὅτι τῆς 'Αγησιλάου ἀρετῆς τε καὶ δόξης οὐ ῥάδιον ἄξιον ἔπαινον γράψαι.

[49] The indication is given in the reference to the biographer's task in the opening words: Clarorum virorum facta moresque posteris tradere. He indicates explicitly before the end of the paragraph that he is writing a life of Agricola.

[50] *Inst. Or.* I Pr. 1: ... de ratione dicendi componerem; see also *Rhet. ad Her.* I,1.1: ... de ratione dicendi conscriberemus; the openings of the didactic or scientific treatises on mathematics by Archimedes and Apollonius of Perga, on medicine by Dioscorides, on agriculture by Varro, etc.; cf. Earl, "Prologue-form", 846, and there n. 18.

Such an indication may also be found in the course of the proemium, as in the case of Philostratus' biography of Apollonius,[51] or towards its conclusion, as in Sallust's two monographs[52] and some of Plutarch's *Lives*.[53] The proemium must be considered as a whole when attempting to establish the literary form or genre of a work from this vantage point.[54] This is not suprising since it is really an expanded title and generally forms a well-defined literary unit.

References to one's predecessors, which are frequently found in proemia, represent valuable indications of literary form or genre. This may be illustrated from the proemia of the historical works of Polybius,[55] Diodorus,[56] Dionysius of Halicarnassus[57] or Josephus.[58] The purpose of a work, which is likewise often given in the proemium,[59] is also a factor that affects literary form or genre. A biography, for example, may have an apologetic,[60] ethical[61] or didactic purpose.[62] Historical works may also have an apologetic purpose,[63] though generally speaking their purpose is didactic.[64]

Finally, since the role of the proemium of a work is introductory, one would expect the nature of the work it introduces to influence the particular themes or motifs it employs. Such indeed is the case. Differences in genre are reflected in the references to subject matter frequently found in proemia to works of all kinds.[65] They may be

---

[51] Cf. *Apoll.*, I,2.

[52]. Cf. *Cat.* 4,3; *Jug.* 5,1.

[53]. Cf. *Pelop.* 2,5; *Dem.* 3,1; see also Diog. Laert., *Lives* I Pr. § 21 (cf. § 1).

[54] Earl's problems in his attempt to ascertain the genre of Sallust's monographs ("Prologue-form", 844-856) stem from an over-reliance on the information given in the first sentence of a work.

[55] Cf. *Hist.* I,1.1.

[56] Cf. *Hist.* I,1.1-3; 3.1-5.

[57] Cf. *Ant. Rom.* I,1.1-2; 4.3; 5.4; 6.2.

[58] Cf. *Ant.* I,1-4; see also Tac., *Hist.* I,1; Diosc., *De Mat. Med.* I Pr.; Quint., *Inst. Or.* I Pr. 1-4; *Rhet. ad Her.* IV,1.1-7.10.

[59] See ch. I, n. 27.

[60] Cf. Phil., *Apoll.* I,2. Whereas Gorgias' encomium of Helen had a predominantly apologetic aspect (cf. Is., *Hel.* §§ 14-15), that of Isocrates' was written strictly to praise her (cf. *Hel.* §§ 14-15).

[61] Cf. Plut., *Aem.* 1,1-3.

[62] Cf. Philo, *De Vita Mos.* I,1.

[63] Cf. Jos., *BJ* I,6-8; *Ant.* I,4; Dion. Hal., *Ant. Rom.* I,5.3.

[64] Cf. Pol., *Hist.* I,1.2; Dion. Hal., *Ant. Rom.* I,5.3. On the level of the smaller literary unit it may be noted, for example, that the nature of Paul's defence speeches in Acts 22-26 is made clear in the proemia of those speeches; cf. 22,1; 24,10; 26,2.

[65] In the case of biography reference is invariably made to the life of the person concerned. Although speaking of Alexander in their proemia, neither Diodorus nor Arrian ever refers to a life of his hero; indeed both make it clear, the former in the proemium (XVII,1.2-5), the latter in the epilogue (VII,30.3), that they are writing history; likewise

reflected, too, in the purpose often given for the literary undertaking.[66] And one can point to proemial themes that are characteristic of certain genres, as for instance the praise of history, frequently found in historical works,[67] or the attribution of the choice of subject matter to a request, a prominent feature of rhetorical and scientific treatises.[68]

3.2 Narrative

The beginning and end of the narrative offer important indications of literary form or genre, particularly in the absence of a proemium or epilogue, or both. The opening of Xenophon's *Anabasis,* which Lucian calls a virtual or potential proemium (*Hist.* § 23: δυνάμει τινὰ προοίμια),[69] suggests by implication its historical genre.[70] The historical monographs written on Alexander begin their narratives with his assumption of power.[71]

The narrative proper of Plutarch's biographies usually begins with an infancy narrative giving an account of the subject's lineage, birth, with any surrounding extraordinary circumstances, and education, continues with his career, noting the beginning of his public life, and concludes with his death and associated events.[72] The narrative of Philo's *De Josepho* does not begin with the subject of his lineage and birth, as does his *De*

Diod., *Hist.* XVI,1.3, in relation to Philip of Macedon. Plutarch, on the other hand, makes it clear in the proemium to his *Alexander* that he is writing biography and not history (1,2); see further the proemia to Plutarch's *Aemelius,* Tacitus' *Agricola* and Lucian's *Demonax*; also Callan, "Preface", 578 and 581 n. 10. In the proemium to an historical work reference is invariably made to the historical events that form the basis of the narrative (see the texts listed in ch. I, n. 21). In the proemia or dedicatory letters to rhetorical, geographical, scientific or medical treatises, such as those of Quintilian, Cicero, Strabo, Archimedes or Dioscorides, the reference to subject matter reflects the technical nature of the work. See the comments of Janson, *Prefaces,* 19-24.64.66-67.94-95.

[66] Compare, for example, the purpose expressed in Her., *Hist.* I,1, Thuc., *War* I,1.1, and Phil., *Apoll.* I,2, or Luc., *Demon.* § 2.

[67] Cf. Janson, *Prefaces,* 66-67; Lieberich, *Proömien,* 17-18.21-22.

[68] Cf. Janson, *Prefaces,* 21-22.64.95.

[69] Cf. Luc., *Hist.* § 52.

[70] Cf. Earl, "Prologue-form", 844.

[71] Cf. Arrian, *An.* I,1.1, and likewise, presumably, the narratives of Ptolemy and Aristobolus (cf. Arrian, *An.* I Pr. 1); also Diod., *Hist.* XVII,1.2; 2.1; similarly his account of Philip (cf. XVI,1.3; 2.1).

[72] See, for example, his *Lives* of Alexander, Demosthenes, Cicero and Theseus, also Lucian's *Demonax,* Tacitus' *Agricola* and Philostratus' *Apollonius.* Suetonius structured his biographies differently, although his narrative opens with a summary of the particular emperor's life. Xenophon's *Cyropaedia* has been descibed as a 'political monograph' (Earl, "Prologue-form", 845), but the narrative proper, which opens with an account of Cyrus' parentage, appearance, natural endowments and education, and closes with his death, points towards biography as its basic genre; this is confirmed by the proemium (cf. A. Momigliano. *Lo sviluppo della biografia greca,* PBE 232: Turin 1974, 57-58).

Vita Mosis, but with Joseph's training in shepherd's craft at the age of seventeen. In this case it is the narrative's conclusion that most clearly points towards the biographical nature of the work, with its account of Joseph's death (§ 268) and a summary that touches his appearance, character, talents, and the general chronology of his life (§§ 269-270).[73]

3.3 *Preparatory Narrative Units*

The beginning of a literary work is often of a complex nature, though not all are as complex as the beginning of Tacitus' *Annals*.[74] As has been noted in the previous chapter, introductory narrative units are to be found in proemia of literary works and also between the proemium and the narrative proper. Their importance for the determination of literary form or genre is well illustrated by Sallust's *Catiline Conspiracy*. In this monograph an account is given of Catiline's life from birth (5,1-8) to death (60-61), and a great deal of interest is shown in his character. Yet the work is not a biography. This is evident from the fact that Sallust places his sketches of Catiline's birth, early career, character and nature not in the narrative proper (17,1 ff.) but in preparatory narrative sections (5,1-8; 15-16) prior to the *initum narrandi* (cf. 4,5).[75]

Neither of the two volumes of Diodorus' *History* devoted to Philip of Macedon (XVI) and Alexander (XVII) can be termed a biography. Apart from the fact that they belong to a larger historical work, there are the proemial declarations of Diodorus' interest in the deeds and achievements of both men which suggest as much (cf. XVI,1.3; XVII,1.2). There is also the fact that the narrative proper in each case opens with the

---

[73] Cf. C. Kraus Reggiani, *Filone Alessandrino. De Opificio Mundi — De Abrahamo — De Josepho. Analisi critiche, testi tradotti e commentati*, BA 23: Rome 1979, 268 ("una vera e propria biografia di Giuseppe"); E. Schürer, *The History of the Jewish People in the Age of Jesus Christ (175 B.C.-A.D. 135)* III.1, eds. G. Vermes, F. Millar, M. Goodman, Edinburgh 1986, 542. Philo's work on Abraham opens with the theme of his character and nature and gives his life story. Philo presents this and his work on Moses as biographies (cf. *De Abr.* § 276; *De Jos.* § 1; *De Vita Mos.* I,1; II,292). The opening theme of Josephus' *Vita* (Ἐμοὶ δὲ γένος ἐστὶν οὐκ ἄσημον) suggests its autobiographical genre. The genre of rhetorical, scientific, philosophical and geographical treatises is made quite obvious from the beginning by virtue of the scientific nature of its subject matter (cf. Earl, "Prologue-form", 846, and n. 18). The initial and concluding themes or motifs are also instructive in small literary units. Initial motifs characteristic of miracle stories may be pointed out in Lk 5,12.18, 7,2, 8,42b-43, 17,12 and Acts 3,2, for example; concluding motifs, in 5,26, 7,10, 8,47-48, 17,19 and Acts 3,8-10; see G. Theissen, *Urchristliche Wundergeschichten. Ein Beitrag zur formgeschichtlichen Erforschung der synoptischen Evangelien*, SNT 8: Gütersloh 1974, 58-62.75-83.

[74] Cf. Leeman, "Prologues", 186-189.

[75] See Giancotti, *Strutture*, 40; also his survey of proposed literary structures of the *Catiline Conspiracy* (pp. 16-28).

beginning of the individual's reign. More importantly, a summary of the life and character of each is found not in the narrative proper but in the proemia of the respective volumes (cf. XVI,1.3-6; XVII,1.3-5).

4. Luke–Acts: Historical Genre?

Bearing in mind the importance for the determination of literary form or genre of the proemium, the preparatory narrative unit, the beginning and end of the narrative proper, the subject matter of the work, its purpose and its overall literary structure, let us attempt to determine the literary form or genre of Luke–Acts.

4.1 *Lk 1,1-4*

It has been argued above that Lk 1,1-4 introduces a two-volume work planned and executed as such. Given the importance of such a proemium for the establishment of the work's literary form or genre, it is to be expected that Lk 1,1-4 would provide valuable information in this regard. And so it does.

A reference to the evangelist's predecessors, one of the surest signs of literary form or genre, is to be found in the proemium's opening words: πολλοὶ ἐπεχείρησαν ἀνατάξασθαι διήγησιν περὶ τῶν πεπληροφορη-μένων ἐν ἡμῖν πραγμάτων. The implication of a work of similar literary form or genre present in this reference is confirmed by the writer himself in 1,3 (ἔδοξε κἀμοί). Consequently a closer look at Luke's description of his predecessors' works, and particularly at the phrase διήγησιν... πραγ-μάτων, should be of considerable assistance in determining the literary form or genre of Luke–Acts.

The noun διήγησις is unique to Lk 1,1 in the New Testament, but parallels to its use in Luke's proemium are not lacking in classical and Jewish Hellenistic literature. In the proemium of his *Roman Antiquities* Dionysius of Halicarnassus applies the term to the historical narrative he is about to begin (I,7.4). Polybius uses it similarly in the proemium to the third book of his *History* (III,4.1); likewise, in the proemia of their works, the author of the *Letter of Aristeas* (§§ 1.8; cf. § 322) and the epitomist of Second Maccabees (2,32; cf. 6,17). It is used with the same meaning, though not in the proemium, by Diodorus (*Hist.* XI,20.1), Josephus (*Ant.* I,67; XX,157; *BJ* VII,42) and Dionysius (*De Thuc.* §§ 7.9.11.12.19). In Lucian's treatise it is used to describe an historical narrative.[76]

---

[76] *Hist.* § 55: ἅπαν γὰρ ἀτεχνῶς τὸ λοιπὸν σῶμα τῆς ἱστορίας διήγησις μακρά ἐστιν.

The term is not confined to historical works. Plutarch, for example, uses it when introducing his biography of Lycurgus (1,3) and when referring to his biographies of Agis, Cleomenes and the Gracchi at the beginning of their comparison (2,6). Tacitus uses an equivalent in the proemium to his life of Agricola (1,3.4). Noted in ch. III above is its use as a rhetorical term to designate the statement of facts in a defence speech.[77] Apart from this technical use, it is most frequently used in reference to an historical narrative.

The only other occurrence in Luke–Acts of the term πρᾶγμα which qualifies διήγησις in Lk 1,1 is the rather uninformative one of Acts 5,4, but parallels to its use in Lk 1,1 are to be found in Hellenistic literature. Polybius refers to the narrative proper of his *History* with the phrase πραγμάτων ἐξήγησιν (I,3.9), and elsewhere he frequently refers to πράγματα as the object of his work (cf. I,4.1.2; 5.4; II,71.10; III,1.7; XII,26d.3; 27.8; 28.5; 28a.7). Josephus makes repeated reference to πράγματα as the object of his inquiry and narrative in the proemium to his *Jewish War* (cf. §§ 1.2.6.9.12.14.30). For Lucian, too, πράγματα are the object of history.[78] Both διήγησις and πράγματα are used by Josephus to describe the narrative of his *Antiquities* (XX,157: ἐπὶ τὴν τῶν οἰκείων πραγμάτων διήγησιν),[79] and by Dionysius in reference to that of his work (I,7.4: περὶ τίνων ποιοῦμαι πραγμάτων τὴν διήγησιν· cf. I,8.4). Such a description recalls the definition of an historical narrative given by Cicero,[80] and Quintilian,[81] and earlier by Aristotle.[82] They suggest that Luke, in referring to a narrative of events that have taken place in the past (διήγησιν περὶ τῶν πεπληροφορημένων ἐν ἡμῖν πραγμάτων), places his own narrative by implication into the same category.

The actual motifs found in Luke's proemium provide another pointer towards the basic historical genre of the work. References to Luke's predecessors, to a narrative of past events, to sources, eyewitness-ship, the accuracy and completeness of the investigation, the decision to write, the care taken in the composition — these represent

---

[77] For this and the equivalent use of *narratio* see ch. III, pp. 105-106, and there nn. 101, 106 and 108.

[78] Cf. *Hist.* §§ 47.55.56.57.

[79] *BJ* VII,42: ἵνα καὶ τῶν μετὰ ταῦτα πραχθέντων εὐπαρακολούθητον ποιήσωμαι τὴν διήγησιν· also V,20: ἀφηγήσεως πραγμάτων· criticizing Justus' history, he wrote (*Vita* § 40): ἐπεχείρησεν καὶ τὴν ἱστορίαν τῶν πραγμάτων τούτων ἀναγράφειν.

[80] *De Inv.* I,19.27: Narratio est rerum gestarum aut ut gestarum expositio; that of *Rhet. ad Her.* I,8.13 (Historia est gesta res, sed ab aetatis nostrae memoria remota) is rather narrow given the contemporary interests of Thucydides and Xenophon.

[81] *Inst. Or.* II,4.2: historiam, in qua est gestae rei expositio.

[82] *Rhet.* I,4.13.1360a35: αἱ τῶν περὶ τὰς πράξεις γραφόντων ἱστορίαι· cf. P. Scheller, *De hellenistica historiae conscribendae arte,* Diss. Leipzig 1911, 9-15; C. W. Fornara, *The Nature of History in Ancient Greece and Rome,* Berkeley 1983, 91-98.

motifs that are typical of, if not exclusive to, the proemia of ancient historical works.[83] The presence of so many in such a brief proemium weighs heavily in favour of it introducing an historical work.

The dedication, it is true, is not found in the writings of the well known Greek and Latin historians.[84] It is typical rather of works of a strictly didactic nature such as scientific and rhetorical treatises.[85] Nevertheless examples of its use are to be found in Jewish Hellenistic writing in the so-called *Letter of Aristeas*,[86] the *Antiquities* of Josephus — an important contemporary parallel for Luke's usage[87] — and in Roman historical writings of minor importance.[88] Its presence in Luke's proemium does not represent a problem for the identification of the basic genre of Luke–Acts as history. But its strong association with didactic works should be borne in mind, especially in the light of Luke's stated purpose (cf. 1,4).

It is also worth noting that Luke's proemium does not present the narrative of his work as a treatise on a particular subject,[89] or as a life of Jesus,[90] or as lives of Jesus and his followers,[91] or as an account of the deeds and achievements of Jesus.[92] It presents it rather in general terms as an account of events that have taken place in the past. Not surprisingly Toynbee included it in his collection of proemia to ancient Hellenistic historical works.[93]

---

[83] See ch. I, p. 11, and there nn. 20-28; also Robbins, "Prefaces", 96.

[84] Cf. Ruppert, *Historiam Dedicationis*, 28; Janson, *Prefaces*, 67.

[85] See ch. I, n. 28; also Ruppert, *Historiam Dedicationis*, 24-26; Janson, *Prefaces*, 18-24.64; Alexander, "Preface", 58-59; art. "Dedications", *OCD*, 259-260. Tacitus provided his *Dialogus* with a dedication (1,1) but not his *Annals* or *Histories*; he dedicated his *Agricola* to the memory of his father-in-law.

[86] On the possible second century B.C. date of the letter see the remarks of R. J. H. Shutt in *The Old Testament Pseudepigrapha* II, ed. J. H. Charlesworth, London 1985, 8-9. Earlier examples of the use of dedication in historical works are to be found in the writings of the third century B.C. contemporaries Berossus, who dedicated his history of Egypt to Ptolemy II, and Manetho, who dedicated his history of Babylon to Antiochus I; cf. Ruppert, *Historiam Dedicationis*, 29-30.

[87] Cf. Lieberich, *Proömien*, 36-37. Josephus also dedicated his apologetic work *Contra Apion* to Epaphroditus.

[88] Velleius Paterculus (19 B.C. — 31 A.D.) dedicated his compendium of Roman history to M. Vinicius, Valerius Maximus, his historical compilation to Tiberius (14-37 A.D.); cf. Ruppert, *Historiam Dedicationis*, 29-31; art. "Dedications", *OCD*, 260. Lieberich, *Proömien*, 37-38, cites the later example of Phlegon of Thralles, a freedman of Hadrian (117-138 A.D.), who dedicated his compilation to a certain Alcibiades.

[89] As happens in the case of scientific and rhetorical treatises; see, for example, Archim., *De Sph. et Cyl.* Pref.; Quint., *Inst. Or.* I Pr. 1; Cic., *De Inv.* I,1.1-2; *Rhet. ad Her.* I,1.1; see also n. 65 above; Janson, *Prefaces*, 20-21.32-33.41.94-95.

[90] See, for example, Plut., *Alex.* 1,1; *Dem.* 3,1; *Thes.* 1.1; Philo, *De Vita Mos.* I,1; Phil., *Apoll.* I,2; Luc., *Demon.* §§ 1-2; Tac., *Agric.* 1,3.4; cf. Callan, "Preface", 581 n. 10.

[91] See Diog. Laert., *Lives* I Pr. 1.12–16.21.

[92] Cf. Arrian, *An.* I Pr. 1-3 (cf. VII,30.3); Diod., *Hist.* XVI,1.3; XVII,1.2.

[93] *Historical Thought*, 57.

But even there it stands very much apart. For it does not introduce a narrative of the notable deeds of men or of peoples in politics and in warfare.[94] The events recounted by Luke are characterized by the fact that they stem ultimately from the group of 'eyewitnesses and ministers of the word' and are associated with the instruction which Theophilus has received. For him these events are related to the message of salvation to which he has positively responded, so that the proemium raises the expectation of a work very different from those presented by parallel proemia in Hellenistic literature. For the non-instructed the references to the 'ministers of the word' and the instruction which Theophilus has received likewise point towards a history of a kind quite different from the usual.[95]

4.2 *Lk 1,5–4,44; 5,1–Acts 28,31*

Leaving aside for the moment the preparatory narrative section 1,5-4,44 and concentrating on the narrative proper of Luke–Acts, a number of points emerge. The gospel's narrative proper opens in 5,1-11 with an account of the call of the first disciples, and more particularly with Jesus preaching the word of God in 5,1-2a. It closes with Jesus' ascension and the disciples in the temple praising God (24,50-53). That of Acts opens with the coming of the Spirit at Pentecost (2,1-4) and closes with Paul preaching the kingdom of God in Rome and teaching "the things concerning the Lord Jesus Christ" (28,31). These are all events set in the past, suggesting a basic historical narrative. The themes of Lk 5,1-2a and Acts 28,31 indicate a prominent role for Jesus in the work, portraying him as the one preaching the word of God.

It must be admitted that the gospel has a marked biographical character, concentrating as it does on the person of Jesus. This is especially true of the infancy narrative which recounts Jesus' conception, birth and presentation, along with the events and the prophecies surrounding each, his growth and a significant incident from his youth. It is also true of the following two chapters. Here one finds an account of Jesus' baptism and the accompanying events which are associated with the explicitly mentioned beginning of his ministry (3,21-23a), a genealogy that conveys the universal significance of that ministry (3,23b-38), and accounts of the temptations in the desert and a visit to Jesus' hometown of Nazareth where the question of his identity is raised.

---

[94] Cf. Fornara, *History,* 96-98, who cites the gory definition of Statius, a poet of the time of Domitian, that history was "armed conflicts and the distinguished deeds of men and fields pouring over with blood" (*Silvae* I,2.96-97); also W. C. van Unnik, "Luke's Second Book and the Rules of Hellenistic Historiography", Kremer (ed.), *Les Actes des Apôtres,* 38-39.

[95] See ch. III, pp. 113-114, and there n. 164.

The rest of the gospel gives an account of Jesus' ministry, concluding with his death, resurrection, appearances and ascension.[96] Various aspects of Jesus' character are indirectly portrayed through his words and deeds: his concern for the poor, the sick and those oppressed by Satan,[97] his compassion for sinners,[98] his life filled with prayer[99] and complete trust in the Father,[100] his attitude towards various groups of people,[101] his fearless warnings to the Jewish leaders,[102] his exacting demands for discipleship,[103] his deep emotions before the passion and his acknowledged innocence and his bearing during it.[105] His character and his behaviour during the passion even form part of the kerygma of Acts (cf. 3,14; 8,32-35). But although the evangelist's biographical interest is evident in a variety of ways, the portrayal of Jesus' character is clearly not his primary concern.[106]

---

[96] See texts cited in n. 71 above.

[97] See ch. IV, pp. 148-149. Through his lifestyle, that of an itinerant preacher or teacher depending on others for support (cf. 8,1.3; 9,3-4.58; 10,4-8), he identified with the poor; cf. Pilgrim, *Poor*, 46-48.96.

[98] See ch. IV, p. 149; note his compassion for the widow of Nain expressed with the term ἐσπλαγχνίσθη (7,13).

[99] For Jesus at prayer see 5,16; 6,12; 9,18.28-29; 10,21; 11,1; 22,17.19.32.41-45; for his teaching on prayer, 11,2-13; 18,1-8.9-14; 22,40.46.

[100] Cf. 22,42; 23,46.

[101] As, for example, towards women (cf. 8,1-3; 10,38-42; 7,36-50) and children (cf. 7,32; 18,15-17); also tax-collectors (cf. 5,27-32; 7,34; 15,1-2; 18,9-14).

[102] Cf. 11,15-54; 12,1; see also his attitude towards the sabbath laws (cf. 6,1-5.6-11; 13,10-17; 14,1-6) and the laws of fasting (cf. 5,33-39) and cleanliness (cf. 11,38), and his remarkable action in cleansing the temple (cf. 19,45a).

[103] Cf. Lk 9,23-25; 14,26-33.

[104] Cf. 22,15.42.44; also his joy in 10,21-24.

[105] Cf. 23,4,14-15.20.22.41.47; his detached bearing is evident in 22,67-70; 23,3.9.28.

[106] This is a crucial consideration when deciding between biography and history. Philo's work on Joseph, which remains faithful to the order of events of Gen 37-50 and includes much that is in these chapters, is a biography, as is clear from his monographic type concentration on the figure of Joseph (note the omission of Gen 38) and especially on his character and nature (cf. Gen 50,15 ff. and Philo, *De Jos.* §§ 261-267). In his *Alexander* Plutarch pursues the objective throughout of bringing out the character and nature of his subject (cf. A. Wardman, *Plutarch's Lives*, London 1974, 4-6). Arrian's *Anabasis*, on the other hand, concentrates on historical facts with character study a subordinate concern. In the narrative proper of his *Catiline Conspiracy* Sallust concentrates on historical events relegating character study to a subordinate, if still important, role. On ancient biographical method see Wardman, *Lives*, 2-10; A. J. Gossage, "Plutarch", *Latin Biography*, ed. T. A. Dorey, London 1967, 57-66; G. B. Townend, "Suetonius and his Influence", Dorey (ed.), *Latin Biography*, 82-85; G. N. Stanton, *Jesus of Nazareth in New Testament Preaching*, SNTSMS 27: Cambridge 1974, 117-129; see also the remarks of Bultmann, *Geschichte*, 228; Dihle, "Evangelien", 402-411.

Acts also has a certain biographical stamp, though not to the same degree, since it does not concentrate on one figure.[107] The witness to the risen Christ and the spread of the word of God among Jews and Gentiles are the stories not only of Peter and Paul, but also of Stephen and Philip, Barnabas and James. Inevitably there is a certain amount of indirect character portrayal.[108] But even in the case of Peter and Paul the author's interest lies in depicting their work at the service of the word of God and the response to their preaching, not in delineating character.[109]

It should be remembered that the presence of biographical elements and character portrayal in an historical narrative was perfectly understandable by the first century A. D. The association between biography and history stretched back as far as the 'biographical profiles' of Herodotus and Thucydides in fifth century Greek historiography.[110] Even before that concentration on the individual was a feature of ancient Eastern writings.[111] In much the same vein Old Testament historiography was very much the stories of individuals such as Abraham, Jacob, Moses, Saul, David, and others.[112]

The type of history taking the deeds of an individual as its explicit subject matter developed with Philip of Macedon[113] and Alexander the Great.[114] The latter's extraordinary career inspired many historical

---

[107] Cf. Momigliano, *Biografia,* 25.66; V. Fusco, "Progetto storiografico e progetto teologico nell'opera lucana", *La Storiografia nella Bibbia,* Atti della XXVIII Settimana Biblica, Bologna 1986, 137.

[108] See, for example, Peter's concern for the sick (cf. 3,1-8; 5,15-16; 9,32-43), his fearless preaching (cf. 4,8-13.19-20.29; 5,29.41), his acceptance of suffering (cf. 5,41); Paul's extreme zeal for his Jewish faith prior to his conversion (cf. 8,3; 9,1-2; 22,3-5), his concern for others (cf. 16,28; 20,34-35), his detachment from material things (cf. 20,33), his courage in facing the dangers that await him in Jerusalem (cf. 21,4.11-14); cf. Stanton, *Jesus of Nazareth,* 52-53.

[109] Note that important biographical information concerning Paul is only to be found as an integral part of his defence speeches (cf. 22,3; 26,4-5); cf. Cadbury, *Making,* 132: "The figures in Acts — Peter, Stephen, Philip and Paul — are neither taken up from their birth nor (except Stephen) followed to their death ... They remain more like actors in a drama than the subjects of biography"; also Schmidt, "Evangelien", 80; Fusco, "Progetto", 137.

[110] Cf. Momigliano, *Biografia,* 14; Dihle, "Evangelien", 37.

[111] Cf. Dihle, "Evangelien", 37.

[112] A. Ehrhardt, "The Construction and Purpose of the Acts of the Apostles", *ST* 12 (1958) 46, even suggests that the portrayal of David is "a model of historical biography, unsurpassed by either Plutarch or Suetonius"! On biographical portrayal in the OT see J. Blenkinsopp, "Biographical Patterns in Biblical Narrative", *JSOT* 20 (1981) 32; Stanton, *Jesus of Nazareth,* 126-127; Scholes, Kellogg, *Narrative,* 123; Culpepper, *Anatomy,* 103.

[113] Cf. Fornara, *History,* 34; Momigliano, *Biografia,* 85; B. Gentili, G. Cerri, "L'idea di biografia nel pensiero greco", *QUCC* 27 (1978) 7.

[114] Philip was the subject of a 58 volume historical monograph by his contemporary Theopompus, a work in which the biographical element is quite evident; cf. Gentili, Cerri, "Biografia", 8-10; also Dion. Hal., *Ep. ad Pomp.* §6.

monographs beginning with those of his contemporaries Callisthenes, Aristobolus and Ptolemy, and continuing on to the first century A.D. works of Arrian and beyond.[115] So much did biography take root in historiography that Dionysius of Halicarnassus could envisage the life and character of famous men as much a part of history as deeds and speeches (*Ant. Rom.* V,48.1), and Cicero likewise (cf. *De Or.* II,15.62-63; *Ep. ad Fam.* V,12).[116] Character portrayal was not the dominant concern in such cases as it was in biographies (cf. Nepos 16,1.1; Plut., *Alex.* 1,2; *Nic.* 1,5).[117] Luke–Acts may be compared to historical works that exhibit a close bond between biography and history but are not biographies. Its subject matter, though, is very different from theirs, and the interest shown in the various aspects of character portrayal very much less.

Even if one were to consider the gospel as a separate work from Acts, the literary structure outlined above provides a crucial argument against its being considered a biography or having a biographical outline. For while the gospel gives an account of Jesus' life from conception to ascension, and would thus appear to satisfy Momigliano's criterion for a biography,[118] many important biographical details including the account of Jesus' infancy, the notice of the beginning of his public life, his genealogy, temptation, and visit to his home town, are placed in the preparatory narrative section 1,5-4,44.[119] This indicates, as in the case of Sallust's *Catiline Conspiracy* (cf. 5,1-8; 15-16) and Diodorus' monographic type volumes on Philip and Alexander (cf. *Hist.,* XVI,1.3-6; XVII,1.2-5), that biography is not the author's primary concern.[120]

The conclusion that history is the basic genre of Luke–Acts finds support in the evangelist's use of literary methods that are common to ancient classical historiography. Apart from the methods of composition noted above such as the parallel and implied comparison in Lk 1,5-4,44, the linking of scenes and the interweaving of matter,[121] the use of Hellenistic-style proemia and preparatory narrative units, there are, for example, the speeches and letters of Acts,[122] the literary imitation present

---

[115] Diodorus devoted volumes XVI and XVII of his *Universal History* to monographic type treatments of the careers of Philip and Alexander respectively. Historical monographs were also written on Alexander's successors and other notable figures; cf. Momigliano, *Biografia,* 86; Fornara, *History,* 34-35. Fornara makes the point (p. 35) that the type of history taking the deeds of an individual as its explicit subject was fully developed by the time of the Alexander-historian Cleitarchus (iii B.C.).

[116] Cf. Fornara, *History,* 116-117; Wardman, *Lives,* 6.

[117] Cf. Wardman, *Lives,* 6-7.

[118] *Biografia,* 13; cf. Hemer, *Acts,* 93.

[119] See ch. I, pp. 31-40, and ch. III, pp. 94-96.

[120] See pp. 164-165 above.

[121] See ch. II, p. 58, and there n. 112; ch. II, n. 197.

[122] Cf. E. Plümacher, "Lukas als griechischer Historiker", *PRE Suppl.* XIV, ed. H. Gärtner, Munich 1974, 243-255.

in both,[123] the elaborate synchronism of 3,1-2a,[124] and the geographical outline of each volume.[125]

Plümacher views Luke–Acts as two historical monographs along the lines of the monograph Cicero tried to wheedle from Lucceius on his part in the Catiline conspiracy (cf. *Ep. ad Fam.* V,12).[126] The genre, exemplified in Sallust's *Catiline Conspiracy* and *Jugurthine War* and well known in Hellenistic literature, provided, according to Plümacher, a literary form with which Luke was able to present salvation history in two clearly distinct epochs.[127]

But Luke and Acts are not two individual works; they do not portray two epochs of salvation history; they are not separated by time and theme as are Sallust's monographs; and given the very selective way in which Acts deals with the spread of the word and the subsequent history of Jesus' individual followers, they can hardly be said to represent or even to attempt to represent an adequate description of the history of Christianity in two loosely linked historical monographs, as Plümacher suggests.[128] Luke and Acts form not two monographs, but two self-contained, profoundly continuous and closely linked parts of the one literary enterprise.[129] The proemium presents Luke–Acts as a monograph, its subject matter and purpose being related to the instruction Theophilus has received.[130] The many parallels and thematic correspondences between Luke and Acts point in the same direction. So too does the dominating presence of Jesus in both, in the gospel as the eschatological prophet preaching the kingdom of God which is present through him and in Acts as the risen Lord whose witnesses preach the message of the kingdom as well as Jesus' ministry, death, resurrection, ascension, exaltation and return.

The division of Luke's work into two volumes followed the custom of the time. Ancient writers mention having to divide their work into two or more rolls due to the extent of their material.[131] The writer had to

---

[123] See ch. IV, n. 82.

[124] See ch. I, nn. 71 and 73.

[125] See ch. II, n. 221; also van Unnik, "Luke's Second Book", 55-59.

[126] "Gattung", 109-123; idem, "Historiker", 262-263.

[127] "Gattung", 116-117.

[128] "Historiker", 263; see Fusco, "Progetto", 135-136.

[129] See ch. III, pp. 98-102, and ch. IV, pp. 125-154.

[130] For the instructed Theophilus it treats of events that have taken place through divine agency (cf. 1,1; see Lohse, "Heilsgeschichte", 261; Luck, "Kerygma", 60; H. Schürmann, "Evangelienschrift und kirchliche Unterweisung. Die repräsentative Funktion der Schrift nach Lk 1,1-4", *Traditionsgeschichtliche Untersuchungen zu den synoptischen Evangelien,* Düsseldorf 1967, 266-270; idem, *Lk* I, 7-15) and are bound up with the word of God (cf. 1,2.4; see ch. III, p. 95, and there n. 47).

[131] Cf. Appian, *Hist. Rom.* Pr. 14; Cic., *De Inv.* I,56.109; Jos., *C. Ap.* I,320; Birt, *Antike Buchwesen,* 130-132; Kenyon, *Books,* 61-62. This monographic type method is to be

tailor the material to fit each roll[132] and, if possible, make each a self-contained unit (cf. Diod., *Hist.*, XVI,1.1-2; V,1.4).[133] Luke's material fell naturally into two parts so that without great difficulty he was able to arrange it to fit into two more or less equal rolls according to monographic criteria.[134] He followed established custom by concluding each on a high point (cf. 24,50-53; Acts 28,17-31)[135] and by ensuring a smooth transition from one to the other.[136]

5. Luke–Acts: Kerygmatic History?

If history is the basic genre of Luke–Acts, its subject matter, as has been noted, differs markedly from that of the ancient historians. A further examination of Luke's proemium and the rest of his work is required in order to define more clearly its literary form or genre.

5.1 *Lk 1,1-4*

For the instructed Theophilus the reference in 1,2 to the ultimate sources of Luke's tradition, namely, those who were eyewitnesses of all that Jesus did and taught, and who were ministers of the word both during and after his ministry, would surely strike a chord. These were men whom Jesus taught and sent to proclaim the kingdom of God and to heal during his Galilean ministry and while on the way to Jerusalem (9,2; cf. 10,9). He later commissioned them to preach repentance in his name to all nations beginning from Jerusalem (24,47).

Luke presents them in Acts witnessing to Jesus, proclaiming the kingdom of God and preaching 'the things concerning the Lord Jesus', and all as part of God's plan revealed in the scriptures. He presents them calling for repentance and proclaiming that in Christ alone lay salvation.

---

distinguished from the bisection of books that is attested, for example, in the LXX (cf. H.St.J. Thackeray, *The Septuagint and Jewish Worship. A Study in Origins,* Munich 1980, 130-136); see also Diod., *Hist.* I,41.10; 42.1

[132] Cf. Birt, *Antike Buchwesen,* 132.

[133] In V,1.4 Diodorus cites the example of Ephorus who, he says, constructed each one of his books so as to embrace events which fall under a single topic. Books XVI and XVII of Diodorus' work illustrate the principle; see also Cic., *Ep. ad Fam.* V,12; Sall., *Cat.* 4,2-3; Appian, *Hist. Rom.* Pr. 14; cf. Burck, *Erzählungskunst,* 193-195; Luce, *Livy,* 25-28; Birt, *Antike Buchwesen,* 137-139.

[134] Luke and Acts would have occupied rolls of about 32 to 35 feet, written in a medium sized hand; cf. Kenyon, *Books,* 62.

[135] Cf. Birt. *Antike Buchwesen,* 132. Tacitus used major turning points and great catastrophies to divide his books; see examples cited by Birt (pp. 137-138).

[136] On the expected provision of such a transition see Birt, *Antike Buchwesen,* 132. It is facilitated by the pause in 24,53 in which the imperfect ἦσαν, the adverbial phrase διὰ παντός, and the pres. ptc. εὐλογοῦντες form a strong contrast with the many aorists of the preceding verses.

In addition to bringing people to faith, their preaching was aimed at strengthening that faith (cf. Acts 14,22; 15,31.41; 16,5; 18,23). The narratives the evangelist used, and upon which he patterned his own work, faithfully transmitted the traditions handed down by these witnesses (cf. Lk 1,2) and doubtless shared their kerygmatic purpose. It is to be expected that a work based on, and claiming to be faithful to, such traditions would be of a similar nature (cf. 1,3).[137]

The term διήγησις, used in v.1 in reference to the narratives of Luke's predecessors, may enable one to specify further the nature of these narratives and by implication that of Luke. Unfortunately this is the only occurrence of the noun in the New Testament. The evangelist's use of the verb διηγέομαι may help to fill the lacuna.

The verb occurs in both the gospel (8,39; 9,10) and Acts (8,33; 9,27; 12,17) where it has as its object events that involve divine intervention. These embrace all that the twelve did on their temporary mission, preaching the kingdom, healing and expelling demons (Lk 9,1-6.10), the risen Lord's appearance to Paul and his bold preaching in Damascus (Acts 9,27), the Lord's rescue of Peter from prison (12,17) and what God had done for the possessed man through Jesus (Lk 8,39). Its use in the latter text is instructive.

The context tells how the healed demoniac is bidden by Jesus (8,39a) to return home and "narrate" what God has done for him. He responds (8,39b) by going forth through the city "proclaiming" what Jesus had done for him.[138] The parallel between v.39a and v.39b suggests that διηγέομαι is closely related to κηρύσσω here. Indeed given its object and its context, διηγέομαι may convey the aspect of proclamation or announcing in 8,39a.[139] This is also a possibility in Acts 12,17 where it is parallel and equivalent to ἀπαγγέλλω, a verb which is used in Lk 7,22, 8,36, 24,9 and Acts 26,20 in a faith-related context.[140] In the event, the healed demoniac's narrative is at the same time a preaching of what Jesus had done for him. It is the narrative of one who believes and who challenges others to believe by his very narrative.[141] This has implications for the use of διήγησις in Lk 1,1.

---

[137] The anonymity of the work would also suggest as much.

[138] 8,39: διηγοῦ ὅσα σοι ἐποίησεν ὁ θεός — κηρύσσων ὅσα ἐποίησεν αὐτῷ ὁ Ἰησοῦς.

[139] Cf. Glöckner, *Verkündigung,* 14 ("ein Erzählen aus dem Glauben"); R.J. Dillon, "Previewing Luke's Project from His Prologue (Luke 1:1-4)", *CBQ* 43 (1981) 209 ("Narrating... refers to the publication of God's wondrous action as experienced by the narrator").

[140] Cf. Glöckner, *Verkündigung,* 14; Dillon, "Prologue", 209; in reference to the closely parallel passages Mk 5,16-20 and Lk 8,36-39, both note Luke's use of διηγοῦ in 8,39a where Mk 5,19 has ἀπάγγειλον and the reverse situation in Mk 5,16 and Lk 8,36.

[141] See Philo's use of the term in *De Spec. Leg.* II,39 where the mere διήγησις of the sabbath laws and customs is said to be sufficient to make the naturally gifted perfect in virtue and to produce some degree of obedience in the rebellious and hardnatured.

The association of λόγος and διήγησις in Luke's proemium is also of note. For the instructed Theophilus the λόγος referred to here is equivalent to ὁ λόγος τοῦ θεοῦ/κυρίου and signifies the fundamental Christian message. It is the λόγος τῆς σωτηρίας (Acts 13,26), the word that demands a response of faith (cf. Acts 13,39-48). It is also the word that strengthens those who have come to faith (cf. Acts 14,22).

The declared purpose of Luke's work is given at the conclusion of the proemium. It is not to give a more accurate account than Luke's predecessors of Jesus' life or the lives of his followers,[142] nor to save the past from oblivion or ensure that the extraordinary achievements of Jesus' era enjoy their just renown;[143] it is not to eradicate erroneous suppositions from the public mind,[144] nor to provide a treatise on the 'Antiquities of the Christians'.[145] Luke's intention is to show Theophilus the reliability or certainty of the instruction he has received.[146] To a certain extent it is didactic. But it is not simply that, for the evangelist's intention is to strengthen faith. This gives his work a kerygmatic setting.[147]

5.2 Lk 1,5–4,44

As was noted in the previous chapter, the preparatory narrative unit 1,5–4,44, which prepares the reader or hearer for the narrative that follows, communicates in various ways the joyful news of the long awaited fulfilment of the promise.[148] It shows God initiating and guiding this eschatological fulfilment, and it sets the rest of the work in the time of fulfilment. As was also shown in ch. IV, it offers a repeated message of hope for Jew and Gentile alike with its good news of salvation that is now present and destined for all. It underlines the kerygmatic aspect of Jesus' ministry (cf. 4,18-19.43) in which the kingdom that he proclaims (cf. 4,43) is shown to be present in word (cf. 4,18-21) and deed (4,32-36.38-41).

Among other things it offers an example of faith in the ready response of Mary to the divine call (cf. 1,38). It provides a message of hope and

---

[142] Cf. Phil., *Apoll.* I,2.
[143] Cf. Her., *Hist.* I,1.
[144] Cf. Dion. Hal., *Ant. Rom.* I,5.3; Jos., *BJ* I,2.6; *Ant.* I,4.
[145] Cf. O. Betz, "The Kerygma of Luke", *Int* 22 (1968) 132; Fitzmyer, *Lk I-IX,* 152.
[146] See ch. III, n. 161.
[147] The term kerygmatic can be used in this manner since it does not refer exclusively to the initial proclamation of the word to non-believers, but is used also in an inner Christian context (cf. Rom 16,25); cf. R. Koch, "Preaching", *Encyclopedia of Biblical Theology* II, ed. J. B. Bauer, London-Sydney, 1970, 692; also J. I. H. McDonald, *Kerygma and Didache. The articulation and structure of the earliest Christian message,* SNTSMS 37: Cambridge 1980, 1-11.133-139.
[148] See ch. IV, pp. 124-128.

consolation for the poor, the oppressed, the sick, the enslaved and the imprisoned. It contains a call for repentance in the fiery preaching of John the Baptist (cf. 3,3.7-9) and conveys a message of comfort in the face of the temptations and assaults of Satan (cf. 4,1-13.33-36.41). It also sounds a note of warning to the Jews (2,34-35; 4,23-30).

5.3 Lk 5,1–Acts 28,31

The opening theme of the gospel's narrative proper (cf. 5,1-2a) and the closing themes of Acts (cf. 28,31) suggest that Luke's work is concerned with the message of salvation. They also suggest that the message of Acts has its origin in the teaching of Jesus and indicate that "the things concerning the Lord Jesus Christ" have been added to the message of Jesus.

As for the rest of the work, the gospel's narrative proper shows God active through the ministry, passion, death and resurrection of Jesus.[149] Salvation is declared and shown to be present in Jesus' words and deeds. The presence of the kingdom in and through him is proclaimed and demonstrated (cf. Lk 11,20). The narrative's faithful record of Jesus' words and deeds, its moving and demanding pictures of repentance, compassion, forgiveness and faith, its portrayal of Christ's passion, death and resurrection represent preaching in narrative form (cf. Acts 2,22-36; 3,13-26; 10,36-43; 13,26-37).[150]

What about Acts, particularly in the light of Overbeck's well known comment?[151] God is again shown to be active throughout, whether in the gift of the Spirit (cf. 2,4.17-21.33; 4,8; 5,32; 11,17), in assisting in difficult situations (cf. 4,8.19; 12,7), or in the spread of the word among the Jews and the initiation and continuation of the Gentile mission (cf. 5,38-39; 10,1-11,18; 15,7-9.11.14-18; 21,19). His role in Jesus' ministry (cf. 10,36-38; 13,23; 2,22), and particularly in his passion, death and resurrection (cf. 2,23-24.32; 3,15.18; 10,40; 13,30.33.34.37), is highlighted, and this time the latter are explicitly shown to fulfil the divine plan enunciated in the scriptures (cf. 2,24-31.33-36; 8,32-35; 13,33-37). Jesus' exaltation (2,33a), his generalized gift of the Spirit (2,33b), a more explicit promise of his return (cf. Lk 21,25-27; Acts 1,11; 3,20-21), and his appointment by God to judge the living and the dead (10,42) are elements added to the message of the gospel.[152]

---

[149] Cf. Betz, "Kerygma", 138-141.
[150] Cf. C.H. Dodd, *The Apostolic Preaching and its Developments,* London 1972³, 26-37.
[151] See n. 4 above.
[152] Cf. Betz, "Kerygma", 138-141.

Acts does not have the same amount of teaching as the gospel, but as in the gospel, Jesus is proclaimed as the Christ (2,36; 3,20), Son of God (9,20), Lord (11,20; 16,31) and Saviour (5,31). Frequent references are made to the proclamation of the kingdom (cf. 1,3; 8,12; 14,22; 19,8; 20,25; 28,23.31), and Paul's words in Antioch to the effect that one enters it through many tribulations (14,22) echo the words of the risen Lord in Lk 24,26 (cf. Acts 20,28-35).[153] As in the gospel, salvation is proclaimed as a present reality (cf. 2,47; 5,31; 13,23.26; 28,28),[154] and repentance and forgiveness are preached to all (2,38-40; 3,19.26; 5,31; 8,22; 10,43; 11,18; 13,38; 17,30-31; 20,21; 26,18.20).

Ecclesiologically Acts has important messages for both Jew and Gentile. From the point of view of Israel, the continued call to repentance and the offer of forgiveness addressed to them are of the utmost importance. The narrative of Acts conveys the crucial message that their treatment of God's anointed has not deprived them of the promise of salvation (cf. 2,38-39; 3,17-26; 4,10-12; 5,30-32; 13,38-41). The universal mission given by the risen Lord to his disciples (Lk 24,47) continues to include Israel despite the hostile reaction of the Jewish leaders to both Peter and Paul (cf. 4,1-21; 5,17-40; 6,12; 9,1-2; 22,30; 24,1; 25,2-3.15) and the repeated rejection by Jews of the preaching of the word.[155]

Acts opens on a note of hope for Israel (cf. 1,6-8; 3,19-21.25-26).[156] The fulfilment of the promise made to it, celebrated in the infancy narrative (cf. Lk 1,32-33.54-55.68-70; 2,30-32), is still preached (cf. 3,18.24), and is emphasized by references to the unwitting role of the Jews and their leaders in bringing the utterances of the prophets to fulfilment (cf. 3,17-18; 13,27-29). Paul can claim to say nothing but what Moses said would come to pass (26,22), and in Rome he can still preach the "hope of Israel" (28,20). More importantly at this point the author still attempts to move Israel to repentance and faith (cf. 28,23-28), and he leaves the Jewish reader with a message that is still not without hope (cf. 28,30-31).[157]

The Gentile mission, although foreshadowed in the gospel's preparatory narrative (cf. 2.30-32; 4,25-27) and in its narrative proper (cf. 8,26-39; 13,29-30; 14,15-24), and ordered by Jesus (24,47), only begins with the conversion of Cornelius and especially with the missionary work

---

[153] For the many parallels between Luke and Acts and the many echoes of the former in the latter see ch. III, pp. 98-101, and the works listed in n. 69 there; also Betz, "Kerygma", 133-134.

[154] Note the aorist tenses of the verbs in 13,23.26 and 28,28 (ἤγαγεν, (ἐξ)απεστάλη); also the pres. ptc. σῳζομένους in 2,47.

[155] See ch. IV, pp. 144-145, and there nn. 194-197.

[156] See ch. IV, n. 187; also Fusco, "Progetto", 140.

[157] See ch. IV, pp. 142-143.

of Paul and Barnabas (cf. Acts 13,46 ff.). But it is shown to be an integral part of God's plan, revealed in the scriptures (cf. 13,47; 15,7.14-18), directed by God (cf. 10,1–11,18; 21,19; 22,21; 26,17-18) and confirmed by the gift of the Spirit (cf. 10,44-45; 11,15; 15,8). The resolution of the problem of circumcision in Acts 15 removes a major problem for this mission. The Gentiles' openness to, and reception of, the word from the beginning are exemplary (cf. 10,1–11,18; 13,48), and their enthusiastic reaction enables Paul to make a statement such as that of 28,28b in an effort to spur Israel on to emulate them.[158]

Like the gospel, Acts contains elements of a pattern of Christian life.[159] Prayer, reflecting that exemplified and taught by Jesus, is a prominent feature of this pattern (cf. 1,14.24; 2,42; 4,24-30; 6,6; 9,40; 12,5; 13,3; 14,23; 28,8) as is the profound commitment of the community to all its members, especially those in need, and to its brethren elsewhere (cf. 2,42-47; 4,32-37; 9,36; 11,29-30; 16,15; 20,35). This commitment gives concrete expression to their sense of unity and fraternity (cf. 2,44). Depicted also is the positive response to the word of God (8,35-38; 16,30-34; 26,19-20), fearless, steadfast preaching even in the face of persecution (4,13.19-20.29-30; 5,29; 6,9-10; 7,2-56; 9,29), the willingness to take up one's cross and follow Christ, even to the ultimate sacrifice (4,19-20; 6,8–7,60; 14,19; 21,13), the tolerance for and consideration of others (15,28-29; 21,25), a readiness to forgive (7,60).

In addition, Acts provides a firm basis for hope in the complete fulfilment of the promise. The gift of the Spirit, the divine assistance in times of necessity, the renewed offer of forgiveness and salvation to the Jews, the Gentile mission, the spread of the word from Jerusalem to Rome — all these show Christ's words being honoured and fulfilled, or well on the way to fulfilment.

Luke and Acts do not carry equal weight, as the parallel drawn by Plümacher with Sallust's two monographs suggests. The gospel clearly has the primary role, and provides the basis for the account of Acts which supplements, and at times confirms, the gospel narrative. Acts has a supporting role. It presupposes the gospel, describing a mission that is given there and resolving a number of problems left over from there such as those of Israel and the Gentile mission.[160] The kingdom and "the things concerning the Lord Jesus Christ" are the object of the preaching

---

[158] Luke's concern to portray the Gentile mission as part of God's plan and his abiding interest in Israel suggest an intended audience that contains both Jewish and Gentile components. Cf. P. F. Esler, *Community and gospel in Luke-Acts. The social and political motivations of Lucan theology*, SNTSMS 57: Cambridge 1987, 30-45.

[159] Cf. Weiser, *Apg 1-12*, 35.

[160] Cf. Fusco, "Progetto", 138-147.

of the witnesses. The proclaimer has become the proclaimed,[161] and he dominates Luke's second volume as well as his first.

How, then, should one describe Luke–Acts whose basic genre, it has been suggested above, is history? Given the indications of the proemium and the content of the narrative, the description 'kerygmatic history' seems appropriate. Luke's work represents preaching in narrative form, just like the narrative in the speeches of Acts or the healed demoniac's narrative in the gospel. It is a proclamation of the salvation accomplished by God in Christ and a call to believe and to be saved.[162] As Jesus' contemporaries were confronted and strengthened by his time-transcending message, so too were the audiences of his witnesses (cf. Lk 24,47; Acts 10,42), and so too are the readers or hearers of this work which constitutes an ever present challenge to faith and discipleship for the non-Christian and a source of nourishment and strength to those who have accepted his message. The term 'kerygmatic' includes both these dimensions.[163] And while Luke's work was primarily addressed to the instructed Theophilus, it also had the non-Christian reader in view.

Conclusion

The evidence from Luke's proemium, from the preparatory narrative section 1,5–4,44, and from the remainder of the two-volume work shows that Luke–Acts may be classified as 'kerygmatic history', with the term 'kerygmatic' expressing the uniqueness of this 'history' both with respect to the purpose of its narration and the nature of the events it recounts. The qualification 'kerygmatic' also indicates the active role of the evangelist who, while respecting the faithfully transmitted multi-layered tradition that has come down to him, is nonetheless intent on strengthening faith and proclaiming the message of salvation in a manner that answers in particular to the preoccupations of the mixed community for which he is writing.

Luke's work is not unique in its kerygmatic intent,[164] nor is it unique in its concentration on the words and deeds of Jesus in the first volume.

---

[161] Cf. R. Bultmann, *Theology of the New Testament* I, tr. by K. Grobel, London 1952, 33.

[162] Cf. P.-H. Menoud, "Preaching", Buttrick (ed.), *IDB* III, 869; Fitzmyer, *Lk I-IX*, 149-162.

[163] See n. 147 above.

[164] For G. Strecker, in "Zur Messiasgeheimnistheorie im Markusevangelium", *SE* III, ed. F. L. Cross, TU 88: Berlin 1964, 104, "Verkündigung als Bericht" characterizes Mark's gospel; see Gnilka, *Mk* 1-8,26, 22-24 (24: "Bericht als Verkündigung oder im Dienst der Verkündigung"); for Matthew see R. Walker, *Die Heilsgeschichte im ersten Evangelium*, FRLANT 91: Göttingen 1967, 149 ("das grundlegende Kerygma-Geschichtsbuch"); H. Frankemölle, *Jahwebund und Kirche Christi. Studien zur Form- und*

However, with its second volume, its particular overall design, and its own specific aims and concerns, this work does represent a Christian contribution to literature, the unique product of an evangelist anxious to confirm and to proclaim, and to impart a message of hope and salvation to a community of varied origins and beliefs.

Traditionsgeschichte des "Evangeliums" nach Matthäus, NTA NF 10: Münster 1974, 380-381; Marxsen takes Mark to be a kerygmatic biography, Hengel, all four gospels (see n. 6 above). On "kerygma' see G. Friedrich, "κῆρυξ κτλ.", *TDNT* III, 713; Koch, "Preaching", 686-693; Fitzmyer, *Lk I-IX,* 146-156.

EPILOGUE

The literary analysis conducted in chs. I and II provides ample evidence for the existence of a major break in the gospel narrative at 4,44/5,1 and for the unity of 1,5–4,44. It puts forward a solution to the problem of where 4,14-44 fits into Luke's presentation of Jesus' ministry, suggesting that it is not chronologically related to the following narrative and does not recount the ἀρχή of Jesus' ministry or of his Galilean ministry (5,1–9,50), but represents a programmatic anticipation of Jesus' ministry placed in an introductory narrative section. This analysis finds further support in ch. III where it is suggested that Luke's proemium points towards 5,1 as the beginning of the gospel's narrative proper.

Evidence of Luke's careful arrangement of his material has been seen in the remarkably similar literary structures of the two volumes. Both have a proemium (1,1-4; Acts 1,1-26), an introductory narrative section that prepares one for the narrative that follows (1,5–4,44; Acts 1,15-26), and a narrative proper arranged in three parts according to geographical considerations (5,1–9,50; 9,51–19,48; 20,1–24,53; Acts 2,1–8,3; 8,4–21,17; 21,18–28,31). This three-part division is a striking characteristic of the literary structure, being found not only in the overall arrangement of the two-volume work, but also in the arrangement of a number of its parts (cf. 1,5-56; 3,21–4,44; 5,1–9,50; 20,1–24,53; Acts 2,1–8,3; 21,18–28,31).

The use of a geographical principle of arrangement for the overall structure of the narrative proper of both volumes, and for their lengthy central sections, gives the whole a strong sense of movement and continuity in keeping with the programme set out in the proemium. Apart from that, the movement from Galilee to Jerusalem and from Jerusalem to Rome emphasizes the holy city's loss of its pre-eminent role in God's plan in the time of fulfilment. The continuity of the narrative underlines the continuity expressed in other ways between Israel and the new people of God.

Hellenistic influence on Lucan composition has been noted in both volumes — in the proemium and secondary proemium, the preparatory narrative or προδιήγησις, the implied syncrisis of Lk 1,5–4,44, the linking of scenes, the rhetorical arrangement of the defence speech of Acts 11,5-17, an arrangement that probably underlies the other speeches of Acts, and elsewhere. As we have seen in ch. III, Luke's Hellenistic-type proemium introduces his two-volume work that was planned and executed as such. Many of motifs of Lk 1,1-4 are common to the proemia of ancient prose writings, and of historiographical works in particular. Its comparison with such proemia highlights its particular characteristics, most notably the intended presentation of the tradition according to a programme that is at once literary, historical and theological, and a positive attitude towards the narratives of Luke's predecessors. Although the question of rhetorical influence on Luke's writing raised in Cadbury's commentary on Lk 1,1-4, and again recently by Güttgemanns, has only been briefly touched upon above and needs to be treated at much greater length, the comparison between Luke's proemium and its Hellenistic parallels reveals its sober tones and modest claims.[1] Given Luke's awareness, evident in the proemia to the speeches of Acts, of the motifs that might have been used, this is all the more striking.

In ch. IV we have seen how Lk 1,5–4,44 prepares the reader or hearer for the narrative proper. The infancy narrative in particular celebrates the dawning of the time of fulfilment and indicates in various ways the advent of the eschatological age. The following two chapters make clear that the ministries of John and Jesus fulfil the divine plan of God as enunciated in the scriptures, each in his own role — John as precursor, Jesus as the eschatological bearer of salvation. As a whole this preparatory section weighs heavily against the scheme of Lucan salvation history proposed in the writings of von Baer and Conzelmann, repeatedly suggesting that the scheme of promise and fulfilment underlies Luke's thought, and that the 'times' of John, Jesus and the Church are all part of the 'time of fulfilment'. Lk 1,5–4,44 also introduces the person and mission of Jesus, indicating his identity and the significance of his mission both for Israel and for the Gentiles and defining his relationship to John. In giving this information at the beginning of his work, the evangelist lends an added vital interest to the development of the narrative, gives it an additional capacity for irony, and creates narrative tensions that hold the attention of the reader or hearer and help to bind the numerous episodes of the two-volume work together.

There are aspects of 1,5–4,44 that have the gospel narrative more directly in view. The programmatic anticipation of Jesus' ministry in 4,14-44, for example, is particularly significant for the gospel, preparing as it does the account of Jesus' ministry in which this programme is realized. But aspects of 4,14-44 also apply to the message of Christ preached in Acts, as, for instance, concern for the poor, the sick and the sinner, the rejection and acceptance of the word of God, the balance between word and deed, the paraenetic use of the Gentiles. The programmatic role of 4,14-44 is not confined to the gospel, therefore, but

---

[1] See ch. III, n. 169.

applies to both volumes. The same is true of Jesus' programmatic victory over Satan in 4,1-13. The close relationship between 1,5–4,44 and the remainder of Luke–Acts is also underlined by the many themes introduced in this preparatory section that run throughout the two-volume work.

Two important Lucan themes are absent from 1,5–4,44: discipleship and eyewitness-ship. All the evangelists attribute great importance to the call of the first disciples, placing it either at the beginning of the narrative proper, as Luke does, or at the beginning of the narrative of Jesus' ministry after an introductory narrative section, as the others do. Luke does give a prominent position to these themes in his introduction, not here but in the proemium.

The final chapter shows how Lk 1,1-4 and 1,5–4,44 play a determinative role in establishing the literary form of Luke–Acts, and its indications are supported by the narrative proper. Proemium, preparatory narrative section and narrative proper make clear that Luke's narrative is not biography but history, and not simply history, but 'kerygmatic history'. It is itself a proclamation of the salvation accomplished by God in Jesus.

As a whole, then, Lk 1,1–4,44 can be said to prepare the reader or hearer for the narrative proper of Luke–Acts. Indeed given the programme for the work and the themes present in its proemium, the wealth of Lucan themes introduced in its preparatory narrative, the anticipations and foreshadowings present there, the extent of its portrayal of the person and mission of Jesus and its programmatic scenes and statements, one may well say that already in 1,1–4,44 the message of Luke is contained *in nuce,* or to put it in terms of an ancient Greek proverb, "the beginning is half the whole".[2]

---

[2] Ἀρχὴ δέ τε ἥμισυ παντός.

BIBLIOGRAPHY

The following bibliography contains all those works referred to above with the exception of editions of the NT and the Loeb editions of classical and Jewish Hellenistic texts (LCL) which were generally used.

Abbreviations for periodicals and series are taken as far as possible from the lists furnished in the *Elenchus Bibliographicus* 64 (1983) 7-26 and S. Schwertner, *Abkürzungsverzeichnis, Theologische Realenzyklopädie*, eds. G. Krause, G. Müller, Berlin-New York 1976. Where abbreviations or acronyms are used above for certain well known works these are given in the course of the bibliography. Commentaries on Luke and Acts are abbreviated Lk, Lc and Apg, according to their linguistic provenance.

1. Reference Works

Aland, K., *Synopsis Quattuor Evangeliorum*, Stuttgart 1973⁸.

Barrett, C. K., *The New Testament Background: Selected Documents*, London 1957.

Bauer, W., *Griechisch-Deutsches Wörterbuch zu den Schriften des Neuen Testaments und der übrigen urchristlichen Literatur*, Berlin 1952⁴ (tr. and adapted in W. F. Arndt, F. W. Gingrich, *A Greek-English Lexicon of the New Testament and Other Early Christian Literature*, Chicago 1974.

Blass, F., Debrunner, A., *A Greek Grammar of the New Testament and Other Early Christian Literature*, tr. and ed. by R. W. Funk, Chicago-London 1975.

Cagnat, R., Lafaye G. (eds), *Inscriptiones Graecae ad Res Romanas Pertinentes*, 4 vols, Paris 1906-1927 *[IGRR]*.

Cary, M., et al., *The Oxford Classical Dictionary*, Oxford 1953 *[OCD]*.

Charlesworth, J. H., *The Old Testament Pseudepigrapha*, 2 vols, London 1983, 1985.

Danby, H., *The Mishnah*, London 1974.

Dittenberger, W., *Sylloge Inscriptionum Graecarum*, 4 vols, Leipzig 1915-1924³ [Ditt., *Syll.³*].

——(ed.), *Orientis Graeci Inscriptiones Selectae. Supplementum Sylloges Inscriptionum Graecarum*, 2 vols, Leipzig 1903, 1905 [Ditt., *OGIS*].

Edgar, C. C. (ed.), *Zenon Papyri in the University of Michigan Collection* (*Michigan Papyri* I), Ann Arbor 1931.

Erbetta, M., *Gli Apocrifi del Nuovo Testamento*, 4 vols, Turin 1966-1981.

Ernesti, I. C. T., *Lexicon Technologiae Graecorum Rhetoricae*, Leipzig 1795.

Grenfell, B. P., Hunt, A. S. (eds.), *The Oxyrhynchos Papyri* III, London 1903 (XIV, 1920) *[P. Oxy.]*.

————, Hunt, A. S., Smyly, J. G. (eds.), *The Tebtunis Papyri* I, London 1902 [*P. Tebt.*].

Hennecke, E. Schneemelcher, W., *New Testament Apocrypha,* 2 vols, tr. by R. McL. Wilson et al., London 1963, 1965.

Huck, A. Lietzmann, H., *Synopsis of the First Three Gospels,* ed. F. L. Cross, Oxford 1972.

————, Greeven, H., *Synopse der drei ersten Evangelien mit Beigabe der johanneischen Parallelstellen,* Tübingen 1981.

Kenyon, F. G. (ed.), *Greek Papyri in the British Museum* I, London 1893.

Le Déaut, R., *Targum du Pentateuque,* 5 vols, Sc 245...282: Paris 1978-1981.

Liddell, H. G., Scott, R., Jones, H. S., *A Greek English Lexicon,* Oxford 1977.

Moraldi, L., *I Manoscritti di Qumran,* Turin 1971.

Morgenthaler, R., *Statistik des Neutestamentlichen Wortschatzes,* Zürich-Stuttgart 1973².

Papiri Greci e Latini IV, Florence 1917.

Pestman, P. W. (ed.), *Greek and Demotic Texts from the Zenon Archives,* PL Bat 20A: Leiden 1980.

Spengel, L. (ed.), *Rhetores Graeci,* 3 vols, Leipzig 1854-1856.

Stephanus, H., *Thesaurus Graecae Linguae,* 8 vols, eds. C. B. Hase, G. and l. Dindorf, Paris 1831-1865.

Wescott, B. F., Hort, F. J. A., *The New Testament in the Original Greek, Text,* Cambridge-London 1890² (1881).

Wettstein, J. J., *Novum Testamentum Graecum,* 2 vols, Amsterdam 1751, 1752.

Zerwick, M., Grosvenor, M., *A Grammatical Analysis of the Greek New Testament,* 2 vols, Rome 1974, 1979.

Zorell, F., *Lexicon Graecum Novi Testamenti,* Rome 1978³.

2. Commentaries on Luke and Acts

Bengel, J. A., *Gnomon Novi Testamenti,* Tübingen 1742.

Bisping, A., *Erklärung der Evangelien nach Markus und Lukas,* EHNT II: Münster 1868².

————, *Erklärung der Apostelgeschichte,* EHNT IV: Münster 1871².

Bossuyt, P., Radermakers, J., *Jésus Parole de la Grâce selon saint Luc,* 2 vols, Brussels 1981.

Bovon, F., *Das Evangelium nach Lukas* 1, EKKNT III.1: Zürich 1989.

Bruce, F. F., *The Acts of the Apostles,* London 1951.

Conzelmann, H., *Die Apostelgeschichte,* HNT 7: Tübingen 1972².

Creed, J. M., *The Gospel According to St. Luke,* London 1930.

De Wette, W. M. L., *Kurze Erklärung der Apostelgeschichte,* ed. F. Overbeck, KEHNT I.IV: Leipzig 1870⁴.

Dillon, R. J., "Acts of the Apostles", Fitzmyer, Brown (eds.), *NJBC* II, 722-767.

Easton, B. S., *The Gospel According to St. Luke: A Critical and Exegetical Commentary,* New York 1926.

Ellis, E. E., *The Gospel of Luke,* London 1966.

Ernst, J., *Das Evangelium nach Lukas,* Regensburg 1977.

Evans, C. F., *Saint Luke,* London 1990.

Ewald, H., *Die drei ersten Evangelien and die Apostelgeschichte*, 2 vols, Göttingen 1871-1872².

Fitzmyer, J. A., *The Gospel According to Luke*, 2 vols, AB 28, 28A: Garden City 1981, 1985.

Geldenhuys, N., *Commentary on the Gospel of Luke*, London 1965 (repr. 1950).

Godet, F., *Commentaire sur L'Évangile de Saint Luc*, 2 vols, Paris 1872².

Grotius, H., *Annotationes in Novum Testamentum* I, *Quatuor Evangelia*, Halle 1769² (1641).

Grundmann, W., *Das Evangelium nach Lukas*, THNT 3: Berlin 1974⁷.

Haenchen E., *The Acts of the Apostles. A Commentary*, Oxford 1971.

Hahn, G. L., *Das Evangelium des Lucas*, 2 vols, Breslau 1892, 1894.

Hanson, R. P. C., *The Acts in the Revised Standard Version*, Oxford 1967.

Harnack, A., *Die Apostelgeschichte*, BENT III: Leipzig 1908.

Harrington, W. J., *The Gospel according to St Luke*, London 1968.

Hauck, F., *Das Evangelium des Lukas*, THKNT III: Leipzig 1934.

Holtzmann, H. J., *Die Synoptiker*, HCNT I.I: Tübingen-Leipzig 1901³.

————, *Die Apostelgeschichte*, HCNT I.II: Tübingen-Leipzig 1901³.

Jacquier, E., *Les Actes des Apôtres*, Paris 1926.

Karris, R. J., "The Gospel According to Luke", Fitzmyer, Brown (eds.), *NJBC* II, 675-721.

Kealy, J. P., *Luke's Gospel Today*, Denville 1979.

Klostermann, E., *Das Lukasevangelium*, HNT 5: Tübingen 1975³ (repr. 1929³).

Knabenbauer, J., *Evangelium Secundum Lucam, Commentarius in Quatuor S. Evangelia Domini N. Jesu Christi* III, Paris 1905².

————, *Commentarius in Actus Apostolorum*, Paris 1899.

Knopf, R., *Die Apostelgeschichte. Die Schriften des Neuen Testaments* I, Göttingen 1907², 526-667.

Knowling, R. J., *The Acts of the Apostles. The Expositor's Greek Testament* II.I, London 1904³, 1-554.

Kremer, J., *Lukasevangelium*, Würzburg 1988.

Lagrange, M.-J., *Évangile selon Saint Luc*, Paris 1921².

Lake, K., Cadbury, H. J., *The Acts of the Apostles* IV, Foakes Jackson, Lake (eds.), *Beginnings* I.IV.

LaVerdiere, E., *Luke*, NTM 5: Dublin 1980.

Leaney, A. R. C., *A Commentary on the Gospel according to St. Luke*, London 1966² (1958).

Loisy, A., *L'Évangile selon Luc*, Paris 1924.

————, *Les Actes des Apôtres*, Paris 1920.

Maldonado, J. de, *Commentarii in Quatuor Evangelistas* II, Mainz 1611.

Marshall, I. H., *The Gospel of Luke. A Commentary on the Greek Text*, Exeter 1978.

————, *The Acts of the Apostles*, Leicester 1980.

Martini, C. M., *Atti degli Apostoli*, NVB 5: Rome 1974³.

Morris, L., *Luke*, London 1974.

Munck, J., *The Acts of the Apostles*, AB 31: Garden City 1967.

Mussner, F., *Apostelgeschichte*, Würzburg 1984.

Pesch, R., *Die Apostelgeschichte*, 2 vols, EKKNT III: Zürich 1986.

Plummer, A., *A Critical and Exegetical Commentary on the Gospel According to S. Luke*, ICC, Edinburgh 1922⁵.

188   BIBLIOGRAPHY

Rackham, R. B., *The Acts of the Apostles*, London 1912[6].
Rengstorf, K. H., *Das Evangelium nach Lukas*, NTD 3: Göttingen 1974[15].
Ricciotti, G., *Gli Atti degli Apostoli, Tradotti e Commentati*, Rome 1951.
Roloff, J., *Die Apostelgeschichte*, NTD 5: Göttingen 1981.
Schanz, P., *Commentar über das Evangelium des heiligen Lucas*, Tübingen 1883.
Schegg, P., *Evangelium nach Lukas*, 3 vols, Munich 1861-65.
Schille, G., *Die Apostelgeschichte des Lukas*, THKNT 5: Berlin 1983.
Schmid, J., *Das Evangelium nach Lukas*, RNT 3: Regensburg 1960[4].
Schneider, G., *Das Evangelium nach Lukas*, 2 vols, ÖTK 3: Gütersloh 1977.
——, *Die Apostelgeschichte*, 2 vols, HTKNT V: Freiburg 1980, 1982.
Schürmann, H., *Das Lukasevangelium* I, HTKNT III.1: Freiburg 1969.
Schweizer, E., *Das Evangelium nach Lukas*, NTD 3: Göttingen 1982.
Staab, K., *Das Evangelium nach Markus und Lukas*, Würzburg 1956.
Stählin, G., *Die Apostelgeschichte*, NTD 5: Göttingen 1962.
Stöger, A., *Das Evangelium nach Lukas*, 2 vols, GS 3: Düsseldorf 1964, 1966.
Stuhlmueller, C., "The Gospel According to Luke", Fitzmyer, Brown (eds.), *JBC* II, 115-164.
Talbert, C. H., *Reading Luke. A Literary and Theological Commentary on the Third Gospel*, New York 1984.
Valensin, A., Huby, J., *Évangile selon Saint Luc*, VS 3: Paris 1952[41].
Weiser, A., *Die Apostelgeschichte*, 2 vols, ÖTK 5: Gütersloh-Würzburg 1981, 1985.
Weiss, B., *Die Evangelien des Markus und Lukas*, Göttingen 1901[3].
Weiss, J., *Die drei älteren Evangelien. Die Schriften des Neuen Testaments neu übersetzt und für die Gegenwart erklärt* I, ed. W. Bousset, Göttingen 1917[3], 392-511.
Wellhausen, J., *Das Evangelium Lucae übersetzt und erklärt*, Berlin 1904.
Wikenhauser, A., *Die Apostelgeschichte*, Regensburg 1961[4].
Zahn, T., *Das Evangelium des Lucas*, Leipzig 1913[1-2].
——, *Die Apostelgeschichte des Lucas*, 2 vols, Leipzig 1919, 1921.
Zigabenus, Euthymius, *Commentarius in Quatuor Evangelia* II, ed. C. F. Matthaei, Berlin-London 1845.

3. Literature on Luke–Acts

Achtemeier, P. J., "The Lucan Perspective on the Miracles of Jesus: A Preliminary Sketch", *JBL* 94 (1975) 547-562.
Agua Pérez, A. del, "El cumplimiento del Reino de Dios en la misión de Jesús: Programa del Evangelio de Lucas (Lc. 4,14-44)", *EstBib* 38 (1979) 269-293.
Alexander, L., "Luke's Preface in the Context of Greek Preface-Writing", *NT* 28 (1986) 48-74.
Anderson, H., "Broadening Horizons. The Rejection at Nazareth Pericope of Luke 4:16-30 in Light of Recent Critical Trends", *Int* 18 (1964) 259-275.
Audet, J.-P., "Autour de la théologie de Luc I-II", *ScEc* 11 (1959) 409-418.
Bachmann, M., *Jerusalem und der Tempel. Die geographisch-theologischen Elemente in der lukanischen Sicht des jüdischen Kultzentrums*, BWANT 109: Stuttgart 1980.

————, "Johannes der Täufer bei Lukas: Nachzügler oder Vorläufer?", *Wort in der Zeit. Neutestamentliche Studien,* Festgabe für Karl Heinrich Rengstorf zum 75. Geburtstag, eds. W. Haubeck, M. Bachmann, Leiden 1980, 123-155.

Bailey, K. E., *Poet and Peasant,* Grand Rapids 1976.

————, *Through Peasant Eyes,* Grand Rapids 1980 (combined ed. Grand Rapids 1983).

Baltzer, K., "The Meaning of the Temple in the Lukan Writings", *HTR* 58 (1965) 263-277.

Barr, D. L., Wentling, J. L., "The Conventions of Classical Biography and the Genre of Luke-Acts: A Preliminary Study", Talbert (ed.), *New Perspectives,* 63-88.

Bartsch, H.-W., *Wachet aber zu jeder Zeit! Entwurf einer Auslegung des Lukasevangeliums,* Hamburg-Bergstedt 1963.

Benoit, P., "L'Enfance de Jean-Baptiste selon Luc I", *NTS* 3 (1956-57) 169-194.

Bernadicou, P. J., "The Lucan Theology of Joy", *ScEs* 25 (1973) 75-98.

Betori, G., *Perseguitati a causa del Nome. Strutture dei racconti di persecuzione in Atti 1,12–8,4,* AnBib 97: Rome 1981.

————, "Alla ricerca di un'articolazione per il libro degli Atti", *RivB* 37 (1989) 185-205.

Betz, O., "The Kerygma of Luke", *Int* 22 (1968) 131-146.

Bihler, J., *Die Stephanusgeschichte im Zusammenhang der Apostelgeschichte,* MTS I.16: Munich 1963.

Blinzler, J., "Die literarische Eigenart des sogenannten Reiseberichts im Lukasevangelium", Schmid, Vögtle (eds.), *Synoptische Studien,* 20-52.

Blomberg, C. L., "Midrash, Chiasmus, and the Outline of Luke's Central Section", France, Wenham (eds.), *Gospel Perspectives* III, 217-261.

Bovon, F., *Luc le théologien. Vingt-cinq ans de recherches (1950-1975),* Neuchatel-Paris 1978.

Braumann, G., *Das Lukas-Evangelium. Die Redaktions- und Kompositionsgeschichtliche Forschung,* WdF 280: Darmstadt 1974.

Brawley, R. L., *Luke–Acts and the Jews. Conflict, Apology, and Conciliation,* SBLMS 33: Atlanta 1987.

Brown, R. E., "Luke's Description of the Virginal Conception", *TS* 35 (1974) 360-362.

————, *The Birth of the Messiah. A commentary on the infancy narratives in Matthew and Luke,* London 1977.

Brown, S., *Apostasy and Perseverance in the Theology of Luke,* AnBib 36: Rome 1969.

————, "The Role of the Prologues in Determining the Purpose of Luke–Acts", Talbert (ed.), *Perspectives,* 99-111.

Brun, L., "Zur Kompositionstechnik des Lukasevangeliums", *SO* 9 (1930) 38-50.

————, "Der Besuch Jesu in Nazareth nach Lukas", *Serta Rudbergiana,* eds. H. Holst, H. Moland, Oslo 1931, 7-17.

————, "Die Berufung der ersten Jünger Jesu in der evangelischen Tradition", *SO* 11 (1932) 35-54.

Bruners, W., *Die Reinigung der zehn Aussätzigen und die Heilung des Samariters Lk 17,11-19. Ein Beitrag zur lukanischen Interpretation der Reinigung von Aussätzigen,* FzB 23: Stuttgart 1977.

Busse U., *Die Wunder des Propheten Jesus. Die Rezeption, Komposition und Interpretation der Wundertradition im Evangelium des Lukas*, FzB 24: Stuttgart 1977.

——, *Das Nazareth-Manifest Jesu. Eine Einführung in das lukanische Jesusbild nach Lk 4,16-30*, SBS 91: Stuttgart 1978.

Cadbury, H. J., *The Style and Literary Method of Luke*, HTS VI: New York 1969 (repr. Cambridge, Mass. 1920).

——, "The Knowledge Claimed in Luke's Preface", *Exp* 24 (1922) 401-420.

——, "Commentary on the Preface of Luke", Foakes Jackson, Lake (eds.), *Beginnings* I.II, 489-510.

——, "The Summaries of Acts", Foakes Jackson, Lake (eds.), *Beginnings* I.V, 392-402.

——, *The Making of Luke-Acts*, London 1968² (repr. New York 1927).

——, "'We' and 'I' Passages in Luke–Acts", *NTS* 3 (1956-57) 128-132.

Callan, T., "The Preface of Luke–Acts and Historiography", *NTS* 31 (1985) 576-581.

Carroll, J. T., *Response to the End of History. Eschatology and Situation in Luke–Acts*, SBLDS 92: Atlanta 1988.

Casalegno, A., *Gesù e il Tempio. Studio redazionale su Luca – Atti*, Brescia 1984.

Cerfaux, L., "La composition de la première partie du Livre des Actes", *ETL* 13 (1936) 667-691.

——, "Les Actes des Apôtres", Robert, Feuillet (eds.), *Introduction* II, 337-374.

Colson, F. H., "Notes on St Luke's Preface", *JTS* 24 (1923) 300-309.

Conybeare, F. C., "Ein Zeugnis Ephräms über das Fehlen von c. 1 und 2 im Texte des Lucas", *ZNW* 3 (1902) 192-197.

Conzelmann, H., "Zur Lukasanalyse", *ZTK* 49 (1952) 16-33 (= Braumann, *Lukas-Evangelium*, 43-63).

——, *Die Mitte der Zeit. Studien zur Theologie des Lukas*, BHT 17: Tübingen 1964⁵ (1954).

Davies, J. H., "The Purpose of the Central Section of St. Luke's Gospel", *SE* II, ed. F. L. Cross, TU 87: Berlin 1964, 164-169.

——, "The Lucan Prologue (1-3): An attempt at objective redaction criticism", *SE* VI, ed. E. A. Livingstone, TU 112: Berlin 1973, 78-85.

Dawsey, J., "The Literary Unity of Luke-Acts: Questions of Style — A Task for Literary Critics", *NTS* 35 (1989) 48-66.

de la Potterie, I., "L'onction du Christ. Étude de théologie biblique", *NRT* 80 (1958) 225-252.

——, *Excerpta Exegetica ex Evangelio Sancti Lucae. Annotationes privatae in usum alumnorum P.I.B.*, Rome 1963-1964.

——, "Le titre κύριος appliqué à Jésus dans l'évangile de Luc", Descamps, de Halleux (eds.), *Mélanges Béda Rigaux*, 117-146.

——, "La notion de "commencement" dans les écrits johanniques", *Die Kirche des Anfangs*, Festschrift für Heinz Schürmann zum 65. Geburtstag, eds. R. Schnackenburg, J. Ernst, J. Wanke, EThSt 38: Leipzig 1977, 379-403.

——, "Les deux noms de Jérusalem dans l'évangile de Luc", *RSR* 69 (1981) 57-70 (= *La Parole de Grâce*, Études lucaniennes à la mémoire d'Augustin George, eds. J. Delorme, J. Duplacy, Paris 1981, 57-70).

Delebecque, E., *Évangile de Luc*, Paris 1976.

Denaux, A., "Het lucaanse reisverhaal (Lc. 9,51–19,44)", *CBG* 14 (1968) 214-242; 15 (1969) 464-501.

de Zwaan, J., "Was the Book of Acts a Posthumous Edition?", *HTR* 17 (1924) 95-153.

Dibelius, M., "Die Herkunft der Sonderstücke des Lukasevangeliums", *ZNW* 12 (1911) 325-343.

——, *Studies in the Acts of the Apostles*, ed. H. Greeven, London 1973.

Dietrich, W., *Das Petrusbild der lukanischen Schriften*, BWANT 94: Stuttgart 1972.

Dillon, R. J., *From Eye-Witnesses to Ministers of the Word. Tradition and Composition in Luke 24*, AnBib 82: Rome 1978.

——, "Previewing Luke's Project from His Prologue (Luke 1:1-4)", *CBQ* 43 (1981) 205-227.

Dornseiff, F., "Lukas der Schriftsteller. Mit einem Anhang: Josephus und Tacitus", *ZNW* 35 (1934) 129-155.

Drury, J., *Tradition and Design in Luke's Gospel. A Study in Early Christian Historiography*, London 1976.

Dumais, M., *Le Langage de L'Évangélisation. L'annonce missionaire en milieu juif (Actes 13,16-41)*, Rech. 16: Tournai-Montreal 1976.

Du Plessis, I.I., "Once more: the purpose of Luke's Prologue (Lk I 1-4)", *NT* 16 (1974) 259-271.

Dupont, J., *Les sources du Livre des Actes. État de la question*, Bruges 1960.

——, "Dieu l'a oint d'Esprit Saint Ac 10,34-38", *ASeign* 12 (1969) 40-47.

——, "Les tentations de Jésus dans le récit de Luc (Luc, 4,1-13)", *ScEc* 14 (1962) 7-29.

——, "Le Salut des Gentils et la Signification Théologique du Livre des Actes", *NTS* 6 (1959-60) 132-155.

——, "La nouvelle Pentecôte: Ac 2,1-11", *ASeign* 30 (1970) 30-34.

——, "La conclusion des Actes et son rapport à l'ensemble de l'ouvrage de Luc", Kremer (ed.), *Les Actes des Apôtres*, 359-404.

——, "La question du plan des Actes des Apôtres à la lumière d'un texte de Lucien de Samosate", *NT* 21 (1979) 220-231.

——, "La structure oratoire du discours d'Étienne (Actes 7)", *Bib* 66 (1985) 153-167.

Egelkraut, H. L., *Jesus' Mission to Jerusalem: A redaction critical study of the Travel Narrative in the Gospel of Luke, Lk 9:51–19:48*, EHS XXIII.80: Frankfurt am Main 1976.

Ehrhardt, A., "The Construction and Purpose of the Acts of the Apostles", *ST* 12 (1958) 45-79.

Erdmann, G., *Die Vorgeschichte des Lukas- und Matthäus-Evangeliums und Vergils vierte Ekloge*, FRLANT 48: Göttingen 1932.

Esler, P. F., *Community and gospel in Luke-Acts. The social and political motivations of Lucan Theology*, SNTSMS 57: Cambridge 1987.

Fabris, R., "La parabola degli invitati alla cena. Analisi redazionale di Lc. 14,16-24", Dupont (ed.), *Invitati al Banchetto*, 127-166.

Farmer, W. R., "Notes on a Literary and Form-Critical Analysis of Some of the Synoptic Material Peculiar to Luke", *NTS* 8 (1961-62) 301-316.

Farrell, H. K., "The Structure and theology of Luke's Central Section", *TrinJ* 7 (1986) 33-54.

Feldkämper, L., *Der betende Jesus als Heilsmittler nach Lukas*, St. Augustin 1978.

Fitzmyer, J. A., "The Ascension of Christ and Pentecost", *TS* 45 (1984) 409-440.

Flender, H., *Heil und Geschichte in der Theologie des Lukas*, BET 41: Munich 1965.

Foakes Jackson, F. J., Lake, K., *The Beginnings of Christianity Part 1. The Acts of the Apostles*, 5 vols, London 1920-33 [*Beginnings*].

Fusco, V., "Progetto storiografico e progetto teologico nell'opera lucana", *La Storiografia nella Bibbia*, Atti della XXVIII Settimana Biblica, Bologna 1986, 123-152.

Gasque, W. W., "A Fruitful Field. Recent Studies of the Acts of the Apostles", *Int* 42 (1988) 117-131.

George, A., "La royauté de Jésus", *Études*, 257-282.

―――, "Jésus Fils de Dieu dans l'Évangile selon saint Luc", *RB* 72 (1965) 185-209.

―――, "Tradition et rédaction chez Luc. La construction du troisième Évangile", *ETL* 43 (1967) 100-129.

―――, "Israël dans l'œuvre de Luc", *RB* 75 (1968) 481-525.

―――, "Le parallèle entre Jean-Baptiste et Jésus en Lc 1-2", Descamps, de Halleux (eds.), *Mélanges Béda Rigaux*, 147-171.

―――, "Le sens de la mort de Jésus pour Luc", *RB* 80 (1973) 186-217.

―――, "Le miracle dans l'œuvre de Luc", *Les miracles de Jésus selon le Nouveau Testament*, ed. X. Léon-Dufour, Paris 1977, 249-268.

―――, *Études sur l'œuvre de Luc*, Paris 1978.

Gibbs, J. M., "Mark 1,1-15, Matthew 1,1–4,16, Luke 1,1–4.30, John 1,1-51. The Gospel Prologues and their Function", Livingstone (ed.), *SE* VI, 154-188.

Giblin, C. H., "Reflections on the Sign of the Manger", *CBQ* 29 (1967) 87-101.

Gill, D., "Observations on the Lukan Travel Narrative and Some Related Passages", *HTR* 63 (1970) 199-221.

Girard, L., *L'Évangile des Voyages de Jésus ou La Section 9,51–18,14 de saint Luc*, Paris 1951.

Glöckner, R., *Die Verkündigung des Heils beim Evangelisten Lukas*, WSTR 9: Mainz 1975.

Glombitza, O., "Die Titel διδάσκαλος und ἐπιστάτης für Jesus bei Lukas", *ZNW* 49 (1958) 275-278.

Goulder, M. D., "The Chiastic Structure of the Lucan Journey", Cross (ed.), *SE* II, 195-202.

Grässer, E., "Die Apostelgeschichte in der Forschung der Gegenwart', *TRu* 26 (1960) 93-167.

―――, "Acta-Forschung seit 1960", *TRu* 41 (1976) 141-194.259-290; 42 (1977) 1-68.

Grimm, J., *Die Einheit des Lukasevangeliums*, Regensburg 1863.

Grimm, W., "Das Proömium des Lucasevangelium", *Jahrbücher für Deutsche Theologie* 16 (1871) 33-78.

Güttgemanns, E., "In welchem Sinne ist Lukas "Historiker"? Die Beziehungen von Luk 1,1-4 und Papias zur antiken Rhetorik", *LingBibl* 54 (1983) 9-26.

Haenchen, E., "Schriftzitate und Textüberlieferung in der Apostelgeschichte", *ZTK* 51 (1954) 153-167.

———, "The Book of Acts as Source Material for the History of Early Christianity", Keck, Martyn (eds.), *Studies in Luke–Acts*, 258-278.

Harnack, A., *Lukas der Arzt. Beiträge zur Einleitung in das Neue Testament* I, Leipzig 1906.

———, "Das Magnificat der Elizabet (Luc 1,46-55) nebst einigen Bemerkungen zu Luc 1 und 2", *Sitzungsberichte der königlich preussischen Akademie der Wissenschaften zu Berlin* 27 (1900) 537-556 [*SPAW*].

Hauser, H. J., *Strukturen der Abschlusserzählung der Apostelgeschichte (Apg 28,16-31)*, AnBib 86: Rome 1979.

Hemer, C. J., *The Book of Acts in the Setting of Hellenistic History*, ed. C. H. Gempf, WUNT 49: Tübingen 1989.

Hilgenfeld, A., "Der Eingang der Apostelgeschichte", *ZWT* 41 (1898) 619-625.

———, "Das Vorwort des dritten Evangeliums (Luc. I,1-4)", *ZWT* 44 (1901) 1-10.

———, "Zu Lucas III,2", *ZWT* 44 (1901) 466-468.

Hill, D., "The Rejection of Jesus at Nazareth (Luke iv 16-30)", *NT* 13 (1971) 161-180.

Hobart, W. K., *The Medical Language of St. Luke*, Dublin-London 1882.

Jeremias, J., *Die Sprache des Lukasevangeliums. Redaktion und Tradition im Nicht-Markusstoff des dritten Evangeliums*, Göttingen 1980.

Kariamadam, P., *The End of the Travel Narrative (Lk 18,31–19,46). A Redaction Critical Investigation*, Diss. Rome 1978.

———, "The composition and meaning of the Lucan Travel Narrative (Lk. 9,51–19,46)", *Biblebhashyam* 13 (1987) 179-198.

Karris, R. J., "Widows and Minors: Literary Criticism and Luke's Sitz im Leben", *Society of Biblical Literature 1978 Seminar Papers* I, ed. P. J. Achtemeier, Missoula 1978, 47-58.

Keck, F., *Die öffentliche Abschiedsrede Jesu in Lk 20,45–21,36. Eine redaktions- und motivgeschichtliche Untersuchung*, FzB 25: Stuttgart 1976.

Keck, L. E., Martyn, J. L., *Studies in Luke–Acts*, Essays presented in honor of Paul Schubert, London 1968.

Kilgallen, J. J., "Luke 2,41-50: Foreshadowing of Jesus, Teacher", *Bib* 66 (1985) 553-559.

Klein, G., "Lukas 1,1-4 als theologisches Programm", *Zeit und Geschichte, Dankesgabe an Rudolf Bultmann zum 80. Geburtstag*, ed. E. Dinkler, Tübingen 1964, 193-216.

Klinghardt, M., *Gesetz und Volk Gottes. Das lukanische Verständnis des Gesetzes nach Herkunft, Funktion und seinem Ort in der Geschichte des Urchristentums*, WUNT 2.32: Tübingen 1988.

Kremer, J., *Pfingstbericht und Pfingstgeschehen. Eine exegetische Untersuchung zu Apg 2,1-13*, SBS 63-64: Stuttgart 1973.

——— (ed.), *Les Actes des Apôtres. Traditions, rédaction, théologie*, BETL 48: Gembloux-Louvain 1979.

Kümmel, W. G., " 'Das Gesetz und die Propheten gehen bis Johannes' — Lukas 16,16 im Zusammenhang der heilsgeschichtlichen Theologie der Lukasschriften", *Verborum Veritatis*, Festschrift für Gustav Stählin zum 70. Geburtstag, eds. O. Böcher, K. Haacker, Wuppertal 1970, 89-102 (= Braumann, *Lukas-Evangelium*, 398-415).

Kürzinger, J., "Lk 1,3: ... ἀκριβῶς καθεξῆς σοι γράψαι", *BZ* 18 (1974) 249-255.

Lampe, G. W. H., "The Holy Spirit in the Writings of St. Luke", *Studies in the Gospels,* Essays in Memory of R. H. Lightfoot, ed. D. E. Nineham, Oxford 1955, 159-200.

——, *God as Spirit,* The Bampton Lectures, 1976, Oxford 1977.

Larrañaga, V., "El proemio-transición de Act. 1,1-3 en los métodos literarios de la historiografia griega", *Miscellanea Biblica* II: Rome 1934, 311-374.

Laurentin, R., *Structure et Théologie de Luc I-II,* Paris 1957.

Le Déaut, R., "Pentecôte et tradition juive", *ASeign* 51 (1963) 22-38.

Legrand, L., "L'Évangile aux Bergers. Essai sur le genre littéraire de Luc, II,8-20", *RB* 75 (1968) 161-187.

——, *L'Annonce a Marie (Lc 1,26-38). Une apocalypse aux origines de l'Évangile,* LD 106: Paris 1981.

Lentzen-Deis, F., "Ps 2,7, ein Motiv früher "hellenistischer" Christologie? Der Psalmvers in der Lectio varians von Lk 3,22, im Ebionäerevangelium und bei Justinus Martyr", *TP* 44 (1969) 342-362.

Lövestam, E., *Son and Saviour. A Study of Acts 13,32-37. With an Appendix 'Son of God' in the Synoptic Gospels,* ConNT 18: Lund 1961.

Lohfink, G., *Die Himmelfahrt Jesu. Untersuchungen zu den Himmelfahrts- und Erhöhungstexten bei Lukas,* SANT 26: Munich 1971.

——, *Die Sammlung Israels. Eine Untersuchung zur lukanischen Ekklesiologie,* SANT 39: Munich 1975.

Lohse, E., "Lukas als Theologe der Heilsgeschichte", *EvT* 14 (1954) 256-275 (= Braumann, *Lukas-Evangelium,* 64-90).

Long, W. R., "The Paulusbild in the Trial of Paul in Acts", *Society of Biblical Literature 1983 Seminar Papers,* ed. K. H. Richards, Chico 1983, 87-105.

Luck, U., "Kerygma, Tradition und Geschichte Jesu bei Lukas", *ZTK* 57 (1960) 51-66 (= Braumann, *Lukas-Evangelium,* 95-114).

Lyonnet, S., "Le récit de l'Annonciation et la Maternité Divine de la Sainte Vierge", *AmiCl* 66 (1956) 33-46.

McCown, C. C., "Gospel Geography: Fiction, Fact, and Truth", *JBL* 60 (1941) 1-25 (= Braumann, *Lukas-Evangelium,* 13-42).

Machen, J. G., *The Virgin Birth of Christ,* New York-London 1930.

Maddox, R., *The Purpose of Luke–Acts,* FRLANT 126: Göttingen 1982.

Mánek, J., "The New Exodus in the Books of Luke", *NT* 2 (1957) 8-23.

Marshall, I. H., *Luke: Historian and Theologian,* Exeter 1970.

——, "Luke and his 'Gospel' ", Stuhlmacher (ed.), *Evangelium,* 289-308.

Martin, J. P., "Luke 1:39-47", *Int* 36 (1982) 394-399.

Mattill, Jr., A. J., "The Purpose of Acts. Schneckenburger Reconsidered", Gasque, Martin (eds.) *Apostolic History,* 108-122.

——, "The Jesus-Paul Parallels and the Purpose of Luke–Acts: H. H. Evans Reconsidered", *NT* 17 (1975) 15-46.

Menoud, P.-H., "Le plan des Actes des Apôtres", *NTS* 1 (1954-55) 44-51.

——, "Les additions au groupe des douze apôtres, d'après le livre des Actes", *RHPR* 37 (1957) 71-80.

Merk, O., "Das Reich Gottes in den lukanischen Schriften", Ellis, Grässer (eds.), *Jesus und Paulus,* 201-220.

Meynet, R., *Quelle est donc cette parole? Lecture "rhétorique" de L'évangile de Luc (1-9,22-24),* 2 vols, LD 99A-B: Paris 1979.

Miller, R. J., "Elijah, John, and Jesus in the Gospel of Luke", *NTS* 34 (1988) 611-622.

Minear, P. S., "Luke's Use of the Birth Stories", Keck, Martin (eds.) *Studies in Luke–Acts*, 111-130 (= Braumann, *Lukas-Evangelium*, 204-235).

——, *To Heal and to Reveal. The Prophetic Vocation According to Luke*, New York 1976.

Miyoshi, M., *Der Anfang des Reiseberichts Lk 9,51–10,24. Eine redaktions-geschichtliche Untersuchung*, AnBib 60: Rome 1974.

Morgenthaler, R., *Die lukanische Geschichtsschreibung als Zeugnis. Gestalt und Gehalt der Kunst des Lukas*, 2 vols, Zürich 1949.

Muhlack, G., *Die Parallelen von Lukas-Evangelium und Apostelgeschichte*, TW 8: Frankfurt am Main 1979.

Mussner, F., "Καθεξῆς im Lukasprolog", Ellis, Grässer (eds.), *Jesus und Paulus*, 253-255.

Navone, J., *Themes of St. Luke*, Rome 1970.

Neirynck, F., "Le Livre des Actes dans les récents commentaires", *ETL* 59 (1983) 338-349.

—— (ed.), *L'Évangile de Luc. Problèmes littéraires et théologiques*, Mémorial Lucien Cerfaux, BETL 32: Gembloux 1973.

Neyrey, J., "The Forensic Defense Speech and Paul's Trial Speeches in Acts 22-26: Form and Function", Talbert (ed.), *New Perspectives*, 210-224.

——, *The Passion According to Luke. A Redaction Study of Luke's Soteriology*, New York-Mahwah 1985.

Nolland, J., "Impressed Unbelievers as Witnesses to Christ (Luke 4:22a)", *JBL* 98 (1979) 219-229.

Ó Fearghail, F., "The Literary Forms of Lk 1,5-25 and 1,26-38", *Marianum* 43 (1981) 321-344.

——, "Rejection in Nazareth: Lk 4,22", *ZNW* 75 (1984) 60-72.

——, "Israel in Luke–Acts", *PIBA* 11 (1988) 23-43.

——, "The Imitation of the Septuagint in Luke's Infancy Narrative", *PIBA* 12 (1989) 58-78.

Oliver, H. H., "The Lucan Birth Stories and the Purpose of Luke–Acts", *NTS* 10 (1963-64) 202-226.

O'Neill, J. C., *The Theology of Acts in its Historical Setting*, London 1970[2].

O'Reilly, L., *Word and Sign in the Acts of the Apostles. A Study in Lucan Theology*, AnGreg 243: Rome 1987.

O'Toole, R. F., *The Unity of Luke's Theology. An Analysis of Luke–Acts*, GNS 9: Wilmington 1984.

——, "Parallels between Jesus and His Disciples in Luke–Acts: A Further Study", *BZ* 27 (1983) 195-212.

Palmer, D. W., "The Literary Background of Acts 1. 1-14", *NTS* 33 (1987) 427-438.

Panimolle, S. A., "Il valore salvifico della morte di Gesù negli scritti di Luca", *Sangue e Antropologia Biblica* 1.II, ed. F. Vattioni, CSSC 1.II: Rome 1981, 661-673.

——, *Il discorso di Pietro all'assemblea apostolica*, 3 vols, SB 1-3: Bologna 1976-78.

Parsons, M. C., *The Departure of Jesus in Luke–Acts. The Ascension Narratives in Context*, JSNTSS 21: Sheffield 1987.

196   BIBLIOGRAPHY

Perrot, C., "Les Actes des Apôtres", *L'annonce de l'Évangile: Introduction Critique au Nouveau Testament* II.2, eds. X. Léon-Dufour, C. Perrot, Paris 1976, 239-295.

Pervo, R. I., *Profit with Delight. The Literary Genre of the Acts of the Apostles*, Philadelphia 1987.

Pesch, R., "Der Anfang der Apostelgeschichte: Apg 1,1-11. Kommentarstudie", *Evangelisch Katholischer-Kommentar zum Neuen Testament* Vorarbeiten 3: Zürich 1971, 7-35.

———, *Der Reiche Fischfang Lk 5,1-11/Jo 21,1-14. Wundergeschichte — Berufungserzählung — Erscheinungsbericht*, Düsseldorf 1969.

Peters, H., "Der Aufbau der Apostelgeschichte", *Philologus* 85 (1929) 52-64.

Pilgrim, W. E., *Good News to the Poor. Wealth and Poverty in Luke–Acts*, Minneapolis 1981.

Plümacher, E., *Lukas als hellenistischer Schriftsteller. Studien zur Apostelgeschichte*, SUNT 9: Göttingen 1972.

———, "Lukas als griechischer Historiker", *Paulys Real-Encyclopädie der Classischen Altertumswissenschaft*, Supplementband XIV, ed. H. Gärtner, Munich 1974, 235-264 [*PRE*].

———, "Apostelgeschichte", *Theologische Realenzyklopädie* III, eds. G. Krause, G. Müller, Berlin-New York 1978, 483-528 [*TRE*].

———, "Neues Testament und hellenistische Form. Zur literarischen Gattung der lukanischen Schriften", *ThViat* 14 (1979) 109-123.

———, "Die Apostelgeschichte als historische Monographie", Kremer (ed.), *Les Actes des Apôtres*, 457-466.

———, "Acta-Forschung 1974-1982", *TRu* 48 (1983) 1-56; 49 (1984) 105-169.

Praeder, S. F., "Luke–Acts and the Ancient Novel", *Society of Biblical Literature 1981 Seminar Papers* I, ed. K. H. Richards, Chico 1981, 269-292.

———, "Jesus-Paul, Peter-Paul, and Jesus-Peter Parallelisms in Luke–Acts: A History of Reader Response", *Society of Biblical Literature 1984 Seminar Papers*, ed. K. H. Richards, Chico 1984, 23-39.

Prast, F., *Presbyter und Evangelium in nachapostolischer Zeit. Die Abschiedsrede des Paulus in Milet (Apg 20,17-38) im Rahmen der lukanischen Konzeption der Evangeliumsverkündigung*, FzB 29: Stuttgart 1979.

Prete, B., "Prospettive messianiche nell'espressione *sêmeron* del Vangelo di Luca", *Il Messianismo*, Atti della XVIII Settimana Biblica, Brescia 1966, 269-284.

———, "L'arrivo di Paolo a Roma e il suo significato secondo Atti 28,16-31", *RivB* 31 (1983) 147-187.

Radl, W., *Paulus und Jesus im lukanischen Doppelwerk. Untersuchungen zu Parallelmotiven im Lukasevangelium und in der Apostelgeschichte*, EHS XXIII.49: Frankfurt am Main 1975.

Rasco, E., "Hans Conzelmann y la 'Historia Salutis'. A propósito de 'Die Mitte der Zeit' y 'Die Apostelgeschichte'", *Greg* 46 (1965) 286-319.

———, *Actus Apostolorum. Introductio et Exempla Exegetica* I, Rome 1967.

———, "Les paraboles de Luc XV. Une invitation à la joie de Dieu dans le Christ", *De Jésus aux Évangiles. Tradition et Rédaction dans les Évangiles synoptiques*, ed. I. de la Potterie, BETL 25: Gembloux-Paris 1967, 165-183.

———, *La Teologia de Lucas: Origen, Desarrollo, Orientaciones*, AnGreg 201: Rome 1976.

————, "Spirito e istituzione nell'opera lucana", *RivB* 30 (1982) 301-321.

Ravens, D. S., "Luke 9. 7-62 and the Prophetic Role of Jesus", *NTS* 36 (1990) 119-129.

Reicke, B., "Instruction and Discussion in the Travel Narrative", *SE* I, ed. F. L. Cross, TU 73: Berlin 1959, 206-216.

Rese, M. *Alttestamentliche Motive in der Christologie des Lukas*, SNT 1: Gütersloh 1969.

Rigaux, B., *Témoignage de l'évangile de Luc*, Bruges-Paris 1970.

Robbins, V., "Prefaces in Greco-Roman Biography and Luke–Acts", *PerspRelStud* 6 (1979) 94-108.

Robinson, Jr., W. C., "The Theological Context for Interpreting Luke's Travel Narrative (9,51 ff.)", *JBL* 79 (1960) 20-31.

————, *The Way of the Lord. A Study of History and Eschatology in the Gospel of Luke*, Basle 1962 (= *Der Weg des Herrn. Studien zur Geschichte und Eschatologie im Lukas-Evangelium. Ein Gespräch mit Hans Conzelmann*, TF 36: Hamburg-Bergstedt 1964).

Rolland, P., "L'organisation du Livre des Actes et de l'ensemble de l'œuvre de Luc", *Bib* 65 (1984) 81-86.

Samain, É., "La notion de APXH dans l'œuvre lucanienne", Neirynck (ed.), *Luc*, 299-328.

Sanders, J. T., "The Salvation of the Jews in Luke–Acts", *Society of Biblical Literature 1982 Seminar Papers*, ed. K. H. Richards, Chico 1982, 467-483.

————, *The Jews in Luke–Acts*, London 1987.

Scharlemann, M. H., *Stephen: A Singular Saint*, AnBib 34: Rome 1968.

Schleiermacher, F., *Ueber die Schriften des Lukas, ein kritischer Versuch*, Berlin 1917.

Schneider, G., "Zur Bedeutung von καθεξῆς im lukanischen Doppelwerk", *ZNW* 68 (1977) 128-131.

Schneider, J., "Zur Analyse des lukanischen Reiseberichtes", Schmid, Vögtle (eds.), *Synoptische Studien*, 207-229.

Schubert, P., "The Structure and Significance of Luke 24", Eltester (ed.), *Studien*, 165-186.

Schürmann, H., "Evangelienschrift und kirchliche Unterweisung. Die repräsentative Funktion der Schrift nach Lk 1,1-4", *Traditionsgeschichtliche Untersuchungen zu den synoptischen Evangelien*, Düsseldorf 1967, 251-271 (= Braumann, *Lukas-Evangelium*, 135-169).

————, "L'Évangile (Lc 5,1-11): La promesse à Simon-Pierre", *ASeign* 58 (1964) 27-34.

Sellin, G., "Komposition, Quellen und Funktion des Lukanischen Reiseberichtes (Lk. IX 51-XIX 28)", *NT* 20 (1978) 100-135.

Siegert, F., "Lukas — ein Historiker, d.h. ein Rhetor? Freundschaftliche Entgegnung auf Erhardt Güttgemanns", *LingBibl* 55 (1984) 57-60.

Sloan, Jr., R. B., *The Favorable Year of the Lord. A Study of Jubilary Theology in the Gospel of Luke*, Austin 1977.

Soares Prabhu, G. M., "'Rejoice, Favored One!' Mary in the Annunciation-Story of Luke", *Biblebhashyam* 3 (1977) 259-277.

Stanley, D. M., "The Mother of My Lord", *Worship* 34 (1959-60) 330-332.

Steichele, H., *Vergleich der Apostelgeschichte mit der antiken Geschichts-schreibung. Eine Studie zur Erzählkunst in der Apostelgeschichte*, Diss. Munich 1972.

Stock, K., "Die Berufung Marias (Lk 1,26-38)", *Bib* 61 (1980) 457-491.

Stolle, V., *Der Zeuge als Angeklagter. Untersuchungen zum Paulusbild des Lukas*, BWANT 102: Stuttgart 1973.

Taeger, J.-W., *Der Mensch und sein Heil. Studien zum Bild des Menschen und zur Sicht der Bekehrung bei Lukas*, SNT 14: Gütersloh 1982.

Talbert, C.H., *Literary Patterns, Theological Themes, and the Genre of Luke–Acts*, SBLMS 20: Missoula 1974.

———— (ed.), *Perspectives on Luke–Acts*, Edinburg 1978.

————, "Prophecies of Future Greatness: The Contribution of Greco-Roman Biographies to an Understanding of Luke 1:5-4:15", *The Divine Helmsman: Studies on God's Control of Human Events*, Presented to Lou H. Silbermann, eds. J. L. Crenshaw, S. Sandmel, New York 1980, 129-141.

———— (ed.), *Luke–Acts. New Perspectives from the Society of Biblical Literature Seminar*, New York 1984.

Tannehill, R.C., "The Mission of Jesus according to Luke IV 16-30", Eltester (ed.), *Jesus in Nazareth*, 51-75.

————, "Israel in Luke–Acts: A Tragic Story", *JBL* 104 (1985) 69-85.

————, *The Narrative Unity of Luke–Acts. A Literary Interpretation* I (The Gospel according to Luke), Philadelphia 1986.

Tatum, W.B., "The Epoch of Israel: Luke I-II and the Theological Plan of Luke–Acts", *NTS* 13 (1966-67) 184-195.

Theobald, M., "Die Anfänge der Kirche. Zur Struktur von Lk. 5.1-6.19", *NTS* 30 (1984) 91-108.

Trites, A.A., "The Prayer Motif in Luke–Acts", Talbert (ed.), *Perspectives*, 168-186.

Trocmé, É., *Le "Livre des Actes" et L'Histoire*, EHPR 45: Paris 1957.

Turner, M.B., "Jesus and the Spirit in Lucan Perspective", *TB* 32 (1981) 3-42.

Turner, N., "The Relation of Luke I and II to Hebraic Sources and to the Rest of Luke–Acts", *NTS* 2 (1955-56) 100-109.

Tyson, J.B., *The Death of Jesus in Luke–Acts*, Columbia 1986.

Untergassmair, F.G., *Kreuzweg und Kreuzigung Jesu. Ein Beitrag zur lukanischen Redaktionsgeschichte und zur Frage nach der lukanischen "Kreuzestheologie"*, PTS 10: Paderborn 1980.

Van Stempvoort, P.A., "The Interpretation of the Ascension in Luke and Acts", *NTS* 5 (1958-59) 30-42.

Van Unnik, W.C., "The 'Book of Acts' the Confirmation of the Gospel", *NT* 4 (1960) 26-59 (= *Sparsa Collecta. The Collected Writings of W.C. van Unnik* I, Suppl. NT 29: Leiden 1973, 340-373).

————, "Der Ausdruck ἕως ἐσχάτου τῆς γῆς (Apostelgeschichte i,8) und sein alttestamentlicher Hintergrund", *Studia Biblica et Semitica*, Theodoro Christiano Vriezen... dedicata, Leiden 1966, 335-349 (= *Sparsa Collecta* I, 386-401).

————, "Remarks on the Purpose of Luke's Historical Writing (Luke i 1-4)", *Sparsa Collecta* I, 6-15.

————, "Once More St. Luke's Prologue", *Neot* 7 (1973) 7-26.

————, "Luke's Second Book and the Rules of Hellenistic Historiography", Kremer (ed.), *Les Actes des Apôtres*, 37-60.

Völkel, M., "Exegetische Erwägungen zum Verständnis des Begriffs ΚΑΘΕΞΗΣ im Lukanischen Prolog", *NTS* 20 (1973-74) 289-299.

————, "Der Anfang Jesu in Galiläa. Bemerkungen zum Gebrauch und zur Funktion Galiläas in den lukanischen Schriften", *ZNW* 64 (1973) 222-232.

————, "Zur Deutung des "Reiches Gottes" bei Lukas", *ZNW* 65 (1974) 57-70.

Völter, D., "Das Angebliche Zeugnis Ephräms über das Fehlen von c. 1 und 2 im Texte des Lukas", *ZNW* 10 (1909) 177-180.

Von Baer, H., *Der Heilige Geist in den Lukasschriften*, BWANT III.3: Stuttgart 1926.

Von der Osten-Sacken, P., "Zur Christologie des lukanischen Reiseberichts", *EvT* 33 (1973) 476-496.

Voss, G., *Die Christologie der lukanischen Schriften in Grundzügen*, SN 2: Paris-Bruges 1965.

Wanke, J., *Die Emmauserzählung. Eine redaktionsgeschichtliche Untersuchung zu Lk 24,13-35*, EThSt 31: Leipzig 1973.

Weinert, F. D., "Luke, Stephen, and the Temple in Luke–Acts", *BTB* 17 (1987) 88-90.

Weiss, J., *Ueber die Absicht und den literarischen Charakter der Apostelgeschichte*, Göttingen 1897.

Wiater, W., *Komposition als Mittel der Interpretation im lukanischen Doppelwerk*, Diss. Bonn 1972.

Wikenhauser, A., *Die Apostelgeschichte und ihr Geschichtswert*, NA 8.3-5: Münster 1921.

Wilkens, W., "Die theologische Struktur der Komposition des Lukasevangeliums", *TZ* 34 (1978) 1-13.

Wilson, S. G., *The Gentiles and the Gentile Mission in Luke–Acts*, SNTSMS 23: Cambridge 1973.

————, *Luke and the Law*, SNTSMS 50: Cambridge 1983.

Winn, A. C., "Elusive Mystery. The Purpose of Acts", *Int* 13 (1959) 144-156.

Winter, P., "The Cultural Background of the Narrative in Luke I and II", *JQR* 45 (1954-55) 159-167.230-242.287.

Zimmermann, H., "Evangelium des Lukas Kap. 1 und 2", *TSK* 76 (1903) 249-290.

Zmijewski, J., *Die Eschatologiereden des Lukas-Evangeliums. Eine traditions- und redaktionsgeschichtliche Untersuchung zu Lk 21,5-36 und Lk 17,20-37*, BBB 40: Bonn 1972.

4. Other Literature

Albertz, R., Westermann, C., "ruªḥ", *Theologisches Handwörterbuch zum Alten Testament* II, eds. E. Jenni, C. Westermann, Munich 1976, 726-753 [*THAT*].

Aloni, A., "*Prooimia, Hymnoi*, Elio Aristide e i cugini bastardi", *QUCC* 33 (1980) 23-40.

Anderson, G., *Ancient Fiction. The Novel in the Graeco-Roman World*, Totowa 1984.

Aune, D. E., "The Problem of the Genre of the Gospels: A Critique of C. H. Talbert's *What is a Gospel?*", France, Wenham (eds.), *Gospel Perspectives* II, 9-60.

———, *The New Testament in Its Literary Environment*, Philadelphia 1989 (1987).

Avenarius, G., *Lukians Schrift zur Geschichtsschreibung*, Meisenheim am Glan 1956.

Balz, H., Schneider, G. (eds), *Exegetisches Wörterbuch zum Neuen Testament*, 3 vols, Stuttgart 1980-1983 [*EWNT*].

Balz, H. R., "Anonymität und Pseudepigraphie im Urchristentum. Überlegungen zum literarischen und theologischen Problem der urchristlichen und gemeinantiken Pseudepigraphie", *ZTK* 66 (1969) 403-436.

Baumbach, G., *Das Verständnis des Bösen in den synoptischen Evangelien*, TA 19: Berlin 1963.

Beasley-Murray, G. R., "The Two Messiahs in the Testaments of the Twelve Patriarchs", *JTS* 48 (1947) 1-12.

Berger, K., "Die königlichen Messiastraditionen des Neuen Testaments", *NTS* 20 (1973-74) 1-44.

———, "Hellenistische Gattungen im Neuen Testament", Haase (ed.), *ANRW* II.25.2, 1031-1432.1831-1885.

Betz, O., "Ἰουδαία", *EWNT* II, 468-470.

Beutler, J., "ἄνωθεν", *EWNT* I, 269-270.

Bieder, W., "πνεῦμα κτλ.", *TDNT* VI, 368-375.

Birt, T., *Das Antike Buchwesen in seinem Verhältnis zur Literatur*, Aalen 1974 (repr. Berlin 1882²).

Blenkinsopp, J., "Biographical Patterns in Biblical Narrative", *JSOT* 20 (1981) 27-46.

Boismard, M.-E., "The Two-Source Theory at an Impasse", *NTS* 26 (1979-80) 1-17.

Bonner, S. F., *Education in Ancient Rome. From the elder Cato to the younger Pliny*, London 1977.

Bornkamm, G., "Evangelien, formgeschichtlich", *Die Religion in Geschichte und Gegenwart* II, ed. K. Galling, Tübingen 1958³, 749-753 [*RGG³*].

Bowra, C. M., *Homer*, London 1979.

Braun, H., "Qumran und das Neue Testament. Ein Bericht über 10 Jahre Forschung (1950-1959)", *TRu* 28 (1962) 97-234.

Brown, R. E., *The Gospel According to John*, 2 vols, AB 29, 29A: Garden City 1966, 1970.

Bruns, I., *Die Persönlichkeit in der Geschichtsschreibung der Alten. Untersuchungen zur Technik der antiken Historiographie*, Berlin 1898.

Brunt, P. A., "Cicero and Historiography", *Φιλίας χάριν. Miscellanea di Studi Classici in onore di E. Manni* I, eds. M. J. Fontana, M. T. Piraino, F. P. Rizzo, Rome 1980, 309-340.

Bucher-Isler, B., *Norm und Individualität in den Biographien Plutarchs*, NR 13: Bern-Stuttgart 1972.

Büchsel, F., "ἄνω κτλ.", *TDNT* I, 376-378.

Bultmann, R., "ἀγαλλιάομαι κτλ.", *TDNT* I, 19-21.

———, "ἀφίημι κτλ.", *TDNT* I, 509-512.

——, *Die Geschichte der Synoptischen Tradition*, FRLANT 29: Göttingen 1921.

——, *Theology of the New Testament*, tr. by K. Grobel, 2 vols, London 1952, 1955.

Burck, E., *Die Erzählungskunst des T. Livius*, Berlin-Zürich 1964².

Burrows, E., *The Gospel of the Infancy and Other Biblical Essays*, London 1940.

Butler, R. C., *The Originality of St. Matthew. A Critique of the Two-Document Hypothesis*, Cambridge 1951.

Buttrick, G. A. (ed.), *The Interpreter's Dictionary of the Bible*, 4 vols, Nashville-New York 1962; Supplement, ed. K. Crim, Abingdon 1976 [*IDB*].

Calboli Montefusco, L. (ed.), *Consulti Fortunatiani. Ars Rhetorica*, ESUFC 24: Bologna 1979.

Cerfaux, L., "Le titre Kyrios et la dignité royale de Jésus", *Receuil Lucien Cerfaux. Études d'Exégèse et d'Histoire Religieuse* I, BETL 6: Gembloux 1954, 3-63.

Chilver, G. E. F., *A Historical Commentary on Tacitus' Histories I and II*, Oxford 1979.

Christ, F., *Jesus Sophia. Die Sophia–Christologie bei den Synoptikern*, ATANT 57: Zürich 1970.

Clark, D. L., *Rhetoric in Greco-Roman Education*, New York 1957.

Colson, F. H., "Τάξει in Papias (The Gospels and the Rhetorical Schools)", *JTS* 14 (1913) 62-69.

——, "Some Considerations as to the Influence of Rhetoric upon History", *PCA* 14 (1917) 149-173.

Coppens, J., "Le Messianisme sacerdotal dans les écrits du Nouveau Testament", *La Venue du Messie. Messianisme et Eschatologie*, ed. É. Massaux, RB VI: Louvain 1962, 101-112.

Cornely, R., *Introductio Specialis in Singulos Novi Testamenti Libros. Historica et Critica Introductio in U.T. Libros Sacros* III, Paris 1897².

Cross, F. L. (ed.), *Studia Evangelica* I (TU 73: Berlin 1959); II (Tu 87: Berlin 1964); III (TU 88: Berlin 1964) [*SE*].

Cullmann, O., *The Christology of the New Testament*, tr. by S. C. Guthrie, C. A. M. Hall, London 1963.

Culpepper, R. A., *Anatomy of the Fourth Gospel. A Study in Literary Design*, Philadelphia 1983.

Dalman, G., *Die Worte Jesu*, Leipzig 1930² (1898).

Da Spinetoli, O., *Introduzione ai Vangeli dell'Infanzia*, Brescia 1967.

De Jonge, M., "The use of the word "anointed" in the time of Jesus", *NT* 8 (1966) 132-148.

——, "χρίω κτλ.", *TDNT* IX, 511-517.520-521.

——, "Christian influence in the Testaments of the Twelve Patriarchs", *Studies on the Testaments of the Twelve Patriarchs. Text and Interpretation*, ed. M. de Jonge, SVTP 3: Leiden 1975, 193-246.

—— (ed.), *The Testaments of the Twelve Patriarchs. A Critical Edition of the Greek Text*, PVTG I.2: Leiden 1978.

——, van der Woude, A. S., "11Q Melchizedek and the New Testament", *NTS* 12 (1965-66) 301-326.

de la Potterie, I., "La notion de "commencement" dans les écrits johanniques", *Die Kirche des Anfangs,* Festschrift für Heinz Schürmann zum 65. Geburtstag, eds. R. Schnackenburg, J. Ernst, J. Wanke, EThSt 38: Leipzig 1977, 379-403.

Denniston, J. D., *The Greek Particles,* Oxford 1954².

Descamps, A., de Halleux, A. (eds.), *Mélanges Bibliques en hommage au R. P. Béda Rigaux,* Gembloux 1970.

Dibelius, M., *Die urchristliche Überlieferung von Johannes dem Täufer,* FRLANT 15: Göttingen 1911.

——, *From Tradition to Gospel,* tr. by B. L. Woolf, Cambridge-London 1971.

Dihle, A., "Die Evangelien und die griechische Biographie", Stuhlmacher (ed.), *Evangelium,* 383-411.

Dilts, M. R., *Claudii Aeliani Varia Historia,* Leipzig 1974.

Dodd, C. H., *The Apostolic Preaching and its Developments,* London 1972³ (1936).

Dorey, T. A. (ed.), *Latin Biography,* London 1967.

Doty, W., "The Concept of Genre in Literary Analysis", *Seminar of Biblical Literature Proceedings 1972,* ed. L. C. McGaughy, Missoula 1972, 413-448.

Downing, F. G., "Compositional Conventions and the Synoptic Problem", *JBL* 107 (1988) 69-85.

Dunn, J. D. G., *Baptism in the Holy Spirit,* SBT II.15: London 1970.

Dupont, J., "La parabola degli invitati al banchetto nel ministero di Gesù", Dupont (ed.), *Invitati al Banchetto,* 279-329.

—— (ed.), *La Parabola degli Invitati al Banchetto. Dagli evangelisti a Gesù,* TRSR 14: Brescia 1978.

Earl, D., "Prologue-form in Ancient Historiography", *ANRW* I.2, ed. H. Temporini, Berlin-New York 1972, 842-856.

Ellis, E. E., Grässer, E. (eds.), *Jesus und Paulus,* Festschrift für Werner Georg Kümmel zum 70. Geburtstag, Göttingen 1975.

Eltester, W. (ed.), *Neutestamentliche Studien für Rudolf Bultmann zu seinem siebsigsten Geburtstag,* BZNW 21: Berlin 1954.

—— (ed.), *Jesus in Nazareth,* BZNW 40: Berlin-New York 1972.

Emmelius, J.-C., *Tendenzkritik und Formengeschichte. Der Beitrag Franz Overbecks zur Auslegung der Apostelgeschiche im 19. Jahrhundert,* FKDG 27: Göttingen 1975.

Engel, G., *De antiquorum epicorum didacticorum historicorum prooemiis,* Diss. Marburg 1910.

Erbse, H., "Die Bedeutung der Synkrisis in den Parallelbiographien Plutarchs", *Hermes* 84 (1956) 398-424.

Farmer, W. R., *The Synoptic Problem. A Critical Analysis,* Dillsboro 1976 (1964).

—— (ed.), *New Testament Studies. The Cambridge Gospel Conference and Beyond,* Macon 1983.

Ferraro, G., "Il Termine 'ora' nei vangeli sinottici", *RivB* 21 (1973) 383-400.

Fitzmyer, J. A., "The Priority of Mark and the "Q" Source in Luke", Miller, Hadidian (eds.), *Jesus and man's hope* I, 131-170.

——, "The Contribution of Qumran Aramaic to the Study of the New Testament", *NTS* 20 (1973-74) 382-407.

———, "The Virginal Conception of Jesus in the New Testament", *TS* 34 (1973) 541-575.

———, Brown, R. E. (eds.), *The Jerome Biblical Commentary* II, London 1970 [*JBC*].

———, Brown, R. E. (eds.), *The New Jerome Biblical Commentary* II, London 1990 [*NJBC*].

Focke, F., "Synkrisis", *Hermes* 58 (1923) 327-368.

———, *Die Entstehung der Weisheit Salomos. Ein Beitrag zur Geschichte des jüdischen Hellenismus*, FRLANT NF 5: Göttingen 1913.

Fornara, C. W., *The Nature of History in Ancient Greece and Rome*, Berkeley 1983.

France, R. T., Wenham, D. (eds.), *Studies of History and Tradition in the Four Gospels. Gospel Perspectives* I-II: Sheffield 1980-81; *Studies in Midrash and Historiography. Gospel Perspectives* III: Sheffield 1983.

Frankemölle, H., *Jahwebund und Kirche Christi. Studien zur Form- und Traditionsgeschichte des "Evangeliums" nach Matthäus*, NTA NF 10: Münster 1974.

———, "Evangelium als theologischer Begriff und sein Bezug zur literarischen Gattung 'Evangelium'", in D. Dormeyer, H. Frankemölle, "Evangelium als literarische Gattung und als theologischer Begriff. Tendenzen und Aufgaben der Evangelienforschung im 20. Jahrhundert, mit einer Untersuchung des Markusevangeliums in seinem Verhältnis zur antiken Biographie", Haase (ed.), *ANRW* II.25.2, 1635-1694.

Freyne, S., *The Twelve: Disciples and Apostles. A study in the theology of the first three gospels*, London-Sydney 1968.

Friedrich, G., "εὐαγγελίζομαι κτλ.", *TDNT* II, 707-737.

———, "κῆρυξ κτλ.", *TDNT* III, 683-718.

———, "Beobachtungen zur messianischen Hohepriestererwartung in den Synoptikern", *ZTK* 53 (1956) 265-311.

Fuller, R. H., "Die neuere Diskussion über das synoptische Problem", *TZ* 34 (1978) 129-148.

Fusco, V., "Tradizione evangelica e modelli letterari. Riflessioni su due libri recenti", *BibOr* 144 (1985) 78-90.

Gaechter, P., *Maria im Erdenleben. Neutestamentliche Marienstudien*, Innsbruck 1953.

Gasque, W. W., Martin, R. P. (eds.), *Apostolic History and the Gospel*, Biblical and Historical Essays presented to F. F. Bruce on his 60th Birthday, Exeter 1970.

Gentili, B., Cerri, G., "L'idea di biografia nel pensiero greco", *QUCC* 27 (1978) 7-27.

George, A., "La royauté de Jésus", *Études*, 257-282.

Giancotti, F., *Strutture delle monografie di Sallustio e di Tacito*, BCC 108: Messina-Florence 1971.

Gnilka, J., "Die Erwartung des messianischen Hohenpriesters in den Schriften von Qumran und im Neuen Testament", *RevQ* 2 (1959-60) 395-426.

———, *Die Verstockung Israels. Isaias 6,9-10 in der Theologie der Synoptiker*, SANT 3: Munich 1961.

———, *Das Evangelium nach Markus*, 2 vols, EKKNT II: Zürich-Neukirchen-Vluyn 1978, 1979.

Gossage, A. J., "Plutarch", Dorey (ed.), *Latin Biography*, 45-77.

Grimm, W., "ἐπιστάτης", *EWNT* II, 93-94.

Grundmann, W., "Sohn Gottes (Ein Diskussionsbeitrag)", *ZNW* 47 (1956) 113-133.

———, "δύναμαι κτλ.", *TDNT* II, 284-317.

———, "χρίω κτλ.", *TDNT* IX, 493-496.527-580.

Guelich, R., "The Gospel Genre", Stuhlmacher (ed.), *Evangelium*, 183-219.

Güttgemanns, E., *Offene Fragen zur Formgeschichte des Evangeliums. Eine methodologische Skizze der Grundlagenproblematik der Form- und Redaktionsgeschichte*, BET 54: Munich 1971² (1970).

Gundry, R. H., "Recent Investigations into the Literary Genre 'Gospel'", *New Dimensions in New Testament Study*, eds. R. N. Longenecker, M. C. Tenney, Grand Rapids 1974, 97-114.

Haase, W. (ed.), *Aufstieg und Niedergang der Römischen Welt. Geschichte und Kultur Roms im Spiegel der neueren Forschung* II.25.2: Berlin-New York 1984 [*ANRW*].

Hahn, F., *Christologische Hoheitstitel. Ihre Geschichte im frühen Christentum*, Göttingen 1964².

———, "Χριστός κτλ.", *EWNT* III, 1147-1165.

Harles, T. C., *Aristophanis Nubes graece et latine una cum scholiis graecis*, Leipzig 1788.

Hawkins, J. C., *Horae Synopticae. Contributions to the Study of the Synoptic Problem*, Oxford 1899.

Hengel, M., *Zur urchristlichen Geschichtsschreibung*, Stuttgart 1979.

———, "Probleme des Markusevangeliums", Stuhlmacher (ed.), *Evangelium*, 221-265.

Hense, O., *Die Synkrisis in der antiken Literatur*, Freiburg 1893.

Hesse, F., "χρίω κτλ.", *TDNT* IX, 496-509.

Holtz, T., "δώδεκα", *EWNT* I, 874-880.

Holtzmann, H. J., *Die Synoptischen Evangelien. Ihr Ursprung und Geschichtlicher Charakter*, Leipzig 1863.

Homeyer, H. (ed.), *Lukian. Wie man Geschichte schreiben soll*, Munich 1965.

Hunger, H., *Die Hochsprachliche Profane Literatur der Byzantiner* I, HAW XII.5.1: Munich 1978.

———, *Aspekte der griechischen Rhetorik von Gorgias bis zum Untergang von Byzanz*, Vienna 1972.

Hunkin, J. W., "Pleonastic ἄρχομαι in the New Testament", *JTS* 25 (1924) 390-402.

Janson, T., *Latin Prose Prefaces. Studies in Literary Conventions*, AUSSLS 13: Stockholm 1964.

Jeremias, J., *Jesus' Promise to the Nations*, tr. by S. H. Hooke, SBT 24: London 1967² (1958).

———, *The Parables of Jesus*, tr. by S. H. Hooke, London 1972³.

Jülicher, A., *Einleitung in das Neue Testament*, Tübingen 1906⁵⁻⁶.

Kee, H. C., "Aretalogy and the Gospel", *JBL* 92 (1973) 402-411.

Kennedy, G. A., *The Art of Persuasion in Greece*, Princeton 1963.

Kenyon, F. G., *Books and Readers in Ancient Greece and Rome*, Chicago 1980 (repr. Oxford 1932).

Kirk, G. S., *Homer and the Oral Tradition*, Cambridge 1976.

Kittel, G., *Theological Dictionary of the New Testament*, 10 vols, tr. by G. W. Bromiley, Michigan 1964-1976 [*TDNT*].

Klein, G., *Die zwölf Apostel. Ursprung und Gehalt einer Idee*, FRLANT 77: Göttingen 1961.

Kleinknecht, H., "λέγω κτλ.", *TDNT* IV, 77-91.

Klingner, P., "Über die Einleitung der Historien Sallusts", *Hermes* 63 (1928) 165-192.

Koch, R., "Preaching", *Encyclopedia of Biblical Theology* II, ed. J. B. Bauer, London-Sydney 1970, 686-693.

Koester, H., "Überlieferung und Geschichte der frühchristlichen Evangelienliteratur", Haase (ed.), *ANRW* II.25.2, 1463-1542.

———, "From the Kerygma-Gospel to Written Gospels", *NTS* 35 (1989) 361-381.

Kraus, H.-J., *Die Psalmen*, 2 vols, BKAT XV: Neukirchen-Vluyn 1978⁵.

Kraus Reggiani, C., *Filone Alessandrino. De Opificio Mundi — De Abrahamo — De Josepho. Analisi critiche, testi tradotti e commentati*, BA 23: Rome 1979.

Kroll, W., "Rhetorik", *Paulys Real-Encyclopädie der Classischen Altertumswissenschaft*, Supplementband VII, ed. K. Ziegler, Stuttgart 1940, 1039-1138 [*PRE*].

Kümmel, W. G., *Introduction to the New Testament*, tr. by H. C. Kee, London 1975².

Kuhn, K. G., "The Two Messiahs of Aaron and Israel", *The Scrolls and the New Testament*, ed. K. Stendahl, New York 1957, 54-64 (rev. repr. of "Die beiden Messias Aarons und Israels", *NTS* 1 (1954-55) 168-179).

Kustas, G. L., *Studies in Byzantine Rhetoric*, AB 17: Thessalonika 1973.

Kyle McCarter, Jr., P., *1 Samuel*, AB 8: Garden City 1980.

Laistner, M. L. W., *The Greater Roman Historians*, SCL 21: Berkeley-Los Angeles 1947.

Lausberg, H., *Handbuch der Literarischen Rhetorik. Eine Grundlegung der Literaturwissenschaft*, Munich 1973².

Leeman, A. D., *Orationis Ratio. The Stylistic Theories and Practice of the Roman Orators, Historians and Philosophers*, Amsterdam 1963.

———, "Structure and meaning in the prologues of Tacitus", *YCS* 23 (1973) 169-208.

Lentzen-Deis, F., *Die Taufe Jesu nach den Synoptikern. Literarkritische und gattungsgeschichtliche Untersuchungen*, FTS 4: Frankfurt am Main 1970.

———, "Methodische Überlegungen zur Bestimmung literarischer Gattungen im Neuen Testament", *Bib* 62 (1981) 1-20.

Leo, F., *Die Griechisch-Römische Biographie nach ihrer Literarischen Form*, Hildesheim 1965 (repr. Leipzig 1901).

Léon-Dufour, X., "Les Évangiles synoptiques", Robert, Feuillet (eds.), *Introduction* II, 143-334.

Lieberich, H., *Studien zu den Proömien in der griechischen und byzantinischen Geschichtschreibung I. Teil. Die griechischen Geschichtschreiber*, Munich 1898.

Livingstone, E. A. (ed.), *Studia Evangelica* VI, TU 112: Berlin 1973 [*SE*].

Lohmeyer, E., *Das Urchristentum I. Johannes der Täufer*, Göttingen 1932.

————, *Das Evangelium des Markus*, Göttingen 1967[8] (1937).

————, *Das Evangelium des Matthäus*, ed. W. Schmauch, Göttingen 1967[4] (1956).

Lorenz, K., *Untersuchungen zum Geschichtswerk des Polybios*, Stuttgart 1931.

Luce, T. J., *Livy: The Composition of his History*, Princeton 1977.

Lührmann, D., "Biographie des Gerechten als Evangelium. Vorstellungen zu einem Markus-Kommentar", *WuD* NF 14 (1977) 25-50.

McDonald, J. I. H., *Kerygma and Didache. The articulation and structure of the earliest Christian message*, SNTSMS 37: Cambridge 1980.

McGiffert, A. G., "The Historical Criticism of Acts in Germany", Foakes Jackson, Lake (eds.), *Beginnings* I.II, 363-395.

McKenzie, R. A. F., "Job", *JBC* I (ed. R. E. Murphy), 511-513.

Mahnke, H., *Die Versuchungsgeschichte im Rahmen der synoptischen Evangelien. Ein Beitrag zur frühen Christologie*, BET 9: Frankfurt am Main 1978.

Manson, T. W., *The Sayings of Jesus as recorded in the Gospels according to St. Matthew and St. Luke*, London 1949.

Marrou, H. I., *Histoire de l'Éducation dans l'Antiquité*, Paris 1948.

Martin, J., *Antike Rhetorik, Technik und Methode*, HAW II.3: Munich 1974.

Marxsen, W., *Mark the Evangelist. Studies on the Redaction History of the Gospel*, tr by J. Boyce et al., Nashville-New York 1969.

————, "Bemerkungen zur "Form" der sogenannten synoptischen Evangelien", *TLZ* 81 (1956) 345-348.

Mays, J. L., *Amos. A Commentary*, London 1969.

Menoud, P.-H., "Preaching", Buttrick (ed.), *IDB* III, 860-869.

Merk, A., *Novum Testamentum Graece et Latine*, Rome 1935[2].

Metzger, B. M., *A Textual Commentary on the Greek New Testament*, London-New York 1971.

Meyer, E., *Ursprung und Anfänge des Christentums*, 3 vols, Stuttgart-Berlin 1921-1923.

Meyer, P. D., "The Gentile Mission in Q", *JBL* 89 (1970) 405-417.

Miller, D. G., Hadidian, D. Y. (eds), *Jesus and man's hope*, 2 vols, Pittsburg 1970, 1971.

Moffat, J., *An Introduction to the Literature of the New Testament*, Edinburgh 1920[3].

Momigliano, A., *Lo sviluppo della biografia greca*, PBE 232: Turin 1974 (tr. with additions of *The Development of Greek Biography*, Cambridge, Mass. 1971).

Murray, R., *Symbols of Church and Kingdom. A Study in Early Syriac Tradition*, Cambridge 1975.

————, "Some Rhetorical Patterns in Early Syriac Literature", *A Tribute to A. Vööbus. Studies in Early Christian Literature and Its Environment, Primarily in the Syrian East*, ed. R. H. Fischer, Chicago 1977, 109-131.

Nicolardot, F., *Les Procédés de Rédaction des Trois Premiers Évangélistes*, Paris 1908.

Norden, E., *Die Antike Kunstprosa. Vom VI. Jahrhundert V. Chr. bis in die Zeit der Renaissance*, 2 vols, Leipzig-Berlin 1909[2] (1898).

————, *Agnostos Theos. Untersuchungen zur Formgeschichte Religiöser Rede*, Leipzig-Berlin 1913.

————, *Die Geburt des Kindes. Geschichte einer religiösen Idee*, Leipzig-Berlin 1924.

Oepke, A., "ἐπιστάτης", *TDNT* II, 622-623.

O'Neill, E. N. (ed.), *Teles (The Cynic Teacher)*, Missoula 1977.

Orchard, B., Longstaff, T. R. W. (eds.), *J. J. Griesbach: Synoptic and Text-Critical Studies. 1776-1976*, SNTSMS 34: Cambridge 1979.

Overbeck, F., "Über die Anfänge der patristischen Literatur", *HZ* 48 (1882) 417-472.

———, *Christentum und Kultur*, Basle 1919.

Pédech, P., *La Méthode Historique de Polybe*, Paris 1964.

———, *Polybe, Histoires* I, Paris 1969.

Pelling, C. B. R., "Plutarch's method of work in the Roman Lives", *JHS* 99 (1979) 74-96.

———, "Plutarch's adaptation of his source-material", *JHS* 100 (1980) 127-140.

Perrin, N., "The Literary *Gattung* 'Gospel' — Some Observations", *ET* 82 (1970-71) 4-7.

Pesch, R., *Das Markusevangelium*, 2 vols, HTKNT II: Freiburg 1976, 1977.

Pestman, P. W. (ed.), *Greek and Demotic Texts from the Zenon Archives (P.L. Bat 20)*, P.L. Bat 20A: Leiden 1980.

Peter, H., *Wahrheit und Kunst. Geschichtsschreibung und Plagiat im klassischen Altertum*, Leipzig-Berlin 1911.

Pope, M. H., "Book of Job", Buttrick (ed.), *IDB* II, 911-925.

Preisigke, F., *Fachwörter des öffentlichen Verwaltungsdienstes Ägyptens in den griechischen Papyrusurkunden der ptolemäisch-römischen Zeit*, Göttingen 1915.

Reese, J. M., *Hellenistic Influence on the Book of Wisdom and its Consequences*, AnBib 41: Rome 1970.

Renehan, R., *Greek Lexicographical Notes. A Critical Supplement to the Greek-English Lexicon of Liddell-Scott-Jones*, Hypomnemata 45: Göttingen 1975.

Rengstorf, K. H., "δώδεκα", *TDNT* II, 321-328.

———, "ὑπηρέτης κτλ.", *TDNT* VIII, 530-544.

Riesner, R., *Jesus als Lehrer. Eine Untersuchung zum Ursprung der Evangelien-Überlieferung*, WUNT 2.7: Tübingen 1981.

Robert, A., Feuillet, A. (eds.), *Introduction à la Bible* II, *Nouveau Testament*, Tournai 1959².

Robinson, J. A. T., *Redating the New Testament*, London 1976.

Robinson, J. M., "On the *Gattung* of Mark (and John)", Miller, Hadidian (eds.), *Jesus and man's hope* I, 99-129.

———, Koester, H., *Trajectories through Early Christianity*, Philadelphia 1971.

Ruppert, J., *Quaestiones ad historiam dedicationis librorum pertinentes*, Diss. Leipzig 1911.

Scheller, P., *De hellenistica historiae conscribendae arte*, Diss. Leipzig 1911.

Schmid, J., Vögtle, A. (eds.), *Synoptische Studien*, Alfred Wikenhauser zum siebsigsten Geburtstag, Munich 1953.

Schmidt, K. L., *Der Rahmen der Geschichte Jesu. Literarkritische Untersuchungen zur ältesten Jesusüberlieferung*, Berlin 1919.

———, "Die Stellung der Evangelien in der allgemeinen Literaturgeschichte", *EYXAPIΣTHPION. Studien zur Religion und Literatur des Alten und Neuen Testaments* II, Hermann Gunkel zum 60. Geburtstag, ed. H. Schmidt, FRLANT NF 19.2: Göttingen 1923, 50-134.

Schmithals, W., *Das Evangelium nach Markus,* 2 vols, ÖTK 2: Gütersloh-Würzburg 1979.

Schniewind, J., *Euangelion. Ursprung und erste Gestalt des Begriffs Evangelium,* 2 vols, BFCT 2.13.25: Gütersloh 1927, 1931.

Scholes, R., Kellogg, R., *The Nature of Narrative,* New York 1966.

Schrenk, G., "βιάζομαι κτλ.", *TDNT* I, 609-614.

Schubart, W., *Das Buch bei den Griechen und Römern,* Berlin-Leipzig 1921².

Schürer, E., *The History of the Jewish People in the Age of Jesus Christ (175 B.C.-A.D. 135)* III.1, eds. G. Vermes, F. Millar, M. Goodman, Edinburgh 1986.

Schulz, S., *Q. Die Spruchquelle der Evangelisten,* Zürich 1972.

Serra, A., "Le Madri d'Israele nell'antica letteratura giudaica e la Madre di Gesù. Prospettive di Ricerca", *Il Salvatore e la Vergine-Madre. La maternità salvifica di Maria e le cristologie contemporanee,* Atti del 3° Simposio Mariologico Internazionale, Rome-Bologna 1981, 303-367.

Shuler, P. L., *A Genre for the Gospels. The Biographical Character of Matthew,* Philadelphia 1982.

Sjöberg, E., "πνεῦμα κτλ.", *TDNT* VI, 375-389.

Smith, M., "Prolegomena to a discussion of Aretalogies, Divine Men, the Gospels and Jesus", *JBL* 90 (1971) 174-199.

Stanton, G. N., *Jesus of Nazareth in New Testament Preaching,* SNTSMS 27: Cambridge 1974.

————, *The Gospels and Jesus,* Oxford 1989.

Starkie, W. J. M., *The Clouds of Aristophanes,* London 1911.

Stein, E., "Ein jüdisch-hellenistischer Midrasch über den Auszug aus Ägypten", *MGWJ* 78 (1934) 558-575.

Stonehouse, N. B., *Origins of the Synoptic Gospels. Some Basic Questions,* London 1964.

Strecker, G., "Zur Messiasgeheimnistheorie im Markusevangelium", *SE* III, ed. F. L. Cross, TU 88: Berlin 1964, 87-104.

————, *Der Weg der Gerechtigkeit. Untersuchung zur Theologie des Matthäus,* FRLANT 82: Göttingen 1971.

————, "Literarkritische Überlegungen zum εὐαγγέλιον-Begriff im Markusevangelium", *Neues Testament und Geschichte. Historisches Geschehen und Deutung im Neuen Testament,* Oscar Cullmann zum 70. Geburtstag, eds. H. Baltensweiler, B. Reicke, Zürich-Tübingen 1972, 91-104.

————, "εὐαγγέλιον", *EWNT* II, 176-186.

Streeter, B. H., *The Four Gospels. A Study of Origins,* London 1924.

Stuhlmacher, P. (ed.), *Das Evangelium und die Evangelien,* Vorträge vom Tübinger Symposium 1982, WUNT 28: Tübingen 1983.

————, "Zum Thema: Das Evangelium und die Evangelien", Stuhlmacher (ed.), *Evangelium,* 1-26.

Talbert, C. H., *What is a Gospel? The Genre of the Canonical Gospels,* Philadelphia 1977.

Thackeray, H. St. J., *The Septuagint and Jewish Worship. A Study in Origins,* Munich 1980 (repr. London 1921).

Theissen, G., *Urchristliche Wundergeschichten. Ein Beitrag zur formgeschichtlichen Erforschung der synoptischen Evangelien,* SNT 8: Gütersloh 1974.

Townend, G. B., "Suetonius and his Influence", Dorey (ed.), *Latin Biography*, 79-111.
Toynbee, A. J., *Greek Historical Thought. From Homer to the Age of Heraclius*, New York 1952².
Tuckett, C. M., "The Argument from Order and the Synoptic Problem", *TZ* 36 (1980) 338-354.
————, *Synoptic Studies. The Ampleforth Conferences of 1982 and 1983*, JSNTSS 7: Sheffield 1984.
Turner, C. H., "Chronology of the New Testament", *A Dictionary of the Bible* I, ed. J. Hastings, Edinburgh 1906, 403-425.
Van der Woude, A. S., "χρίω κτλ.", *TDNT* IX, 517-520.521-527.
Vanhoye, A., "Structure et théologie des récits de la Passion dans les évangiles synoptiques", *NTR* 89 (1967) 135-163.
————, *La structure littéraire de l'épître aux Hébreux*, Paris-Bruges 1976².
————, *Prêtres anciens, prêtre nouveau selon le Nouveau Testament*, Paris 1980.
Van Unnik, W. C., "Jesus the Christ", *NTS* 8 (1961-62) 101-116.
Vielhauer, P., *Geschichte der urchristlichen Literatur. Einleitung in das Neue Testament, die Apokryphen und die Apostolischen Väter*, Berlin-New York 1978.
Völter, D., *Die evangelischen Erzählungen von der Geburt und Kindheit Jesu kritisch untersucht*, Strassburg 1911.
Volkmann, R., *Die Rhetorik der Griechen und Römer in systematischer Übersicht*, Leipzig 1885².
Von Soden, H., *Die Schriften des Neuen Testaments in ihrer ältesten erreichbaren Textgestalt* I-IV, Göttingen 1902-1913.
Votaw, C. W., "The Gospels and Contemporary Biographies", *AJPh* 19 (1915) 45-73.217-249 (repr. *The Gospels and Contemporary Biographies in the Greco-Roman World*, ed. J. Reumann, BS 27: Philadelphia 1970)
Walker, R., *Die Heilsgeschichte im ersten Evangelium*, FRLANT 91: Göttingen 1967.
Walker, Jr., W. O. (ed.), *The Relationships Among the Gospels. An Interdisciplinary Dialogue*, San Antonio 1978.
Wallbank, F. W., *A Historical Commentary on Polybius*, 3 vols, Oxford 1957-79.
Walsh, P. G., *Livy: His Historical Aims and Methods*, Cambridge 1961.
Wardman, A., *Plutarch's Lives*, London 1974.
Weiser, A., "ἀγαλλιάω κτλ.", *EWNT* I, 17-19.
Weiser, A., *The Psalms. A Commentary*, tr. by H. Hartwell, London 1971.
Wellek, R., Warren, A., *Theory of Literature*, London 1956.
Wendland, P., *Die Urchristliche Literaturformen*, HNT I.3: Tübingen 1912²⁻³.
Westermann, C., *Isaiah 40-66. A Commentary*, tr. by D.M.G. Stalker, London 1969.
————, *Genesis*, 3 vols, BKAT I: Neukirchen-Vluyn 1974-1982.
Wikenhauser, A., *Einleitung in das Neue Testament*, Freiburg 1953.
Wilder, A. N., *Eschatology and Ethics in the Teaching of Jesus*, New York-London 1939.
Wink, W., *John the Baptist in the Gospel Tradition*, SNTSMS 7: Cambridge 1968.
Wolter, M., "Die anonymen Schriften des Neuen Testaments. Annäherungsversuch an ein literarisches Phänomen", *ZNW* 79 (1988) 1-16.

INDICES

1. Old Testament

2. Jewish Writings

3. New Testament

2,46	76, 130, 131, 152	4,27	76, 132, 133, 137
2,46-47	128	4,29	73, 99, 170
2,47	75, 177	4,29-30	147, 178
3,1	130	4,30	137
3,1-8	149, 152, 170	4,31	32, 73, 76, 95, 99
3,1-10	147	4,32-35	109
3,1-26	147	4,32-37	108, 149, 178
3,1–4,2	76	4,32–5,42	76
3,2	164	4,33	76
3,6	147	4,34	149
3,8-10	164	5,1-11	108
3,10	32	5,3	120
3,11	130	5,4	166
3,12-26	147	5,11	109
3,13-15	151	5,12	76, 130
3,13-18	109, 125	5,12-16	109
3,13-26	176	5,12-42	147
3,14	169	5,13	144
3,15	176	5,15-16	170
3,17	144, 151	5,16	76, 148, 149
3,17-18	177	5,17	32
3,17-26	177	5,17-18	144
3,18	125, 176, 177	5,17-40	130, 177
3,18-26	110	5,18	100, 125
3,19	177	5,20	152
3,19-21	143, 152, 177	5,20-21	76, 130
3,20	177	5,21	76
3,20-21	110, 176	5,25	76, 130, 152
3,21	125, 137	5,27	76, 100
3,22-23	136	5,28	76, 144
3,23	143	5,28-32	125
3,24	104, 177	5,29	170, 178
3,25	109	5,29-32	149
3,25-26	143, 152, 177	5,30-32	177
3,26	76, 109, 177	5,31	76, 149, 177
4,1-21	130, 144, 177	5,32	100, 176
4,3	100	5,33	144
4,3-21	125	5,34	76
4,4	95, 99, 144, 147	5,38-39	176
4,5	76	5,40	144
4,8	32, 100, 176	5,40-41	100, 125
4,8-12	100, 147	5,40-42	76
4,8-13	170	5,41	76, 149, 170
4,10	76	5,42	69, 74, 76, 78, 99, 109, 152
4,10-12	177	6	73
4,12	125, 149	6,1	70, 82, 108
4,13	73, 178	6,1-3	149
4,15	76	6,1-6	74
4,15-18	100	6,1–8,3	74, 76, 77, 108
4,19	176	6,2	76, 95, 99
4,19-20	149, 170, 178	6,3	32, 148
4,23	82	6,4	95, 99
4,24-30	178	6,5	32, 74, 76

4. Classical Authors

I,2.1-3.6	112	II,13-15	111
I,3.6	11	**Hecataeus**	
I,4.3	162		
I,5.1-2	112	*Historica* fr. 332	158
I,5.1-3	11, 112	**Hermogenes**	35
I,5.3	94, 112, 162, 175		
I,5.4	162	Περὶ Εὑρέσεως II,1	153, 154
I,5.4-6.3	112	**Herodotus**	170
I,6.1	114, 115	*Historia*	
I,6.1-2	11	I,1	11, 112, 158, 161,
I,6.2	112, 162		163, 175
I,6.3	11, 112	I,1-5	11, 154
I,6.3-4	112	I,2-5	112, 153
I,6.3-5	11	I,5	94
I,7.1	11	II,35-37	34
I,7.1-3	11, 112	**Hippocrates**	
I,7.1-8.2	114	*Vetera medicina*	
I,7.2	92, 112	3,10	90-92
I,7.4	165, 166	3,20-21	91, 92
I,8.1	94	**Homer**	
I,8.1-2	108, 112	*Illiad*	158
I,8.4	94, 166	*Odyssey*	158
V,48.1	171	**Isocrates**	
De Thucydide		*Evagoras*	
7	165	Pr.	11
8	115	34-38	34
9	84, 107, 108, 165	*Helen*	
10	94, 107, 108	14-15	162
10-12	108	16	94
11	165	*Panegyricus*	
12	165	15	94
19	165	19	94
De Lysia 17	111	**Livy**	
Ep. ad Pompeium		*Ab Urbe Condita*	
3	107, 108	Pr. 1	11, 94
6	170	6	11
De Isaeo		9-10	112
15,1	153	**Longinus**	
15,3	153	*De Sublimitate*	158
Dioscorides		**Lucian**	
De Materia Medica		*Historia*	
I Pr.	11, 97, 112, 162,	6	107
	163	7-9	115
II Pr.	11, 71, 97	14	111
III Pr.	11, 97	23	163
IV Pr.	11, 97	47	166
V Pr.	11		
Fortunatus			
Ars Rhetorica			
II,12	105		

5. Early Christian Authors

6. Greek Words

7. Selected Topics

8. Modern Authors

Achtemeier, P. J., 145, 157
Agua Pérez, A. del, 4, 19, 24, 145
Aland, K., 6-7, 10, 14, 64, 81, 159
Albertz, L., 124
Alexander, L., 113, 167
Aloni, A., 111
Anderson, G., 157
Anderson, H., 4, 31
Arndt, W. F., 18, 90
Audet, J.-P., 3, 9
Aune, D. C., 156, 160
Avenarius, G., 58, 77, 102, 108, 111, 112

Bachmann, M., 27, 119, 120
Bailey, K. E., 48, 53, 57, 60, 61
Baltensweiler, H., 159
Balz, H. R., 158
Barrett, C. K., 132
Bartsch, H.-W., 114
Bauer, J. B., 175
Bauer, W., 18, 27, 90, 103, 139
Baumbach, G., 122
Beasley-Murray, G. R., 138
Bengel, J. A., 7, 46, 102
Benoit, P., 3
Berger, K., 131, 157
Bernadicou, P. J., 128
Betori, G., 68, 69, 73, 76
Betz, O., 99, 175-177
Beutler, J., 90
Bieder, W., 124
Bihler, J., 100
Bisping, A., 5, 9, 24, 40, 43, 44, 47, 49, 54, 56, 62, 68, 69, 74, 76, 78, 83, 89, 93, 102, 157
Birt, T., 99, 172, 173
Black, M., 14
Blass, F., 21, 133
Blenkinsopp, J., 170
Blinzler, J., 48, 52, 53
Blomberg, C. L., 52, 53, 60
Böcher, O., 119
Boismard, M.-E., 7
Bonnor, S. F., 35
Bornkamm, G., 158
Bossuyt, P., 5, 9
Bousset, W., 4

Bovon, F., 1, 6, 44, 99, 124, 150
Bowra, C. M., 158
Braun, H., 136
Brawley, R. L., 143
Brown, R. E., 3, 4, 9, 12, 14, 15, 17, 20, 36, 40, 68, 126-129, 132, 134, 141, 143
Brown, S., 93, 103, 120, 148
Bruce, F. F., 68
Brun, L., 25, 44, 54, 55, 56
Bruners, W., 37
Bruns, I., 34
Brunt, P. A., 115
Büchsel, F., 90
Bultmann, R., 128, 148, 155, 169, 179
Burck, E., 7, 173
Burrows, E., 12, 13, 15
Busse, U., 4, 24, 25, 28, 136, 145
Butler, R. C., 7
Buttrick, G. A., 158, 179

Cadbury, H. J., 1, 68, 71, 75, 85-89, 91-93, 97, 104, 109, 113-115, 127, 156, 170, 182
Calboli Montefusco, L., 105
Callan, T., 113, 163, 167
Carroll, J. T., 143
Casalegno, A., 131
Cerfaux, L., 67-69, 74, 134, 135
Cerri, G., 170
Charlesworth, J. H., 167
Chilver, G. E. F., 153
Christ, F., 14
Clark, D. L., 35
Colson, F. H., 107, 108, 115
Conybeare, F. C., 2
Conzelmann, H., 1, 2, 22, 24, 27, 48, 50, 67, 68, 78, 82, 96, 117-123, 125, 126, 145, 146, 147, 155, 157, 182
Coppens, J., 129
Cornely, R., 9, 55, 68, 69, 78, 83, 102
Creed, J. M., 6, 9, 18, 24, 40, 48, 63, 141
Crenshaw, J. L., 9
Cross, F. L., 6, 49, 52, 54, 179
Cullmann, O., 136
Culpepper, R. A., 150, 151, 170

Dalman, G., 139

Finito di stampare il 27 settembre 1991
Tipografia Poliglotta della Pontificia Università Gregoriana
Piazza della Pilotta, 4 – 00187 Roma